Going There

Going There

Katie Couric

Little, Brown and Company
New York Boston London

Little, Brown and Company
Hachette Book Group
1290 Avenue of the Americas, New York, NY 10104
littlebrown.com

First Edition: October 2021

Little, Brown and Company is a division of Hachette Book Group, Inc. The Little, Brown name and logo are trademarks of Hachette Book Group, Inc.

The publisher is not responsible for websites (or their content) that are not owned by the publisher.

The Hachette Speakers Bureau provides a wide range of authors for speaking events. To find out more, go to hachettespeakersbureau.com or call (866) 376-6591.

ISBN 978-0-316-53586-1 (hc) / 978-0-316-59331-1 (large print) / 978-0-316-42398-4 (signed edition) / 978-0-316-42387-8 (Barnes & Noble signed edition)
LCCN 2021935494

Printing 1, 2021

LSC-C

Book design by Abby Reilly

Printed in the United States of America

For Ellie and Carrie

Contents

Going There

Prologue

My PETER PAN collars and sensible pumps didn't exactly scream *Miami*. It was a whole new world: causeways stretching across sparkling bays, cigarette boats, Cuban coffee, women roller-blading in bikinis. The pulsating city was about as far as you could get from my wholesome hometown of Arlington, Virginia.

It was also one of the hottest news markets in the country. I was a general-assignment reporter at WTVJ, where a normal week might mean covering a pit-bull attack, a tropical storm, a drug deal gone bad, and the Calle Ocho festival in Little Havana. For a young journalist looking to make her mark, Miami had everything.

My learning curve was steep. The run-and-gun of covering spot news was all new to me, while the terror of reporting live practically turned me to stone. But in Miami, you couldn't dwell on your mistakes. The stories came fast, which meant lots of airtime and plenty of practice.

One day after work I was buying a birthday card at Burdines department store downtown when the woman at the register started examining my face. "You look just like that girl on TV!" she said.

Cue the choir of angels. My first time being recognized.

"Actually, I *am* that girl on TV," I said with a smile.

The woman smiled back. "You know, dear, your skin looks so much better in person."

* * *

BEING ON TELEVISION brings instant familiarity: People feel like they know you. They assess you, analyze you, project on you; they develop strong feelings about who they think you are. If you become a fixture in their home, like another member of the family, they even start to care about you. And you start to care about them too. Loyalty is pledged, bonds are built. I am still so moved by the power of television to make connections between people who've never met. Perhaps like you and me.

Over the years, whenever I ran into *TODAY* show viewers, they'd tell me they felt like they knew me. And in so many ways, they did. Because the parts of me they saw were real—the joy and frustration, the bloopers and belly laughs, the genuine affection I felt for my colleagues. They saw me become a mom to two daughters and grieve the loss of my husband and sister; they even got a good look at my colon. But it was two hours a day in a manufactured setting. There's so much the audience didn't see.

I've been a public figure for 30 years, a journalist for 40. The journey has exceeded every ambition I ever had. It's allowed me to witness seismic events and huge societal changes up close, and help people—on a grand scale—understand them. It has been the privilege of my life.

But the journey has also been deeply personal: Summoning the grit to make my way in the male-run media business. Adjusting to the thrilling, chilling world of sudden fame. Learning on the job, and occasionally stumbling—with millions watching. Experiencing institutional sexism at the highest levels; hanging in long enough to see things start to change. Telling other people's stories while complete strangers tried to tell mine. Doubting myself, forgiving myself, being proud of myself. As I say, it's been a journey.

I'VE LOVED EVERY second of being on TV. And yet, it has a way of squeezing you down to a shape and size designed to fit comfortably in the nation's living rooms, bedrooms, and kitchens. In other words, the box can put you in a box; the flat-screen can flatten. On TV, you are larger than life but somehow smaller, too, a neatly cropped version of who you are. Real life—the complications and contradictions, the messy parts—remains outside the frame.

It's magical, television; I know it made my dreams come true. But it is not the whole story, and it is not the whole me. This book is.

PART I

1

Moxie

THE SUMMER AFTER I graduated from college, my skin turned orange. I was on the Scarsdale Diet, a high-protein fat-melter that let you eat as many carrots as you wanted. The idea was to look as good as possible for my wet hot American summer, a sticky, sandy final fling before finding a job—maybe even a career—in TV news.

My plan was to wait tables in a picture-postcard beach town where the smell of fried fish mingled with the salt air; where my friends and I would spend the day slathering ourselves with Johnson's baby oil and lying out on beach towels, listening to the Bee Gees on our transistor radios. Then I'd shower, throw on a uniform, and hustle for tips at a restaurant on a shimmering inlet with skiffs scooting by.

That was the plan. Instead, I found a job at H. A. Winston's, located on a scrubby stretch of Route 1 in Delaware. The chain specialized in burgers with ambitious toppings (the Society Hill had blue cheese and chives; the Russian was dressed with sour cream and caviar). I loved the controlled chaos of the kitchen, shouting to the cooks over the pop and sizzle of the fryers, navigating the dining room while balancing dinner plates up and down my arm.

One night, a party of about seven or eight rowdy locals came in. They ordered round after round of daiquiris and beers, then burgers and fries plus onion rings and more fries, and I cheerfully kept it all coming.

After they left, I started piling their dirty dishes on a tray and saw my tip sitting there on the dark wood table: a quarter.

I put down the tray and headed outside, still in my apron, and scanned the parking lot. Then I spotted the guy I'd seen handling the check getting into his truck.

I walked up to the driver's-side window.

"I don't need your money," I said, and tossed the quarter into the cab.

Then I headed back to the restaurant, walking a little taller in my Tretorns.

I HAD SENT MY resumé to ABC News in Washington, where I figured it got sucked into the black hole of forgotten candidates. So I asked my mom if she'd drive me to the bureau in downtown DC. I liked the idea of having a getaway car (her cream-colored Buick station wagon) idling at the curb if things didn't go my way.

"Hi!" I said to the security guard at the bureau, busting out the biggest smile in my arsenal. "Is Davey Newman here?"

"Do you have an appointment?" she said, looking bored.

"Not really...I'm an old friend of his," I said, even though I'd never actually met Davey Newman.

"But you don't have an appointment."

"There's a phone over there," I said, pointing to a beige one hanging on the wall. "Do you mind if I call him?"

Heavy sigh. "Go ahead."

"Newman" came a gruff voice on the other end.

"Hi, it's Katie Couric!" I said and launched into the many minor ways our lives had intersected, including the fact that my sister Kiki went to high school with his twin brothers, Steve and Eddie. Shockingly, he let me up.

Davey looked at me over some wire copy he was reading; a cigarette smoldered in the ashtray on his desk. After the smallest of small talk, he passed me off to Kevin Delaney, the deputy bureau chief in charge of hiring—the same guy I'd sent my resumé to.

"Tell me about yourself," Delaney said, staring me down through lenses perched on the tip of his nose.

Knowing I was on borrowed time, I flew through my bona fides: recent graduate of the University of Virginia, American studies major, wrote for the college newspaper, interned at three different DC radio stations during the summers. I ended my spiel with "I really want to work in TV news."

"How did you get up here?" Delaney asked.

I confessed to the tenuous Davey Newman connection.

"Well," he said, smiling, "I admire your tenacity."

And with that, Kevin Delaney sifted through a thick stack of resumés on the corner of his desk, found mine, and put it on top.

BACK HOME, MY dad was at the kitchen table, eating a chipped beef sandwich with a glass of milk. I told him every detail as my mother chuckled quietly while stirring some Campbell's tomato soup at the stove. His blue eyes brightened, the corners of his mouth turning up ever so slightly.

"That's wonderful," he said in his soft Southern accent. "Katie, you've got moxie."

Moxie. I liked the sound of it.

A few days later, ABC called: "Can you start next week?"

2

ABC News, May I Help You?

I CAN STILL HEAR the cacophony of the newsroom—the clattering type-writers, the ringing phones, the whirring copier, the syncopated conversations between producers, reporters, assignment editors, camera-men. Discordant and thrilling, like a symphony orchestra tuning up.

I'd been hired as a desk assistant—a not-so-glorified girl Friday (and Monday through Thursday too). On my first day a gangly guy with a mustache named Mike showed me the ropes: how to make coffee, where to distribute the day's newspapers, how to collate the run-downs and change the ribbon on the teletype machine while wearing white cloth gloves so the purple ink didn't get all over your fingers. Everyone had an air of *I belong here and I'm doing important things;* men sauntered around in safari jackets, exhaling cigarette smoke and confidence. I felt so out of place. But you have to start somewhere, and I was determined to make the best damn pot of coffee these people had ever tasted.

Desk assistants didn't have actual desks, so I found a vacant seat and started answering phones (the first time I said, "ABC News, may I help you?" I got goose bumps). And suddenly a tall, eagle-eyed figure with dramatically arched eyebrows and a shellacked comb-over bounded in—White House correspondent Sam Donaldson. He came to a screeching halt when he saw me.

"You!" he bellowed. "What is your name?"

I felt the whole newsroom look my way. "Katie," I squeaked.

"Katie! Katie!" At which point, Donaldson literally jumped on the desk and started crooning, *"K-K-K-Katy, beautiful Katy / You're the only g-g-g-girl that I adore / When the m-m-m-moon shines, over the cowshed / I'll be waiting at the k-k-k-kitchen door."*

My cheeks started burning while everyone else just rolled their eyes and went back to their work—Sam being Sam, apparently. Then he jumped down and said, "Come with me!"

We hoofed it to the White House, about a half mile away, for the daily briefing. I was huffing and puffing in my summer shift and heels, desperately trying to keep up with Sam's long strides, as we approached the West Wing entrance. He grabbed my hand and whisked me past security, barking, "She's with me."

The press room was packed with pros holding reporter's notebooks and tape recorders. Sam plunged into the crowd while I stood stiffly against the wall, hoping no one questioned what the hell this 22-year-old nobody was doing there. I spotted legendary Helen Thomas in the front row looking like a harried housewife in a sea of men. Then they started lobbing questions at Jimmy Carter's press secretary, Jody Powell, fighting for information the nation needed to know. Afterward, Sam went off to his White House cubicle and sent me on my way. Returning to the bureau, I felt a bit dazed. *Did that actually just happen?*

Back in the newsroom, Mike pointed out Kevin Delaney's secretary, the person who'd be giving me my weekly schedule. Blond and so thin she was practically concave, Wendy Walker looked like she had just stepped out of *Town & Country*. I introduced myself and whispered conspiratorially, "Today is my first day."

"It's my first day too," she whispered back. I felt like grabbing onto her like a life raft. "Want to get lunch?" I asked.

Over salads, Wendy told me about her recent breakup with a curator at the National Gallery, about working for Ethel Kennedy and seeing Walter Cronkite do the limbo at Jackie Kennedy's 50th-birthday party in Hyannis Port. It all sounded so upper-crusty and out of my league. But later she'd tell me how her father had lost his job. After graduating from Hollins, a women's college in Virginia, she headed to Washington with $40 in her bank account and instructions to marry well. Coming from a frugal family, I realized we had more in common than I'd thought.

We shared something else too—the desire to succeed not by finding a husband but by having a career. It was the '70s—the decade of *Roe v. Wade,* Title IX, fiery debate over the Equal Rights Amendment, Barbara Walters becoming the first woman to co-anchor a Big Three evening newscast. I'd spent many a Saturday night for seven years watching *The Mary Tyler Moore Show,* transfixed by the ambitious, independent heroine setting out for a career in TV news.

Gee, I thought, *I want to turn the world on with my smile too!*

FRANK REYNOLDS, THE anchor of ABC's *World News Tonight,* gave off an air of old-school manliness. After the broadcast, he and his posse would sip scotch in his office and compare notes about what the competition had led their newscasts with. I'm pretty sure he spoke to me only once—in front of a *Washington Post* reporter who was writing a profile of him. I'd been asked to fetch him a ham sandwich from the deli next door, and when I returned, Reynolds looked up from the interview and said, "Thank you, dear." Largely, I guess, for the benefit of the reporter.

The backdrop of *World News Tonight* was the newsroom. To make sure viewers saw that it was a real, live, *working* newsroom, we were asked to be seat-fillers behind the anchor desk. I would always volunteer and pretend I was engaged in serious business—holding the phone to my ear, earnestly nodding and taking notes—when in reality, I was talking to my parents, urgently telling them to turn on the TV. "Can you see me? Look! I'm behind Frank Reynolds's right shoulder!"

Wendy and I did everything we could to get ahead. We memorized the office floor plan, learned everyone's names and what they did.

We came in on Sundays to do extra work (we called it "Sunday school").

One of those Sundays when no one was around, I slipped into the anchor chair. Wendy handed me a script she'd found in a trash can by the teleprompter operator's perch. I proceeded to deliver a mock newscast in full-on Ted Baxter mode, before collapsing in laughter at how ridiculous we were.

3

Let 'Em Know You're There

OUR FAMILY TREE was just a sapling when my parents, John and Elinor, bought a tidy four-bedroom brick Colonial for $30,500 in 1957. I was 6 months old. It had shutters the color of Georgia clay and three windows facing the street on the second floor. When I was a teenager, the middle one would be aglow until I came home at exactly 11:50 p.m., just before my curfew. Our house exuded a modest solidity that also described my family.

Emily was 10 years older than me. She always seemed to be racing around with important things to do—studying for exams, going on dates and college tours. Clara was born three years after her. She was named for my maternal grandmother, but my father didn't love the name, so we all called her Kiki. She and I shared a room; Kiki would comb my hair, put it in pigtails, and treat me like a little doll. I remember watching her rush off to a football game in her cheerleading uniform, tossing her pom-poms and megaphone in the back of our dad's Sunbeam Alpine convertible (his one midlife indulgence), thinking, *I want to be just like her.*

Johnny came next. When he was 5, he stuffed pebbles up his nose; my mom had to take him to the hospital to have them removed with giant tweezers. We were partners in crime, getting into pillow fights—one of which brought down a ceiling light, shattering it into a million pieces—and giving each other wedgies, which we called "creepers." Sometimes he'd pin down my shoulders with his knees and let a loogie drip dangerously close to my face before sucking it back up. "Stop roughhousing!" my mom would scream from downstairs.

No one seems particularly surprised to learn that I was the baby of the bunch. My parents would put my infant seat on the dining-room table so the whole family could stand around and watch me—my first audience. Later, my sisters would entertain their suitors by instructing me to do a cartwheel and the splits on the living-room floor or sing "Jolly Old Saint Nicholas" while they accompanied me on the piano. I was more than happy to perform.

In summer, over corn on the cob and sliced tomatoes at the glass table on the screened-in porch, I'd hold court, telling a bawdy joke or making a racy comment; my mom's eyes would turn into tiny crescents as she laughed so hard her shoulders shook, barely making a sound except the occasional snort. Attempting to maintain some dinner-table decorum, my father would suppress a smile and say, "Elin-*ah!* Don't encourage her!"

OUR MOTHER WAS the ultimate protector and defender—a homemaker in the most concrete sense, always doing for us, pulling for us, waiting for us to come home. She'd tell me, "Everyone needs a cheerleader. I'm yours." She was sturdy in every way. When I was little, I'd spring up and wrap my legs and arms around her and hold on like a koala bear in a eucalyptus tree.

After two years at Sophie Newcomb College in New Orleans, my mom moved to Chicago and lived at the Three Arts Club while working as a cartographer at Rand McNally and doing layout for *Coronet* magazine. All of which seemed pretty exciting to me. My dad was nearby at officer candidate school; they met at a tea dance in 1943. My mom thought he was dashing in his navy whites; he thought she was "a dish" in her red paisley dress. While she waited in Chicago, he did a tour of duty on a naval destroyer in the Pacific, once operating a smoke machine to hide his ship from kamikaze pilots. Less than a year later, they were married, and his life became hers.

The mothers I knew growing up didn't have careers, with the exception of Christine Hughes's mom. (Dr. Hughes helped us with our sixth-grade science-fair project, which entailed pumping cigarette smoke into a fishbowl to show how nicotine would cause a goldfish to lose its equilibrium, sending ours into an aquatic barrel roll.) My mom's job was us—fixing our breakfasts, packing our lunches (sometimes including little notes like *Don't get stuck in your peanut butter sandwich!*), driving whatever I'd forgotten (my purse, my sweater, my homework, my permission slip) to school, bringing me to piano lessons and Johnny to guitar. My mother was the family concierge, making sure we all had what we needed.

She'd always say, "Let 'em know you're there." The woman who ran our household like a boss, but had neither the opportunity nor the self-confidence to let the world know *she* was there, wanted more for us.

Not that my mom and dad were helicopter parents—I was given plenty of freedom to roam and make mistakes. It was the '60s and '70s, when you could hop on your bike in the morning and not come home until dinner. (My dad would holler "Katieee!" on the front step, while Mr. McMullan had perfected a whistle that signaled my friend Janie to head inside.) But if there was any hint I was seriously veering off course, my mother would swoop in.

In tenth grade after school one day, I was making out with my boyfriend, Steve Elliott, in his basement. He went to another high school, was two years older, was the product of divorce, and his mother worked—all of which sounded a bit dicey to my parents.

Suddenly, we heard banging.

Steve and I untangled and sat up. He craned his neck and saw my mom's Keds through the window well. I quickly collected myself, ran upstairs, and opened the front door.

"Mom," I said, my face flushed, my hair a mess.

"Come with me," she ordered and threw my orange Schwinn Varsity bike into the back of the station wagon. I wanted to crawl under the vinyl seat. We didn't say a word the entire way home.

My mom was born in 1923, just three years after women won the right to vote, decades before we'd enter the workforce in real numbers.

Sometimes I wonder: What if little Elinor Hene had been told the sky was the limit? If she'd come along a generation later, what might she have been—a graphic artist? She loved to sketch and paint. A stockbroker? When the AIDS crisis hit, she bought shares of Trojan condoms. Head of operations at some big company? She certainly ran a tight ship. Who knows—maybe she wouldn't have changed a thing.

My HOURS AT ABC were brutal. Going from the morning shift to afternoons to overnights totally screwed up my body clock. Driving down Canal Road after work one afternoon, I felt certain my life was over.

I'd been living at home. The Peter Max bedspreads I'd begged my mom for in junior high had been replaced by granny-friendly rayon quilts; the chartreuse walls had been repainted cream. As much as I enjoyed my mother's home cooking, I wanted to be on my own. Fortunately, one of Wendy's roommates was moving out, and she asked if I wanted the spot. What could be better than rooming with Wendy, her friend Margaret, who worked on Capitol Hill, and Leslie, who had a golden retriever named Amy?

They lived in a townhouse on Dent Place across the street from the fire station, a 15-minute drive from my parents and just a few blocks from the heart of Georgetown. On weekends we'd grab turkey and Brie on baguettes from the French Market or head to Au Pied de Cochon (the Pig's Foot—yum) for omelets and fries and to flirt with the sexy French waiters. At some point, Wendy started dating Sam Donaldson (back when no one batted an eye at workplace relationships). One day he showed up at our door in a white shirt, white pants, white belt, and white shoes. I turned around and yelled, "Hey, Wendy, the Man from Glad is here!"

I was a total slob and Wendy was meticulous—she almost had a coronary one day when I balanced a mug of coffee on her crisp white duvet. I'd sometimes rifle through her sweaters, disrupting her elaborate system, everything organized by color and pattern. Knowing the Oscar/ Felix thing might not be working for Wendy, my mom drove over to Dent Place one day and pleaded with her not to kick me out. Wendy told her not to worry.

THERE WERE A handful of female correspondents at ABC, and I studied their every move: Bettina Gregory, a Rosalind Russell–style toughie; motherly Ann Compton, who covered the White House with Sam and hired me to babysit her kids when I was looking to supplement my $7,000 salary; tall, striking, platinum-blond Cassie Mackin, who practically glided through the newsroom on her cool confidence.

I was just as fascinated by the male reporters: Rising stars Charlie Gibson and Brit Hume calling in on the "hotline" (a literal red phone with a special ring) from Capitol Hill with big scoops; Lou Cioffi, a foreign correspondent who got so miffed when I asked if he was a cameraman (honest mistake—at the time, he was wearing a Members Only jacket and xeroxing his expense report). Don Farmer was a *20/20* correspondent, married to Chris Curle, a gorgeous and talented local anchor at the ABC affiliate WJLA. During one high school summer, I had taken a journalism class that included a field trip to the station. I remember walking by Chris Curle's desk and seeing, alongside legal pads and pens, hot rollers and a Clairol makeup mirror. *Wow,* I thought. *So glamorous.*

One afternoon, I snuck upstairs and poked my head into Don's office. "I have some story ideas for *20/20* I'd love to show you," I said. He smiled encouragingly, knowing the chutzpah that required, and invited me in.

I read him the six ideas I had typed out, including one about a treatment center for gambling addicts in Pikesville, Maryland. Don listened and nodded, then thanked me. I left him the list and headed back to the newsroom.

I don't know if he ever actually used any of my ideas. But I do know that getting on Don Farmer's radar changed my life.

IN THE SPRING of 1980, 10 months after I started, Carl Bernstein became bureau chief of ABC News. He strutted around the place like the big deal he was, having broken Watergate with Bob Woodward seven years earlier. He'd replaced George Watson, who was leaving to run a brand-new cable news operation. Watson invited Wendy to come with him, promising he'd put her on the producer track.

Then he said, "You know the young people here; is there anyone we should take with us?"

Wendy said there was.

I nervously walked into Carl Bernstein's office, nearly blinded by his royal-blue crushed-corduroy three-piece suit.

I told him that I had accepted an offer at a new cable news network— CNN. He looked confused.

"Why are you going to the minor leagues when you've already made it to the majors?" he said.

"I know, Mr. Bernstein—but I think I need to learn how to play baseball first."

Yep. I actually said that.

4

Chicken Noodle News

I DIDN'T KNOW MUCH about Ted Turner. I knew he was a swashbuckling sailor who'd won the 1977 America's Cup, held up bottles of champagne at his victory press conference, and appeared to be three sheets to the wind. And I knew he was a millionaire crazy enough to start a 24-hour cable news channel at a time when no one really knew what cable was.

The entire network had been built from scratch in less than a year. The Atlanta headquarters were in a plantation-style mansion on Techwood Drive known as "Tara on Techwood," after Turner's favorite movie, *Gone with the Wind*. Meanwhile, the Washington bureau was crammed into a two-story building in Glover Park with a piece of paper on which someone had scribbled in Magic Marker *Cable News Network,* taped to the front door. There was a cemetery across the street, where we ate our salad-bar concoctions from Safeway on pretty days, and a strip club called Good Guys a few blocks up. All an easy walk from our bachelorette pad on Dent Place.

Ted Turner's idea of interior design was to ship old, stained sofas and chairs from his other offices; Wendy and I cleaned them up as best we could. Staffers doubled as carpenters, nailing together the anchor desk. The tech crew hoisted a giant satellite dish onto the roof; we ordered legal pads, reporter's notebooks, Bic pens, and Rolodexes. We'd heard that Turner didn't like Styrofoam, so Wendy brought in coffee mugs from home. The penny-pinching could get aggressive: one day a memo came around warning against the overuse of toilet paper.

Stories began to circulate about Turner that gave us all pause. During an orientation for anchors and producers in Atlanta, he showed up unannounced. All eyes turned to their fearless leader, eager to hear his words of wisdom and inspiration.

"I just want to tell you, we are going to beam this shit all over the world," he said in a slurry drawl. "And I'm gonna do this because Russia is gonna bomb our ass."

SINCE THE SHOP was nonunion, we could do anything—write, produce, edit, run equipment—without fear of a grouchy tech guy yelling at us for touching something we weren't supposed to. You'd often hear, "Hey, we need someone on the camera!" and whoever was available would jump up, stand behind the massive cantilevered thing, and swing it in the direction of the person sitting at the anchor desk. We were also the makeup artists, rolling giant tubes of beige goo down guests' faces.

But there were a few pros in the mix. Bernie Shaw, our lead Washington anchor, commanded the newsroom like Captain Kirk. When he was preparing to do a cut-in, if the sound of keys clacking in the background started to build, he'd wheel around and boom, *"Typewriters!"*—and everyone would pretend to type until he was done. Dan Schorr, who won an Emmy for his coverage of Watergate (landing him at number 17 on Nixon's enemies list), was our senior correspondent. Because he was (*gasp*) 62, people referred to him behind his back as "Dan Schorr, Senile Correspondent."

Bloopers were us: A director cutting to a live shot of a monkey at the Atlanta Zoo, who happened to be masturbating. Studio cameras crashing into anchor desks; a correspondent caught wiping his nose (sorry, Mike Boettcher). Our White House reporter, stationed outside the hospital where President Reagan was recovering after being shot by John Hinckley, began extolling the awesomeness of another network's catering spread—unaware that he was on live television. No wonder we were nicknamed "Chicken Noodle News."

And yet even at CNN there were fairy-tale moments. Somehow, Wendy and I managed to snag a pair of seats at the Radio and Television Correspondents' Association Dinner. It was a big deal among the Washington press corps and the hottest ticket imaginable for "underlings and young idiots like us," as Wendy later put it, all aflutter in the semiformal dresses we'd bought at Loehmann's. The Hilton glittered with big-name talent—Tom Brokaw, Connie Chung—although none more glittery than Jane Pauley in a taffeta ball gown, a sleek French braid trailing down the nape of her neck. Wendy and I were obsessed with her—every morning we huddled in front of Wendy's portable TV to watch Jane co-anchor the *TODAY* show. In the lobby, people tried to get close to her and grab a brief audience, maybe even a photo.

Standing several people behind Jane in the line to enter the ballroom, we gawked. "I want to touch her," I said. Wendy dared me.

I started snaking my way through the black-tie throng. As I got closer, I saw Jane throw her head back and laugh—what a thrill to see her legendary warmth and graciousness in the flesh. About a foot away, I summoned my nerve and squeezed past, getting close enough to graze her gown with my knuckles.

After that night, Wendy and I would French-braid each other's hair, just like Jane's.

5

Binge, Purge, Repeat

M Y NEIGHBORHOOD GROWING up was the postwar suburban
dream: hilly streets teeming with kids riding bikes and playing
capture the flag, roving house to house on Halloween dressed up as cowboys and witches. Striving middle-class families who'd moved there for
the good schools.

My parents had high expectations for the four of us; they were
demanding and strict, and poor Emily was the guinea pig. One night
when I was five, I heard her sobbing in her bedroom—she was in big
trouble for something. So I tiptoed into the bathroom, wrapped a wad
of toilet paper around my chubby hand, and brought it to her so she
could blow her nose and dry her tears. I remember feeling so useful.

Our parents expected her to be a leader. When Emily ran for
student council, the kitchen became her campaign headquarters. Our
dad helped write her speeches, and our mom oversaw the posters. One
of my favorites, tacked up over a water fountain at school, read FREE
WATER COURTESY OF EMILY COURIC. (Kiki, Johnny, and I followed in
her footsteps, turning our family into a political dynasty—at least in the
Arlington County public schools.)

By the time I was born, my parents were slightly more relaxed, but
they still kept us in line. When my dad asked a question and we answered, "Yes," he'd say, "Yes, what?" Our conditioned response: "Yes,

sir!" (Though Johnny's slight lisp made it "Yeth, thir!") Thankfully, the Captain von Trapp phase didn't last very long.

My father had a bit of that midcentury-dad mystique, driving off to some serious place with a big typewriter and a leather chair that swiveled. On weekends, he tended to manly duties like mowing the lawn and raking leaves (the sum total of his handiness). His favorite spot was an olive-green wingback chair in the den surrounded by hundreds of books and his beloved toby jugs—Farmer John, Admiral Nelson, John Barleycorn... And while he had an air of gentility and formality about him, he was always our loving dad. I think of him helping us so patiently with our homework and telling us to "boat your oars" at the dinner table (a navy term that means placing your silverware across the center of your plate to show you are finished). I can still picture his khaki trunks billowing in the local pool as I dog-paddled frantically toward his outstretched arms.

But when things got serious, he put the fear of God in us. I remember getting whacked a couple of times when I did something that might hurt me—once when I glanced up at the solar eclipse after I'd been warned it could make me go blind, a second time when I swallowed a plastic bead I'd been chewing on. It was less painful than humiliating. I got the message.

Our parents wanted us to be good citizens... and have strong extra-curriculars for our college applications. Among other things, that meant being camp counselors at the Columbia Lighthouse for the Blind every summer at Mount Vernon College in DC. Kiki did it first and staged a full-fledged production of *Peter Pan,* starring her campers. I remember sitting with my mom in the audience and being so moved by the performances, I cried. A few years later, my group of 6- and 7-year-olds formed a band; I played "The Entertainer" on the piano while the campers accompanied me on bongos and tambourines. The job also required me to apply ointment to the eyes of a little French boy named Didier every day at lunchtime. For a 16-year-old busy collecting Bonne Bell Lip Smackers and perfecting the Hustle in Janet Taff's basement, it was intense. To this day I thank my mom for insisting we "experience life beyond 40th Street."

Good grades were paramount: My parents regarded getting into a prestigious college as a critical rung on the ladder of life. Emily nailed it, accepting an offer from Smith, one of the "Seven Sisters" and the pinnacle for women before the Ivy League started routinely accepting them. (I knew all about it from studying the *Barron's Guide* in junior high, memorizing which colleges were "most selective" versus "selective" and the median SAT scores for each.) I'll never forget the excitement of our family heading to New York City, having dinner at Schrafft's, and seeing Emily off as she boarded an ocean liner to Paris for her junior year abroad.

She set the bar high, and Kiki cleared it, going to Smith a few years later. But I was less disciplined than my sisters, my youngest-child charm helping me get away with things like handing in assignments late and faking my way through a piano lesson. (I could play by ear, so it was easier than you might think.) Yes, I worked hard and did well enough, but my superpower was my emotional intelligence— I learned at a very early age how to win friends and influence people, something that doesn't necessarily come through on a high school transcript.

It is burned in my memory, coming home from school one day and seeing an envelope addressed to me sitting on the mahogany dresser in the living room that doubled as a mail table. It was from Smith. It was thin. I knew what that meant.

Apparently, Smith *loved* sisters, and having an alum in the family— not to mention two—was supposed to give you a leg up. Emily was Phi Beta Kappa, for God's sake. But I didn't even get wait-listed. (Maybe it had something to do with my interview, when I nervously told the admissions lady I admired FDR and the "Big" Deal.)

It was my first real disappointment. Which I dealt with by turning on myself.

Stealthily, I grabbed a glass from the kitchen cabinet and a spoon from the drawer, then rooted around in the refrigerator until I spotted the marigold-colored box with the Arm & Hammer logo. I headed to the bathroom, mixed some baking soda in water, chugged it, jumped up and down, and stuck my finger down my throat. A classmate had given me the secret recipe.

Body issues had been brewing long before Smith weighed in. I was nine when a waifish Twiggy frugged onto the scene in her Union Jack minidress. Stick-thin models pranced across the pages of my sisters' *Glamour*s and *Mademoiselle*s; their gazelle-like figures seemed fantastical.

Dieting was a way of life in my house—my mom and sisters subsisted on cottage cheese and Tab. I remember making a tuna fish sandwich one night and Kiki, at a world-weary 17, saying, "Enjoy it, because you're not going to be able to eat like that forever."

My mom would regularly slip up, tossing a giant Hershey bar into the shopping cart; when one of us went searching for it, she'd sheepishly admit she'd finished it off. Her mother was that rare thing, petite *and* buxom, and I'm sure she got on her less petite daughter about what she ate.

And my mom got on me. Call it generational body-shaming. When I went off to UVA (which turned out to be a much better fit than Smith would have been), she'd send me sweet letters in her controlled, blocky handwriting with advice and admonitions tucked in:

> *Do not get angry with me when I say to watch your diet— stay away from fried foods, starches and just use your head about keeping healthy.*

My mother passed down so many wonderful traits, a positive relationship with food not being one of them.

The cycle started with deprivation. Knowing food was my enemy, I'd swear it off. Then I'd get hungry—famished, actually—which drove me to make terrible choices, grabbing a cookie (or 12) or a big handful of chips. Self-loathing and resignation came next; *I blew it,* I'd think, *I'll start again tomorrow,* and eat anything that wasn't nailed down— doughnuts, ice cream, cold spaghetti, bread slathered with butter— followed by panicky desperation to rid myself of the calories.

Now at the townhouse on Dent Place, the alluring packages of chocolate-covered graham crackers that Leslie kept in our refrigerator were taunting me. I'd finish off one of the sleeves—that's 16 crackers, minus a couple that Leslie had eaten (the normal way people consume such things). Furious with myself, I'd reach for the baking soda and gulp the concoction while holding my nose, then expel my guilt. Afterward, it was off to the grocery store to buy another package, tossing out the top four to cover my tracks.

Starve, cheat, binge, purge—the cycle would take years to break.

6

Who Is That Girl?

M Y TITLE AT CNN was assistant assignment editor—not much of a step up from desk assistant. But there was one big difference: Here, I actually got to be on TV (not the vote of confidence it might sound like—there was a lot of airtime to fill and they were desperate for people to fill it).

On camera was where I wanted to be. After all, I'd been "on" my entire life, whether it was at dinner with my family or at the lunch table with my friends. I can't remember a time I ever shied away from the spotlight. Which made me wonder: Why would I come up with the ideas, write the scripts, find the visuals, pick the sound bites, and not be front and center? Determined to get on camera, I would settle for scraps, gladly covering an obscure hearing on Capitol Hill or a no-news press conference at the Department of Transportation, hoping they'd turn into stories.

My big break came in the fall of 1981 when Washington Bureau Chief Stuart Loory, who looked a little like Groucho Marx, said, "I know you're interested in becoming a reporter. So here's your chance: Tomorrow morning I want you to go live from the White House and report on the president's schedule for the day."

I panicked. *Live?* As in *live from the White House?* I'd never gone live before. Live TV is working without a net—no do-overs.

"Really?" I said incredulously. "Okay, great." While inside I was thinking, *Oh. My. God.*

That night I laid out my light blue pin-striped pantsuit. Then I grabbed my hairbrush Marcia Brady–style, stared into the mirror, and said in earnest, measured tones over and over, "Katherine Couric, CNN, at the White House…Katherine Couric, CNN, at the White House," hoping my given name would lend an air of authority my face and voice lacked. My stomach churned. I spent most of the night in the bathroom.

I woke up at 4:30 a.m., got dressed, and drove to the bureau to rip the AP daybook off the wire machine that detailed the president's schedule. Unfortunately for me, President Reagan was meeting with former national security adviser Zbigniew Brzezinski—a nightmare to pronounce.

At the White House, a crew member helped me insert my IFB, the earpiece that allows the control room to communicate with reporters in the field. With minutes to go before my "hit," I stood there practicing under my breath, waiting for the anchors to throw to me. Through the earpiece I could hear them reading the headlines, then going to a commercial break. As I listened to a jingle about the joys of orange juice, I suddenly heard the anchors' voices.

"Who is that girl?"

"She looks like she's 12 years old."

And suddenly I was on. One of them said, "Katherine Couric is standing by at the White House with more…"

I heard myself reciting the president's schedule, my voice so high, it was as if I'd inhaled two balloons' worth of helium.

Everything was off—my tone, my pacing, the way I looked down at my notes instead of at the camera (although I did pronounce Zbigniew Brzezinski correctly). After I threw back to the anchors, I looked at the crew for positive reinforcement. They didn't say a word.

Back at the Washington bureau, I hoped someone, anyone, would tell me I had done a good job. I walked to the assignment desk, where Bill Hensel was sitting.

"Hi, Bill!" I said eagerly.

"Reese Schonfeld"—president of CNN—"just called. He never wants to see you on the air again."

"Did he say anything else?"

"No. That's it." Bill looked at me sympathetically and shrugged. As I slunk away, some Sandra Boynton wisdom on a coffee mug caught my eye: DON'T LET THE TURKEYS GET YOU DOWN. Even though they had, and I was. I looked around at the other reporters and wondered, *What do they have that I don't?* Then it hit me: experience.

I'd been at the DC bureau for a year and my reporting future wasn't looking particularly rosy. By now, Don Farmer and Chris Curle were at CNN in Atlanta and looking for an associate producer for their noon-to-two broadcast *Take Two*. They asked me if I was interested.

Uh, yeah. Not only had I found my mentors, I'd found my next chapter.

7

The State of the Onion

I HEADED SOUTH ON I-95 in the white Toyota Corolla my parents had bought me—a gift for going to an affordable state school (my first year at UVA cost less than $2,000). But the car was bare-bones, with no AC, and by the time I passed the giant peach on the big blue sign welcoming me to Georgia, I had a serious case of swamp ass.

My father grew up 140 miles south of Atlanta, in Dublin, where he spent hot, lazy afternoons shooting squirrels with a 12-gauge shotgun and reading. He was bespectacled and studious; at Mercer University in Macon, he was editor in chief of the school newspaper, the *Cluster.*

His great-grandfather Charles Mathurin was an orphan, left on the doorstep of a hospital in Brittany, France. He was taken in and given the name Cour, which in Gaelic means "the smallest little person"; the *ic* was tacked on as an endearment. *Et voilà*—Couric.

In 1831, when he was just a teenager, Charles stowed away on a ship bound for America. Onboard, he met a woman named Henriette Fontaine, who was traveling with her husband and child. Before the ship docked in Pensacola, Charles jumped overboard to avoid getting caught. Soon, he and Henriette crossed paths again— her husband and child had both died not long after they'd arrived. Charles and the widow Fontaine (12 years his senior, an early cougar) fell in love, married, and took a wagon train to Eufaula, Alabama, near the Georgia border, where they settled and raised four children. One of them, Alfred Alexis, was my dad's grand-father.

Atlanta figured in my mother's side of the family too, after a lengthy detour in the Midwest. Her mom, Clara Frohsin (Nana to us, pronounced "Nah-nah," the French way), married Bert Hene, a successful architect and contractor primarily in a neighborhood of Omaha called Happy Hollow. They raised my mother and her younger brother, Buddy, like high-class nomads, occupying the fancy homes Bert built and moving on when they were sold (a particular point of family pride: my grandfather built the boyhood home of the future Oracle of Omaha, Warren Buffett). When Bert died of a heart attack at 58, Nana joined her brothers Leon and Lewis in Atlanta, where they had opened a pair of high-end women's clothing boutiques.

As a child, I loved when Nana came to visit. The minute she arrived, she'd unzip her sky-blue Skylark suitcase and start pulling out gifts— cute outfits and stuffed animals wrapped in tissue for the girls; sugared jelly candies shaped like orange slices for Johnny. I'd sit on her bed and chatter away while she got dressed, rolling a nylon stocking up each shapely leg and attaching it to the snaps dangling from her girdle (that medieval precursor to Spanx). Then she'd step into some formfitting dress (the lavender ultra-suede was my favorite) plus heels. Always heels. Even her slippers had kitten heels. Nana was so accustomed to her calf-flattering heels that when she was barefoot, she walked on the balls of her feet.

We'd play gin at the kitchen table. Nana would have a tissue tucked under her sleeve at the wrist or in her cleavage. She'd hold a Tareyton between her lips, the ever-lengthening ash threatening to dump on the floor, the cards, my head. Sometimes she'd tap it into an ashtray shaped like a cast-iron kettle on three little legs that now lives in my kitchen. (In seventh grade, I'd retrieve the butts and smoke them in the woods behind my elementary school with my friend Betsy.)

By the time Nana was in her eighties and started complaining about all the cats she was seeing under her bed, she was moved to a nursing home. Now that I was living in Atlanta, I visited often, playing the piano for her and the other residents, then giving my mom a full report.

AS AN ASSOCIATE producer on *Take Two,* my job included thinking of teases for upcoming segments, like cooking demonstrations with British chef Graham Kerr. One time, the recipe involved onions, and because President Reagan had just delivered his State of the Union address, I came up with "Next...the state of the onion."

"I love that!" said one of the middle-aged bookers, which put a little pep in my step.

But I was always on the hunt for opportunities to report. To get past my disastrous debut at the White House, I paid a visit to a voice coach. It was kind of a revelation—she told me not to project from my throat, which resulted in a high-pitched nasal sound, but to relax my belly and speak from my diaphragm. My tone instantly got lower and my voice more mellifluous, but it veered dangerously close to James Earl Jones territory. It would take me another few years to find just the right register.

I also had to learn the craft of interviewing: how to put people at ease, ask the right questions (nothing that could be answered "Yes" or "No"), act interested (99 percent of the time, I was), listen carefully (but never nod as if I'm agreeing), recognize a sound bite, and write to the pictures.

Don and Chris knew how much I wanted to be on-air and happily supplied the training wheels. They sent me to interview Ray Charles, Liberace (we played a duet of "Heart and Soul"), and newcomer Boy George as well as former Alabama governor and segregationist George Wallace. I did a story on the outlet malls in Reading, Pennsylvania, putting together a montage of bargain-hunters to the tune of the "William Tell Overture." When I showed it to Don, he pointed out that the editing wasn't in sync with the music. I'd never make that mistake again.

I started dating the show's director, Guy Pepper. Raven-haired, bearded, and newly separated from his CNN anchor wife, he was not my usual straight-arrow preppy type. But he was so clever and quick (he called me Katrina), and we had a blast soaking up all things Southern: grits and biscuits at the Silver Skillet, horseback riding in Dahlonega (we were almost thrown when our horses got spooked), the laser-light show at Stone Mountain. For me, it was a fun, 20-something extended fling—which reminds me of the time I flung several shoes at Guy when I thought he was cheating on me.

Taking *Take Two* on the road always felt like the big time. We went to Dallas–Fort Worth and I did a feature on Billy Bob's Texas, the massive honky-tonk. I headed home on Christmas Day. Wandering the deserted airport, wearing the black cowboy hat Billy Bob had given me, I remember missing my parents terribly but thinking it was all for a good cause—i.e., my career.

In the spring of 1982, thanks to a budding bro-ship between Ted Turner and Fidel Castro, we broadcast for a week from Havana—the first American network to do so since Castro took over. A crew that included Don, Chris, me, and Guy chartered a DC-3 to Cuba. I marveled at the pastel-hued buildings and vintage Chevys with their Batmobile fins in a land untouched by time since the '62 embargo. The hotel buffet was laden with salads drowning in mayonnaise, and everyone drank Coca-Cola by the gallon.

The embargo had apparently extended to toilet seats. When we got to our hotel, we discovered that nobody had one. Except me. Everyone was so jealous. I'd never won anything, but I guess you could say I hit the jackpot.

And I got to do some stories, including one on Hemingway in Cuba and his love of the fishing village Cojímar, the setting for *The Old Man and the Sea*. When I watch that piece now, it sounds more like an eighth-grade book report than an artfully crafted feature, but I gave it my all, and it showed.

"Your piece was brilliant, Katie!" said Reese Schonfeld over the phone—the same guy who'd banned me from the airwaves a year before.

8

Breast Size

AT CNN WE worked hard and played hard. One of the anchors hosted an annual Halloween party with instructions to come as your "favorite" story of the year. My friend Bonnie came as Grace Kelly, who'd died in a car crash that September; Bonnie wore a ball gown she'd picked up at a thrift shop, a rhinestone tiara, and a steering wheel around her neck that she'd found at a junkyard. A producer came as Vic Morrow, the actor who'd been decapitated while filming the *Twilight Zone* movie; he wore fatigues and what looked like helicopter blades protruding from his neck. Someone else showed up as a tampered-with bottle of Tylenol.

I was a flight attendant in a blazer, khaki skirt, and shoulder bag. And ripped stockings and a single shoe. The previous January, Air Florida Flight 90 had crashed into the icy Potomac shortly after takeoff—78 people died, including heroic passengers who'd drowned while saving others.

I know what you're thinking. But we were newspeople with a twisted sense of humor whose jobs sometimes required ironic distance. Still, what the hell was wrong with us?

Clearly, it was a less enlightened time. Especially when it came to women in the workplace. With a new generation looking to get a toehold in the industry, there were easily as many *Mad Men*–era leftovers who wanted to get the broads out of broadcasting.

One week, I filled in for a *Take Two* producer while she was on vacation, attending an editorial meeting in her place. I was running a few minutes late, per usual, so when I got to the conference room, the eight male executives and lone young woman (in charge of promos) were already seated. The number-two man at the network, Ed Turner (no relation to Ted), was running the meeting. As I walked in, he picked up on my arrival and said to the room, "That's not why Katie is successful. She's successful because of her determination, hard work, intelligence, and"—here Turner paused—"breast size."

I froze. The place went quiet. Some people laughed nervously. Others looked down uncomfortably. I took my seat.

I couldn't focus. It wasn't the first time I'd had to deal with this kind of BS: There was the customer at Gifford's ice cream parlor who, while I athletically scooped his mint chip, asked if my right breast was larger than my left; the teenage boy who walked by me at a crowded high school football game and casually but firmly cupped my crotch; the GM at a radio station I visited after interning there one summer who leered at my chest and asked, "Did you go on the pill? Your breasts are much bigger than they used to be."

After the meeting, I walked into the office Don and Chris shared.

"You won't believe what just happened," I told them, and described what Ed had done. They looked incredulous, then disgusted.

I was still stewing about it the next day. Don fed a piece of paper into his IBM Selectric. Together we composed the following:

```
TO: Ed Turner
FROM: Katie Couric
DATE: December 14, 1983
SUBJECT: Tuesday's Morning Meeting


I found your remark that I had succeeded because
of my determination, hard work, intelligence and
breast size insulting, demeaning, embarrassing,
humiliating and totally uncalled for . . . If you
```

were intending to be humorous, you failed . . . I
request that you apologize to me and that you
somehow indicate to the others who heard the
remark that you have so apologized.

I hand-delivered the memo to Ed Turner's office. Within a half hour, he was on the line.

Hummina, hummina... "I am so terribly sorry!" he said, his voice saccharine, sounding less regretful than like someone who'd been caught. "I was just being funny. I'm so sorry I offended you."

I liked the feeling of having his nuts in a vise. "Well, Ed," I said finally, "it was really offensive. And really inappropriate."

He promised it would never happen again.

"Thanks for calling. I appreciate it." What else could I say? The guy controlled my fate.

"What a creep," Chris said when I replayed the conversation.

"Good," Don said. Then, somewhat triumphantly, "Good!"

For every young woman starting out, I wish you a Don and a Chris. And no Ed Turner.

THE JOB GAVE me a chance to focus on politics, something I had come to love growing up in the DC area. I did some stories on the Reagan-Mondale campaign and even covered the conventions in Dallas and San Francisco. Apparently, Al Buch, the news director of WTVJ in Miami, was watching; he called and offered me a job on the spot.

The timing couldn't have been better. The new president of CNN, Burt Reinhardt, made it known he didn't think I had the right stuff to be on-air. So I applied for a job in the writers' pool and got rejected from that too. By Ed Turner. While Wendy found her professional home at CNN—she'd stay 32 years, producing *Larry King Live* for 18 of them— it was time for me to move on.

By now my relationship with Guy Pepper had petered out, so before flying south, I had one last adventure in Atlanta—and my first brush (well, more than a brush) with fame.

I was covering a press conference featuring the cast and crew of the movie *The Slugger's Wife* as well as the screenwriter, Neil Simon, the genius auteur behind such American classics as *The Odd Couple, Brighton Beach Memoirs,* and *The Goodbye Girl,* which I loved. The idea that I'd be in the presence of such an icon was thrilling. I was determined to get him to notice me.

I sat in the front row, wearing a white cotton dress with black stripes under a black knit jacket. I'd swiped on my go-to Max Factor Frosty Cola lipstick (I'd read that Connie Francis liked it too). I thought I looked pretty cute. Simon, sitting in a director's chair, glanced my way several times. I knew he knew that I knew that he noticed me.

The next day at CNN, the show's hilarious secretary, Mary, gave me a look as she handed me a pink While You Were Out slip. In her thick cursive, she had written *Neil Simon* and put a little check in the box next to CALLED.

I was completely, utterly, and crazily starstruck, laughing with my co-workers, wondering how I'd be able to go grocery shopping without being mobbed by fans when I became the next Mrs. Neil Simon.

He took me out to dinner. I remember him gazing at me and sighing audibly, his elbow on the table and his chin in his hand, looking like a smitten schoolboy. A bit over the top, but I was flattered to be the object of his momentary infatuation.

We had dinner again, after which he invited me back to his hotel. It was strange, being with someone 30 years older, but I was all for new experiences. He started kissing me and—well, that's as far as it got.

Neil Simon's three-word explanation: "Blood pressure medication."

9

Rainy Days and Mondays

THERE WAS AT least one thing I left behind in Atlanta.

Bulimia had plagued me throughout college. I remember gorging on chocolate chip cookies in my dorm room, then throwing up in a paper bag and stealthily discarding it in a dumpster outside. Sometimes I'd do it three times a week, then months would go by when I wouldn't succumb to the urge. But the cycle always started up again.

I shared an apartment in Atlanta with a cardiac rehab nurse. We weren't especially close, but our quarters were. One night, after hearing me retch in the bathroom, she confronted me. "I'm worried about you," she said. "I think you've got a problem."

I felt exposed and ashamed. So I moved out. But the confrontation forced me to face what I was doing to my body. I learned that my eating disorder could wreak havoc on my teeth, my esophagus, my overall health. Then Karen Carpenter died.

She was a huge star when I was in middle school—I can still remember her distinctive low vibrato in hit after hit, like "Top of the World" and "Rainy Days and Mondays." I'd say to my friends, "Listen, I sound just like Karen Carpenter," and perform a few bars of "Close to You," provoking eye-rolls. Thirteen years later, in 1983, her heart gave out, the result of anorexia. She was just 32 years old.

I studied Karen Carpenter's gaunt face on the cover of *People* magazine at the supermarket checkout. To think this gifted, wildly successful person was so sick she couldn't save herself and reverse what was happening to her.

That flipped a switch. *Get over this while you still can,* I thought. Which I did, and somehow managed to do it on my own. While body-image issues would dog me for years, the death of a childhood idol helped me escape the grip of an illness that, for far too long, had controlled my life.

10

Good Night, David! Good Night, Chet!

MY FATHER LOVED journalism. While he often said the pay was "lousy," he believed it was important work. He also liked being in the center of the action and thought the people were fun. He once told me being a reporter "feeds your ego, in a funny sort of way." When my dad covered politics for the *Atlanta Constitution,* he got such a kick out of the fact that he was on a first-name basis with state legislators.

But with a homemaker wife and a fourth kid (me) on the way, his chosen career just wasn't sustainable. So, after working in newspapers and two stints at the United Press, he put away his reporter's notebook and became a PR man, writing press releases and giving speeches for the National Association of Broadcasters. He was 37 years old.

Among ink-stained wretches, shifting to PR is like going to the dark side. But for our family, it meant much-needed stability. At roughly 6:30 every night, my dad would come through the door in his felt fedora and trench coat and drop his briefcase on the plastic carpet protector. As my mom welcomed him home, Johnny and I would run into the living room and squeal, "Kissing again!"

Then my mom would return to the kitchen to finish cooking dinner while my father made himself a drink. Picturing him pouring the Cutty Sark over crackling ice, I sometimes wonder if he was dulling the disappointment, knowing the days of tracking down sources, grilling politicians, and writing a kick-ass lede were behind him.

I INHERITED MY FATHER'S love of words (for a few months there, he had us bring a new word to the dinner table every night—I was particularly proud of *incongruous*). He once gave me a dictionary inscribed *To Katie, the wordsmith*. Like so many girls of my era, I determined early on that math wasn't my thing. I remember getting off the school bus in first grade and bawling all the way home because I had gotten a 2 instead of a 1 in arithmetic. It set me on a path—as far away from numbers as I could get and into the arms of words.

My dad also passed down a love of news. At the breakfast table over a bowl of Wheaties, he'd be poring over the *Washington Post,* pointing out important things that were happening locally and nationally and reading particularly powerful paragraphs out loud.

Following the news became something we shared. At bedtime, he'd call out, "Good night, David!" I'd yell back, "Good night, Chet!" Chet Huntley and David Brinkley, NBC's big anchor duo in the 1960s. Soon I was spending every Sunday night eating leftover fried chicken on the floor of my parents' bedroom, watching a riveting new show called *60 Minutes.*

My very first news story is preserved in my paisley-cloth-covered diary from fourth grade:

Dear Diary,

On Friday, January 27, 1967, all three astronauts got burned to death on the Apollo rocket. They were Grissom, White and Chaffee. It was very sad.

That same year I started mocking up my own version of the *Washington Post* in blue ballpoint pen, with news, weather, sports, even obituaries. A few years later, I created my own magazine, called *Now,* with important articles about the value of a good appearance, nutrition, movie reviews, a crossword puzzle, and original illustrations by yours truly.

My father noticed it all, including my ability to get my homework done under the wire. On many mornings, he'd find me sitting cross-legged against the front door, finishing a book report with seconds to spare, then slamming my notebook shut and running to catch the bus. He might have been exasperated, but he appreciated my ability to work on deadline.

I wrote for my high school paper, the *Sentry*. In college at the *Cavalier Daily*, I became the associate features editor and launched a series of professor profiles. There was something about getting beneath their academic facade that really appealed to me. With a bulky tape recorder sitting between us, I was good at disarming them and accessing another side.

My first profile was of an art history professor. The opening sentence: "Ralph Waldo Emerson once wrote, 'We put our love where we have put our labor.' This certainly holds true for Frederick Hartt."

I sent a copy to my parents. As reliably as the sun coming up, my father had feedback. A typed critique arrived in the mail:

Dear Katie,

Just a brief note from the office to tell you how much your mother and I enjoyed your first faculty profile. It was excellent. I had the feeling I was talking to him. The typography was lousy but that's not your problem. I also liked the photo.

A good profile article gives insights into an individual's personality. You achieved this to some degree on your first effort but keep digging. Ask some of your subjects about their thoughts for the future. Where is the University heading? What problems do they foresee?

Again, you did a good job and we are proud of you.

Love,
Dad

I was grateful for my father's guidance through the years. He was almost giddy when I told him my eighth-grade English teacher had read my essay in front of the class. It was his idea for me to intern at radio stations in the summers during college. But I also understood his vicarious interest. Not only had he been forced to give up journalism, but what he'd given it up *for* wasn't really working out either.

It was a Saturday during high school. My mother was making sandwiches for lunch, stacking the tuna and egg salad several deep on a platter, as my dad and I sat down at the kitchen table. I distinctly recall babbling on in a very me-me-me kind of way about something I wanted to buy or do. And I can still see my mother standing stock-still by the table and fixing me with a look.

"Katie," she said, "your dad lost his job."

It was one of those indelible moments from childhood when you realize your parents are fallible. Vulnerable. They're hurt—maybe even scared.

There was no rush to reassure me that everything would be okay like they normally would. I wasn't the priority here—my parents had bigger things on their minds. My typically loquacious father was speechless, eyes downcast. I can never unsee his head bent in shame.

I'm not sure what happened. In retrospect, I don't think schmoozing, a job requirement in PR, was my dad's strong suit. But he got back on his feet, writing speeches and handling the media for various organizations—nursing homes, podiatrists, the National Association of Retarded Children (at a time when the nomenclature was far less enlightened); he was also an adjunct professor at American University, teaching journalism and public relations, which he seemed to enjoy.

But it's not an overstatement to say I pursued journalism for my father. Yes, the excitement of it quickly won me over. And yet the pleasure he took from my success in a profession he'd loved but had to leave was never lost on me. He couldn't believe the stories I covered, the people I got to interview, the books I had inscribed for him by some of his favorite authors, from David McCullough to Sue Grafton. And, of course, the money I eventually made, so beyond anything we could ever have imagined. I never wanted that to be awkward between us, but the fact is, he reveled in it.

I was living the dream. Mine. And his.

11

Hot, Hot, Hot

MIAMI WAS FULL of flavor and color and noise in a way Atlanta and Washington just weren't. My mom had always wanted me to work in a market like Chicago; she thought my friendly openness would play well in the Midwest. But there was just one problem: When I interviewed for a job in Chicago, the news director had zero interest.

Two other newcomers to South Florida at the time: Crockett and Tubbs, the Metro-Dade police detectives on *Miami Vice,* chasing down drug dealers and gunrunners in the blazing sun. Who could forget the pink and teal logo, the sexy title sequence that played like a music video with shots of Rolls-Royces, windsurfers, the Hialeah racetrack...everyone, including me, started pushing up the sleeves of their blazers to the elbow.

My embrace of the whole *Miami Vice* ethos included dating a Metro-Dade cop of my own—Commander Bill Johnson. As the police department spokesman, Bill was the person local reporters got the scoop from at a crime scene. Local reporters like me.

We first kissed on a rainy night in the parking lot of my apartment building in Coconut Grove, the kind of kiss where everything around you peels away. When we detached, Bill saw the rivulets of mascara staining my cheeks and said, "I think your eyebrows are running down your face." I liked the way his tongue tasted after he'd been smoking.

Bill was divorced, with two towheaded boys. I brought him home to Arlington for Christmas and my mom took an instant dislike to him. Perhaps it was the gold chain or the mesh tank top or the fact that he went to the sidewalk outside our house to smoke. After we left, she was so unsettled, she called Wendy to make sure this wasn't "serious."

She didn't have to worry. I really liked Bill, but I knew he wasn't for the long haul—that's one of the reasons I went out with him. I didn't want anything or anyone getting in the way of my career.

MIAMI WAS A great news market for a young reporter. It had crime, immigration, hurricanes, a lush ecosystem under constant threat—once I covered a story about the Everglades from a pontoon boat. Local stories were often national news. It was action central, which made Miami a feeder for the big leagues. So many reporters who'd learned the ropes in South Florida went on to long careers as network correspondents.

By the time I left CNN, I had a number of features under my belt. What I didn't have were the chops that come with covering spot news, jumping in the back of a van and hauling ass to a live shot, churning out two stories a day. In other words, I was a rookie, and treated that way. For one of my first stories, I remember dashing out with a cameraman named Carlos Rigau. I pointed at the protest we were covering and said, "Hey, Carlos, can you zoom in?" Then: "Hey, Carlos, can you pan over here?" If looks could kill...he clearly wasn't enthralled by the new girl literally calling the shots.

I'm not being modest when I say I was terrible live. I just couldn't get over people who could stand there and talk off-the-cuff in full sentences, without notes, hitting their "roll cue" (the words that signal the director to roll the tape). If I wanted to do this for a living, I had to get some experience, pronto.

They put me on the night beat, where I got plenty of opportunities to go live: two dead drug dealers who'd been stuffed in the trunk of a car (a fellow reporter described the corpses moldering in the Miami heat as smelling like "rotten chicken"); an uprising at the Krome

Detention Center, where undocumented workers were warehoused; crazed Dolphins fans before a big game, mugging and jumping around behind me (I finally understood why newspeople called TV cameras "asshole magnets"). I went live from fires, home invasions, DOAs on the interstate (proving the adage "If it bleeds, it leads"), and slowly but surely got more comfortable.

As much as I loved breaking news, I was happiest sinking my teeth into in-depth features. I did a story on the pathology of shoplifters, and another on child-abuse laws that in some cases wrongly separated kids from their families. But the one that will live in infamy was about the homeless in Miami. Whatever you do, please, I beg you, don't google it.

It was an era of enterprising stunt journalism, of reporters strapping on "fat suits" and going undercover. I made the boneheaded decision to infiltrate the homeless subculture by pretending to be part of it. That meant buying dingy clothes at the Salvation Army, having my face spackled with wrinkle makeup, donning a curly wig, a knit cap (with a fork stuck in it, for some reason), plus ripped knee-high hose. Then I loaded up a shopping cart with my supposed worldly goods and pushed it down the street, asking passersby for spare change.

It gets worse. I cleaned windshields and dived for pennies in a hotel fountain. At one point I stretched out flat on the sidewalk. I waited in line with other homeless people for a free meal (and pronounced it fairly tasty). Under the Miami sun, my makeup started to melt; one man I met at the shelter asked me if I was a burn victim. By nightfall, things got a little tense when someone challenged me about who I was and suggested I might be muscling in on his turf. When he reached into his pocket, the cameraman rushed over, blasting us with light.

I was desperate to go deep on important stories. And, yes, I pointed out how difficult it was to get into a shelter (which required an ID) and how dangerous this life was. But it was just so poorly done, an insult to homeless people everywhere. The spectacle of me shuffling around the mean streets of Miami in costume was bad enough, although some of the writing was even worse: "This is the American dream gone bad," I noted gravely. "These people only wish they weren't awake."

I don't even know what that means. I'll be atoning for that piece for the rest of my days.

ALL IN ALL, I loved being at WTVJ. Tammi Leader (aka Tammi from Miami) and Lisa Gregorisch, who ran the Broward bureau, would become lifelong friends. But after two years I was nearing the deadline I'd set for myself—to become a network correspondent by the time I turned 30. And I couldn't see myself settling down in Miami.

There'd been a few nibbles, so I decided to get an agent who could help me figure things out. It just so happened the woman I hired was dating the general manager at a TV station (that kind of cross-pollination was typical of the news business). Even better, the station was WRC in Washington, DC—a local shop in another news-making city. I interviewed with the GM and the news director. They offered me a job as a general-assignment reporter, bumping up my salary from $45,000 to $60,000 a year. I packed up my apartment, loaded my gray Persian, Frank, into his cat carrier, and headed north.

12

Nice Writing, Ms. Couric

THE HEADQUARTERS OF WRC-TV had all the personality of a munic-
ipal building behind the Iron Curtain, with its squat, concrete
facade and matrix of windows. And yet I knew I was right where I
needed to be, figuratively and physically: WRC was just one flight up
from the mighty Washington bureau of NBC News.

If we were middle school, the first floor was where the cool seniors
hung out. Sometimes you'd see Andrea Mitchell or Tom Brokaw walking
around as you headed to the stairs. Lining the wall by the entrance were
huge posters of TV-news stars, perfectly coiffed with airbrushed skin,
staring out of the frames. I'd wonder why Tim Russert seemed to be
scowling at me and consider Garrick Utley's resemblance to a butler in
a black-and-white movie. I'd silently greet Bryant and Jane and Willard
and Gene Shalit as I passed. And sometimes I'd fantasize, *Maybe I'll
have my picture up there someday too.*

WRC was full of characters. Lovable assignment editor Milton
Shockley looked like an extra from *Duck Dynasty* who apparently wasn't
eating much duck—his skinny frame, long auburn beard, plaid shirts,
and saggy jeans seemed out of place in a newsroom in the middle
of the nation's navy-blazered capital. Gruff Kenny Gamble was always
glued to the police scanners, while excitable Ed Fishel, who resembled
a Berenstain Bear with hearing aids in both ears, got everyone whipped

up when news was breaking. My fellow reporter, Beltway fixture Pat Collins, had the twinkly-eyed, ruddy face of someone who'd wandered in from County Clare. Had we met a century earlier, he would be happily dipping my braids in the inkwell.

The newsroom teemed with strong, smart women: assistant news director Kris Ostrowski, who could have doubled as a high school basketball coach and yelled "Couric!" whenever she saw me; warm, impeccably dressed morning anchor Barbara Harrison (the first time I ever saw Bulgari jewelry in the wild); saucy, sassy assignment editor Dana Rudman, whom I bonded with instantly; no-no-nonsense Nannette Wilson, the producer of the 6:00 p.m. broadcast; Susan Kidd, a ballsy anchor with an Angela Davis vibe. Looking back, I realize that racial and gender diversity ruled at WRC before it was even a thing.

The minute I walked into the newsroom, an assignment editor would bark orders: *You're going with Mike Swann to shoot a school-board meeting/protest/fire*—name that news event. Adrenaline pumping, I'd jump in the live truck or crew car and head out, gathering as much information as I could before getting to the scene. Then I'd leap out of the vehicle, assess the situation, grab some sound bites, send some material back to the station, get wired up to do a live shot, throw to a "Sony sandwich" (sound bites or B-roll of the scene that I'd narrate live or play as a stand-alone element). And that was just for "the five and six" (the 5:00 and 6:00 p.m. broadcasts); the 11:00 still loomed.

As usual, I was a wreck when I had to go live. With seconds to spare, I'd slap on some lipstick, pat my face with powder, and run a comb through my hair. On days I forgot eyeliner, I'd use a black felt-tip pen. And then, showtime!—as the anchors back at the station uttered those five sphincter-tightening words—"Katherine Couric is there live." I was still incapable of describing things off-the-cuff—I had to write down everything in my reporter's notebook, then memorize and regurgitate. When I was done, I'd walk around the live truck, mouthing every word I had just said.

"What are you *doing*?" the cameraman would ask.

I'd tell him I was decompressing.

Reporting stories for the 11 was a whole different animal: There was glamour and edge to covering news at night, especially if you were a woman—racing around the city Brenda Starr–like in our pumps and pantyhose, thrusting mics in the faces of cops at the scene of the crime (crime being the bread-and-butter of the night shift). Out in the field I'd see Nancy Mathis from the CBS affiliate, Channel 9, and Penny Daniels from ABC's Channel 7. We were fiercely competitive, trying to beat each other with better shots and sound bites, bigger interviews—anything to stand out. Oh, how my heart would sink if I arrived on the scene and one of them was there first. We were faux-friendly, more often sniffing around one another like dogs.

One of my first big stories was a horrific tragedy: A stalled dump truck filled with hot asphalt suddenly started to roll, crushing the Toyota idling behind it, killing two of the teenage girls inside. I was sent to track down the victims' families, find out more about them, and retrieve some photos we could use in our story.

Thinking about invading those people's privacy still makes me anxious. I remember walking up to one of the girls' houses and knocking tentatively, hoping no one would answer—when a tearstained woman opened the door.

"I'm so sorry about your daughter," I said. I wasn't much older than the child she'd lost; I thought about my own mother. "We're covering what happened, and I was wondering if you might have a picture..."

To my profound surprise, the woman asked me to come in. She led me downstairs to the basement and pulled out a photo album full of pictures of her daughter—smiling, clowning around, posing with loved ones. I asked about a few of them. Then this grieving mother carefully extracted a pretty photo and told me I could take it. I remember her saying, "Thank you for coming by and being so nice."

In that moment, I was struck by how two complete strangers could find a way to connect in a crisis. In the best of worlds, reporters are people first, and I quickly learned the role we can play in helping validate a life lost. Journalists are often berated for their mercenary hunt for raw emotion—*How did it feel to lose your job/husband/legs/child/home?* But the human drama of these stories spoke to me, bringing out my ability to form a bond—albeit temporary—with people I had only just met.

NEWS DIRECTOR BRET Marcus made a habit of leaving encouraging notes and feedback for me, calling out a turn of phrase that nailed it. I still have them in a box of mementos. When I flew to Detroit to cover the crash of a Northwest Airlines jet, I described the debris-strewn site like this: "In the wreckage below, a baby doll, a man's shoe, a coffeepot—remnants of the lives lost on Flight 255." Bret jotted, *Ms. Couric, very nice writing.*

Another time, the face of the broadcast, local legend Jim Vance, walked by and dropped a note he'd scribbled on a legal pad: *FYI. I think your work is great. You really lite up the screen with good stuff!* I still have that one too.

I loved that other people were feeling what I was feeling—that this was where I belonged. The news business was perfect for me: the fast pace (I thrived in chaos), the opportunity to write (turning what I'd witnessed into a compelling script), the chance to help viewers understand what was going on and sort through the emotions that came with it.

The positive feedback gave me the courage to take it up a notch. One day I asked Bret if I could try anchoring. "I could do the morning cut-ins," I suggested, the ones that would run at 25 minutes past the hour during the *TODAY* show.

He looked skeptical. "Sure...you can try."

I got to the newsroom at 4:00 a.m. to write the script, cut the tape with the editor, and try to get comfortable in the anchor chair. I had no idea the gig would require me to operate the prompter myself, turning a knob under the desk to scroll the script. Of course I didn't time it properly. So there I was, staring into the camera and earnestly reading the copy when the director said in my earpiece, "Katie, we're already in a commercial."

Later that morning, I stepped into Bret's office. "What did you think? Can I try again?"

Bret paused. "Maybe if you go to a really, really, really small market somewhere."

MILTON SHOCKLEY LOOKED embarrassed and spoke in a hushed tone so no one else could hear. "They want you to do a series called 'No Time for Sex.'"

Ugh. Sweeps, the months when advertising rates are set, were all about eyeballs, and apparently someone thought it would be grabby to explore the dearth of intimacy plaguing two-career couples. But why me? Did they think I was going to appear on camera sitting seductively on a bed, legs crossed, in a short skirt? No thanks.

"Why not ask I. J. Hudson?" I suggested. "He's married with children; *he* probably doesn't have time for sex. I'm 27 and single. I have plenty of time!"

I agreed to do a series that was more in my wheelhouse—about the difficulty young professional women were having finding a man. We called it "Lonely Too Long" and opened each segment with the song of the same name by the Young Rascals.

It was a hot, zeitgeisty topic. At the time, a culture war was raging, with a new generation of women delaying marriage and motherhood to pursue careers. Armed with the pill and college degrees, many women my age were focused on making their marks.

And yet if our beloved Mary Richards embodied those tentative early steps (tongue-tied when trying to ask Mr. Grant for a raise), the face—or caricature—of our generation was morphing into something else: Alex Forrest from *Fatal Attraction,* whose steely, career-obsessed selfishness had turned her into a homewrecking bunny-boiler.

There had already been relentless hand-wringing in the media about the ways the women's movement had supposedly backfired. The thinking was that all of this hard-won self-sufficiency was making us anxious, lonely—maybe even infertile (a whole laundry list of woes methodically debunked in Susan Faludi's 1991 book *Backlash*).

But nothing struck a nerve quite like a *Newsweek* article in June of 1986 with the blaring headline "The Marriage Crunch." Right there on the cover was a graph indicating that a woman's chances of getting married plummet as she ages (and pretty much flatline after her thirties). The story inside, "Too Late for Prince Charming?," put it more colorfully: Women over 40 "are more likely to be killed by a terrorist than to get married."

Two decades later, *Newsweek* actually apologized for the article's faulty research and analysis. But at the time, it was a shot through the heart of single women everywhere, including me. I bought a T-shirt that was all the rage among us working girls, featuring a Roy Lichtenstein damsel in distress with the thought bubble I CAN'T BELIEVE IT. I FORGOT TO HAVE CHILDREN!

Around that time, Cassie Mackin, the ABC correspondent I'd idolized, died of cancer at 43. I remember watching her funeral on TV. VIPs like Ted Kennedy, Frank Reynolds, and David Brinkley carried her coffin. No husband or children in sight.

Perhaps that was her choice. But the scene helped clarify *my* choice: yes, a career. And a husband and kids too.

13

Finding Ted

TICK-TICK-TICK-TICK-TICK. I was in my late twenties and I knew I had to put myself out there. That meant saying yes to everyone, even men I was certain would never be the father of my children. In other words, even Larry King.

I was at a reception at Duke Zeibert's on L Street, the late, lamented power-lunch mecca of presidents, lobbyists, and pro athletes. I spotted the CNN host, in his trademark aviators and suspenders, moseying over, which might have had something to do with the chocolate-brown leather skirt I was wearing. We chatted, and at some point he said, "Can I take you out to dinner?"

"Sure," I said. Why not? Larry was already a big player on- and off-screen with a slew of ex-wives. A pretty fascinating character, and I was eager to pick his brain.

I looked down from my ninth-floor apartment at 1100 Connecticut Avenue and saw a black sedan snake into the circular driveway. As I slid into the passenger seat, I was greeted by the smooth sounds of Jack Jones on the tape deck. (Yes, I'm that old.)

We headed to a posh Italian place on K Street. The maître d' sat us next to each other at a table by the wall, an arrangement you often see in the dark corners of romantic restaurants—a middle-aged man hip to hip with his "niece."

I asked Larry what it was like at CNN now, hosting his popular talk show *Larry King Live*. Our media chitchat was mixed with daughterly concern about my dinner partner's health; Larry was 24 years older than me and had recently come through quintuple-bypass surgery. He ordered veal poached in chicken broth and ate it with gusto. Nothing gets a single gal's juices flowing quite like a man slurping a heart-healthy dish and splattering it all over the napkin tucked into his collar.

After dinner, we got back in the sedan. Suddenly I saw that we were making our way across Memorial Bridge, in the opposite direction of Connecticut Avenue.

"Where are we going?" I asked, a little croaky from all the conversation.

"My place!" Larry exclaimed, a little croakier.

Mayday! Mayday! *Dear* Cosmo: *My dinner date is an aging horn dog and he's detouring me to his place. How do I extricate myself, stat?*

We pulled into his parking garage in Rosslyn and headed to his apartment. Inside, I was greeted by the biggest brag wall ever: keys to cities great and small, commendations, photos with the rich, famous, and infamous everywhere.

Larry invited me to sit on the sofa. I was trying to figure out an exit strategy when suddenly—*boom!*—the lunge. The tongue. The hands.

The whole scene was such a cliché, I began to laugh and gently pushed him away. "Larry, you are so nice and I enjoyed getting to know you," I said. "But I'm really interested in meeting someone a little closer to my age."

Deflation—on all levels. He stopped what he was doing.

Then he got up, grabbed his car keys, and smiled. "No problem," Larry said. "But when I like, I really like."

Duly noted.

Larry and I were one and done. Every time we ran into each other in the years that followed, it gave us a big laugh.

THE SEARCH FOR Ted was on. That's what my friend Carmela called my imaginary future husband.

Mark Levinstein, a UVA classmate, now a lawyer, invited me to a big party at his house in Falls Church. Sure, I said, suspecting the place would be swimming with eligible yuppies.

It was a bitterly cold night. I slid into some black tights, threw on a white ribbed turtleneck, and finished the look with yet another leather skirt, this one black.

Mark's undergraduate experience planning university events had clearly paid off. He was a convener—he took pride in the fact that so many friendships and love connections had been forged at his parties. He'd filled the place with booze, soda, and snacks, and created several continuous hours of mixtapes, from Motown to Springsteen.

I was excited about the possibilities. So excited, in fact, I was the first person there. Mark's girlfriend, Terri, and I went downstairs to the bachelor-pad bar area, perched on some stools Mark and Terri had bought from Ikea and assembled the day before, and did shots of tequila, licking salt off our hands and sucking on wedges of lime.

The place started to fill up...with beautiful blondes fresh out of college. I was a little mad at Mark for stocking the party with them, feeling self-conscious about being 30. So I got to work trying to get noticed.

Fueled with liquid courage, I headed to the pool table, cue in hand, and proceeded to bend over the edge and slide the stick suggestively between my fingers, tented on the felt. Then I strolled around the table and teasingly grabbed the end of someone's cue as he was about to take a shot. I was teetering precariously between adorable and obnoxious.

As I called the eight ball in the corner pocket like Minnesota Fats, I spotted two guys walking down the stairs. They were both really attractive, but I was drawn to the one with curly brown hair wearing a cocoa-colored fisherman's sweater. Whenever I tried to look into my future, I envisioned a man with curly brown hair walking down the street, holding the hand of a little girl in a pink tutu—our daughter.

Curly Brown Hair and his friend lingered on the basement steps—strategically, perhaps, holding back and being cool, surveying the scene—then finally made their way down. Emboldened by a what-the-hell attitude, I walked right over. After some perfunctory introductions—the object of my affection was named Jay—I tried something really original. "So, what do you guys do?" I asked.

"I'm a lawyer," Jay's friend David said. At Mark's law firm, Williams & Connolly.

Pretending to stifle a yawn, I turned to Jay. "And you?"

"I'm a painter," he replied.

"Like an artist?"

"No, I paint houses."

Intriguing, I thought. "I feel like I'm the oldest person here," I lamented. "I bet I'm older than both of you."

Jay bit. "I bet you're not. Whoever's wrong has to get the other person a drink." Jay whipped out his driver's license. I read the small print: *January 9, 1956.*

"We almost have the same birthday!" I said. "I was born on January 7th the year after you."

"I'll have a beer," Jay said.

I didn't want to seem too available, so after a flirty conversation, I played a little more pool, well aware that Jay was watching me. Then I headed upstairs and chatted with someone else, keeping one eye on the basement steps.

Finally he appeared. I went over.

"Are you dating anyone?" I inquired, shamelessly.

"Not really."

I asked him if he wanted to have lunch sometime. God, I was brazen.

"Maybe," Jay said.

Soon, he and David headed out the door. I ran after them and gave them my business card—chintzy and thin, printed with a big blue 4 (as in, News 4). They both gave me theirs, engraved on thick stock. Yup, Jay was a lawyer at Williams & Connolly too.

"Call me!" I yelled before heading back inside.

I put Jay's card on my bedside table. I couldn't stop thinking about his Irish good looks and slightly brooding, Heathcliffian air.

Several days went by with no call. So I decided to call him.

"Jay Monahan."

"Hi, Jay Monahan, this is Katie Couric. I met you at Mark Levinstein's party last weekend. We compared driver's licenses."

"Of course, hi," he said, sounding as if he was actually glad to hear from me. "I was going to call you."

"But you didn't."

"I guess I didn't have to."

Oh, brother, he's confident. "Would you like to have dinner with me?" I asked. He said sure.

Jay and I made plans to go to a Thai restaurant a few blocks from my apartment. A school night. Less pressure.

He was already seated when I arrived.

"Hi!" I said enthusiastically and shook his hand while he stayed glued to his chair.

"I'd stand up," he said, "but I ripped my pants getting out of the cab." I loved his honesty. And he was even more handsome than I remembered, wearing a sharp suit with a neatly folded white handkerchief peeking out of his breast pocket.

Jay ordered a Thai beer and told me about growing up in Manhasset on Long Island in a big Irish Catholic family; he was the oldest boy in a brood of seven. He'd gone to college at Washington and Lee, where he played football and lacrosse, which allowed us to compare notes on going to school in Virginia. Then things took a fascinating turn. He told me about joining the navy and flying jets in Pensacola, working on a dude ranch, modeling, acting, going to law school at Georgetown... Jay was so smart, a polymath, an adventurer. After dinner, as I rode the elevator to my apartment on the ninth floor, I thought a thought I hadn't thought in a while: *This has potential.*

But Mark Levinstein wasn't so sure. As he later told me, Jay always dated the same type: tall, thin, blond, with a father who had a big job at some embassy.

Katie isn't anything like them, he thought. *It won't last.*

OUR NEXT DATE was lunch at Bread and Chocolate, a restaurant on Connecticut Avenue. Over ham and cheese on baguettes, Jay explained the history of the conflict in Northern Ireland. I was enthralled. (Or at least I acted like it.) Then we took a big step: The following Saturday we spent the whole day together, in Pennsylvania Dutch country. We ate shoofly pie and bought preserves at a farm stand. Everything felt new and tasted delicious, and the grass was Easter-basket green. Jay had picked me up in his brand-new maroon Jeep Cherokee—he was so proud of it. I'd put my coffee cup on the floor of the passenger seat and promptly kicked it over. He pretended not to mind.

We went to Williams & Connolly parties and softball games and had dinners out in Georgetown. One time when Jay came to pick me up, I looked out the window and saw him standing by the car—and noticed his hair looked a bit thin on top.

Later I asked innocently, "Do you think you'll be bald when you're older?"

"I don't know," Jay replied. "Do you think you'll be fat and ugly?"

Touché.

About a month into our relationship, a serious test: Jay was my date at a college friend's wedding. When he brought me out on the dance floor, I was, well, floored. The guy could dance! The way he held me, guiding our every move, spinning me effortlessly ... finally, I didn't have to lead.

14

I Can Do This

JUST BEFORE CHRISTMAS, NEARLY a year after we met, Jay and I went to a party in Arlington at my friend Betsy's house. A whole cadre of childhood buddies were there—it was great seeing them and reconnecting with my fun, handsome boyfriend in tow.

At some point, Jay asked me to make sure my parents were home. Then he dashed out of the party, saying he'd be back soon. Hmmm...

As I'd later learn, gallant Jay wanted to ask them for my hand in marriage.

My father's reaction: "We would be delighted!"

My mother's reaction: "That would be swell!"

They broke out the scotch and continued the conversation. My dad confessed I did have a flaw—"Sometimes she can be a pouter," he said, quickly adding that was my *only* flaw. My mom, who'd stared suspiciously at Jay's striped socks the first time I brought him home, had since been won over and was pleased as punch.

Back at the party, Jay said he needed to talk to me and took me into an empty room at Betsy's. Suddenly he pulled out that heart-stopping object—a small black velvet box. He didn't get down on one knee, but he did snap it open and say, "Will you marry me?"

I was completely and utterly thrilled, although not all that surprised (you didn't have to be Inspector Clouseau to know that something was up). Jay looked like he might burst from excitement as I slipped the beautiful, one-carat-diamond ring on my finger.

I had finally found my Ted. The yin to my yang. Jay could be serious and a tad standoffish, making it even more special that he was so affectionate toward me. I, on the other hand, always seemed to be running for class president. I made Shirley Temple seem like an introvert. Jay often told people, "Katie was born on a sunny day." Somehow, it just worked.

We rejoined the party and shared our news. Cheers, hugs, and toasts. As the last of my friends to get married, I was happy to be joining the club. Now I had the next six months to focus on work, plan a wedding, and have plenty of premarital sex.

SHORTLY BEFORE OUR big day, Tim Russert called and said he wanted to talk to me. I couldn't imagine why. We'd seen each other in the cafeteria, but we'd never had an actual conversation.

Although it would be another two years before Tim became a household face as host of *Meet the Press,* he was already a force at NBC. He'd just been made Washington bureau chief—he had a lot of power and could make things happen, like brokering Bryant and Jane's meeting with Pope John Paul II at the Vatican for the *TODAY* show.

His sweet secretary, Barbara Fant, greeted me. She directed me to Tim's spacious office, where I spied a bin of individually wrapped Twizzlers and resisted the urge to pluck one out.

"I have an opening at the Pentagon," Tim said. "I'm looking for a deputy correspondent to work with Fred Francis. What do you think? Do you think you could do this?"

Holy shit, I thought.

"The Pentagon, wow," I said. But I had to be honest. "I don't really have a strong background in military affairs."

"You can learn," Tim said. "Fred will take you under his wing. I've watched you covering Marion Barry" (the DC mayor caught on tape smoking crack with a supposed lady friend in a downtown hotel). "You're relentless."

Tim told me he had already asked the WRC general manager for permission to offer me the job. "He said by all means, go ahead."

That hurt. I couldn't believe there was so little interest in keeping me.

Tim continued: "At first he wanted me to talk to Wendy Rieger"—a leggy looker at WRC and my complete opposite—"but I said no, I want Katie."

I knew I liked this guy.

In no time we were talking turkey, figuring out logistics. I told him I was getting married in a couple of months and had planned a two-week honeymoon.

"We can wait," Tim said, fixing me with his patented penetrating stare. "You're ready for this."

I wasn't so sure. Then I remembered what George Watson told me when I'd sought his advice about becoming a reporter: "Whatever you do, don't be typecast as the cute girl who does features."

I thought about those words every time I did a story. And you can't get more hard-news than the Pentagon.

When I reached the door, I turned around.

"I can do this," I said.

OUR WEDDING WAS on June 10th at 2:00 p.m. at the Navy Chapel, right next door to the WRC/NBC building.

Something I hadn't counted on: Jay wanted the Monahans' family friend John Kelly—a Catholic deacon—to marry us. That meant I would need to be confirmed in a Christian church, something I had rejected in seventh grade.

I'd met with our local Presbyterian minister, Reverend Birdsall, at the drugstore, where he bought me a Coke and shared the benefits of a prayerful life. He pulled out a pamphlet with a diagram showing Jesus on a throne surrounded by symbols for parents, siblings, friends, and community. I just couldn't accept the idea that Jesus was more important than my family and announced to my dad that I didn't want to become a member of the church. But now, almost 20 years later, I was asking him to go through the confirmation process with me.

Together, we joined the National Presbyterian Church, which was on the other side of WRC. We were mesmerized by the minister's sermons. Sharing a hymnal and reciting the Lord's Prayer made me feel so close to my dad. I loved those mornings with him, not as father and daughter but as contemporaries, talking about faith and life.

I shelled out $1,100 for a wedding dress at the Bethesda boutique Claire Dratch: white silk with a shawl collar, a spill of tiny covered buttons down the back, and a train that hitched up to make a bustle. On my head, a lightly sequined pillbox hat with a pouf of tulle. The whole effect was more jaunty than elegant, which felt right. I carried a pretty bouquet of gardenias that my mom made. She had a side hustle doing floral arrangements with women we referred to as "the flower ladies," providing companionship and a bit of spending money.

We had 230 guests. The ceremony was lovely, although not without drama: Just as Jay uttered those immortal words "I do," a fire alarm went off in the chapel. Apparently, someone who worked there was smoking in the balcony.

"Did I give the wrong answer?" Jay ad-libbed.

As for the reception, neither of our families could afford a super-snazzy affair with a soup-to-nuts sit-down dinner. I'm remembering stuffed mushrooms, Swedish meatballs in chafing dishes, and strawberries you could dip in a vat of chocolate mousse. There was a '40s-type swing band that kept taking smoking breaks at the most inopportune times, which ticked me off; Jay would say it was his first taste of me as "a pouter" (he'd picked the band, so I was mad at him too). Steve Doocy emceed. Long before he became the host of *Fox and Friends,* he was a benignly funny features guy at WRC. There's a priceless photo of my mother near the end of the wedding looking anxiously at her wristwatch. Not because she hadn't had fun but because she knew that if the band played on, she and my father *paid* on. Time to wrap it up.

Jay and I were driven off in a friend's car, our heads and arms popping out of the sunroof as we waved to the crowd.

We took a two-week honeymoon in Italy, my first time. I ate it up, literally, developing a lifelong obsession with prosciutto and melon, which somehow always tastes better at an outdoor café at dusk, overlooking a medieval square dotted with old ladies in shawls and nuzzling lovers. Rome was magical: St. Peter's Basilica, the Colosseum, the Vespas darting down the narrow cobblestone streets…at CNN I'd met the fabled Sammy Cahn, who'd written the lyrics to "Three Coins in the Fountain," so of course as soon as we got to the Trevi Fountain, I serenaded Jay while throwing spare *lire* over my shoulder.

We ended up speed-dating the Sistine Chapel the next morning before heading off to Pompeii, Florence, Siena, and the quaint town of Ravello on the Amalfi Coast, where we stayed at a palazzo Jay's parents had discovered. We loved eating on the balcony, inhaling the scent of the lush lavender fields below. I have never had so much sex in my life, before or since, but that's what honeymoons are for, right?

Along the way we made a detour to Monte Cassino, where Jay's father had fought during World War II. He had told us stories of lying in dank trenches for days during a horribly bloody, drawn-out battle; more than 200 civilians seeking shelter in the 16th-century abbey were killed in a bombing raid after British intelligence wrongly determined that German soldiers were camped there. History, a family connection, an epic battle. For Jay, Monte Cassino was the trifecta.

Between the romantic dinners and sightseeing, I was determined to be ready for my new job at the Pentagon, so along with sundresses and comfortable walking shoes, I had packed homework: thick military manuals that would help me learn a new language of jargon and acronyms like IBS—not *irritable bowel syndrome* but *inflatable boat, small.* FAN—*feet, ass, and nuts,* to describe the smell of the barracks (who knew?). And, of course, *snafu,* which most civilians don't realize stands for *situation normal all fucked up.* And I steeped myself in core military values about never making excuses or leaving a man behind; about the bedrock significance of esprit de corps and the Marine Corps motto Semper Fidelis ("always faithful").

And I drilled down on weapons of war so I could tell an M1 tank from an M1A1, a Chinook helicopter from an Apache, an F-16 from an F/A-18 by the time we got home. At flight school, Jay had learned how to land an A-6 on an aircraft carrier (his description of barely hooking it was so harrowing, I think he still had PTSD), so he found my new obsession amusing. Then slightly annoying. Whizzing down the Autostrade as I bore into the page describing gun turrets on destroyers, he glanced down at my homework and said, "This isn't exactly the kind of hardware I was hoping you'd be focused on."

15

The E-Ring

JUST TURNING IN TO the parking lot of the Pentagon, the world's biggest office building, was daunting. I'd passed it countless times on my way to National Airport; actually working there was a different matter altogether. Checking in at security and getting my laminated credentials made me feel so...*official* as I passed men and women walking briskly in uniform.

I loved working with Fred Francis, NBC's senior Pentagon correspondent. Swarthy and raspy-voiced, with an easy smile, he had also toiled in local news in Miami. Fred was a fixture at the Pentagon and a damn good reporter. The walls of our cubby, right next to CBS veteran David Martin's, were lined with soundproofing gray foam for when we tracked our stories. We'd grab one of the big mics on our desk and read a script while editors at the NBC mothership put the piece together.

"Hey, kid!" Fred would say when I walked in, twirling around in his chair to take a look at me. There was a ubiquitous smoky haze in the cubicle—he puffed Kools nonstop. At times it was so unbearable, my baffling default was to revive a habit I had occasionally indulged in at UVA fraternity parties: I'd grab one of his Kools and puff right along with him. *If you can't beat 'em, join 'em,* my idiotic thinking went.

Naomi Spinrad was Fred's longtime producer. She clearly disliked me and my eager-beaver shtick. She definitely did not think I was up to snuff.

The place was teeming with testosterone—at the time, you could count the female Pentagon correspondents on half a hand. And of course, the officials were almost exclusively stone-faced males, starting with Dick Cheney, the secretary of defense, and Colin Powell, the chairman of the Joint Chiefs of Staff. In that world, a cute girl in a short skirt was a novelty. Sometimes David Martin would walk by as some public affairs guy was hovering around our cubicle and just shake his head. I think it drove him a little crazy that I was making inroads so quickly.

On my third day there, I was on the steps overlooking the parking lot, feeling turned around, when I spotted a couple of civilian women around my age—such a rarity—who worked at the Department of Defense. They pointed me in the right direction.

When I ran into one of them the next day, she shared a tip: Classified documents had been discovered in the West Berlin home of air force captain John Vladimir Hirsch, now under investigation for espionage. This was new territory for me, so I consulted Fred, who made a flurry of calls and said we should go with it.

A week later I was on the air with my first exclusive. I quoted a source, saying the case had "all the familiar earmarks of an American selling secrets to the Eastern bloc." David Martin was quietly irritated.

Then we learned the investigation was the result of a glitch in a routine lie-detector test. Hirsch was cleared and would eventually receive an honorary discharge.

Whoops. I was terrified I had screwed up royally. That I'd let down Tim Russert, who took a big chance on me, and Fred, who allowed me—the neophyte—to run with the story. Not to mention the entire news division of NBC, many of whom might have been skeptical about me to begin with. Maybe Naomi Spinrad was right.

Then Hirsch slapped the network with a $10,000,000 defamation lawsuit. That meant I would have to be deposed. The only depositions I had ever witnessed were on *L.A. Law,* and I was beside myself. Kevin Baine, a colleague of Jay's at Williams & Connolly, spent many hours coaching me on how to handle whatever Hirsch's lawyers threw at me. I kept Jay up all night practicing.

On D-day (deposition day), I sat behind a massive mahogany table and tried not to incriminate myself or reveal my sources. For so many years, I'd wanted a seat at the table, but Jesus—not *this* one. Mercifully, Hirsch and his lawyers dropped the lawsuit.

That night, I thanked God profusely, but also Jay, who'd held my hand through it all. It was an early lesson in the high stakes of the profession I'd chosen and the enormous responsibility of getting it right.

I SPENT MY DAYS in press briefings and taking endless laps around the E-ring, the outer corridor of offices, chatting up officers and flacks, earning their trust and trawling for leads. But airtime was hard to come by, especially for the new kid who still *looked* like a kid; I'd heard about a *Nightly News* producer, a bespectacled veteran, who flat-out refused to put me on the air.

Then Noriega happened. In December 1989, the U.S. invaded Panama (code name Operation Just Cause, in case anyone had any doubts), and Fred was assigned to the Pentagon's press pool. That left me to mind the store. *Nightly* had no choice but to use me, which meant regular stand-ups. But I was so green. I did everything I could to project substance, clinging to my serious-sounding sign-off: "Katherine Couric, NBC News, the Pentagon."

Across the Potomac, Jay was working crazy hours, coming home at midnight, heading to the office on weekends. I remember going to church one Sunday with my dad, singing the familiar "Praise God, from whom all blessings flow," and out of nowhere starting to cry, missing Jay, missing the fun of playing house with my new husband—and feeling overwhelmed at work. My dad grabbed my hand. By the time we reached the parking lot, my tears had dried.

16

Velveeta

JAY AND I were living in my small apartment at 4707 Connecticut Avenue, and hankered for a place where we could stretch out. Convinced we would never be able to afford anything in DC or even the nearby suburbs, we decided to keep the apartment and buy a weekend house in Maurertown, a cozy hamlet in the Shenandoah Valley. It was an easy drive from Washington and much more affordable than places like Middleburg and Upperville, the tony, horsey getaways of social fixtures like the Mellons and Senator John Warner (who was married to Elizabeth Taylor at the time).

Despite the fact that he typically dressed like a pheasant-hunting Anglophile, Jay hated pretense. His strong preference was for grounded middle- and working-class people—like our new neighbors. In Woodstock, the next town over, the big attractions were a Ben Franklin five-and-ten, a Food Lion, and an 18th-century courthouse supposedly designed by Thomas Jefferson.

Our Federal-style farmhouse was built in 1803 from bricks made of local clay with actual horsehair visible in the mortar (used back then to strengthen it). The house was situated on 10 peaceful acres on a sloping hillside between our neighbor Betty Carey's barn and a small tributary where the Shenandoah River gurgled beneath a concrete bridge, our favorite place to take walks and pictures.

The home came with a name: Valhalla, the word from Norse mythology meaning "a place of great glory" or "heaven," which is what it was for Jay. We built fires in the winter (there were four fireplaces, including one in the kitchen the size of an SUV where we kept a big vase of dried flowers) and swatted away gnats in the summer as we dipped our young, toned bodies in the less-than-high-end pool, our toes sinking into the vinyl bottom.

We were right where we wanted to be. Jay and I had moved out of the "skyrockets in flight, afternoon delight" phase and into the steady rhythms and comfortable familiarity of marriage.

BACK AT NBC, things were decidedly less tranquil. Tom Brokaw's newscast was stuck in third place, and the *TODAY* show, which had dominated the morning for years, was starting to shed its young female viewers—the demo most coveted by advertisers.

The trouble started in February of 1989, when The Memo, as it will always be known around the network, Bryant's unsparing assessment of the show's strengths and weaknesses, was leaked to the press. Among other things, it went after beloved Willard Scott, saying that he "holds the show hostage" with his centenarian birthday tributes ("What a beautiful lady, 104 years young!") and corny jokes before getting to the weather.

Talk about a cold front. It seemed to rally viewers to Willard's side and made Bryant look churlish and petty. It also made it seem like *TODAY* had become *Family Feud.* As NBC scrambled, the corporate gaze fell on Jane Pauley.

I couldn't understand it. She had the winning combination of Midwestern approachability and East Coast sophistication. I even loved her assorted hairstyles, including the ponytail that draped over her shoulder like a squirrel's tail. She'd been anchoring the show for 13 years, the first four with Tom and the last nine with Bryant. Now the network brain trust wondered if she was a little long in the tooth for the job (Jane was 39; Bryant, 41).

Dick Ebersol, the newly minted president of NBC Sports who'd also been put in charge of *TODAY*, had an idea. Deborah Norville, the blond, pillowy-lipped former pageant winner from Dalton, Georgia (the carpet capital of the world), eight years Jane's junior, had bumped up the ratings as anchor at *NBC News at Sunrise*. Now she was the newsreader at *TODAY*, bringing an air of uber-confidence and glamour to the role.

I mean, Deborah was stunning. She was also whip-smart, Phi Beta Kappa from the University of Georgia, and incredibly hardworking. As if that weren't enough, she made her own clothes. Curtains too.

It wasn't surprising that all the male executives at the network saw Deborah as Jane's inevitable successor. That included Jack Welch, chairman of GE (which owned NBC at the time), who apparently watched her on *Sunrise* from his exercise bike. But the way they set the process in motion became an infamous object lesson in how *not* to handle beloved talent. One morning as the cameras rolled, Deborah showed up on the couch next to Bryant and Jane—much to Jane's visible surprise (she would later describe it as a complete humiliation). The *Washington Post*'s feared media columnist Tom Shales put it this way: "Watching the three of them on screen together is like looking at a broken marriage with the homewrecker right there on the premises."

After four months of awkwardness, Jane said her classy and moving on-air goodbyes and headed off to a newsmagazine show, *Real Life* (short-lived, unfortunately).

The audience took it personally. They'd been through a lot with Jane, including her two pregnancies (one with twins). They cared about her and resented the way she had been treated. So instead of attracting the larger, younger audience of NBC's dreams, the Bryant/Deborah team repelled them: After nearly five years at number one, the show fell to second place, behind *Good Morning America*. Soon, *TODAY* was bleeding viewers, down nearly 20 percent from the previous year.

The press blamed Bryant, along with NBC management. In a familiar PR move at the time for anyone in need of a little reputation repair, Bryant submitted to a Barbara Walters interview on ABC's *20/20*, during which he talked openly about how much he missed Jane. Viewers could see why—he and Deborah had zero rapport; Bryant's brow crinkled uncomfortably whenever she spoke. And suddenly, NBC was in panic mode.

Elena Nachmanoff, who recruited journalists for NBC, reached out to gauge my interest in subbing as newsreader on *TODAY*. Shortly after I'd arrived at the Pentagon, she and Don Browne, whom I got to know in Miami when he was the NBC bureau chief, had become big boosters.

All I could think of was the day the San Francisco earthquake hit in the fall of 1989. I was a newbie at NBC and happened to be the only one still in the bureau when an assignment editor pointed at me and said, "You! We need you to do a special report!"

I froze, then looked around the empty newsroom for someone, anyone, more experienced. I sat at the desk and muddled my way through a news brief while terrifying shots of burning buildings flashed on the screen. I prayed no one was watching.

The idea that NBC might actually want me to read the news in front of the huge *TODAY* show audience seemed absurd. But I didn't feel like I could say no, so I practiced, reading off a prompter a few times in the Washington bureau after the evening news, once the place had emptied out. I learned the importance of turning the pages of the script on the desk as I was reading the words on the screen. Everyone's afraid of the prompter crapping out, and knowing you can default to the script if necessary is crucial. The other thing, which is harder than it sounds, is to make it look like you are talking instead of reading. Newspeople joke about "seeing God in the prompter"—the gobsmacked look you get if you're fixated on the screen. I dedicated myself to avoiding that look.

Soon enough, I got the call, and hopped on the shuttle to New York.

CROSSING ROCKEFELLER PLAZA in the heart of Midtown, I felt like Marlo Thomas in the title sequence of *That Girl*. The colorful flags whipping in the wind, the sun glinting off the gilded *Prometheus* statue, the art deco skyscraper with its bronze and marble lobby and massive *American Progress* mural, made the mere act of showing up for work feel exhilarating.

The studio itself was a revelation. TV Land has an otherworldly quality; the cheerfully artificial sets bathed in cheerfully unnatural light create a sense of hyper-reality. It was like the scene in *The Wizard of Oz* when suddenly everything is in Technicolor.

Also otherworldly: Meeting Bryant Gumbel. Despite how confrontational he could be in interviews, he was incredibly welcoming and friendly to me. In retrospect, I think it had a lot to do with the fact that I came from the Pentagon, giving me instant street cred with him. Furthermore, at the time he was in ratings hell, and grateful, probably, for anything resembling a lifeline.

Reading the news that first time out, I was stiff as a board, although not a disaster, and they kept asking me back. Eventually, I got more comfortable and started relying on my sense of humor to bring a little levity to the proceedings. Whenever possible, I ended the newscast with something light and funny, a so-called kicker that gave the anchors something to react to. One time, the last story involved a skier who got lost on the slopes. Desperate to signal a search plane, he'd lit his money on fire. The pilot spotted the flame and the skier was rescued. When I threw back to Bryant, I said, "With my luck, I'd only have change."

The crew hooted; Bryant practically belly-laughed. To be able to make Bryant laugh was a major test, and I passed. I can still remember how good that felt. From then on, my news producer Jim Dick and I were always on the hunt for a funny story to end the newscast with.

Then the producers asked me to take part in a cooking segment with Deborah. Michael Lomonaco, the chef at the venerable 21 Club, had come in to whip up some fondue. Stirring ingredients in a silver tureen atop a Sterno flame, he described the fancy European cheeses he used. With Deborah gorgeously standing by, I asked, "So this is better than Velveeta?" I grew up eating that brick of cheese-like substance, and knew much of America had too.

Again, the crew laughed, and so did Lomonaco. Maybe I was onto something.

17

A Two-Bagger

I N MAY OF 1990, Jay and I were at the University of New Mexico for his sister Sally's graduation when I was summoned to 30 Rock for a meeting. Like, now. We saw her get her sheepskin and raced to the Albuquerque airport.

"What do you think it's about?" I asked Jay as we settled into our coach seats. Were things so bad with Deborah they wanted to make a change? We almost couldn't let ourselves go there.

We rode the elevator to Dick Ebersol's leather-upholstered executive man cave. Before we even had a chance to sit, Dick got down to business.

"We love your work," he said. "We think you're doing a great job. Which is why"—*Here it comes*—"we want to offer you the newly created position of national correspondent for the *TODAY* show."

I was confused. It didn't sound like much of a promotion; why would they go to so much trouble to get me here for that? But okay. If they liked me enough to create a job for me, that had to mean something.

Then Ebersol opened a closet in his office and loaded us up with NBC Sports goodies: umbrellas, mugs, and tote bags bearing peacocks. I'd later learn the plan had been to offer me the co-anchor job—Deborah's job. But somewhere in the air between Albuquerque and

New York City, things changed. It turned out that Deborah's grand-mother had died, and NBC was worried about the timing fueling yet more bad press. Instead, they grew the team, adding Faith Daniels as newsreader; Bryant's friend Joe Garagiola, to help him seem more warm and fuzzy; and me.

In my new role, I'd need a very capable producer. The network suggested a whippersnapper named Jeff Zucker. At just 25, he had already made a name for himself as an NBC researcher at the Seoul Olympics, where he prepared thick binders of background and trivia for Jane and Bob Costas. Jane became Jeff's champion, guiding him toward a writer-producer gig at *TODAY*.

He showed up to meet me in a gray sweatshirt—the kind you'd wear in high school gym class—and lace-up Keds. *Why is he wearing girls' tennis shoes?* I wondered. Beneath a mop of frizzy brown hair, he screamed *nerd,* but he also seemed a little cocky, espe-cially for someone so young. *Well, this is going to be interesting,* I thought.

Just two months after I became national correspondent, simmer-ing tensions over oil erupted in the Persian Gulf. Iraq invaded and annexed Kuwait; Saddam Hussein defied the UN Security Council's demand that he withdraw. President George H. W. Bush swiftly mobilized an international coalition—by August, the military-buildup phase known as Operation Desert Shield was underway. For me, this meant a steady stream of high-octane, attention-getting assignments.

For one of the first, I went to Shaw Air Force Base in Sumter, South Carolina, to profile pilots and take a spin in an F-16 fighter jet that would be used in military operations in the Gulf.

I was zipped into a flight suit and fitted with a helmet, oxygen mask, and all-important G suit, which keeps blood flow semi-normal as the force of gravity, or number of g's, increases. I then met the pilot who was going to take me for the ride of my life: Captain Jeff Connors, 28, straight out of *Top Gun,* with aviator shades and perfect white teeth. I hadn't eaten anything that morning, so on my way out to the tarmac, I grabbed two slices of white bread that were sitting unappealingly on a random tray of cold cuts, slapped a piece of American cheese between them, and choked it down. Then I crawled into the cockpit and gave Captain Connors a half-hearted thumbs-up.

The plane had been rigged with cameras, and I wasn't sure I was ready for my close-up. Suddenly, the engines roared and the jet shot off into the South Carolina sky.

Then came the not-so-fun part: We did loops, the equivalent of backflips, before launching into a spin, where the plane corkscrews around its axis. As if I weren't feeling shitty enough, the aircraft then bolted like a rocket—I felt like my breasts would soon be protruding out of my back. It's called pulling g's, and I wasn't a fan. Asked by my personal Tom Cruise if I was okay, I could barely form words, given the force field that was compressing my face and vocal cords, but I mustered a labored "Yes" through clenched teeth.

Finally, we landed. Before I got off the plane, I took out a plastic vomit bag and promptly made use of it. Luckily there were two, so I pulled out the second one and made use of it too. As I wobbled down the metal stairs, there was a welcoming party from the base to greet me as I triumphantly raised my arms and exclaimed, "Look, everyone! A two-bagger!"

Jeff was in the crowd, howling with laughter. It made for damn good TV and proved I was game for anything.

LATER THAT MONTH, Jeff and I were deployed to Dhahran, Saudi Arabia, where the U.S. military forces were headquartered. We bonded during the 16-hour flight as only people can when they're about to jump into a journalistic foxhole together.

It was blisteringly hot—110 degrees. That it was a "dry heat" didn't help. Pallets of bottled water were everywhere, providing almost no relief since the contents were as warm as bathwater.

One of our most attention-getting stories came on September 18th when I interviewed the commander in chief of Operation Desert Storm, General Norman Schwarzkopf. Stormin' Norman, a soldier's soldier and bona fide rock star. He talked candidly about the 150,000 troops in his care—how soon (or not) they'd be going home and how critical it was that the American people were behind them (Schwarzkopf himself was a Vietnam vet and admitted in our interview that he still felt bitter about the lack of support).

It was a real coup. The truth is, I got lucky. The year before, I'd attended another Radio and Television Correspondents' Association Dinner, where news organizations try to outdo each other with the big-wigs at their tables. When I asked Beth Wilkinson, a lawyer friend from the Pentagon, who'd be a great guest, she suggested Schwarzkopf, then commander of U.S. Central Command in Tampa.

We got to know each other over hotel beef and had a nice rapport, so when I came calling in Saudi Arabia, Schwarzkopf was happy to grant me an interview.

I RETURNED TO THE region in November and did a piece on how it felt to be away from home, in a war zone, over the holidays, and spent Thanksgiving with the 82nd Airborne, stationed outside of Dhahran; they were so disciplined and motivated (not to mention well mannered and well groomed), the experience filled me with a whole new level of respect for the armed forces. A bunch of turkeys were cooked and served out of a trailer. I slept in a tent they'd set up for me beneath a celestial dome of the brightest stars I'd ever seen. Before I left the next day, the guys presented me with a T-shirt that said I SLEPT WITH THE 82ND AIRBORNE.

It was a challenge being a female reporter in a country that treated women like third-class citizens. There were rules about whether we could swim in the hotel pool and where we could eat; at a Baskin-Robbins, women reporters were told the tables were reserved for men. Driving was out of the question.

Here's the irony: While we were subjected to misogyny, the experience was a glass-ceiling-shattering, star-making opportunity, with women correspondents at the forefront in unprecedented ways. Thanks to her plummy-voiced, levelheaded explanations of conflicts in the Middle

East, my former fellow neophyte at CNN Christiane Amanpour became a cable news supernova.

In my case, my Pentagon training served me well. I reported with authority on the war effort while injecting my stories with humanity. At 34, I was in the spotlight, getting prime placement on *TODAY* every morning. My career was on the F-16 track—full throttle, straight up.

18

Horny Toads

THINGS JUST WEREN'T working out with Deborah Norville. On top of residual bad feelings from the Jane Pauley debacle and the absence of chemistry, there was a major relatability problem. Viewers wanted to feel comfortable at that hour. They had morning breath, they were stumbling out of bed, they were wriggling into their pantyhose and trying to separate the damn Mr. Coffee filters. In that state, maybe they didn't want to be greeted by relentless perfection. As a colleague once told me, "With Deborah, people feel like they need to get dressed before they turn on the TV."

When Deborah took maternity leave, NBC asked me to fill in for her. The big job. Live interviews. Charming chitchat. A whole new level of scrutiny.

My college friend Kathleen Lobb, now working at a PR firm in New York, came to my room at the Essex House and played stylist. I'd throw on a jacket and kneel behind a chair so that the seat cut me off about where the bottom of the TV screen would in a close-up. "Scarf or no scarf?" I'd ask. "Is this jewelry too much?"

Meanwhile, nailing the mechanics of live television wasn't easy—it's like learning to juggle, recite "The Song of Hiawatha," and tap-dance all at the same time. It means paying rapt attention to the person you're interviewing while someone's in your ear telling you to throw to a clip as the stage manager gives you time cues in a newfangled sign language (a crisp twist of the fist means "Wrap it up"; if it comes with a thrust, it means *"Now"*), graciously thanking your guest, smoothly teasing the next segment, and effortlessly hitting the commercial break with seconds to spare. It was an art form that would take me months, if not years, to learn. Luckily I was in the presence of a master: Bryant was the Michelangelo of live broadcasting.

At least my sense of humor was fully developed. When Willard Scott was doing the weather from, believe it or not, a horny-toad convention somewhere, and threw back to the anchor desk, I piped in with "Hey, speaking of horny toads, Gene Shalit just walked into the studio."

The director, Bucky Gunts, put the camera on Gene, who was hiding sheepishly behind a monitor. It was a daring and saucy thing to say, but I went for it and it worked—guffaws broke out in the studio. It reminded me of those times at the dinner table when I'd say something cheeky and my dad would call me "irrepressible" while my mom shook with laughter. Now it was paying off—the ratings jumped almost immediately.

And soon I was mastering the serious part of the job too. A month into Deborah's leave, Stormin' Norman gave me his first postwar interview, which helped us win a different kind of war: That half hour, *TODAY* beat *GMA* in the ratings.

All in all, life was going pretty swimmingly—except for one teeny, tiny thing: While I was in Dhahran, I didn't get my period.

I'd confided to Wendy, who was there with CNN, that I had been feeling a little off. My breasts hurt, and I'd lost my appetite. She asked me if I could be pregnant.

Oh God... I hadn't thought of that. Did they even have EPTs in Saudi Arabia? I wasn't quite up to the reconnaissance that finding one might require.

When we got back to DC, Wendy came to my apartment carrying a brown paper bag; inside was the telltale pink box. I went to the bathroom and peed on the stick. Then we ate bologna sandwiches and waited for the results. A few minutes later, I looked—in the little round window, a plus sign.

I remembered a cool October morning in Maurertown—the smell of damp leaves in the air and a dozen eggs sitting by the stove, waiting to be freed from their cardboard compartments and fried up. Jay and I were so happy. We'd taken a walk down to the river, and when we saw a neighbor, we asked him to snap our picture. I still have it in a frame—Jay looking pensive and casual-chic, as always, wearing a dark denim coat with a corduroy collar; me in a sweater the color of merlot and a jean jacket, looking like an unmade bed. I'm pretty sure I hadn't showered. I radiate a happy calm. If I've got the math right, I was about 12 hours pregnant.

Now, staring at the little plus sign, all I could say was "Shit." Given the beloved, beautiful, brilliant daughter that would result, I feel terrible even writing that now—God knows I wouldn't have it any other way.

I hopped in the Honda Accord I'd traded up for in Miami and drove to Williams & Connolly. When I walked into Jay's office in the middle of the day, he was surprised to see me.

I cut to the chase. "I can't believe it. I'm fucking pregnant."

His face lit up instantly. Jay was thrilled—until he saw that I was borderline apoplectic. We both really wanted a family, but now? Just when my career was taking off?

I stewed for a week and finally got used to—even excited about— the idea. The way things were going, if I had delayed getting pregnant until there was a lull in the action, I never would have had children. It really was such a lucky mistake. But who knew if NBC would be on the same page?

I WASN'T SHOWING, AND I wasn't telling.

As national correspondent, I still covered the Pentagon. It seemed like the bathrooms were several miles away. Add morning sickness and bladder-control issues, and it felt like they were in the next state. I'm sure some of the generals and their staff strutting down the cavernous hallways wondered about the girl they often saw sprinting to the head.

One day, after devouring a package of Twizzlers, I was at a stop sign just a few blocks from our apartment when suddenly I projectile-vomited all over the dashboard and steering wheel. I pulled into the circular driveway and called Jay, who was already home, on my clunky mobile phone. My voice trembling, I said, "I just threw up all over my car."

"Don't worry," he said. "I'll come down and clean it up."

I had never felt so loved.

19

I Am Woman

THE *TODAY* SHOW was in limbo. Then came the mother of all photo shoots: For an interview with *People* magazine during her maternity leave, Deborah posed for celebrity photographer Harry Benson while breastfeeding her new baby. It was a lovely, tasteful picture, but this was 1991 and the network definitely was not jiggy with it.

There was a growing clamor in the press that I was being groomed to replace Deborah: "Will Katie Couric Be Deborah Norville's Substitute— or Successor?" said *TV Guide.* "Today Show Plots to Replace Debbie with Katie," declared *Star.* It was all very flattering, but I couldn't imagine what must have been going on in Deborah's head with all of this swirling around her. Now she was home with a new baby— what should have been a magical time—probably wondering if she still had a job.

Following the homewrecker narrative Deborah had (unfairly) been written into, I was a very different kettle of fish. Not a bombshell by any means; more Mary Ann than Ginger, and that was on a good day. I didn't look like I'd shown up at the party to steal your husband.

The first big piece about me ran in the *Washingtonian,* my hometown magazine. Reporter Barbara Matusow spent the day with me. We did a long interview over lunch, and she reached out to some of my friends.

There is nothing quite as nerve-racking as having someone analyze your every move and utterance for a profile. No matter how charming you try to be, everything is filtered through the POV of the writer, and for whatever reason, she or he may just not be that into you. Furthermore, writers don't want to be accused of doing a "puff piece." They love to find the wart in the story, and I lived in terror wondering what mine would be.

Jay was visiting NBC when we finally got hold of a copy. I paced the halls near the deserted studio as he read it. When he finished, he looked up and said, "What were you worried about, silly? It's a home run!"

I exhaled. I would have settled for a double.

IN EARLY MARCH 1991, I was summoned to the office of Michael Gartner, president of NBC News. The bow-tied former editor of the *Des Moines Register* had a no-nonsense Midwestern style that may have been better suited to River City than 30 Rock. After exchanging pleasantries, he looked me in the eye and changed my life with these words: "I'd like you to replace Deborah on the *TODAY* show."

It may not have been a total surprise, but still, it was an out-of-body experience. All the naysayers in my career flashed before my eyes.

"Wow," I said. *Holy crap,* I thought.

And then suddenly—I don't know where it came from—I channeled my inner Helen Reddy and said, "I'm really only interested in this job if Bryant and I split the big interviews 50/50. I don't want to be relegated to cooking segments and fashion shows."

It always struck me how Jane Pauley took a back seat to Bryant. Why was he so clearly in charge of the show when she'd been there longer? I was keenly aware of how the media—TV shows, ads, billboards, magazine covers—conditions us to see gender roles a certain way. It's where the seeds of implicit bias are sown. I realized how something as seemingly benign as a morning show could shape the perception of what a woman could do and be.

After some deliberation, Gartner said, "How about 49/51?"

Close enough—I'd made my point.

"Okay," I said. "Oh, I almost forgot. I'm pregnant."

Gartner bowed his head like a man who'd been played. "You have really lousy timing," he said.

"So I guess you're not going to be knitting me baby booties anytime soon," I shot back with a smile.

Ultimately, Bryant would have it written into his contract that he was the anchor, I was the co-anchor, and he would open every show. It was also understood that only he could throw to Willard Scott. That seemed strangely territorial to me, but I could live with it. The bottom line: I was going to be a key part of this broadcast.

"YOU'RE MAKING HOW much?"

My dad was on the phone, marveling at my new mid-six-figure salary, probably picturing how different my life was going to be.

I guess you'd have called us solidly middle class. As kids, we were well taken care of—new shoes from Hahn's in Clarendon every September, good winter coats from Woodie's, birthday parties, Girl Scout camp. Vacations weren't a given; my friend Sara Crosman's family let me tag along with them to Disney World and Quoddy Head, Maine. It was such a treat when my family did get away, the six of us piling into the station wagon, eating the cream cheese and olive sandwiches my mom had made and carefully packed in a Lord and Taylor box by 9:00 a.m., heading to a hotel called Far Horizons on Longboat Key, off Sarasota. (My dad had met the owner, who I'm sure gave him a deal.) When I was 10, we rented a house for a week in Rehoboth Beach; it had a big porch out front with worn wicker furniture. I loved the board-walk, where we got Thrasher's french fries in paper cups and saltwater taffy at Dolle's. At night, I could hear happy screams wafting over from Funland and see the top of the Ferris wheel from my bedroom window.

We didn't belong to clubs—certainly not country clubs, but not even one of the local swimming pools. Instead, I'd go with my friends and pay the $3 guest fee, with enough left over for a frozen Milky Way from the snack bar. My mom was always coupon-clipping, bargain-hunting, and tracking our expenses, unfurling the grocery receipt and checking off each item with a pencil to make sure she'd gotten what she'd paid for.

When I went to the movies, she sternly reminded me not to buy candy, telling me the movie itself was enough of a treat. (One Saturday there was hell to pay when she found a Planters Peanut Bar wrapper in my snow jacket pocket after a matinee.) Sometimes my friends would pass me their empty popcorn buckets, knowing I liked to stick my face in and inhale the buttery scent. Since I looked so young, my mother had no problem letting me take advantage of the under-12 ticket price long after I was over 12. When my dad found out, he made her drive me back and pay the extra quarter.

My parents wanted us to understand the value of a dollar and be responsible with money. When Johnny finished at UVA, they set up a bedroom for him in the basement, installed a toilet and shower in the cold concrete laundry room, and charged him $200 a month. When he was finally ready to buy his own place, they gave it all back for him to use as a down payment, satisfied that he'd learned to live within his means.

Every year on our birthdays, Nana sent each of us a card with a $5 bill inside; we were expected to put it right into the college fund. Yet another lesson in saving and planning: Our parents so diligently socked away money for college that when the time came for us to choose one, they said we could go anywhere we wanted. They had it covered.

THE SKIN ON my belly was stretching tighter by the day. I craved creamed spinach and chocolate milk, which sounds like a revolting combination now.

As it turned out, being with child could not have come at a better time. NBC had already ditched beloved mother of three Jane Pauley; now they were pushing out new mom Deborah Norville. How convenient that they had another mom-to-be on deck.

The excitement of an impending birth only made the morning-show audience feel more connected to me. I was a bright, shiny symbol of a new breed of woman—happily, successfully merging career and family.

A congratulatory note from General Schwarzkopf came in the mail. He suggested that Norman might be a good name for the baby. And if it's a girl, he wrote, I could call her Stormy Norma.

20

Katherine or Katie

APRIL 5TH, 1991, my first day as co-anchor of the *TODAY* show. With most of my life still in Virginia, NBC had put me up in a furnished apartment at Bristol Plaza on East 65th Street. My alarm went off at 4:15 a.m. I got up, threw up, and jumped in the shower. There would be a number of challenges in this huge new role, although at the moment, the biggest one was how to cover my ever-growing belly.

Places like A Pea in the Pod and Mimi's Maternity were newish resources for pregnant professionals, offering slightly more sophisticated styles than the flowy, boho frocks of the '70s or the baby-doll smocks of the '50s and '60s, which I always saw as society's infantilizing of mothers-to-be, a way to camouflage the sex act that had taken place. In terms of my wardrobe, I remember a lot of lime green, fuchsia, shoulder pads, and buttons the size of poker chips—I don't know how I left the house thinking I looked presentable.

That first day, I opted for a tomato-red number with little gold buttons shaped like pretzels. Hearing my heels echo across the slick floor of the Bristol Plaza lobby before dawn, I imagined the cleaning crew thinking I was some sort of baby-faced woman of the night.

Looking out the car window, I took in the sight of New York City waking up from its slumber: Doormen hosing down the sidewalks. The café owner noisily rolling up the metal gate protecting his storefront.

The sun peeking through the skyscrapers, casting a coral hue on the concrete below. A yellow cab picking up an early riser headed to the airport. An intrepid runner who'd hauled himself out of bed at dawn heading to Central Park. I paused to inhale the sights and sounds, marveling that I was part of it.

The raspy-voiced Bobbi, who'd seen it all, did my makeup. A hair-stylist named Catherine blew out my short 'do; a wardrobe woman, stout and stern, steamed my dress. I reviewed my notes, walked into the studio, and sat in my chair. The audio engineer clipped on my mic. Bryant looked over and said, "You good?" I said yes, even though I wasn't so sure. Jimmy Straka, the stage manager, boomed, "Thirty seconds to air!"

At the stroke of 7, against the theme music's staccato trumpets and swelling strings, the announcer intoned for the first time ever, "From NBC News…this is *TODAY* with Bryant Gumbel, Katherine Couric, and Joe Garagiola."

If there was any confusion among the audience about why I was sitting there, Bryant dispelled it, with perhaps a little less tact than the moment required: "In case you haven't gotten the message, Katie Couric is now a permanent fixture up here, a member of our family, an especially welcome one. Deborah Norville is not." YIKES.

As for that "Katherine" in the intro…I still used it to counteract my Campbell's Soup Kid looks. In real life, though, nobody called me Katherine (except my dad when he was mad at me). I was conflicted.

When Bryant asks me how it sounds, hearing my name in the intro, I tell him, "It sounded good! But I still can't decide whether I'm Katherine or Katie," grabbing my head with both hands in a playful gesture of confusion.

Watching it now, I can hardly believe what a prescient comment it was: Katherine or Katie, the serious journalist or the smiley cutup…the tension between those two sides of my nature would run like a fault line through my career.

21

A Defiant Mop

I WAS QUEEN of the May, as my mother might say. Reporters wanted to talk to me; photographers wanted to take my picture. My old station WRC asked to interview me from New York while my parents were interviewed at their house. They sent a live truck and wired them up, and my friend Barbara Harrison started asking us questions. My parents looked so uncomfortable and confused, sitting on their living-room sofa. I later learned the audio was screwed up and the feedback they heard was throwing them off. I vowed never to do that to them again, telling them that if a reporter ever knocked on the door, slam it in their face.

A stringer with the *National Enquirer* reached out. "I don't need to warn how aggressive the *Enquirer* can be," he wrote, then assured me I could easily satisfy them with things like "baby pictures, personal recipes, an occasional frank-sounding disclosure of some minor personal problem, etc." Then he offered to broker an introduction to the articles editor. The hint of a threat, wrapped in supposed advice and help...it was a chilling welcome to my new world. (I didn't reply.)

Friends were calling, people were writing, flowers were arriving, and men I didn't know were claiming to have dated me.

Everyone had an opinion, including a self-described "83-year-old Scotsman," who wrote:

Dear Katie:

Your hair-do is for the birds. You have it puffed up on the left-side, then combed at a straight 45 degree angle. It could readily be the ski-slope for an adventurous sparrow. It is totally lacking in symmetry.

Word came down that Dick Ebersol also had some hair advice; he wanted me to grow mine out and wear small earrings and fuzzy sweaters for a "softer" appearance. I sent word back that I liked the way I looked and was sticking with it, but thanks for the suggestion. (A *Washington Post* reporter astutely described my do as "a defiant mop.")

My world was changing fast. A blazered airline representative whisking me away on a cart, tearing through the terminal, beeping at pedestrians who were in our path. At Disneyland, a solicitous VIP guide offering to kick a family out of a live Cinderella show so we could have their front-row seats (I said absolutely not). Walking down Broadway with a friend, glancing at a newsstand and seeing a beaming face on a magazine cover, and realizing it was me.

Then there was the time I was flipping through the latest copy of *The New Yorker* and saw a cartoon with the perpetually gloomy donkey, Eeyore, watching TV with a smile on his face. Next to him, Winnie-the-Pooh. The caption reads, *Katie Couric will do that to you.*

One morning when I was lying next to Jay in bed, I said the kind of thing you'd confess only to your closest friend: "I used to want to be the most popular girl in school. Now I'm the most popular girl in the country!"

He turned to me. "You're gross," he said, then hit me with a pillow.

SOMETHING I KNEW instinctively—if I was going to be successful at this, I had to be myself. The pioneering John Chancellor confirmed it in a note he sent when I got the job: "The only way it can work is for you to throw yourself on the mercy of the audience and hope they like you for what you really, truly, honestly are. The camera is the world's most sophisticated lie detector."

For me, that included a willingness to be clueless about sports. Rather than earnestly try to keep up with Bryant's keen analysis the morning after a big game, I decided to have a little fun. With Jeff in my earpiece telling me what to say, I started offering my two cents on things like "calling an audible at the line" or "throwing a bomb as the pocket was collapsing." Bryant would look at me, stunned. The third time it happened, he was onto me—and leaned over and pulled out my earpiece.

We had reached cruising altitude. Not that there wouldn't be occasional turbulence.

The day before I went on maternity leave, Bryant commemorated the occasion by giving me a hard time—on camera.

He's in country-club khakis and a blazer; I'm in shoulder-padded Crayola-blue shapelessness. He starts by asking how long I'd be gone. Nine weeks, I say.

> Bryant: Why so long?
> Me: It's a major shock to your body, I hope you realize, when you
>   have a baby...
> Bryant: Your ancestors didn't worry about that "shock to your
>   body"; they came right back and worked.
> Me: Yeah, and they died when they were, like, 32 years old.
> Bryant (incredulous): You're 34; you've already beat that! What are
>   you worried about?...How many men *get nine weeks off*?

I noted that he did—every summer.

Classic Bryant. He loved to needle me, and I had no choice but to smile gamely and play along. The guys in the control room sometimes encouraged him by piping a whip-cracking sound effect into the studio.

Bryant was a macho, macho man. But I deeply respected his talent and work ethic. He came in every morning with his interview notes highlighted and color-coded. And in the TV universe, he was a historic figure—the first Black person to anchor a morning show.

NBC executives had hesitated about moving Bryant from sports to news. But once he got the anchor job on *TODAY* in 1982, he settled into his hyper-professional, hard-ass persona—a preening, stogie-smoking, alpha male (David Letterman, with whom he had a long-running feud, once described Bryant as the kind of guy who spends the weekend "alphabetizing his colognes"). In his horn-rims and gorgeously tailored Joseph Abboud suits, he was the cock of the walk. And while he sometimes bristled at my assertiveness, we developed a mutual respect and affection that came out at surprising moments.

After Bryant's great friend Arthur Ashe died, he was narrating a montage when his voice started to shake so much, he couldn't continue. Instinctively, I jumped in and picked up where he'd left off. He returned the favor when Audrey Hepburn died. I'd found her so gracious when I interviewed her on *TODAY*—before she sat down, she walked around the studio and shook every person's hand. During our taped tribute, I began to sob.

"Don't worry, I've got this," Bryant said, smoothly stepping in and throwing to a commercial break.

That was Bryant: tough, sensitive, competitive, prickly, brilliant. All of which I'd learn to navigate.

22

It's a Girl!

IWAS PLANNING TO give birth at Arlington Hospital, four miles from where I grew up, a short drive from the 7-Eleven where my lifelong friends Bruce and Janie McMullan and I would stock up on bubble gum and Turkish taffy, then drive around while we were supposed to be at church.

In anticipation of the baby's arrival, Jay and I had sold my apartment and were renting a place in McLean, a modest ranch house with more room, close to my folks. I braced myself for the drama I'd long pictured—my water breaking in some comically public place, the mad dash to the hospital with a frantic Jay at the wheel. But...nothing. Despite taking long walks to speed things along, my due date came and went.

Then a sonogram revealed that our baby's efforts to make its way down the birth canal were being obstructed by my coccyx. The doctor gave us a choice: He could either break my coccyx—which didn't sound like a ton of fun—or I could have a C-section. We chose option B.

When they came in with that epidural needle, big enough to inflate a basketball, I put on sunglasses—anything to obscure the sight. Then I was laid out on the operating table and my arms were strapped to the extensions jutting from either side, a little like Jesus on the cross. I can still feel the pressure of the knife on my skin cutting me open and hear the squishing sound of the surgeon pushing my bladder and intestines aside so he could get to the baby. And I will never forget Jay saying, "Your uterus looks like a portobello mushroom." Seriously?

Then the doctor lifted Ellie from my guts. "She's beautiful," Jay reported. "And she's peeing." Welcome to the world.

Something else I hadn't counted on: The *TODAY* audience became deeply invested. People from all over the country sent gifts—bonnets and booties by the truckload; one grandmother sent a baby blanket with a note that said she'd been knitting it for her granddaughter but decided to give it to Ellie instead. It was sweet, albeit a little strange; it felt like I was having America's baby.

I'D NEVER BEEN particularly maternal, had never been one of those women who were desperate to get their hands on other people's newborns, nor had I been big into babysitting; as the youngest of four kids, I was always the one being looked after. Yet now I found myself in the position of caring for a wriggling bundle of need.

I like to think I have a few talents, but I'll tell you what isn't one of them: breastfeeding. My nipples bore no resemblance to the pert, squared-off latex ones I'd seen on those Playtex Baby Nurser commercials. Getting Ellie to "latch on" was like a military maneuver, and my breasts had swollen to the size of melons. Not cantaloupes, not honeydews, but watermelons—and having 20 pounds of produce strapped to my chest was every bit as painful as it sounds. In my version of a "stupid human trick," I'd sometimes give myself a squeeze and squirt milk across the room, much to my amusement (and Jay's chagrin). And when I used my electric breast pump, making that pneumatic sucking sound as I kept the cones pressed to my yarmulke-size areolas, I felt like Elsie on a factory farm. It was all pretty disgusting. Trapped in my stained green velour robe, I'd wonder, *Can I please just take a shower?*

On top of everything, Jay was on his way to making partner at Williams & Connolly. We agreed he should gut it out, then parlay that prestigious credential into a job at a New York firm. That meant a commuter marriage for at least a couple of years. (Jay and I always thought one day we'd put his career first. If he realized his dream of running for office, we agreed we'd move back to Virginia.) For now, NBC was paying the rent on our Manhattan apartment—a double-height artist's studio with a giant window in the living room, a white circular staircase, and the actor Robert Duvall living across the hall. My life had taken a strange and wonderful turn and I was still catching my breath.

There were a lot of moving parts, but we thought we could make it work. Little did I know I was about to be cast in a sequel to *The Hand That Rocks the Cradle.*

23

Brains After Babies

IN THE DOG days of new parenthood, I never took for granted how lucky I was to have Jay. I remember talking to exhausted, frustrated friends from college who suddenly realized that "having it all" meant "doing it all"—holding down a job while handling the lion's share of the housework and child-rearing. It's just the way it was. In the early '90s, the glaring inequity wasn't even questioned.

Yes, some husbands were beginning to understand the importance of being full-fledged partners, but with Jay, there was no learning curve—he was a full-fledged partner from the start. He handled the logistics and paperwork of family life, and at our new weekend place in Millbrook, New York, he'd be the one cleaning the kitchen, making sure everything was in order, packing up the minivan (which we'd nicknamed the Monavan) while I was practically comatose on the sofa. It was an unspoken arrangement: Jay understood the demands of my job, the homework and constant sleep deprivation, and stepped up.

Whether or not I was truly conscious of it, when the time came to find someone to build a life with, I went for a guy I knew would be supportive, someone with a progressive attitude toward the division of labor in a marriage. Even today, all these years later, women spend an average of seven more years, as Melinda Gates tells us, cooking, cleaning, and taking care of the kids. That just wasn't my reality. Without Jay, our girls wouldn't have gotten their rock-solid start in life, and I may never have launched my *TODAY* show career.

I STARED INTO THE Tupperware bin full of Legos.

"Paul loved Legos. Would you like to see the bathtub?"

I shuddered. "No, thank you," I said quietly. "I just don't think I could do that."

I was in Clear Lake, Texas, getting a tour from Rusty Yates, whose wife, Andrea, had recently drowned each of their five children in the bathtub Rusty had just offered to show me.

I couldn't stop thinking about those innocent kids—held underwater, one by one, by their mother, right after she'd fixed them breakfast. Noah, the oldest, at 7, came last; she had to chase him around the house before catching and killing him too. I couldn't bear to think about how terrified he must have been.

I also couldn't stop thinking about Andrea—the shell-shocked, hollow-eyed expression, the stringy hair and wire-rim glasses, looking like a husk in an orange prison uniform. She, too, was one of five children. She was also class valedictorian, captain of the swim team, a member of the National Honor Society, and went on to become a registered nurse—before pumping out five babies in seven years.

She suffered from postpartum psychosis, an extreme case of what can go wrong with a new mother. Andrea's doctor had warned her that her postpartum depression would get worse with each child, and yet they kept at it, something Rusty wanted. I found it so upsetting to learn that two weeks before the murders, she'd been taken off the antipsychotic Haldol but, according to Rusty, was still on antidepressants. Some medical experts claimed that left her contemplating heinous, delusional acts—killing her children in order to save them—and functional enough to carry them out.

It was an American tragedy. And it scared me to death.

When Ellie was a baby, I sometimes worried I might just leave her in her car seat by the side of the road or drop her from the top of the staircase in our apartment onto the hardwood floor below. I never seriously considered doing either, but it terrified me to think that I could. I was just so overwhelmed, knowing this tiny creature depended on me for her survival.

Experts call them "intrusive thoughts"—dark fantasies that can pop into a new mother's head about the terrible things that could happen to her child, causing her to tiptoe into the nursery every 28 seconds and stare into the crib to make sure the baby is still breathing. Even scarier: fantasies in which *she's* causing the harm. I never told anyone I had those thoughts. No one really talked about those things back then; no one wanted to admit she wasn't the "good mother," bonding effortlessly and breastfeeding like a pro. Softly lit, as if in a baby-powder commercial, gazing adoringly at the infant on the changing table, who is gazing adoringly right back.

I'd later learn that intrusive thoughts sometimes come with post-partum depression and anxiety, where your hormones are wildly out of whack, wreaking havoc on your brain chemistry. I'd come to understand they might even play a beneficial evolutionary role, putting moms in a state of hypervigilance as a way of keeping their babies safe. Had I known that at the time, it would have made me feel less ashamed.

RUSTY YATES, A NASA engineer, was sitting across from me in the *TODAY* studio a week after Andrea was convicted of capital murder (later overturned; she was retried and found not guilty by reason of insanity). Wearing a blue button-down shirt and patterned tie, his hair close-cropped, his all-American face clean-shaven, Rusty looked like a high school jock after a postgame shower.

"Andrea wasn't overwhelmed," he said plainly. "Go to my website and look at our videos"—heartbreaking footage of two giggling tots hopping across the floor like rabbits (one in bunny ears); Andrea in bed cuddling a newborn, then tenderly touching one of the boys who's just scurried onto her lap to kiss his new baby sister. "There was no mounting pressure in our family or anything like that. I mean—"

I broke in: "Five children at home, homeschooling them, a small home…that's an awful lot of pressure to put a woman under."

"But like I said, you can see for yourself. Go look at the videos. We managed fine."

Four years later, in 2005, when Matt Lauer interviewed Brooke Shields, she spoke openly about her struggles with postpartum depression and the fact that she had turned to antidepressants. That led to a famously heated segment where Tom Cruise—biceps bursting out of a too-tight black T-shirt—went on an anti-pharma tirade, blaming Matt for being uninformed. Cruise earned a lifetime spot on the highlights reel with "Matt, Matt, Matt, Matt, Matt…you're glib."

However bizarre that all was, the issue of postpartum depression and anxiety was finally coming out of the shadows. While celebrity magazines will never be able to resist those "bodies after babies" photos, it's encouraging to see increased cultural interest in "brains after babies" and how we can better support new mothers. For those in deep trouble like Andrea Yates, who was tragically failed by the medical establishment, her insurance, and, to some degree, her husband, a fuller understanding of what they're going through might allow them to get the help they need.

In many ways, I've witnessed this gradual but necessary evolution firsthand. The Women's Health Initiative was launched in the early '90s, just as I was starting at *TODAY,* after the hue and cry over the fact that most medical research was conducted on white men. It's no surprise that it took a woman—Dr. Bernadine Healy, the first to head the NIH— to implement it. Even more heartening, female doctors have plenty of company today—more than half of med school students are women.

When it comes to reducing the stigma around women's health, mommy bloggers deserve some credit too, building vast, vibrant communities of women who used to be ashamed about things like infertility, divorce, a breast cancer diagnosis, substance abuse, hating their kids sometimes, mental illness. On top of everything else ravaging Andrea Yates, she just seemed profoundly alone.

I had a massive support system: a flexible employer, the wherewithal to afford childcare, health insurance, a wealth of loved ones—all of which provided the scaffolding that helped me raise healthy, happy children. For so many American women, this simply isn't the case. After all, we live in the only industrialized nation that doesn't guarantee workers paid family leave, sending a clear message that the hard work of building a family just isn't valued. I was one of the lucky ones. Every time I look at my girls, I can't help but think how different life might have been.

24

Paging Mary Poppins

DURING THOSE DISCOMBOBULATING first weeks of parenthood, we had a baby nurse to help us out. Now, though, we needed to find a full-time nanny.

The idea of household help was really alien to me. Growing up, my only experience with someone handling so-called domestic duties was Emma Mudd, a soft-spoken woman with a patient smile that revealed a gold tooth who came every Tuesday to clean the house. I think my mom appreciated her company as much as her help.

The adult me found the notion of having anything resembling "staff" a little absurd; it seemed so pretentious, so upstairs/downstairs, when I knew I'd be more comfortable downstairs. But out of necessity, I was quickly adapting to the ways of the modern working mother, and if that meant outsourcing, I was prepared to do it.

Someone had recommended a firm called the International Nanny Agency, which sounded like a place that knew what it was doing. My contact there was a woman named Denise. With her elegant accent (South African or British, I was never sure which), she seemed like just the person to help us find our "practically perfect in every way" Mary Poppins.

Denise sent a steady stream of candidates to my office at 30 Rock. One after another, they'd take a seat on my chintz sofa. I'd pull up a chair and start the interview, fumbling around while asking questions about their work experience, doing my best to explain what they'd be walking into: a first-time mom with a high-wattage job and a husband living 240 miles away.

Initially, I was drawn to a fresh-faced Irish woman, but Jay wanted someone more mature. He was interested in meeting a candidate we'll call Doris who, at 46, was not only more experienced but also had celebrities like Bianca Jagger and Diana Ross on her resumé. Impressed (and slightly intimidated) by her pedigree, we figured she understood the unique challenges of caring for the offspring of well-known people. Denise assured me Doris would be just right and that her references were stellar. So we offered her a job as Ellie's live-in nanny Monday through Friday; she'd have the weekends off to do as she pleased.

We decided to spend a few days in Maurertown with my parents and Doris to acclimate her to the Couric/Monahan universe. In her khaki shorts, oversize T-shirts, tube socks, and sneakers, she exuded competence, moving about the house with military-style efficiency as she saw to Ellie's every need.

One afternoon, Doris and I went grocery shopping while Jay stayed behind with Ellie, giving us a chance to get to know each other. It was slightly awkward—we were strangers, after all, at the beginning of a relationship that was both transactional and oddly intimate. On the way back from the Food Lion, we chatted about our lives—she told me she had never been married, had no children, and wasn't close to her parents or siblings. She didn't mention any other relatives, good friends, or a partner, past or present. And then, as we made our way along the bucolic country road leading to the house, she blurted out, "I don't want to go away on the weekends. I want to feel like I'm part of a family."

My immediate reaction was a combination of *Wait a second…* and sympathy. I quickly filled the silence with an overly upbeat response: "Oh, that's okay, of course you can be part of our family!"

A few days later, Doris, Ellie, and I drove to New York and got our new nanny settled in our apartment. We gave her a small room near the kitchen; I'd be upstairs near Ellie's nursery.

It wouldn't be long before Doris convinced us to convert the TV/ playroom upstairs into a bedroom. For her.

DORIS BROUGHT STRUCTURE and expertise to our routine, putting Ellie to bed at precisely 5:30 p.m. That seemed a little early to me, but the truth is, I was exhausted from getting up before 5:00 a.m. every day, and it was nice to have the evening to relax a little and prepare for the roughly six interviews I'd be doing the next morning. Besides, Doris was the expert. I trusted her judgment.

With Ellie asleep and everything in the apartment tight as a drum, Henry from NBC would deliver "the packet"—a giant white envelope bearing the peacock logo and my name in Magic Marker. Then I'd shake out the contents, including the rundown for the next day, research for the heavy-hitting "Close Up" segment at 7:09, a book synopsis for an author interview, perhaps a new CD if there was a musical act, and background on dependable topics like nutritious after-school snacks and hormone replacement therapy. Once I'd gone through it, Doris and I would eat dinner, just the two of us—maybe a rotisserie chicken she'd picked up at Williams Bar-B-Q on Broadway—while watching *Nightly News.* I spent more time with Doris than anyone else in my life, and I was completely unguarded around her, making funny/snarky asides about this or that person, ducking in to tell her something while wrapped in a towel post-shower.

The next morning, she'd hand me my research, fetch my coat, and send me off into the predawn darkness, down to the curb, where my driver, the brusque but sweet Jack Sturm, was waiting, his black sedan purring, taillights glowing red.

I sometimes joked that Ellie had two moms. Monday through Friday, when Jay was in Virginia, Doris and I really were a couple, in a weird kind of way.

THE SHOW HAD so much momentum, but soon it was clear that the executive producer, Tom Capra (son of Frank, of *It's a Wonderful Life* fame), wasn't the guy to capitalize on it. Conveniently, Jeff Zucker was on deck. Everyone, including Michael Gartner, saw how smart, hungry, and ambitious he was. So, early in my tenure, Gartner made a bold move: He replaced Capra with Zucker. At just 26 years old, he'd be the overlord, tasked with having a vision, mixing the perfect cocktail of stories, and constantly innovating and sweating the details, all of which Jeff was built for.

By this point, Jeff and I were very tight. Ideas spilled out of us as we planned and schemed and brainstormed interviews and stunts that would attract yet more attention. (I always said if Edward R. Murrow and P. T. Barnum had a baby, it would be Jeff Zucker.) Jeff and I would hunker down in the newsroom before the show, going over questions for some of the tougher interviews. We talked about how I should calibrate my tone, depending on whom I was talking to.

But there were challenges, like how to funnel important stories my way without enraging Bryant and vice versa. And whenever Bryant got miffed at me during the broadcast, Jeff would whisper in my earpiece, "ROYB," code for "Let it roll off your back." He knew how to manage egos. Imagine being a brand-new EP in your twenties and having to tell Bryant Gumbel no. (Not fun at any age.)

Me, though—I was good. Not only did I have a shrewd and loyal producer in my corner; suddenly I had a very powerful one too.

25

Perky

WHEN FREUD SAID, "Anatomy is destiny," I'm pretty sure he wasn't talking about the zygomaticus major—a muscle beneath the cheekbones that, when activated by the facial nerve, pulls up the corners of the mouth. Not that I've ever had this checked out, but I think my zygomaticus major might be major. I smile big and I smile a lot—even my resting bitch face is a smile.

When I was little, my sisters nicknamed me Smiley—I'd be the thousand-watt welcome wagon when their friends came over. In a fifth-grade production of *The Tempest* (why they had a bunch of 10-year-olds doing Shakespeare, I'll never know), I played the brooding sorcerer Prospero with a gummy grin, surveying the audience the entire time. That same year when I ran for student-council president, I delivered a stump speech that began "People wonder why I'm always smiling. It's because I'm happy. Happy to go to such a wonderful school." (Oh, brother.)

Years later, the media would go to creative lengths to describe my smile; the *Washington Post* said it "slides across [my] face like a puppy on linoleum." Ironically, my two front teeth aren't even my own—one got chipped when I was 6 and went flying over the handlebars; the other when Chris Foley tripped me on the blacktop in third grade. (My mother cried both times—worried about the dental bills as much as my pearly whites.)

My smile, and the ebullience that came with it, had become my defining feature. And at a certain point, reporters decided the word for me was *perky*—the adjective stuck like powdered sugar to a jelly doughnut. I hated it. I thought it made me sound unserious.

The thing that had opened so many doors now threatened to close others. So I vowed not to let that happen, to be a journalist in full, pursuing the meaty, difficult issues that obsessed me, as aggressively as necessary. No matter what my zygomaticus major might be doing.

SOME SEGMENTS I could do in my sleep (and sometimes did)—back-to-school shopping, Super Bowl snacks. And some sent me into the preparation bunker with stacks of research and calls to experts (including my dad). One of those was David Duke, white supremacist, former grand wizard of the Ku Klux Klan, and, in 1992, a candidate for president of the United States.

Duke was at the NBC affiliate in New Orleans; I interviewed him from New York. His blow-dried weatherman look, helped along by plastic surgery, betrayed little of his vile ideology.

I greet him the way I would any other guest on *TODAY* and pose the sort of questions you typically ask a candidate—about reducing the deficit and foreign policy.

Then I pivot, channeling Tim Russert. Tim had an incredibly effective way of using things his guests had said to uncover falsehoods or hypocrisy. So I researched a number of inflammatory statements Duke had made through the years, then offered them up to see how he'd react.

Me: I'd like to repeat something you said in 1985: "I think the Jewish people have been a blight and they probably deserve to go into the ash bin of history."
DD: Well, I don't agree with that quote—that certainly doesn't sum up my feelings accurately—
Me: That was just six years ago.

On the split screen, Duke looks defensive as I bear down and offer a more recent example.

> Me: You've often said you're a changed man, so I'm wondering why just yesterday you made this comment about the Japanese...

We play a clip from a press conference in which Duke said, "I come from Louisiana. We produce rice. We must go to the Japanese and say, 'You no buy our rice, we no buy your cars.'"

> Me: Hm. "You no buy our rice, we no buy your cars"—isn't that a modernized version of "No ticky, no laundry," a pretty blatant ethnic slur?

My dad had suggested that question, an insult that was more from his era than mine.

> DD: No, I don't think it is; I think I'm simply saying we've gotta open our markets to the Japanese. And it's certainly humorous, but you know, a lot of people talk in broken English...

At the same press conference the previous day, Duke had said, "We cannot let this country go to the party of the Democrats, go to the party of Jesse Jackson and Ron Brown." That sounded like a dog whistle to me.

> Me: Did you intentionally invoke the names of two Black men when describing the Democratic Party?
> DD: Well, I—I...I invoked who I think are the future of the Democratic Party, the liberal policies of the Democratic Party—

I point out that Jackson wasn't even running for president, wondering in what sense he was the future of the Democratic Party.

Me: Why didn't you mention George Mitchell, Tom Foley, Bill
    Clinton, Geraldine Ferraro?

Duke looks a bit befuddled as I curtly wrap things up, giving him the morning-show equivalent of the bum's rush.

Almost immediately, calls came flooding into NBC saying I had been "too angry" and "too harsh" with Duke. A viewer in Marion, Illinois, wrote:

Dear Fathead,

I watched David Duke make a fool of you today. Instead of being objective, you became antagonistic, almost strident! Your ignorance made him all the more reasonable. Shame on you.

My demeanor was about as far from perky as you could get. If Bryant had done that interview, it would have been seen as Bryant being Bryant—appropriately combative, holding someone's feet to the fire. With me it was more like, *Holy smokes, Martha, what happened to that nice Katie Couric?*

So there I was, in the teeth of a dilemma: Do I run the risk of alienating viewers by doing what journalism often requires—going hard, calling BS? Here I am, face to face with a white supremacist attempting to become the leader of the free world. Would it be better to ask about his role models or how he keeps his energy up on the campaign trail?

Amid the bins of unhappy viewer mail, there was one letter that made it all worthwhile.

Dear Ms. Couric:

As an American, a journalist and a Jew, I watched in horror as the big guns of network television news let David Duke barrel through with his own, virtually unchallenged agenda in interview after interview. What you did this morning was not only right, but also smart and courageous—a true example of hard-hitting journalism, built on a solid command of the facts and a desire to uncover the truth.

This from Frank Rich, on *New York Times* letterhead. Rich was the theater critic; his unsparing reviews had earned him the epithet "the Butcher of Broadway," so I knew compliments from him didn't come easily. The framed letter still hangs in my office.

But the reaction I was waiting for was my father's. After the show, we'd frequently do postmortems. Sometimes he'd have small corrections: They're called *Canada geese,* not *Canadian geese.* And people feel *nauseated,* not *nauseous.* Sometimes the critique was more serious. Following a safe-sex demonstration with an AIDS counselor during which I put a condom on a life-size rubber penis, he called to say, "Katie, I'm afraid this time you've gone too far."

When I called him after the Duke interview, I was worried he thought I'd gone too far this time as well.

Instead, he picked up and exclaimed, "Bravo, bravo," clapping his hands as he cradled the phone between shoulder and ear. "Excellent work. An interview in the tradition of Edward R. Murrow. Well done." I'd be hard-pressed to remember a time I felt more proud.

HE WAS MY journalistic North Star. I still go through his clippings, preserved in the plastic sleeves of the scrapbooks my mother had lovingly assembled. As I turn the fragile pages, I scrutinize the articles for evidence of my father's perspective in stories about the South's stubborn resistance to change. He despised the segregationist Georgia governor Lester Maddox and was both disgusted and amused by Strom Thurmond, the anti–civil rights crusader from South Carolina who served a mind-boggling 48 years in the Senate (humorist Dave Barry once satirized Thurmond in his syndicated column, saying he colored his hair with Tang). On one occasion, my father found himself in Thurmond's office while reporting a story and witnessed an interaction between the senator and a female aide that Dad would reenact to my delight: Putting his arm around an imaginary woman, he'd drawl, "Purty guhl. Smaht too."

Our father's voice was rich and loamy, like the soil in Eufaula—a reminder of his heritage, and ours. He was one of the most fair-minded people I've ever known. Which is saying something, given that he grew up in the segregated South.

His willowy mother, Wilde, had an air of Southern formality. On birthdays and holidays she'd send Hallmark-y cards always signed *Your devoted grandmother.*

I remember going with my dad to see her in Dublin. We had lunch at a restaurant with a screened-in porch—it was hot, and there was a fly buzzing around her salmon croquettes. Wilde yammered on about who knows what; at the time I'd never heard the word *dementia,* but it was clear to me she was losing her marbles.

She was a teacher, a devout Presbyterian, and an adoring mother who handwrote multipage love letters to her two children. She was also that unusual thing at the time, an educated woman, an early graduate of the University of Alabama. And yet she was a racist. My grandmother bequeathed my father a first edition of the 1905 novel *The Clansman* (subtitled *An Historical Romance of the Ku Klux Klan,* the basis of D. W. Griffith's *The Birth of a Nation*). Her inscription:

> *This is such a valuable and beautiful book. Never destroy it. I want someone to own it who realizes how marvelous this book is…It is absolutely true.*
> *Mother*

Ellie discovered it in a bookcase in my father's study when we were cleaning out my parents' home. She's still processing the shock, as am I.

The daughter of a Confederate soldier, Wilde had been indoctrinated with fierce if misguided ancestral pride. And yet she also took on the cause of a Black child in the neighborhood, teaching him to read, giving him food and my father's hand-me-downs. There must have been some sort of cultural logic to her contradictions—I'll never know how she squared the ill-fitting pieces.

Our family tree was blighted with racists. At first glance, there were fascinating characters—my great-grandmother Sallie, for instance, whose mother and two brothers went to New Orleans to buy a piano. On the journey they contracted yellow fever and died; their bodies were shipped home in the piano crate. Because Sallie hadn't joined them, she survived. I was taken with the gothic quality of her story.

But Sallie was a descendant of the slave-owning Shorter family; her father, Reuben Clark Shorter, was known as an "ethnic cleansing specialist" and "renowned Indian fighter." Sallie married a cotton broker, Alfred Alexis Couric; their son, A. A. Couric, was also a cotton broker—and a mean drunk who, evidence suggests, participated in a lynching. He was my father's uncle. I will never be at peace with the fact that I share a bloodline with such a person.

As a child, I was oblivious to these things. My fondest memories were of time spent with relatives in the magnolia-scented South—the Tolkien-like cypress trees draped in Spanish moss and the gracious, pretty women who "bathed before noon, after their three o'clock naps, and by nightfall were like soft teacakes with frostings of sweat and sweet talcum," as Harper Lee wrote.

My mom's Southern heritage also has its roots in Alabama. She descended from German immigrants, Isaac and Emma Frohsin, who left Germany in the late 19th century and made their way to Alexander City, where they opened the department store bearing their last name. My great-uncle Ralph took over the store, making Alex City his lifelong home. I have vivid memories of picking blackberries in his backyard, pulling puffer fish out of Lake Martin, and eating pimento cheese sandwiches.

When I was 10, we drove to Uncle Buddy's house in Atlanta for Nana's 70th-birthday party. We were all hanging out in the family room, goofing around, playing games. At one point, my eyes locked on a foreign-looking silver sculpture nestled high up in the bookcase. A menorah.

My young brain tried to process it. I remember thinking, *Wow—they're Jewish*. Quickly followed by *Oh my God*—we're *Jewish*. The suddenly terrifying Tom Lehrer lyrics filled my head:

Oh the Protestants hate the Catholics
And the Catholics hate the Protestants...
And everybody hates the Jews

I guess it shouldn't have come as a huge surprise with names like Abraham and Isaac in the family mix and beef tongue being sliced in the kitchen, two of my cousins fighting over the tip. Going through my mother's papers, I find plentiful evidence of our Jewish lineage and Nana's involvement in a lively Jewish community in Atlanta: an invitation to a luncheon at Ahavath Achim Synagogue; a Yom Kippur prayer card; Nana's wedding announcement noting that Rabbi David Marx officiated. She'd met her future husband, Bert, at a "Jewbilee"—a social where Jews could mingle with other Jews. The homes my grandfather built were in the Jewish enclaves of Omaha. My mom and Buddy were both confirmed at their local synagogue.

They were clearly Reform Jews, putting up a Christmas tree every year. When they asked the rabbi if that was okay, he said sure, "it's just like celebrating someone's birthday." And yet they knew that feeling of "otherness." In a letter to my mom during her freshman year at Sophie Newcomb, her father wrote, "We would be glad to know if your style is being cramped by association with young folks of your own faith or have you been able to knock down the barriers?"

Jewishness was not something my mother talked about. And I know she suffered a million slights over the years, something I became more attuned to as I got older. When my cousin married into a wealthy WASPy family, the wedding was at a "restricted" country club in Birmingham. When our family went to find our table, it was on the outskirts of the action. We heard there was a big party at the new in-laws' house afterward—we weren't invited. I felt so bad for Nana, the grandmother of the groom.

Then there were "the flower ladies." One day when I was visiting my parents, I found my mom sitting alone, crying. When I asked what was wrong, she hesitated, then told me that, while making bouquets and small talk, one of them casually said something anti-Semitic. She wouldn't say what. The flower ladies didn't know my mother was Jewish, but that didn't make it any less painful.

"Mom, why didn't you say something?" I asked. She just shook her head. Perhaps she thought that keeping our Jewish heritage under wraps would protect us, that it would be better for my dad professionally and better for the kids socially (in my entire grade, I knew of only two Jewish girls, both named Sandy). For my mother, her parents, and their parents before them, assimilation was often the key to survival and success.

My mother's anxious ambivalence stayed just below the surface. I remember going through a phase on *TODAY* where I'd react to something vexing by ad-libbing, "Oy."

One day after the show, my mom called.

"Please don't say that," she said. "It makes you sound so...New York."

26

Florence and Normandie

IF I'D CLAIMED the moral high ground in the Duke interview, another story about race showed me just how much I (and so many others) had to learn. Only a few months later, in downtown LA, unarmed Rodney King was savagely beaten by four members of the LAPD—the whole thing caught on tape. Some call it the first viral video. The cops would be acquitted by a mostly white jury in a mostly white California suburb.

When the outrage boiled over into the streets—small businesses torched, police cars overturned and set ablaze—Bryant opened our broadcast this way:

"We'd like to say good morning on this Thursday, but frankly there is nothing good to be said about this last morning of April of 1992. This one's a tough one." Bryant never lost his cool, although sitting just inches away, I could feel how troubled he was. The riots would go on for six days and claim 63 lives.

Some of the worst violence occurred in downtown LA, where groups of young Black men dragged white drivers from their vehicles and beat them mercilessly. A hovering helicopter caught a skinny, long-haired white man at the intersection of Florence and Normandie being pulled from the shiny red cab of his tractor trailer and thrown to the ground. Then his assailants took turns delivering the beatdown—a roundhouse kick to the head, balletic leaping jabs; one dropped a cinder block on the man. The pavement around his limp body was coated with blood; the men picked his pockets before leaving him for dead.

The trucker, Reginald Denny, was immediately held up as the sacrificial victim, the face of phase two of this tragedy.

IN APRIL OF '93, nearly a year after the riots, I was given the opportunity to interview Denny. That's when I got to know Johnnie Cochran, Denny's flamboyant Rolls-driving attorney—I became friendly with him and his wife, Dale. Johnnie had argued many police-brutality cases and had serious civil rights credentials. I couldn't really see where a white trucker fit in that mix, except for the fact that he'd be at the epicenter of a media firestorm, and there was nowhere Johnnie would rather be.

I sat down with Denny in Cochran's law-book-lined LA office. I wondered what kind of shape he'd be in and was relieved that he seemed okay in spite of a few dents in his face (he had pins in his cheeks and pieces of reconstructive plastic under the skin beneath his eyes) and a lower lip that didn't match up with the top one, a result of his jaw being shattered. But Reggie was open, funny, and sweet—I liked him immediately.

At one point I laid my hand against the right side of his face. "It feels like some of your head is missing," I said.

"It is," Denny responded, putting his hand over mine and guiding it along the crater where his skull had been crushed.

Denny talked about the men who'd assaulted him, hoping they'd find a way to step out of the bad groove they were in—what he called the "fast train to nowhere."

"I think what people find so remarkable about you, Reggie," I said, "is that you don't harbor any bitterness or resentment or hatred toward these people who have changed your life forever...what do you think should happen to them?"

"Oh God, I don't know. What can be done to make them better people?" Denny said as the camera cut to me shaking my head. "That's something that has to happen within themselves. They have to want to be productive and be good citizens."

Going from the taped piece back to being live in the studio, I said, "He's the sweetest man. I mean, I was just overwhelmed by him and the level of forgiveness and understanding that he was able to have toward the people who beat the living daylights out of him *for no reason*...he's an incredibly special person."

And it's true—he *was* an incredibly special person. But watching the interview today makes me squirm.

As does much of the coverage, which focused on the sensational details, like the graphic violence and the nearly $800 million in property damage. Bryant did the best he could to tease out underlying attitudes and misconceptions when he interviewed one of the jurors who'd acquitted the LAPD cops, a woman who explained that Rodney King "was directing the action. He was the one who determined how long it took to put him in handcuffs."

"At what point when he was lying there taking blows do you think he lost control of the action?" Bryant asked.

I'm writing these words in the wake of George Floyd. As our eyes have finally been pinned wide open to the systemic injustice that has derailed the lives of Black people since slavery, I am appalled at the cluelessness I now see in the way we covered the Rodney King story (starting with the optics—many carefully coiffed, white correspondents delivering their uninflected reports). No one, myself included, was able to interrogate what any of this was actually about on a societal level. Almost no one could ask hard, sustained, well-informed questions about the source of the anger. Instead, we dedicated major airtime—a two-part interview— to the plight of the white victim. (Why do you think we committed so many hours to stories like Laci Peterson, Natalee Holloway, and Trisha Meili, the Central Park jogger? Tragic victims, yes, but pretty white women all. I never heard anyone say it explicitly, but I know it was assumed that's what most viewers wanted to see, and the predominantly white people behind the scenes complied.)

It's hard to be an apologist for what those four men did to Reginald

Denny, on display in all its viciousness, just as it was with the cops who beat Rodney King. To this day, the footage makes me want to throw up. Denny was in the wrong place at the wrong time, and those men were out for blood and worse. And yet I come back to the word *clueless*. The cluelessness of growing up in a de facto segregated Virginia suburb, being friendly with the Black girls I ran track with, girls I loved…yet I never went to their houses in the "Black part of town" (Halls Hill, behind the McDonald's). The cluelessness—no, malevolence—of a fraternity at UVA having pledges work as waiters in blackface. I was at that party. I was disgusted, and yet at the time I didn't have the guts to just get up and leave. The cluelessness, born of intractable white privilege, about institutional racism—about redlining and voter suppression and predatory lending and maternal mortality and the criminal justice system and police brutality.

As educated and progressive as many of us in the mainstream media thought ourselves to be in the '90s, very few had the awareness or life experience to provide any nuance about what was happening and push the reporting to go deeper. It was: white trucker good, Black assailants bad. Case closed. Thinking about it now mortifies me.

A DEEPLY DISTURBING OVERCORRECTION would come two years later in the form of OJ Simpson. I'd met OJ and Nicole during the Barcelona Olympics in '92 as they were getting off a hotel elevator; I remember thinking how beautiful Nicole was. OJ and I had been photographed together when I covered the First Gulf War and he was visiting the troops. Both times he was gregarious, radiating charisma. He hosted an NFL pregame show with Bob Costas, which made him a member of the NBC family.

Five days after Nicole and her friend Ron Goldman were brutally murdered outside her Brentwood home, the Knicks faced the Houston Rockets in game five of the playoffs. I'm not a big basketball fan but Jay badly wanted to go. Of course there were no seats left at Madison Square Garden, but Dick Ebersol came through, and arranged for us to sit with Bob on the platform he was broadcasting from, behind one of the baskets.

Things got weird fast. It started rippling through the stands that a phalanx of LAPD cruisers was on the 405 tailing a white Ford Bronco carrying Simpson, with his friend and former Buffalo Bills teammate Al Cowlings at the wheel. Suddenly, Bob was toggling between game commentary from Marv Albert and updates from the news division on the bizarre scene playing out in LA, along with images of the SUV looking like some ghost car headed for the abyss. (NBC normally would have just stayed on the breaking news, but a playoff game, especially between teams from two really big markets, was ratings gold. Not even a real-time drama involving a big celebrity was going to get in the way of that.)

These being the days before iPhones, everyone was scrambling for information. Fans were craning their necks to get a look at Bob's screen and shouting over to him, "Bob, what's happening with OJ?" It turned out Simpson was holding a .38 to his own head; his friend and lawyer Robert Kardashian, father of Kim and company, had read what sure sounded like a suicide note and thinly veiled confession written by Simpson. And yet, somehow, throngs of OJ fans were packing the overpasses and pressing up against the guardrails on the freeway, cheering him on.

What was happening? Why was this plainly guilty person being celebrated like a modern-day folk hero? Bob and I just looked at each other, speechless, knowing this might be the strangest thing we'd ever witnessed in our broadcasting lives.

The trial lasted almost a year; deliberations, less than four hours. The courtroom was packed; reporters and spectators jammed the hallway outside. Like pretty much everybody else in the news business, I'd been consumed by this saga for months.

The words "Not guilty" reverberated throughout the room, followed by gasps, yelps, and sobs. OJ's son Jason Simpson doubled over, weeping with relief; a distraught Kim Goldman, sister of Ron, wept too. The scene in the hallway revealed an equally stark divide: Black people cheering and throwing up high fives, white people standing by, speechless, shell-shocked. Just like the rest of the country, we'd soon learn.

Looking back, I find it much less difficult to comprehend. The

Rodney King verdict was a slap in the face to Black Americans and the abuse they routinely took at the hands of the police. Acquitting OJ may have seemed like a measure of delayed racial justice (despite the feeling that he'd turned his back on the Black community long before; as Ta-Nehisi Coates wrote in the *Atlantic,* "Simpson should have been the last person in the world to reap a reward from the struggle waged against the LAPD").

Meanwhile, all the aghast white people knew was that a murderer had gotten off. It would take years for them, us, me to fully see what lay beneath.

27

The Coast of Casablanca

IN RARE MOMENTS when the country wasn't blowing up, I allowed my-self to enjoy what was happening in my little corner of the world. The ratings were climbing, the reviews were glowing, and the requests for interviews were coming in by the second. Even Johnny Carson wanted one. Chatting with him on *The Tonight Show*—making *the* Johnny Carson laugh about my dad's reaction to the condom demonstration—was a pinch-me moment.

But I wasn't the only one getting noticed.

Part of the job of co-anchor was popping up on local morning shows to tease segments that were coming up later on *TODAY*. The idea was to give viewers a reason to stick around, have another cup of coffee, and maybe even be late for work. And make them feel that the people at NBC and its affiliates across the country were all one big, happy family, which required a heavy dose of playful banter with local anchors.

There was a guy doing *Today in New York* we were all checking out. He seemed to be a natural at the chummy, unscripted back-and-forth. And he was good-looking, with a rakish smile and a nice head of hair. At a certain point, everyone was talking about Matt Lauer.

Whatever *it* is, Matt had it—that ability to reach through the screen and make people watch. I remember visiting Kiki in Boston years earlier and catching a local show called *Talk of the Town,* and checking out the host. *Wow, that Matt guy is smooth,* I said to myself, both of us nobodies at the time.

Matt co-anchored *Today in New York* with warm, capable Jane Hanson. As the story goes, one morning they were preparing to chat about the previous night's big hockey game where one of the teams had staged a major comeback. Jane didn't know anything about hockey, so during the taped piece, Matt gave her an assist: He said that after he mentioned the final score, she should say, "Wow! They are really on the coast of Casablanca."

"It's a sports thing," said Matt. "People will be impressed."

Sure enough, when Matt reported the score, Jane did as he'd suggested, saying, "Wow! They are really on the coast of Casablanca."

At which point Matt turned to her and said, "What? What does that mean? I have no idea what you're talking about."

Punk'd. On live TV. Jane turned beet red and laughed. So embarrassing, yet so hilarious—and so Matt.

He started filling in as newsreader on *TODAY* in 1992 and officially got the job two years later. The first time Matt covered for Bryant, we kicked it around effortlessly—the chemistry was obvious.

After one particularly jocular exchange, Jeff jumped to his feet and pointed at the monitor. Anyone within a mile radius of the control room could hear him shout, "That, ladies and gentlemen, is the future of the *TODAY* show!"

MEANWHILE, BACK ON 86th Street...one night after dinner, with the dishwasher humming and Ellie sound asleep, I was heading to my room when Doris approached me in the hallway. She said she wanted to ask me a question.

"Of course," I replied. "What is it?"

"I was wondering if you could give me a hug before I go to bed."

The thought bubble above my head read *What the hell?* "Really?" I said.

"Yes," she replied. "It would just make me feel better."

I immediately started rationalizing, trying to process what she had just said. She seemed to have no friends, no one special in her life. She wanted to be part of the family. What would be the harm in giving her a little hug at night? (I know, I know…)

"Okay, I guess so," I managed. Then I lightly embraced her, like you do when saying goodbye to a friendly acquaintance, hands fluttering awkwardly around her shoulder blades.

Then Doris hugged me back—a little too tightly, resting her head on my chest like a child.

Maybe she was having an especially bad night. Maybe this was a one-off. Testing the theory, the next few nights I went directly to my bedroom, calling out, "G'night!" Without fail, Doris would pipe up, "Katie, aren't you going to give me a hug?" I'd oblige, then walk back to my room thinking, *How weird is this?*

It all felt so creepy. And yet I let it go for many reasons—the main one being I was completely dependent on her. My job was ridiculously unpredictable and demanding, but here we were, settled into a comfortable domestic routine.

Doris was available to me basically 24/7, which came in handy on countless occasions. And she was my proxy—even at those tender, milestone moments, like Ellie's first birthday. When I was in Barcelona covering my first Olympics, it was Doris who planned the party and celebrated with Jay, my parents, our friends, and a (possibly drunk) clown in a multicolored wig while I was interviewing the U.S. gymnastics team and eating tapas.

And yet, I had the nagging feeling that something was not right, as Miss Clavel would say. I'll never forget watching the Chilean family drama *The House of the Spirits* and feeling a shock of recognition as bizarre Férula (Glenn Close), obsessed with clueless Clara (Meryl Streep), ultimately sneaks into her bed one night…

But the thought of firing Doris and starting over, going through the time-consuming process of finding someone else, was daunting. Giving her a hug at bedtime seemed a small price to pay. Who cared if sometimes when I walked by her room late at night, I saw her lying on the bed, eating a Baby Ruth, staring at the ceiling? During the day, Doris whipped up baby food and did puzzles on the floor with a happily gurgling Ellie. Our daughter was in good hands. So, rather than establish some boundaries, I pretty much erased them.

On the weekends, it was baby makes three...and Doris makes four. Most times we were frequent fliers, hopping on the Delta shuttle to visit Jay and stay in the former tobacco warehouse we'd bought in Old Town, Alexandria. I still had a lot of friends in the area; later on, they'd tell me about coming by to visit and Doris not letting them in. One of those times, when Wendy and Dana, my friend from channel 4, stood at the front door, Dana heard me call out from the other room, "Who is it?," like some gaslit woman in peril in a Lifetime movie. Doris turned them away.

An alarming level of codependency had been achieved. In such a subtle, crafty way, Doris had managed to grow deep, twisted roots into our family—and my psyche, leaving me to imagine I couldn't function without her. And she made me feel completely responsible for her happiness and well-being. Once, when my friend Tammi came to visit, I actually asked her if she could watch Ellie for a few hours because I hadn't spent much time with Doris lately, and I was going to take her to a movie.

Tammi from Miami said what a lot of my friends were thinking at the time: "This is insane. You're insane."

WE TOOK DORIS with us on fancy vacations (Cap Juluca, a resort in Anguilla; Lost Creek, a dude ranch near Jackson Hole, Wyoming; Little Dix Bay—I would joke with Jay that it took a very confident man to go there). We bought her expensive presents—sweaters, boots; Jay gave Doris an antique silver perfume bottle he'd found on one of his treasure hunts, serendipitously engraved with her name. My mom was 100 percent Team Doris, and no wonder—Doris would spend hours on the phone chatting her up, filling her in on what was happening. (My mother *loved* to talk on the phone.)

But I was Doris's main focus. More than once, she said she had something really important to tell me—voice trembling, tearing up. "Doris, what is it?" I'd say, genuinely concerned. We'd sit down and I'd wait for her to tell me some deep, dark secret that never came. Because, I realized later, she'd gotten what she wanted: my rapt attention.

When a team from *Good Housekeeping* came to our apartment to do a story about our family, I insisted Doris be included in the photos. Mother of God.

Even the editors agreed with Miss Clavel; despite my protestations, they photoshopped Doris out of the picture. Ellie's back is to the camera, with only her wavy brown baby hair visible. I had followed Jane Pauley's sage advice to protect my child's identity. So why did my good sense desert me with Doris?

28

Movin' Out

WITH THE 1992 presidential race gearing up, I needed help on the home front more than ever.

At the time, politics were bleeding into the popular culture in unprecedented ways—Bill Clinton in Blues Brothers shades blowing his sax on *Arsenio Hall*, a self-made Texas billionaire who looked like a Keebler elf announcing his candidacy on *Larry King Live*...we couldn't have ordered up better ratings bait. Especially when Ross Perot accused me and NBC's Lisa Myers of "trying to prove our manhood" with our tough interview questions. The *New York Post* blared the phrase on the front page.

But my biggest moment of the campaign happened in the Blue Room, somewhere between Dolley Madison's tea set and a portrait of James Monroe. In October, First Lady Barbara Bush gave me a live tour of the White House on the occasion of its 200th anniversary. I had spent days studying every nook and cranny of 1600 Pennsylvania Avenue, from the ball-and-claw feet on the Chippendale chairs to the bronze doré clock on the mantelpiece. It was the interview equivalent of a ladies' lunch until I heard the pitter-pat of little paws—the unmistakable sound of an excited canine running down the hall. Suddenly, the president's English springer spaniel Ranger came tumbling in. Followed closely by the president himself.

It never occurred to me that George H. W. Bush might show up. And yet here he was, the leader of the free world, standing a couple of inches away. Even though my prep for the First Lady hadn't included politics, I knew I had to seize the moment, and swiftly pivoted to Bush's charismatic opponent; I got Bush to say that Clinton should come clean about why he hadn't served in the armed forces and mock his claim that he didn't inhale. I was afraid I was going to run out of questions, but I had Jeff in my earpiece, urging me toward Iran-Contra. When I asked Bush about the Justice Department's questioning of FBI head William Sessions, I saw the patrician grin fade and his upper lip start to twitch.

Jeff had made the game-time decision to kill the commercials and run the whole interview, an unimaginable 19 minutes and 38 seconds. It was nerve-racking—and one of the most exhilarating experiences of my life. As I tried to squeeze in a few final questions, the First Lady was losing her patience—at a certain point, it looked like she might forcibly separate us and drag her husband out of the room. Bush smiled and playfully remarked, "I know what Ross Perot said about you..."

The impromptu grilling was a huge win. A few days later, I received a handwritten note on snappy Jazz Age letterhead. It read:

Dear Katie,

You were terrific with Mrs. Bush (you knew far more than she did) and nabbing the President was a real coup. You are so darn good! Bravo!

Barbara

As in Walters. She was always so supportive—she liked to say we were similar in that neither of us was particularly glamorous. I never quite knew how to take that, although being in Barbara's mold was nothing but a compliment.

Tom Shales also weighed in: "Couric proved again yesterday that she's worth her weight in gold. Actually, more. She doesn't weigh all that much."

In a piece overflowing with praise, that last sentence might have been my favorite part.

LABOR DAY WEEKEND. I was disappointed that Jay had to stay in DC and work, so I decided to rent a house on Martha's Vineyard, a place I'd never been, where Doris, Ellie, and I could relax for a few days. The charming cottage, overlooking the water in Menemsha, belonged to Billy Joel. By then I'd met my fair share of famous people, but for some reason that really tickled me.

With Doris playing photographer, we took some funny pictures for my friends—me lying in Billy's bed "smoking" a Bic pen, looking like I'd just had a roll in the hay; me looking shocked while holding a bottle of Sun In I'd found in the medicine cabinet (presumably his then-wife Christie Brinkley's); me pretending to sniff Billy's gym shorts. Juvenile but harmless. Doris snapped away, snorting with laughter. She'd truly become my partner in crime.

By now, Jay had grown tired of commuting. He had tried to hang in there at Williams & Connolly, but living apart was too hard and not the life we wanted, so he took a job in the New York offices of Hunton and Williams.

Finally, we were going to be together as a family. Jay started working on a book about his abiding passion, the Civil War. He was even a re-enactor, meaning that he and some equally obsessed buddies in Virginia would dramatize important battles on weekends, having researched every detail, from the type of muskets that were used to the patina of the buttons on the uniforms. I thought it was a little strange; I used to tell him, "I hope you don't expect me to follow you around in a hoop skirt and snood," which made him laugh.

"It's better than gambling, drinking, and chasing women," he'd say.

I was excited for this new phase. Doris, not so much. She didn't enjoy having Jay around, intruding on *our* relationship, and the atmosphere in the apartment grew tense. "You won't believe what he said about you," she'd murmur to me, attributing some bogusly hurtful remark to Jay. What pushed her over the edge was Jay thinking aloud that he might take a break from practicing law to focus full-time on his book.

"If you think I'm going to keep working here while he sits around the house doing nothing, you've got another thing coming," Doris said.

The scales fell from my eyes. She was delusional, and she was trying to destroy my marriage. I'd never been more sure of anything.

"Get out," I said, as angry as I'd ever been. "Pack your things and leave."

Hastily, she did.

That's when things got *really* crazy.

Doris was like a wounded animal, thrashing about, hoping to hurt us in any way she could—which meant trying to embarrass me and going after my reputation. Imagine the spit-take I did when I saw the headline on the front page of a tabloid: "Exposed! Katie Couric's Wacky Hubby: He Walks Around the House Half Naked Blowing a Bugle, Says Nanny." The article goes on to poke fun at Jay for his (admittedly large) bugle collection, vintage military uniforms, and how much he supposedly spent on it all. Another one shares the fact that I'd happily go the whole weekend without showering (guilty as charged). It is so not fun when someone who's had an all-access pass to your private life decides to hurt you.

Then Doris got creative. One day, my parents received a call from someone who introduced himself as a salesman from the McCormick spice company. "I was just at a rest stop in New Jersey and all the pay phones there have stickers on them that say 'Why does Katie Couric care more about her job than her child?' And 'Why is her husband a pedophile?' 'For more information call...' and then it shows your phone number. I watch your daughter on the *TODAY* show and she seems like a very nice girl. I wanted you to know I took the stickers off."

As for the pedophile claim: One night during our trip to Lost Creek, after we'd all pigged out at a family-style dinner, I took a photo of Jay lying on the bed with a smiling Ellie sitting nearby. He'd undone the top button of his khakis to give himself room to breathe. Doris xeroxed the photo, made flyers, and delivered them to the lobby of the apartment building we were about to move into, warning residents that a pedophile would soon be in their midst.

We hired a retired policeman to keep an eye on things outside Ellie's preschool for a few weeks, worried what Doris might do. We thought about getting a restraining order, but that legal step would make it part of the public record and accessible to the tabloids; "Couric's Nanny Accuses Husband of Pedophilia" was a headline we could live without. Everyone—lawyers, psychiatrists, security experts, the PR people at NBC—agreed that I should ignore her. Starve the beast and it'll slink away. Which, eventually, it did.

As for the photo shoot at Billy Joel's house...One night my friend Pam was behind him in line at an ice cream place on the Upper East Side; they started chatting and she mentioned she was on her way to see me.

"Oh," Billy Joel said, "please tell Katie I got the photos from her vacation." Doris had mailed them to him. Oy. (Sorry, Mom.)

In the darkest days of the Doris debacle, I'd frequently think, *This is the worst thing that's ever happened to me.* I had no idea.

29

Martha, Dear Martha

BEING A FRENZIED working mother in the mid-'90s meant being a soldier in the so-called mommy wars. Career women were on the rise in unprecedented numbers, while an equally defiant contingent stayed home to take care of their kids. The whole thing got so politicized, with the two camps eyeing each other warily across the divide—questioning each other's choices and sometimes secretly questioning their own.

I had no problem whatsoever with stay-at-home moms. After all, that's what my mother had done, and many of our viewers had made that choice too. I didn't really understand why people were so quick to take it personally when someone decided to walk a different path than they had. I loved connecting with the full-time moms in our audience and doing what we could on the show to help them feel supported.

At the same time, I'd become a very public face of the opposite—a working woman trying to keep it all together, joking on-air about sometimes falling short. In other words, not Martha Stewart.

By now a fixture on *TODAY,* the former stockbroker and model had become the doyenne of domestic perfection: rib roasts that took days to prep, elaborate craft projects involving beeswax and wildflowers, paint colors serene enough to put you in a trance. Never mind that she'd run a media conglomerate and amass a net worth exceeding half a billion dollars. Her message of making your homelife your masterpiece spoke to many women on a deep level.

Martha was *very* serious about her work. She had a group of diligent helpers who came early to set up her segments. For a spot on decorating Easter eggs, one poor assistant was tasked with blowing out the contents of a dozen eggs through a pinhole without passing out. Lacking the bandwidth for such projects, I was always happy to grab whatever leftovers she didn't pack up and take with her—once I took home an entire ham she'd prepared and served it to Jay's relatives on Easter Sunday. (It was delicious.) We were a funny combo: goddess of the hearth and frazzled career gal, who was unlikely to spend Saturday dipping candles while listening to Gregorian chants.

In 1996, Martha won a Matrix Award, a big deal for women in media that used to pack the ballroom of the Waldorf Astoria with names like Liz Smith, Whoopi Goldberg, Amy Tan, Ann Richards. That's whose eyes were following me as I made my way from the dais to the podium to present Martha with her award. I didn't know her that well, so I wouldn't be able to tell moving personal anecdotes. Frankly, I'd been a little apprehensive about the whole thing, so I'd come up with an idea: Martha was everything I wasn't—why not play off that?

Poems were my specialty. Whether for birthdays or wedding toasts, I had a way with clever couplets that affectionately tweaked the honorees and caught the mood. My dad dismissed my efforts as "doggerel," a lowly form of verse, though I like to think I raised it to an art form. I worked on Martha's poem for weeks, employing the kind of care she'd bring to needlepointing a dog collar. The result:

Martha, dear Martha, what shall I do?
These people have asked that I introduce you.
I haven't eaten, I haven't slept,
Talk about making a girl feel inept.
Anything I can do, you can do better,
Potting a plant or knitting a sweater.
Dipping a candle, tiling a table,

You're always ready, willing and able.
A room needs repainting? You'll make it sing
With robin's egg blue…cause it's a good thing.
Marzipan, tarte tatin, coq au vin too,
Bruschetta, pancetta's not all you can do,
Your holiday meals are a feast for the eyes,
Can't you use Stove Top and Mrs. Smith's pies?

And on and on, for two pages. The women in the room—working women almost exclusively—roared.

I hadn't set out to write a treatise on the escalating mommy wars, but the poem subversively nailed where a lot of us were back then and what we were anxious about. I felt like the applause in the room was driven by a sense of recognition.

Martha, however, seemed a little miffed.

"Well, Katie," she said, turning to me as I settled back into my seat on the dais, "would you know what pancetta *was* if it weren't for me?" I theatrically shook my head no. "Would you know what bruschetta *was* if it weren't for me?" Again, no, Martha, I wouldn't. By way of thanks, she had a very small bouquet delivered, and her office sent over a cookie-decorating kit.

It took a few years and some prison time for Martha to develop a sense of humor. She slayed at the Justin Bieber roast, and by the time Martha was co-hosting a cooking show with her unlikely BFF Snoop Dogg, her ironic appreciation of her place in the culture was complete. Nothing delights me quite like Martha Stewart poking fun at herself in her own tasteful way.

DURING THOSE DAYS on *TODAY,* it felt like there was nothing we couldn't do. We took the show to the South of France on the occasion of the Cannes Film Festival; I remember the tricky time the cameramen had trying to shoot around the topless sunbathers.

We stayed in the medieval town of Saint-Paul-de-Vence on the French Riviera, which gave me the feeling of reconnecting with my roots. Then it was on to Monaco—me in a turquoise suit and oversize sunglasses, with a scarf tied behind my neck like Grace Kelly—where I dined at three-star Le Louis XV with my stage manager / epicure Mark Traub. I think I might still be digesting that meal.

We also broadcasted from Normandy on the 50th anniversary of D-Day. A paratrooper in his eighties signed and gave me a piece of the parachute that had dropped him into history. I finished out the week in Paris, my first time, staying at the Prince de Galles Hotel on Avenue Georges V and doing the show from the banks of the Seine. At one point Andy Lack, president of the news division, told me, "Go buy yourself a Chanel suit." On NBC.

I was quietly flabbergasted.

When I walked into the store on the Rue Cambon, it felt like the first time I went to a fashion show in New York City, wearing a heinous hot-pink knit maternity dress, carrying a canvas L.L. Bean book bag. At Chanel, I picked out a tropical-weight-wool navy jacket with black trim and gold buttons bearing tiny interlocking *C*s and a skirt that hit just below the knee. Twirling in front of the mirror, I felt like Audrey Hepburn. I can't remember how much it was, although I do know it was *beaucoup* bucks—more than I'd ever spent on a single item of clothing in my life.

I wore it on the show the next morning. At the end I yelled, "Taxee," jumped in, and instructed the driver, *"Vite, vite!"*—the cameras following until the cab drove out of frame.

When I called my dad and told him about my Parisian escapade and my new Chanel suit, he laughed—I could almost hear him shaking his head.

I WAS ON THE way up, and Bryant was on the way out. After 15 years anchoring *TODAY,* the last six with me, he was moving on.

Andy Lack would later tell me he'd informed Bryant that he wanted us to be 50/50 partners. When Bryant balked at the idea, Andy showed him the door. Although maybe Bryant was ready to go anyway.

And there was something else: his heir apparent sitting 15 feet away. Matt was nine years younger than Bryant and born for this job.

Also helpful was the fact that Matt and Bryant had become close friends, sharing an obsession with golf and an easy, jokey, locker-room rapport; both thrived in the boys' club atmosphere at NBC. Once, when Michelle Pfeiffer was coming on the show, they went on and on during the commercial break about how hot she was; Bryant even said, "I'd drink her bathwater." When we were back on the air, I teased the segment with something like "Also coming up, Michelle Pfeiffer—Bryant, didn't you say you'd drink her bathwater?" He was furious. I thought it was funny.

Another time, *TODAY*'s wildlife wrangler Jim Fowler was waiting in the wings with a primate. Bryant, Matt, and I were chatting on the sofa when I innocently remarked that Jim was backstage "petting the monkey." They both burst out laughing like a couple of 13-year-olds.

On and off camera, Matt worshipped Bryant, even emulated him— his smooth style of both interviewing and dressing. And Bryant seemed genuinely happy about Matt's rise. As succession plans go, this one was flawless.

IT WAS SUCH a heady time in my life—full of amazing surprises, including this one: swollen breasts, a missed period…Jay and I hadn't been trying to get pregnant; we were so overwhelmed with everything we had on our plates, it was pretty much the last thing on our minds. But we were psyched. I'd seen firsthand that motherhood wasn't a career killer. And I wanted Ellie to have a sibling. When we told her the news at a nearby pizza joint, she reacted like the neighborhood gossip, exclaiming, "You've *got* to be kidding me!" She was so excited (until the baby came and she wanted to put her in the oven, but that's another story).

I gave birth during "the storm of the century!" as the local weather folks called it; we were lucky there was anyone in the hospital to help us. I remember the wind howling and the windows rattling in the old, unrenovated maternity wing, like something out of *A Farewell to Arms*.

I can still recall the relief of it all being over and Carrie having safely come into the world. While trying to get her to latch on, I glanced up at the TV bolted to the wall, tuned to the *TODAY* show. I kept one eye on my breast and the other on Elizabeth Vargas, who was filling in for me, looking comfortable standing next to Bryant, Matt, and a giant snowdrift, yukking it up.

Don't get too comfortable, I thought.

The sidewalks were thick with ice. Jay inched his way so carefully to the lobby of our building, clutching the baby carrier. But within the sun-dappled walls of 1100 Park, all was safe and warm. I took the girls into my bed, Carrie the size of a bag of sugar on my chest, Ellie nestled in the crook of my arm, her head on my shoulder. Strains of a Brahms nocturne rolled in from the living room—Jay was playing the Steinway we'd given each other for our birthdays. *This is what happiness feels like,* I thought.

With two little girls and all four of our parents alive and thriving, we were in the happiness bubble—buffered, generationally, by the people we loved most in the world. Nothing made my heart sing like seeing a young couple pushing a stroller alongside vibrant grandparents. My mom would visit and come with me to pick up Ellie from school. My parents stayed with us in Maurertown and, later, Millbrook. We loved double-dating with them.

Jay's equally fun folks had a house in Rehoboth Beach. His siblings' kids were around the same age as ours, so it was always cousin central when we visited (there's a funny photo of me and Jay's sisters Barbara and Clare and his brother Chris's wife Kathy all pregnant at the same time). They had a piano and a fireplace; we'd bust out the chips and salsa and watch old movies like *How Green Was My Valley* and *Mrs. Miniver.*

At the time, it didn't occur to me that one day, the bubble would burst. That's what bubbles do.

PART II

30

Jay

I SOMETIMES WONDER what he would look like now. Would he be trim or portly? Would his hairline have stopped receding just short of his crown or retreated to a ring of salt and pepper? Would he have shaved his head and embraced his baldness, à la the Wall Street guys who look like Mr. Clean? Would we still hold hands underneath the duvet and celebrate our birthdays by splitting the difference on January 8th? Would we still be in love or would it have worn thin, like the rust-colored riding pants I kept on a hook in a closet in Millbrook for eight years after he died?

Then I see flashes of his smile and the creases that ran from the edges of his eyes to just below his ears. I remember watching him hang up his winter coat one day and turn to me, grinning, me thinking, *If those are wrinkles, I could learn to love wrinkles.* It was Valentine's Day and he had brought Ellie, Carrie, and me—each of us—little bouquets. They were nothing special, probably purchased from a bodega on his way home, but the fact that there were three of them for his three girls moved me so. Our last Valentine's Day.

THIS WAS NOT supposed to happen to us.

Everything was picture-perfect. A rarefied Upper East Side existence of private schools and mothers sporting sweater sets and Belgian loafers, their banker husbands in horn-rimmed glasses and alligator belts. In our case, two beautiful children, two busy careers, one Park Avenue apartment. If only I'd had a little warning, enough time to say, *Remember this feeling.* Because it's all going to get swept up in an instant and land in a heap of splintered beams and shattered glass, like the towns I'd covered, leveled by storms with nice names like Gloria and Andrew.

On the third day of April 1997, I ran up from the studio just after 9:00 a.m. to greet two women from the Gap. They were waiting outside my office, holding a half dozen white shopping bags overflowing with spring clothes. Six years in, I had solidified my approachable, girl-next-door persona by wearing labels my female viewers could afford (Ann Taylor, Dana Buchman, the so-called bridge lines), avoiding anything that even slightly whispered *haute couture.* It wasn't difficult, considering that my five-foot-three, 125-pound physique would inspire few designers to choose me as their muse.

Soon my dressing room was strewn with T-shirts, khakis, cotton skirts, and summer-weight sweaters—I tried things on while we chatted and laughed like preteens at the mall.

I have a clear mental picture of what happened next, like remembering where you were when the *Challenger* exploded or the first plane crashed into the North Tower. It started with a phone call. Our new nanny, Nuala, a young woman from Armagh in Northern Ireland, was unflappable, with the scrappy look of a female boxer, so her agitated voice quickly got my attention.

"Katie," she said, the Irish brogue tumbling out with an urgency I had never heard before. "Jay is doubled over in pain. It's really bad. You need to come home."

I quickly changed back into my pantsuit, ran downstairs, and jumped into Jack's car, waiting at the curb. My heart beating double time, I told him to head home as fast as he could. Our morning ritual over the years—him seeing me looking like a sleepy wet rat as I crawled into the car and we drove to 30 Rock—had created an intimacy I was especially thankful for now.

Once at the apartment, I burst into the bathroom. Jay was just getting out of the shower and wrapping himself in a towel. I tried not to gasp. *Jesus, he's thin. How have I not noticed how thin he is?*

I called my internist, Dr. Tom Nash, and told the receptionist I needed an appointment immediately. Not for me, but for my husband. Like so many seemingly healthy men his age, Jay didn't even have his own doctor. *Why hadn't I made sure he was getting annual physicals?*

Jack rushed us to East 72nd Street. Jay winced from the stabbing pain as he was led into Dr. Nash's examination room. I lingered in the waiting area, too sick with nerves to even leaf through a gummy copy of *Men's Health,* whose name and buff cover model seemed to mock our situation. In his office afterward, Dr. Nash tried to keep us calm but couldn't hide his concern, sending us immediately to New York Hospital. There, Jay handed me a piece of paper on which he'd written the names and phone numbers of our insurance broker and the lawyer who'd drafted our will.

He was admitted right away. That's when our nightmare officially began.

I WALKED INTO THE apartment and hugged the girls—Ellie was 5, Carrie 15 months. I quickly packed a bag for Jay, threw on a pair of jeans, and headed back to the hospital.

I was greeted in the hallway by a young gastroenterologist named Mark Pochapin. Displaying a bedside manner I would rely on for months, even years, to come, he gave me his assessment.

"Your husband has a tumor the size of an orange that is completely blocking his colon," he said. "He needs a bowel resection so we can remove it before we even begin to discuss what kind of treatment is possible."

The words swirled around me—normally an acute listener, quick with a follow-up, I couldn't focus. Until he added: "We believe it's cancer."

Cancer.

A sucker punch to my gut.

Cancer? Handsome, athletic, 41-year-old Jay? This couldn't be happening. My future flashed before my eyes: Christmases, birthday parties, graduations, weddings—all of it suddenly replaced by uncertainty.

Cancer was supposed to happen to older people—pancreatic for my great-uncle Leon, ovarian for my mother-in-law, Carol, undergoing treatment as her son was being diagnosed. Growing up, I thought it only happened to characters in movies and TV shows, like Carol Brady's phantom first husband, who (I assumed) had died of it before she met Mike, or *Love Story*'s Jenny Cavilleri, who made succumbing to a fatal illness look so, well, beautiful. Or *My Life,* in which the terminally ill character played by Michael Keaton reconciles with his father and makes a heartbreaking video for his future son.

When I saw that movie, my own bad news was years away, and yet it gutted me, exposing my greatest fear—losing someone I loved.

Now, *my* life was that movie. But I couldn't simply wipe my eyes, pitch my popcorn bucket in the trash, and head home. This was about as real as it gets. Cancer, it turned out, happened to people like us.

THEY RUSHED JAY INTO emergency surgery, which involved excising the tumor, then reconnecting the two pieces of his large intestine. The smell of disinfectant, the fluorescent lights, the beige vinyl chairs, the loudspeaker paging a doctor, the sad, leftover flowers at the nurses' station— this would become my new normal.

I walked across York Avenue in a thick haze, barely capable of operating my limbs. I'd heard a horrible story about a bereft man who'd left the same hospital after learning his wife was dying of cancer. As he crossed the street, he was struck by a car and killed. Tragic, ironic— and now completely conceivable to me. Jay's sister Clare came and slept on the pullout couch in the den; I was so restless and upset, I joined her. We held hands through the night. I mentioned how dry hers were, which, for a brief moment, made us laugh.

I thought about all the clues I'd overlooked. The fact that Jay had a perpetually sensitive, sour stomach. He popped Tums like cocktail peanuts; I remember discovering a roll of them in his pocket on our first date. He'd even stopped drinking coffee, hoping it was the caffeine that was causing his stomach to declare war on itself.

Jay was also tired a lot. But we had two little girls and he traveled frequently, most recently to Denver to cover the run-up to the Oklahoma City bombers' trial for MSNBC, where he'd become a legal analyst. Who *wouldn't* be tired? And, yes, he was steadily losing weight—but like most neurotic New Yorkers, we were always trying to drop a few pounds.

Why hadn't I given any of this a second thought? Why hadn't I noticed that Jay's pants had grown baggy and that his skin seemed slightly jaundiced? If I'd just pressed pause long enough to look at him, *really* look at him...we were too busy living to see that he was dying.

I had woken up that morning with a healthy husband, our lives stretching out before us. I went to sleep with a husband who had colon cancer and a colostomy bag.

31

Mr. Katie Couric

I HADN'T BEEN ATTENTIVE enough. That stung, especially at this moment in our marriage. I never discussed it with anyone except a complete stranger—a guest on the show who had written a book on intimacy. After our interview, I approached her in the hallway and asked quietly, "My husband and I haven't been intimate in a while...is this something I should be worried about?"

Jay and I had been growing apart. Some of it was the natural ebb and flow of a relationship. But it was also the stress that my celebrity put not just on him or on me but on *us*. It took up residence in our marriage like an overbearing houseguest.

I was never ambivalent about being recognized. I liked it when people stared at me as I strolled to a great table at a nice restaurant that I'd snagged at the last minute by giving my name to the snooty hostess who suddenly turned charming. Or when people whispered and craned their necks when I walked down the aisle of a Broadway theater.

Having the identity of *TODAY* show anchor inured me to the insecurities that had long been percolating just below the surface. For a regular girl suddenly catapulted to the highest strata of the New York media world, it functioned like armor. In virtually any room I entered, everyone already knew who I was; I didn't have to try to ingratiate or impress. They were all atwitter just to meet me. Johnny Carson once said the best part of being famous is that if people approach you at a cocktail party and you don't say anything interesting, they walk away thinking *they* are boring.

At first, Jay got a kick out of it. When someone did a double take as we walked down the street, he'd jokingly whisper, "HRF," our code for "high recognition factor." It was both strange and exhilarating.

But the bigger I got—the more I was photographed and splashed across magazine covers and gossiped about—the smaller he felt. Everywhere he went, he was treated like Mr. Katie Couric. At a State dinner at the White House, I was seated at President Clinton's table while Jay laughed—sort of—about being at "the kids' table" on the other side of the room. But the truth was, the imbalance had become destabilizing.

In those early days, I ran on a bottomless supply of adrenaline. The *TODAY* show was just so much fun to do—it was such a rush to be one of the stars of a program that was creating tons of buzz. And I was getting increasingly close with Jeff Zucker. But sometimes that all-consuming partnership—and Jeff's singular focus—threatened to eclipse my marriage. When Jay would poke his head in my home office while I was on the phone with Jeff going over the show, taking apart the competition, gossiping about the business, I'd wave and keep chatting, too obsessed with work to hang up and attend to my real life.

It started to make Jay feel less-than, which was crazy. He was far more interesting than I was—smarter, deeper, with more intriguing things to say. But in starry-eyed New York, those qualities are no match for fame. People are drawn to it; they want that white-hot light reflected back on them. And it can be a very tricky thing for the lesser-known spouse. In social situations, I used to feel so grateful when somebody genuinely engaged with Jay instead of giving him the once-over and turning swiftly back to me.

As a wife who was also the primary breadwinner, a rarity at the time, I did everything I could to protect Jay's ego. Once when I was on *Letterman,* Dave said something like, "So you make all the money and your husband pays the bills?" It was such a random question and felt so off base. After all, Jay was successful in his own right.

I knew Dave's crack, put out there on national TV, would bother Jay. So after the taping, I called the executive producer, Rob Burnett, and tearfully begged him to take that part out, which he did. And yet when Jay got the chance to raise his profile and show his smarts by becoming an on-air legal analyst, I bristled. My churlish gut reaction was *Stay in your lane.*

Jay and I still had a solid marriage, especially when it was just us or with family and old friends. Within the walls of our apartment, we were really happy. But the difference in our take-home pay sometimes caused tension, compounded by the fact that Jay was a spender and I was a saver, just like my parents. When he bought antiques and uniforms that satisfied his passion for wars, Civil and otherwise, I'd feel an occasional surge of resentment. I'd get upset when he gave money to a friend or a family member without telling me. Of course, it was something we should have discussed.

I wish we had gone to couples' therapy. If Jay hadn't gotten sick, I hope that we would have, so we could get help working through such a big change in our lives. When we started out, we were on an equal footing—a local news reporter and a promising young law associate. Then my career took off, overshadowing everything.

But none of that mattered now. In the face of a horrific diagnosis and the unthinkable prospect of losing Jay, my ambivalence and misgivings fell away. The only thing I wanted in this life was for him to get well. And I dedicated myself to doing anything I could to save him.

32

"Shit."

THE DAY AFTER Jay's surgery, Dr. Nash summoned me to one of those nondescript rooms at the end of a hospital hallway; the kind with a Naugahyde sofa and a random poster of a sunset on the wall. He had looked at the scans. I could barely breathe, waiting for him to speak.

His eyes locked on mine. "This is much tougher than I thought," he said. "The cancer has spread. Jay has tumors all over his liver. His prognosis is very bleak."

Writing this, I'm hurtled back to that paralyzing moment. Dr. Nash hadn't told Jay. And I didn't tell him either. That was the first in a series of omissions, half-truths, and outright lies I allowed in order to protect him. Which I had no right to do.

Jay's mom, Carol, came to see us at New York Hospital. She had a buzz cut after months of chemo. I asked her if she would take a walk with me down the hall while Jay rested. I told her what Dr. Nash had told me.

I loved Carol, the Monahan matriarch, who'd raised her seven children—all with wildly different personalities—in a lively, loving home. Her response was out of character.

"Shit," she said.

* * *

THE URGENCY OF Jay's situation propelled me into relentless "I've got to fix this" mode. Every advantage I had gaining access to the top people at the top institutions, I exploited without apology. I called Steve Rosenberg, the chief of surgery at the National Cancer Institute in Bethesda, Maryland, who'd pioneered immunotherapy. I asked him if he could take a look at Jay's scans.

A few days later, we were back on the phone. "This is very, very serious," Dr. Rosenberg said, actually sounding shaken. His words knocked the wind out of me. But they also strengthened my resolve to leave no stone unturned.

The questionable ethics didn't keep me from letting colleagues turned close friends fan out, using "I'm calling from NBC News" to open doors and gather information from research institutions and drug companies. I turned the makeup room at the *TODAY* show—deserted after 10:00 a.m.—into a call center, reaching out to far-flung specialists. I contacted a pharmaceutical company in Israel to ask about a monoclonal antibody they were developing. Tim Russert introduced me to Dr. Alan Rabson, deputy director of the National Cancer Institute, who was so supportive and had helped many desperate family members during their ordeals. I'd call him regularly with questions that came up in the research I was doing: "Dr. Rabson, what about this new drug oxaliplatin that's being developed by Sanofi?"—a pharmaceutical company in Paris. "What's the latest on Avastin?"—an experimental drug designed to kill tumors by cutting off their blood supply. "Could Jay be a candidate for ablation?"—a treatment using high-energy radio waves to pulverize tumors. It got to the point where he greeted my call with "Dr. Couric, good morning!" Jay didn't want to fixate on his treatment or his chances, so I took that on for him.

I negotiated with God and anyone else within earshot to keep the cancer in check until a scientific breakthrough was announced to the world. I searched the term *cancer* every day on my computer, hoping that I'd see a promising new clinical trial or drug on the market that would give hope to thousands of patients, starting with Jay. I inhaled *JAMA, The Lancet,* and any other scholarly publication I could get my hands on, trying to decipher the language of cancer. Powered by fear, desperation, and love, I was a quick study.

The pressure, the dread, were constant. Sometimes when the *TODAY* show was over, I'd collapse on the floor of the bathroom in my office, bum a cigarette from my hairdresser, and sob. Ridiculous, I know— my husband has cancer and I'm smoking, but that's how completely undone I was. I'd keep it together for the show, the only two hours of my day when I wasn't obsessing over Jay's fate. And then at 9:02 a.m., I'd fall apart.

33

The Worry Cup

IT WAS MORE than my mind could process, the idea that I might lose my best friend and partner. And the girls—how would they be without a father? Ellie was old enough to have already stockpiled many sweet memories of her dad: awkwardly brushing her unruly hair and putting it in a ponytail; walking her to school (skipping over sidewalk cracks to avoid breaking her mother's back); riding in his Jeep through the fields of Millbrook as night fell, searching for deer, their eyes reflecting the beam from the giant flashlight Jay kept in the back seat for just such occasions, counting how many pairs shined back.

Then there was the singing—Jay's highly vibrato rendition of the cheesy theme from *The Swan Princess* and the little rhyme he'd made up about Ellie when she needed changing: *Elinor Tully Monahan the first / is the cutest little baby but her diaper smells the worst!* And of course, reading *The Napping House*, one of their favorite bedtime books: "There is a house, a napping house, where everyone is sleeping." Then the house would come to life with crashing, booming, screeching sounds that Jay acted out with Tony Award–worthy theatrics.

Carrie was so little, not yet a year and a half, but Jay had already made memories with her too—chasing her down the hall saying, "I'm going to get you!" as Carrie's peals of laughter ricocheted off the apartment walls. But his favorite trick was catching a sunbeam with the face of his wristwatch, refracting the light and making it jump around on the wall of Carrie's bedroom.

"Look!" he'd say. "It's Tinker Bell!"

I DEVOURED BOOKS ABOUT how you help your children deal with sickness and loss. A lot of them told the frantic reader to be as honest and concrete as possible. So whenever Ellie asked me, "Is Daddy going to be okay?" I'd respond by saying, "I really, really hope so. The doctors are doing everything they can." I didn't want to overpromise. While Carrie couldn't understand what was happening, I knew that Ellie was at a very tender stage, when a girl's relationship with her father is formative, when death seems reversible, when you hate to feel different from your peers.

One book suggested an exercise called "the Worry Cup." I asked a social worker from CancerCare to facilitate it for Ellie's class. Twenty 6-year-olds sat cross-legged in a circle on the floor. She placed a cup in the center and gave each child a big plastic "gemstone." One by one, the girls walked up to the cup, dropped in their gem, and shared what they were worried about: an aging grandma, their dog, parents divorcing, the dark. In Ellie's case, a sick father. The girls took it so seriously, revealing their deepest fears. Her teacher told me it was the most profound experience she'd ever witnessed during her years in the classroom. I could only hope it made Ellie feel less alone.

I brought her to a therapist. They mostly played Candy Land and checkers, but I wanted her to have a safe space where she could just feel her feelings without worrying that she was upsetting me, a common concern of children with a sick parent. I started seeing someone, too, and discovered my sleepless nights and lack of appetite were the result of something called situational depression. I had no idea this kind of debilitating shock could actually change your brain chemistry. The therapist prescribed Zoloft, which dulled the pain, making my heart feel like it was coated in wax.

One morning on *TODAY* after I'd interviewed Herbert Benson, a Harvard cardiologist who had popularized the idea of a mind-body connection, I asked him if he would join me in my studio office. I told him about Jay and how unbelievably difficult the situation was. He recommended that I come up with a seven-syllable mantra that I could repeat while breathing deeply every time I started to feel unhinged.

Counting out the syllables on my fingers, I chose *God, please heal Thy servant Jay.*

While an abiding faith may have eluded me, that mantra was helpful. I'd breathe deeply and say, *God, please heal Thy servant Jay…God, please heal Thy servant Jay…God, please heal Thy servant Jay…*Then steel myself for whatever was coming next.

34

"Katie's Private Pain"

JAY WANTED TO GO to Millbrook. Liam Neeson and Natasha Richardson invited us to their house, not far from ours. I wasn't sure if Jay was going to be up to it, but he badly wanted to resume normal life, so we said yes.

Their house was super-British, impeccably shabby-chic. Along with Liam and Natasha were Natasha's sister Joely and their legendary mother, Vanessa Redgrave—it felt like an honor to be in their presence. Although my main memory of that afternoon was how brave Jay was. I knew he was worried about his colostomy bag, that it might be visible under his shirt or emitting an odor. But when I looked over at him like a concerned mother, I saw him conversing with Joely as if nothing were wrong. Jay's MO was to ignore what was happening to him as much as possible. A few weeks later, he was back in Denver for Timothy McVeigh's trial, colostomy bag and all.

Early on in my research, I discovered something called a hepatic artery infusion pump, a hockey puck–like device that would be implanted southwest of Jay's navel and filled with chemo; the medicine would then be delivered via the hepatic artery to his liver, where it would attack the tumors. He'd also receive systemic chemo through an IV in his arm every other week. I prayed this one-two punch would shrink the tumors while keeping the microscopic disease circulating throughout his body at bay.

His CEA levels, a measure of how much cancer is in your blood, plummeted, making my spirits soar in inverse proportion. I heard the chemo he was on, 5-FU and leucovorin, had something like a 23 percent response rate, and I couldn't believe how lucky we were. But the crash came just a few weeks later when his levels started to tick up again. Why didn't anyone tell me that a response is often short-lived and doesn't take into account cancer's sinister ability to outwit its most determined foe?

I was leading a double life. On the show Monday through Friday, I put on a brave front for an audience of millions. And not just a brave front—I had to be the upbeat, cheerful Katie viewers had come to expect. During the brief commercial breaks, I'd shoo away my anxiety and fear, chatting up the crew, running upstairs to survey the now-tired platter of bagels in the greenroom—anything to keep my mind from going to the dark place. My makeup artist would come and powder me with such tenderness it left me feeling loved and cared for, although so many times, I was just one tender-powdering away from losing it.

I didn't want people to know how serious Jay's situation was. This was his body, his life. I guarded his privacy fiercely because insider information about me, about us, was trading high.

One day, a mother from Ellie's preschool stopped me on the street and said, "A friend who was visiting her mother at the hospital told me about Jay. She said it was really, really bad." The idea of anyone gossiping about something so personal infuriated me. *What is wrong with people?*

As I waited in Jay's room during the surgery to reverse his colostomy, a nurse walked in, pulled out a tabloid, and said, "Look, you're in the paper!"

In fact, I was on the cover looking grief-stricken next to the screaming headline "Katie's Private Pain." I wanted to kill her.

This was the dark side of celebrity. I hadn't realized how little privacy we had until we desperately needed it.

Earlier that morning, I'd picked up a cup of coffee at the hospital café on the first floor. And I'll never forget walking down the cavernous marble hallway, rounding the corner, and seeing the unmistakable shock of white hair and wire-rimmed glasses, the seersucker suit…my dad, waiting for me on the bench situated between two elevator banks. He had taken the train from DC to New York to be with me. It was so unlike him—he was not a spontaneous person. My surprise gave way to overwhelming gratitude.

He sat with me during the surgery and made me feel safe enough to fall apart. I told him I couldn't believe what we were going through. "Why is this happening to me?" I said two or three times, catching my breath between sobs.

To which my father gently replied, "Katie, this isn't happening to you. It is happening to Jay."

NOW THAT JAY'S illness was public, a steady stream of supportive letters poured in from around the country. Some viewers sent literature about natural therapies—the magic of milk thistle, the beauty of bee propolis. Other notes overflowed with optimism bordering on naïveté: *You should have every faith in the world that Jay is going to be just fine,* a neighbor shared in neat print. Jacqueline Onassis's nephew Anthony Radziwill wrote about his own metastasizing nightmare (which would kill him less than two years later). Jay's reaction: "I don't know why people think they have to take me through every detail of their treatment. I know they are well intended, but it doesn't help me. I don't want to be part of this club."

His hair was falling out in clumps. My makeup artist Barbara Kelly's father, a famous wigmaker whose creations were featured in a number of Broadway shows, made a piece for Jay that looked amazingly like his real hair (with a little less gray). Jay wore it for his TV appearances and even for a job interview at another network. He also recorded his daily caloric intake in a small leather notebook: *Ensure—250 calories. Banana—80 calories. Yogurt—290 calories.* It seemed like Jay had his eye on the future. But his cancer was on the march, surging northward; that summer, a scan revealed tumors in his lungs. The sword of Damocles was getting closer.

* * *

WE SPENT AS much time in Millbrook as possible. It's where Jay could do the things he loved—go riding; plop Ellie on a pony at a nearby farm, hoping she'd one day share his equine passions; chase Carrie around on the rolling lawn behind the house. The three of them would sit on the sofa watching *The Little Rascals,* Jay's favorite show from childhood, which he wanted to share with his girls. After they went to bed, we'd watch some of Jay's favorite movies, like *Gunga Din,* all about bravery and battle; he knew the Rudyard Kipling poem by heart.

One muggy August day in Millbrook, I came the closest I ever would to acknowledging that this might not end how we desperately hoped. I was splashing around in the pool with Ellie; the way the late-afternoon sun filtered through the trees made me feel an almost spiritual connection to something bigger than us. Somehow I mustered the courage to say, "I just can't imagine coming to this house if you're not here."

Jay looked at me with an expression I couldn't quite decipher. "Well," he said, "I hope it will be full of happy memories."

Maybe he knew all along how bad it was. And letting me handle it my way was something he did for me.

35

Diana

*H*OPE. *HOPE. HOPE.* "The thing with feathers," as Emily Dickinson wrote.

I held on to it for dear life, worried that if I let go, Jay would too.

So I stayed positive. When Tom Nash pulled me into that anodyne room and said there were tumors all over Jay's liver, I stayed positive. When the cancer spread to his lungs, I said, "We will fight this." When Jay met me in the waiting room, so gaunt and courageous after yet another procedure, I smiled and slipped my hand in his, once again pretending to be strong and that it was going to be okay.

One weekend, Jay was in his riding clothes, having returned from an afternoon on horseback. Even though he was rail-thin, he still looked Ralph Lauren–handsome in his polo shirt, jodhpurs, and boots. We were packing up the car when out of nowhere he said, "Something's wrong. I can't really see."

On Monday we went to yet another specialist: an ocular oncologist, something I'd never even heard of. After he examined Jay, we assumed the familiar position of terrified couple sitting across a desk from a doctor.

This one would tell us why Jay's vision was blurry: he had a tumor growing behind his right eye. How many more ways could Jay's body betray him?

* * *

MY PRODUCER AND friend Lori Beecher, her husband, Marc, and their kids came to Millbrook for Labor Day weekend. On Saturday around 8:00 p.m., Marc's beeper went off—he was head of special events at ABC, and the news desk needed him to come in right away: Princess Diana had been in a car accident. After midnight in Paris, she and her boyfriend, Dodi Fayed, were being pursued at high speed by paparazzi when their driver crashed into a concrete pillar in the Pont de l'Alma tunnel.

We were glued to the TV. It being a holiday weekend, the networks were short-staffed (I wasn't the only one who had escaped the city). Brian Williams, then the face of the young and struggling cable channel MSNBC, rushed to the set at 11:00 p.m. to continue coverage while Tom Brokaw headed to London. At 11:46 p.m., Williams reported that Princess Diana had died.

I had met the princess a year earlier, at a luncheon at the Drake Hotel in Chicago. She'd been invited by Northwestern University to spend three days helping raise money for breast cancer research. Diana sat between Anna Quindlen and me, glowing in a sleeveless cream-colored dress with a single strand of pearls. Anna and I were struck by her girlish charm, still looking like the rosy-cheeked, bashful, part-time kindergarten teacher Prince Charles introduced to the world when she was just 19. At one point she turned to me and said, "I like your lipstick," which took me by surprise. I was flattered that she'd noticed.

Then the subject turned to parenting.

"How do you keep your children from watching too much telly?" Princess Diana asked us. "I'm having a terrible time with William and Harry" (then 13 and 11). I think we told her to hide the remote.

"This must be an exhausting trip," I said, "with so many people to meet, shaking hands with all those strangers. Are you excited to go home?"

"I would be," Princess Diana responded, "but I'm going home to an empty house."

As we all knew, she was in the process of finalizing her divorce from

Prince Charles. I was surprised by her openness and sensed a deep sadness. "Why don't you invite some friends over for a slumber party?" I asked, half joking.

Princess Diana cocked her head quizzically at the idea of it, like a dog hearing a high-pitched whistle. At the time, I had no idea how miserable she really was.

Now, 15 months later, I was flying to London to broadcast her funeral live from Buckingham Palace. Bereft Londoners and tourists were leaving bouquets outside the gates; by midweek, they'd cover acres.

The service was on Saturday at Westminster Abbey. NBC had built a platform directly across from the entrance where Tom Brokaw and I sat, along with Tina Brown. After an hour, the cortege came into view; the casket, laden with lilies, had a simple white card on top that said *Mummy*—handwritten and placed there by Harry. Mourners wailed at the sight of the princes walking behind the casket, heads bowed. And I realized that what I was seeing was not the passing of the most famous woman in the world; it was two boys who'd lost a parent. And I thought of my girls.

Tears started to flow. I leaned over to Tom and whispered, "I'm having a really hard time."

He put his hand on my back and nodded—he understood. So did the control room, which instructed the cameraman to get a two-shot of Tom and Tina while I wiped my face and tried to pull myself together. Diana and Jay—I was mourning them both.

36

A Pony for Ellie

THE QUOTIDIAN RITUALS of a new school year came without the usual excitement. Ellie returned to Spence in her plaid jumper, a sweater-clad Carrie watched the leaves go from green to orange from the comfort of her stroller. We went through the motions of being a happy young family, but sadness gripped me like tentacles I couldn't pry off. Jay insisted on going to a reenactment of the Battle of Antietam, near Hagerstown, Maryland. I was worried yet grateful he was doing what he loved.

One weekend in Millbrook, Liam and Natasha stopped by and took us to a farm in Red Hook for a hayride and pumpkin-picking, Jay doing his best as the bumpy tractor jostled his thin frame. There is a photo of us from that day: him in a bomber jacket, me in his denim jacket, holding Carrie under a canopy of leaves; she's leaning over and cradling Ellie's smiling face in her dimpled hands. I look at that picture now and wonder what Jay was thinking.

We had late, lazy breakfasts of omelets and french fries at the Millbrook Diner. One Sunday, Carrie was sitting in a baby seat clipped to the linoleum tabletop when she barked at the waitress, "More bacon, lady!" We couldn't stop laughing (to this day, when my girls and I have bacon, one of us is guaranteed to call out, "More bacon, lady!"). When Jay and I went to see *Titanic* at the Ziegfeld, he had grown weaker, although not too weak to point out that the saga of Rose and Jack paled in comparison to the stories of the real-life passengers on board the doomed ship. He was weaker still when he walked into Spence for Ellie's holiday concert wearing a big, furry trapper hat to ward off the cold—by now Jay had no body fat. I still remember the uncomfortable feeling of people trying not to stare but staring anyway.

"Cancer," Jay told me one night, "is the loneliest experience in the world."

I understood. As much as I loved him, took him to doctor appointments, urged him to eat, ran to the grocery store to replenish the Ensure, was by his side for every relentless piece of bad news, if—when—he lost this fight, I'd still be here. With the living.

In late fall, Jay's closest friend from Williams & Connolly, David Kiernan, spent the weekend with us to take some pressure off me and be with Jay. On Saturday morning, they headed to the barn, where Jay kept the remnants of his life as a young lawyer. They sorted through boxes of his work stuff—a stapler, his nameplate, a framed photo of him holding a squirming, laughing Ellie at the Boar's Head in Charlottesville, no doubt for a UVA football game. They found the Spuds MacKenzie mug I'd given him when we first started dating, a nickname bestowed by some of his fellow associates for being such a "party animal." There were stacks of notebooks, briefs, and manila folders related to Williams & Connolly cases from years back. Then they discovered a box of VHS tapes—hard-core pornography from a case Jay had worked on in, of all places, Salt Lake City.

"Oh my God," he said to David, "if anyone finds these after I'm gone, they're going to think I was some kind of pervert."

After I'm gone . . . a rare acknowledgment that time might be running out. David joked that he'd be happy to take them off his hands, but they ended up throwing them in a dumpster.

After a few hours going down memory lane, they walked back to the house.

"In the spring," Jay told David, "I'm going to buy Ellie a pony."

His words hung in the air.

They jumped in the Jeep and started down one of the winding roads that fanned out like tributaries from our house, the roads Jay loved exploring that always seemed to offer up something new for him to marvel at—a quaint church, a sunlit field, a picturesque barn. These two friends, now older, perhaps wiser, who should have been sliding into middle age, with the graying temples and softer bellies that come with it, were dealing with something else altogether. On a stretch of road with few houses, Jay pulled over and turned off the ignition.

He looked at David. "I'm not going to make it, am I?"

"You have to make it," David said. "You have a wife and two beautiful little girls. You have to make it."

"I'm not going to, though, am I?"

"You have to make it," David repeated.

Jay looked out the window, frustrated. "Well, I guess that's my answer."

They drove in silence back to the house. As they pulled into the driveway, David said, "You really need to talk to Katie."

THAT THANKSGIVING WE piled into the Monavan and drove to Clare's khaki-colored Arts and Crafts house in Darien, Connecticut, where Jay's extended family had gathered. He was so skinny, but he'd made a huge effort to look as good and as much like himself as possible in his quilted Barbour jacket and tweed sport coat. An English driving cap covered his bald head.

Whenever the Monahans and their cousins the Conroys gathered, a touch football game followed. I stayed inside with the girls and watched from the living-room window. It was so hard seeing my once healthy, athletic husband sidelined. But Jay was right in it, clapping and cheering everyone on, calling plays, even trash-talking his brothers.

We were also celebrating Jay's father's 75th birthday. Jay gave a toast full of color and wit. Gripping his wineglass, even his fingers looked thin and fragile, as his entire extended family watched, transfixed by the poignancy of that moment. Jay's illness lived among us, especially at the holidays. Instead of joyful benchmarks of our evolving lives, each one had become a gut-wrenching "last."

January came, along with our birthdays: Carrie's 2nd, my 41st, Jay's 42nd. He was on a new chemo regimen that knocked him out. He spent his days in his bathrobe, lying on the sofa in the den watching the History Channel, surrounded by prescription pill bottles, his wig resting on a Styrofoam head on a shelf in our closet. When I came home one day, he turned to me and said, "This is no way to live."

All these years later, I realize how delusional I'd willed myself to be. I recently found a letter I'd written to my great-aunt Carrie Hibbler:

> *He's been having a pretty rough time of it lately, feeling pretty miserable in general. The good news is, the chemo seems to be working, so keep your fingers crossed and say a prayer that it will continue to work.*

It was dated January 21st.

ON JANUARY 23RD, I met with Earl Kramer, the president of the co-op board in our building. New York co-ops are notoriously picky about who can live there; they rarely allow an apartment to be subleased, but we had gotten special dispensation to rent in the building for two years. The lease was almost up, and I was worried about having to move out while Jay was sick—or worse. The owners of the apartment had told me they were going to be in London for another year, and they would be happy to let us stay on. But I needed permission from the board.

"My husband is very, very sick," I told Mr. Kramer, breaking down in front of a man I barely knew. "I'm so worried about him, and I'm worried about our girls if something terrible happens. It would be so helpful if we could stay here just one more year."

He looked at me sympathetically. "I'm so sorry you're going through this," he said, "but rules are rules, and we just can't allow you to stay."

I went downstairs, washed my face, and didn't tell Jay. It would be our last night together.

37

Saturday Morning

Janu). ANUARY 24TH, 1998—it was freezing outside. Jay was coming off a particularly bad night, although I thought he might rally if he ate something. But he just couldn't; food, even water, felt terrible on his tongue. I wasn't sure what was ravaging his body more, the cancer or the medicine.

By now, Jay was emaciated, and his legs could barely support what was left of his body. As a result of something called bitemporal wasting, his skull almost seemed visible through his skin.

"I look like a Holocaust victim," he'd say, regarding his sunken cheeks and protruding cheekbones in the mirror.

"Stop," I'd say. "No, you don't." Even though he did.

That morning, I finally convinced him to have a few sips of club soda. Then I went to the kitchen to make a cup of tea.

Standing at the stove, I heard a glass shatter. I ran to the powder room—Jay had collapsed on the marble floor. I whirled into crisis mode and dialed 911. Then I called our upstairs neighbors Gail and Lenny Saltz.

"Lenny, please," I said frantically, "come downstairs. Hurry, please."

Gail grabbed Ellie and Carrie and took them to their place to play with their three daughters, who had a dollhouse mine loved; Lenny, a GI oncologist at Memorial Sloan Kettering, rushed into the powder room.

Jay was sprawled out on the floor. Lenny crouched at his feet, saying softly, "It's okay, it's okay." I cradled his head. "Please breathe, Jay," I said, "just breathe." I still wonder if he heard me. His eyes were wide open, directed at the ceiling. Lenny attempted mouth-to-mouth resuscitation.

Then—the commotion of EMTs arriving with their equipment. The sound of the gurney's squeaky wheels rolling across the hardwood floor, the clanking of the metal, the technicians trying to jump-start Jay's heart. They passed information back and forth in shorthand as they lifted him, strapped him down, and swiftly rolled him into the elevator.

Out on the street, they loaded Jay into the back of an ambulance. I wanted to be with him, but instead they had me ride in a waiting police car, sirens blaring the 20 blocks to Lenox Hill Hospital.

I don't know how long I was sitting in the empty waiting room in my Gap sweatshirt and jeans, barely able to breathe, before a doctor walked in. I knew what he was going to say. All I remember is "I'm sorry." I felt like my spirit had left my body too.

I thought we'd have more time. Time for me to lie next to him. Time for him to tell me he was scared; to tell me his hopes and dreams for Ellie and Carrie. Time to say goodbye.

"Can I see him?" I said.

The doctor brought me in. Standing over Jay's pale, lifeless body frightened me. Tentatively, gently, I kissed him for the last time.

I called my parents.

My mom made a quiet ululating sound I'll never forget, an "Oh-oh-oh-oh" so redolent of love and despair, so helpless and sorry she couldn't protect her child from this pain. As for Jay's parents, it turned out they'd already received a call about their son's death—from the tabloids, looking for a comment. I cannot put into words how that sickened me.

Jeff Zucker and his wife, Caryn, came to the hospital. After I left to be with the girls, they stayed until Jay's siblings arrived.

Back at the apartment, I knelt down so I could be eye to eye with Ellie. "Honey," I said softly, "Daddy died."

She giggled. At 6 years old, Ellie was unable to process what I was saying.

When Clare arrived, Carrie shrieked, "Clare's here!" and ran and leapt into her arms—a joyful, oblivious toddler.

For the three of us, it was all so new.

38

Ashokan Farewell

WENDY HAD PICKED up my parents and flown with them from DC. She quickly became the head of operations—fielding calls, keeping track of who sent flowers, and making room in the refrigerator, which would soon be packed with casseroles and honey-baked hams and pasta salads in giant Tupperware tubs. There was an influx of bagels and brownies and cookies that I would have feasted on for weeks if only I had an appetite. Our doorman called to say that Sarah Ferguson, the Duchess of York, was in the lobby. I'd interviewed her on the show, but I didn't know her nearly well enough to see her now. She had come bearing white tulips that the doorman brought up. Bob Wright, the CEO of NBC, and his wife, Suzanne, sent over a giant stuffed Mickey Mouse that Ellie would use as a chair.

Matt came by. He looked so sad, so serious, so sorry—there wasn't much either of us could say. Our conversation turned to the interview I was supposed to do in a few days with Hillary Clinton, that now fell to Matt.

I could tell he was nervous—the Monica Lewinsky scandal had just broken, and he'd have to ask the First Lady about it. I gave him a few pointers—listen carefully and have a range of follow-ups at the ready for every possible answer. Matt would do fine, providing a pivotal moment in the impeachment saga when Hillary railed against a "vast right-wing conspiracy."

* * *

SITTING AMONG THE tony shops and restaurants on Madison Avenue, Frank E. Campbell has been New York's funeral home to the stars for over a century, preparing luminaries like Judy Garland, George Gershwin, and Ed Sullivan for their final act. Clare and I were greeted by a mortician who was born for the role, with his jet-black hair and large, hooded eyes.

He guided us to the second floor, where a variety of caskets were on display, sitting on platforms and opened to show you the plush, tufted comfort in which your loved one would rest in peace. Each had a name—Renaissance, Promethean, Lincoln, Embassy, Ambassador. We were looking at the Concord, classic and masculine, just like Jay.

While we attended to this grim task, the funeral director approached, his tone urgent and serious. "Hillary Clinton is on the line—your office put her through. She wants to express her condolences," he said. Clare gave me a look. A bit later he was back. "Al Gore is calling." My public and private worlds were colliding like never before. I felt both touched and embarrassed.

Before we left, the funeral director convinced me that I needed to buy the Monticello—a concrete vault that would protect the Concord— for an additional $2,000. When my dad learned of the purchase, he was over the undertaker, furious he had upsold me. But all I could think of was that song I'd learned in Girl Scouts: *The worms crawl in, the worms crawl out, the worms play pinochle on your snout*...the Monticello seemed like a small price to pay.

Back at the apartment, Clare and I went to Jay's closet to choose his final ensemble. I rubbed the fabric of a plaid Paul Stuart sport jacket, the one he wore to a school cocktail party. The one he was wearing when I fell asleep on his shoulder at *A Streetcar Named Desire* on Broadway. I pulled a sleeve to my nose, inhaling deeply.

I stroked a tawny suede vest. I sorted through a rack of trousers, mostly gray flannel, all arranged neatly on their wooden hangers. I gazed at the belts hanging from brass hooks—black and brown leather, a few western-style, with ornate buckles...Jay selected his outfits with such care, and now here I was, hoping I'd pick something he'd approve of.

I told Clare I wanted Jay to wear khakis so he'd be comfortable. I also told her I was worried that if we chose the Paul Stuart blazer, he might be hot in the summer. We allowed ourselves to laugh at the thought.

Should he wear his wedding ring? I wondered. Ultimately, I decided to put it on a chain around my neck to keep him close to me. Although I did pick out a tiny brass bugle he had taught Ellie to play and a stuffed bunny of Carrie's to go in the casket to keep him company. I also put in a poem I wrote thanking him for loving me, loving us, and for always making me feel "safe, sane and secure." I'd felt so protected in his presence, whether he was giving me a reassuring play-by-play of what a plane was doing during turbulence or positioning himself between me and the street when we strolled down the sidewalk despite the fact that mud-splattering horse-drawn carriages were few and far between.

THE WAKE WAS held on the third floor of Campbell's, where the line snaked around the corner. At one point, the overloaded elevator dropped to the basement, leaving the shaken occupants to take the stairs. It was a strange assortment of friends and family and the world of media and politics, some who knew and loved Jay and some probably hoping to be mentioned in Page Six, the juicy (if not always accurate) *New York Post* gossip column.

In the middle of it all, the archbishop of New York, Cardinal O'Connor, a big personage in the city, glided in, his white vestments flowing behind him. Wendy and I just looked at each other, our eyes as big as Communion wafers. Could this get any weirder? The strange high-profile-ness of it all drove home such a humbling lesson: Grave illness doesn't care how well known you are, how powerful your connections, how big your salary. We're all made of the same flesh and blood and bone that keeps working or turns against us for reasons even the most brilliant scientists don't fully understand. A successful career had given me so much, but it couldn't help me here.

I was intent on having the funeral reflect the many sides of Jay, the man I had imagined growing old alongside, even though "till death do us part" would come just six months shy of our ninth anniversary. I thought that if I hadn't always shown him how much I loved him in life, perhaps I could show it by giving him the perfect send-off.

Judy Collins sang "The Battle Hymn of the Republic" and "Amazing Grace," a cappella. I asked Jay's reenactor buddy Todd Kern to reach out to some of the others in the Stonewall Brigade to see if they'd come to the service in uniform, which Jay would have loved—especially the sight of them walking down Park Avenue in full military regalia.

The Mass was held at St. Ignatius, just a few blocks from our apartment, a house of worship neither of us had ever set foot in. I selected two Bach pieces I loved and the Navy Hymn to play as people were taking their seats. Jay's dad said "On Eagle's Wings" would wreck him, so we didn't include it. During the service, people passed around a framed photo of Jay holding Carrie in a swimming pool when she was just a few months old. I saw Rosie O'Donnell crying as she handed it to someone in front of her.

In her eulogy, Clare spoke about Jay's sense of fairness and compassion for the underdog. "When Jay was in the fifth grade, he took it upon himself to teach an awkward and unpopular boy the proper technique for throwing a baseball in an attempt to help him be more readily accepted by his peers." His brother Chris poked fun at Jay's idiosyncratic musical tastes. "While my friends were listening to Jimmy Hendrix, Led Zeppelin, and the Allman Brothers with *their* brothers, I was stuck listening to such classics as Scott Joplin's greatest hits, 'John Jacob Jingleheimer Schmidt,' and John Philip Sousa's 'Marches to Dress By.'"

David Kiernan told a funny story about Jay's strategy for attracting women at bars during their single days. "Girls would walk by. Jay warned me not to act too interested. If you're interested and they make eye contact, don't look back right away. About a year later…Jay spotted Katie. That night, Jay moved." Geraldo Rivera said Jay "had the sharpest legal mind TV ever saw."

I had spent days writing my eulogy. Then I realized I wouldn't be able to get through it, so I asked my sister Emily to read it for me: "When

I freeze-frame the happiest moments of our lives, they are when we are a family—all snuggled in bed together, watching cartoons on a Saturday morning. The smile that lit up Jay's face, even on his darkest days, when Carrie toddled into the room or Ellie showed him a picture she had drawn." I remember being irritated by her delivery. It didn't sound like me—because it wasn't.

Finally, Jay Ungar and his wife, Molly Mason, who had come from their home in New Hampshire, performed "Ashokan Farewell," the melancholy melody they had composed for Ken Burns's Civil War series. Jay loved the fiddle, guitar, and banjo piece so much, he often played it in the car to and from Millbrook on repeat.

In the series, the song serves as a backdrop for the reading of a letter written in 1861 by Sullivan Ballou, a Union army officer, to his wife, Sarah, as federal forces were about to move into Virginia. I'd asked Todd Kern to read Ballou's beautiful words—in his Civil War finest— while Jay and Molly played:

Dear Sarah,

The indications are very strong that we shall move in a few days, perhaps tomorrow. Lest I should not be able to write you again, I feel impelled to write lines that may fall under your eye when I am no more.

I have no misgivings about, or lack of confidence in the cause in which I am engaged. And my courage does not halt or falter. I know how American civilization now leans upon the triumph of the government and how great a debt we owe to those who went before us through the blood and suffering of the Revolution. And I am willing, perfectly willing, to lay down all my joys in this life to help maintain this government and to pay that debt.

Sarah, my love for you is deathless. It seems to bind me with mighty cables that nothing but omnipotence can break. And yet my love of country comes over me like a strong wind and bears me irresistibly with all those chains to the battlefield.

The memory of all the blissful moments I have enjoyed with you come crowding over me, and I feel most deeply grateful to God and you that I've enjoyed them for so long. And how hard it is for me to give them up and burn to ashes the hopes, the future years, when, God willing, we might still have lived and loved together and see our boys grown up to honorable manhood around us. If I do not return, my dear Sarah, never forget how much I loved you, nor that when my last breath escapes me on the battlefield, it will whisper your name. Forgive my many faults and the many pains I have caused you. How thoughtless, how foolish I have sometimes been.

But oh, Sarah! If the dead can come back to this Earth and flit unseen around those they love, I shall always be with you in the brightest day and the darkest night always, always. And if there be a soft breeze upon your cheek, it shall be my breath; or the cool air fans your throbbing temple, it shall be my spirit passing by. Sarah, do not mourn me dead; think I am gone and wait for me, for we shall meet again.

Sullivan Ballou was killed a week later at the First Battle of Bull Run. Now I was Sarah. But it was 1998, not 1861.

THE SOMBER CONVOY wended its way to the Cemetery of the Holy Rood in Westbury, Long Island. On that bitterly cold day, we lowered Jay's casket into a plot near his grandparents John and Mina Tully. I felt like I was watching myself in a movie.

39

From Hope to Hope

TWENTY YEARS AFTER Jay died, I walk into Cognac, a bistro on the Upper East Side, and greet two ghosts of cancer past: Joe Ruggiero, Jay's oncologist, slightly stooped now, his close-cropped beard peppered with gray, and Mark Pochapin, the gastroenterologist who was on call that terrible first night we spent at New York Hospital, still boyish-looking in his late fifties. We say hello with the warmth of comrades who've been through a war, because in many ways, we had.

We tuck into a banquette toward the back. Joe orders a Sancerre and Mark a chardonnay. I ask the waiter for a cup of tea. Black tea is fine.

I invited them here to talk about what happened with Jay; even two decades later, it feels so unresolved. As I look into their expectant, sympathetic faces, my voice starts to tremble, which takes me by surprise.

"I wanted to ask you about your relationship with Jay during his illness. Did he tell you he was frightened? Did he know he was dying?"

Joe gives me the kind smile that thousands of patients have seen and no doubt tried to read in his office.

"There was just so little time," he says. "We just never settled into a treatment routine. The cancer was like a tornado that ripped through Jay's body."

He was an ideal patient, Joe tells me. Meticulous, intent on doing everything right. And he was curious, wanting to understand why certain treatments were being prescribed and asking all the right questions. Jay wasn't as willfully in the dark about his situation as I'd thought. "But he never asked if he was going to die," Joe says.

As I listen, the tears come. Joe and Mark explain that many patients, particularly young ones, avoid discussing the possibility of death.

"People want hope and direction," says Joe, his glass of wine untouched. "They don't want to talk about dying. I always quote Samuel Johnson: 'The natural flights of the human mind are not from pleasure to pleasure, but from hope to hope.' "

I can tell from Mark's expression that he knows how much I am struggling.

"Listen, Katie," he says, "there are different kinds of hope. One is the hope that the cancer can be cured. If it can't, there is the hope that the disease can be managed. And finally, there is the hope for comfort and grace."

Mark tells me he gave Jay many opportunities to talk. He sat in his hospital room as Jay recounted his most recent Civil War reenactment, describing the mist coming over the valley, how the soldiers had been scattered across the berm behind the trees. It makes me smile. That was so Jay, going into every detail about a fight to the death that had taken place more than a hundred years before. Just as he was facing his own.

Years later, I discovered a legal pad on which he had made a list of all our assets, including our house in Millbrook (how much we paid for capital improvements highlighted in yellow), our minivan, his beloved Jeep, our bank accounts, IRAs, life insurance policy. In the right-hand corner was the date: October 30th, 1997, three months before he died. He knew.

THERE ARE MANY things I would do differently if I had the chance. Being more honest with Jay is the first one. I thought I was protecting him. And his surgeon at New York Hospital was all too willing to follow my lead. I'd told him to be careful when describing to Jay how much the cancer had spread. So he talked about seeing "shadows" on the X-rays rather than using the word *tumors*. It's one reason I didn't want Jay treated at Sloan Kettering, which has a reputation for being cold and clinical and sparing no details. I felt like I could co-opt the doctors more easily at New York Hospital and manage Jay's information flow.

Why was I so afraid to talk to Jay about the inevitable? Why weren't we straight with each other and admit that this was not solvable, not fixable, and that our storybook life together would end after just a few chapters? I remember thinking I did not want to destroy the time Jay had left by admitting defeat, leaving him with little choice but to wait for death to take him. But in hindsight, I think I was a coward.

There's no playbook for how to handle the devastating things we all, sooner or later, will have to face. Death may come suddenly, out of nowhere. My friend Diane lost her husband, Mark, in a car accident one summer morning when they were on their way back to the city from Long Island. Her life changed in an instant. Other people's loved ones simply fade away. Both bring their own unbearable pain. However it happens, you do the best you can.

I wish we had sought out the help of a minister, a social worker, anyone. Perhaps then we could have said the things we wanted to say, needed to say, but were too afraid to say.

John Kelly, who officiated our wedding, wrote to us the summer before Jay died:

> *Don't let the fear of your vulnerability result in the building of a wall that blocks your talking to each other. Don't stay behind a wall trying "to be strong for the other." Rather begin from your mutual weakness, your vulnerability, so that together you can show the strength that can be found in the stories of your relationship.*

It's too late for us. But consider this my gift to you or anyone you know facing a terminal illness.

I did everything I could to keep Jay alive. Looking back, I wish I had done a better job helping him die.

* * *

I GOT SO ANGRY with people when Jay was sick. I felt like they couldn't do anything right. If they stayed away, I resented it. If they got too close, it only strengthened my resolve to circle the wagons. I was furious that the church across the street from us in Millbrook, where Carrie was baptized, never sent over a note or a casserole—never even called to see if we needed anything. *Not very Christian of them,* I would silently seethe. (I was later told that the congregation didn't want to intrude on our privacy, especially since I was a public figure.) I think I often defaulted to anger because it was easier to feel and express than pain or fear.

Even though I told myself to stay positive, it drove me crazy when others counseled Jay to do the same. Yes, I believe there is a powerful connection between body and mind. But I take issue with the notion that somehow, through sheer determination, people in Jay's situation would be able to muster "the will to live" and cure their own illness. I hated those four words. Cemeteries are full of people who had the will to live. Sometimes biology and the limits of modern medicine conspire against you.

I had read an article about how more children would be dealing with this because couples were having children later—parents were just older than they used to be. I worked with the Child Mind Institute to put together a handbook for New York private schools that provided support for anyone who suddenly found themselves a single parent. Years later, I hosted a video called "When Families Grieve" for *Sesame Street* in which real families shared their stories of loss (and Elmo came to terms with the passing of his uncle Jack).

IN THE YEARS following Jay's death, Ellie was in denial. At summer camp in Maine, she sent letters home addressed to Mr. and Mrs. Jay Monahan. My heart sank whenever I saw one on the mail table. On visiting day, always a huge deal for campers, Ellie told friends her dad was on a business trip. But when she was 11, she had a breakthrough. The camp directors wrote to tell me that during an assembly of 300 people to discuss what good cause the camp should make a donation to, Ellie addressed the group. Her recollections of her father, her explanation of colorectal cancer and the lifesaving importance of early detection, reduced the room to tears; her peers chose to donate to our cancer awareness campaign. The directors called it a "miraculous growth step."

Just a toddler when her father died, Carrie had her own way of processing the loss. One morning when she was 3, she told me her dad had flown through her bedroom window the night before, knelt down at her bedside, and said, "Carrie, I'm so proud of you." I imagined her innocent, uncalcified heart being open to just such a visitation. A teacher told me that when a kindergarten classmate asked Carrie where her father was, Carrie said, "He's sitting in this chair, right next to me." Then the hard questions came. "Why," Carrie asked, "did my dad die of Kansas?"

I tried to bring Jay up the most natural way I could as often as I could. Over hamburgers at a neighborhood place, I'd talk about how much ketchup their dad slathered on his. When Carrie smiled, I'd tell her she smiled just like him. We'd attempt to play his bugles, managing a few breathy squeaks before dissolving into giggles. Of course there were framed photographs of Jay everywhere in the apartment, endless configurations of him with the girls—holding them, hugging them, like there was no tomorrow.

40

Safe, Sane, and Secure

AFTER FOUR WEEKS on autopilot signing preprinted thank-you cards at the dining-room table with a brigade of moms, I knew it was time to go back to work. Although I still felt disoriented, I thought resuming a routine was probably the best thing I could do. And I wanted to express my appreciation to all the viewers who had kept me in their prayers, sending Mass cards by the bushel and deeply personal notes from widows preparing me for what lay ahead.

Tuesday, February 24th. I wore a black suit and Jay's wedding ring on a chain around my neck. Jeff decided we would tape the open instead of doing it live. That way, if I broke down, we could just do it again. The first time I tried it, I sounded shaky and my words came cascading out.

"Do you want to try again?" Jeff asked in my earpiece. Before I could answer, he said, "Let's do it again. Try to slow down a bit. You're doing great." Somehow I managed.

Five, four, three, two, one—cue Matt.

"Good morning. President Clinton says he welcomes the UN's new agreement with Iraq and will wait to hear the final details later today, February 24th, 1998."

Cue theme music. Our director, Joe Michaels, takes a wide shot of the studio, then a two-shot as Matt greets the audience: "Welcome to *TODAY* on this Tuesday morning, I'm Matt Lauer. And nothing makes me happier than to say *along with* Katie Couric. We missed you, welcome back."

I pat Matt's hand and thank him for his support. Then, a single on me speaking into the camera: "Many of you know that I lost my husband, Jay Monahan, my loving and beloved husband, last month after a courageous battle with colon cancer. Words, of course, will never describe how devastating this loss has been for me and my daughters, and for all of Jay's family as well. But the heartfelt and compassionate letters and cards that so many of you sent to me were enormously comforting and I am so grateful. I am also grateful to those who have made contributions to the National Cancer Institute in Jay's memory. It is my profound hope that the money can be used to help eradicate this terrible disease, which is second only to lung cancer in the number of cancer deaths in this country every year."

Finally, I address certain viewers in particular: "For all of you who may be struggling with a life-threatening disease right now and wondering how the world can keep going, business as usual, just know that my heart goes out to you."

Matt throws to Ann at the news desk, and once again the show is live.

I interviewed former Secretary of State James Baker and Monica Lewinsky's lawyer William Ginsburg. In the sofa area, our attention turned to Pop-Tart flavors; I laughed and said how much I'd missed these conversations. It felt good to be back.

In *Time* magazine, Roger Rosenblatt complimented the way I'd handled my return, calling it a much-needed "tasteful" break from the incredibly tawdry news cycle the American people were stuck in. Michele Greppi of the *New York Post* saw it differently, suggesting I'd worn Jay's ring around my neck to drum up sympathy, which left me feeling wounded and angry.

What won the day was the indescribable kindness that made me feel as "safe, sane, and secure" at work as Jay had made me feel at home. From the executives to the camera crews to the producers to the people in the control room, everyone at NBC was so gentle with me, leaving notes on my desk, hugging me. It gave me a soft landing as I tried to adjust to my new life—dealing with my pain behind the camera, trying to do my job as well as I could in front of it.

Thomas Jefferson said, "The earth belongs to the living." I was determined to heed those words and build on the life Jay and I had started. I couldn't bring him back. But I was still here, and so were my daughters. God willing, we had many years ahead of us.

41

The Aloneness

*W*IDOW.

The word conjures the image of a ghostly woman in Victorian black, her face obscured by a lace mourning veil. There but not there—shattered by loss.

I hated the word. And now it described me.

I tried to summon Jay in my dreams. Before I succumbed to the emotional and physical exhaustion I felt every day, I'd ask him to show me some kind of sign—to make his presence known. By daylight, I could never remember if he had. I do remember waking up at the strangest times: 1:11 a.m., 2:22 a.m., 3:33 a.m. Was that Jay's way of telling me he was watching over us?

I wanted to believe that he was in a better place, that death had brought deliverance and eternal life. I longed for the kind of deep faith that could ward off the bitter chill of grief.

As we'd learned, the tragic death of a fellow resident who'd left behind a wife and two small children was no match for the bylaws of a Park Avenue co-op. That said, looking for a new place to live provided a welcome distraction.

I didn't want to disrupt the girls' lives any more than they already had been. The adventure of moving from one apartment to another (we'd lived in four over the past six years, as leases longer than two years were hard to come by) was getting old. I yearned for something permanent, where the three of us could put down roots.

I wanted to find something cozy, cheerful, and, most important, in the Carnegie Hill neighborhood, home to our favorite playgrounds, coffee shop, children's shoe store, and families.

By some miracle, a real estate agent told me, a nice apartment on Park, just two blocks away, was about to go on the market. It was around the corner from the 92nd Street Y, where Carrie would be going to preschool, and close to Spence, where Ellie would spend the next nine years. I felt lucky to have found it—the first time in nearly a year I'd felt lucky about anything.

The only problem with the apartment was that it needed a lot of love—updating, freshening up, a new kitchen—and the renovation would take a year. I wanted it to be our home for a long time and really needed it to feel right. So while the work was being done, we decided to pull an Eloise and live in a hotel—the Surrey, about 15 blocks away.

It was a strange existence. My *TODAY* show wardrobe hung on long racks right there in the living room. We'd cook macaroni and cheese on the small stove in the kitchenette or go around the corner to Three Guys for burgers, omelets, and fries at Madison Avenue prices. It felt a bit like we were camping out—in style.

Even in my grief haze, I was well aware of how fortunate I was to have these options and care for my girls free of financial worry. So many women, whether divorced or widowed, have found themselves blindsided by circumstances that pushed them to the brink of poverty.

But financial security was little comfort when one of the girls got sick and Jay wasn't standing by to absorb my distress and help devise a plan of action. One night my friend Nancy Armstrong, an ABC producer who'd married one of Jay's childhood friends, came to visit. Carrie had a terrible, barking cough that grew worse as the night wore on (the croup, of course). When it got to the point where she was having trouble breathing, I swung into action, bundling her up and asking Nancy to stay with Ellie, then rushing downstairs and heading to the ER. Nancy remembers looking out the window and seeing me on the deserted avenue cradling my inconsolable child while trying to hail a cab—not a celebrity with a team of assistants tending to her every need, but a scared single mom doing the best she could.

The aloneness was a huge adjustment, especially when it came to school functions—going to parent-teacher conferences and class cocktail parties solo. (At Carrie's preschool orientation, I looked at all the couples sitting on folding chairs and was seized by sadness—they glanced at me uncomfortably as I broke into a full-on ugly cry.) Figuring out what to do on a Saturday night, often asking married friends if I could join them for dinner—grateful for their willingness to let me tag along. Taking in the day's ups and downs alone, in the dead quiet of the apartment after the girls went to bed.

Staying busy was my elixir. We'd head to Arlington and spend the weekend with my parents. We'd drive to Darien to visit Clare, her husband, Jeff, and their kids. We'd hop on the shuttle to Boston to visit Kiki and her family. Anything to outrun our sadness. In the city, we had a busy rotation of dinners with friends. On some weekends, we'd get in the Monavan and drive to Millbrook.

It was hard to be there. Jay had adored that house and cared for it so lovingly—poking around antiques shops for the perfect umbrella stand for the entryway, walking the property, trimming the grass around the paving stones with fingernail scissors. His office was full of the militaria he collected: soldiers' hats on stands, the document box that had belonged to Union officer Joshua Chamberlain when he became president of Bowdoin College, daguerreotypes of young men headed to war whose uncertain fates are reflected in their stares. I remember walking by and feeling a chill go down my spine, a kind of "rabbit ran over my grave" sensation.

The whole house scared me a little, so I imported friends, whose children brought diverting chaos and kept my mind from going there.

We'd drop into the Millbrook Diner, where the sweet waitresses always asked me how I was doing. We'd sled down the big hill near town—

the same hill where we'd watched the Fourth of July concert with Jay describing every troop movement as the "1812 Overture" played. We'd visit the bookstore, lap ice cream cones at a picnic table outside the Dairy Queen, and get elephant ears or sticky buns at the Mabbettsville market on Sunday morning. I'd make dinner in the kitchen Jay and I had designed, filling the house with the smell of roast chicken. We'd build a fire and watch DVDs of *Faerie Tale Theatre*. I had become a strange hybrid of grieving widow and camp counselor.

One weekend when my mom and dad came to visit, we were drinking tea at the kitchen table when I saw my father's hand start to shake. He placed his other hand on top to try and still the tremor.

"Dad," I said, "what's the matter?"

"I'm just a little nervous," he told me.

Later, my mom called and said he'd been diagnosed with Parkinson's. In the terrible aftermath of Jay, they had tried to keep it from me as long as possible.

WHEN JAY FELL in love with the Millbrook house, I told him we could buy it under one condition: that we spend two weeks every summer at the beach.

We rented a place on Ocean Road in Bridgehampton with charming English flower beds and a thick rope for a banister; Jay threw me a surprise baby shower there when I was pregnant with Carrie. After he died, we found a cottage on Quimby Lane. Summer dresses and dining alfresco, barbecues and bonfires, a warm group of friends cycling through at all times...I just wanted to feel normal.

That October, Matt married Annette Roque, a sleek Dutch woman whose model name had been Jade. The wedding was in a little church in Bridgehampton, and the party was on the panoramic lawn of one of Matt's wealthy friends. Jeff and Caryn were my dates; I tried to have fun. The newlyweds looked so glamorous and Matt seemed happy. What more could he want?

The one-year anniversary of Jay's death fell on a Sunday. After the girls went to sleep, I opened the Maeve Binchy novel I had started dozens of times. Grief made it impossible to concentrate. After reading the same paragraph over and over and over again, I gave up and settled in to watch *Rushmore,* the quirky coming-of-age movie starring Bill Murray. I don't remember much about it, except feeling my organs twist. The loneliness, longing, and sadness that had set in a year earlier were attacking me from the inside.

42

"There's Been a Shooting"

B Y SPRING, OUR new apartment was ready. I'd been intent on making it as warm and inviting as I could. No shades of eggshell and slate— I wanted it to look like a color wheel had exploded all over our living room.

The apartment was a large prewar four-bedroom with great light. While higher floors are more coveted, I liked that this one was on the third, with its catty-corner view of Brick Church, which I had joined, and cherry blossom boughs reaching skyward. To me, it felt more like a house than an apartment, which I loved. Come April, the Park Avenue median just outside was a carpet of blooming tulips—the girls and I would take an annual family photo there for years to come. Every Christmas, I'd open my bedroom window and listen to the throngs of Upper East Siders singing carols at the annual lighting of the Park Avenue Christmas trees. Tight-knit and family-friendly, the neighborhood had the feel of a quaint town within the big, bad city.

Once we'd settled in, I ramped up my search for a new nanny—Nuala had quit shortly after Jay was diagnosed. I'll never know exactly why. We'd been so lucky to have a wonderful family of Bahamian women helping us while Jay was sick: Nell, and later her sister Emily, then her caring daughter Charlene, who'd pitched in at the Surrey. I loved them all and found it comforting that they were a family, helping ours.

But I needed someone who could live in and be there for us in every imaginable way—covering for me when I had to travel at a moment's notice, helping with meals, homework, and everything else.

An agency sent me Lori Beth Meyer. When we met at Sarabeth's, my favorite neighborhood spot for brunch and lunch, I found her unassuming and charming. In the last half hour of the show we'd done a segment on hairpieces, including extensions and falls, which were very trendy at the time. I had luxurious, flowing locks clipped to my crown, and I was so strangely delighted by the princess-y effect that I'd decided to leave them in for a little while—even during my interview with Lori Beth. We had a great conversation despite the fact that I looked like an aging Barbie. (Lori Beth would tell me later that she assumed I was trying to be incognito—although she was confused about why I was smiling and waving at everyone who recognized me.)

I invited Lori Beth over to meet the girls. Watching her and Ellie play computer games, I knew we were a match.

WITH OUR NEW life taking shape, we decided to get a dog—a cairn terrier like Toto in *The Wizard of Oz,* which played on a loop for a month in the playroom. (That Halloween, all three of us dressed up as Dorothy.) Our puppy was blonder than Toto, and one of her ears folded over, prompting my mom to say we should name her Flopsy. Instead, we called her Maisy, after the cute mouse from the kids' books we loved.

I'd never owned a dog before and quickly learned how high-maintenance they can be compared to a sleep-and-sun-loving feline like the incomparable Frank, my roommate in Miami. A dog trainer came in and suggested I put a match in Maisy's bottom, noting that the sulfur on the tip would activate her sphincter and train Maisy to do her business. I know. I could barely use a rectal thermometer on the girls when they were babies—thank God they invented the ear kind—much less stick a match up Maisy. (I'm sorry to say she had more than a few accidents on Jay's grandparents' Oriental rug.)

Our all-chick apartment would become an unlikely bachelor pad for my nephew Jeff, Emily's younger son. He'd graduated from Dartmouth the previous spring and I had asked him if he wanted to come stay with us while he figured out his next move, hoping to break into the film business. "You can live here rent-free," I told him. "Plus, I think it will be really nice for the girls to have a guy around the house." Jeff got a job assisting Pierce Brosnan while he was in New York shooting a remake of *The Thomas Crown Affair.*

At night, the playroom became Jeff's bedroom; he hung his clothes among the plastic bins full of toys and costumes and slept on the pull-out couch. Sensibility-wise, he was the male version of me—I suspected he'd easily channel our humor and inject some much-needed fun into our lives.

We started calling him our "manny." He walked Ellie to school while Lori Beth tended to Carrie; he'd impersonate a gorilla and chase the girls throughout the apartment or dance while Carrie jumped around with two oranges stuffed in her tank top singing "Oops!...I Did It Again." He was Gaston to Ellie's Belle and a frequent guest at tea parties. It may not have been what he envisioned as a 20-something single guy in New York, but I know he had fun. So much so that when Pierce Brosnan asked Jeff to join him on the London set of his next James Bond movie, *Die Another Day,* Jeff turned him down, clearly thinking life with a 42-year-old widow and her two little girls was more exciting.

One of his main responsibilities was to help me get some sleep. I was burning the candle at both ends and in the middle—just perennially exhausted. After the girls were in bed, he'd sit at the desk in the play-room, with a clearer view of the hallway than Lori Beth had from her room. Jeff would chase down any little night creatures who had escaped their bedrooms and were headed to mine.

Much to Jeff's chagrin, the girls' playroom never became his, er, playroom—the living arrangements seriously cramped his dating style. He joked that when he met potential hookups, he'd say, "Hey, do you wanna come to my place and do a puzzle?" I tried to make it up to him by taking him to cool parties and premieres, where I couldn't resist introducing Jeff as my "boy toy." When people found out he was actually my nephew, they'd try to set him up with their daughters and nannies.

Jeff infused our apartment with laughter and light that year before breaking our hearts by heading to USC film school in LA. On so many occasions, he'd been a lifesaver. One time, I was called out of town to cover a breaking story and wasn't able to attend Parents Night. I couldn't bear the idea of Ellie finding the picture she'd drawn for me still in her cubby the next morning, so I called Jeff in a panic. He canceled his plans and sprinted to Spence, by far the cutest "dad" in the classroom.

THE STORY THAT kept me from Parents Night was one of the biggest of my career.

I'd been at an AIDS fundraiser in a Broadway theater when I got a call from Jeff Zucker: "There's been a shooting at a high school in Colorado," he said. "A lot of kids are dead. You've got to get on a plane ASAP."

Horrific details were emerging. Two students in black trench coats carrying assault weapons had opened fire.

The community was shell-shocked, barely able to absorb what had happened. Finding anyone to talk about it was almost impossible. My tireless producer, Jen Brown, tracked down two people in the throes of grief: 16-year-old Craig Scott, whose sister, Rachel, had been murdered, and Michael Schoels, who'd lost his son Isaiah.

Time sometimes erases the details of the interviews I've done through the years, but I vividly remember everything about the morning of April 22nd. The show started at 5:00 a.m. mountain time. A small set had been erected overnight—the giant klieg lights illuminated a steady snowfall.

Craig and Michael were a study in contrasts. Everything about Michael was big—his Dallas Cowboys jacket, his eyeglasses, his gold rings. Craig was slight and blond with a boy-band haircut, looking younger than he was. He was white; Michael was Black.

Michael started to talk about his son, a football player, just five feet tall. "Isaiah was very outgoing; he had a lot to live for," he said. At the time of the shooting, Isaiah normally would have been at lunch, but instead, he went to finish a paper at the library—where the worst of the carnage took place.

Craig was sitting near Isaiah when a teacher ran in screaming at everyone to get under the tables. The shooters came in, brandishing their guns, and spotted Isaiah. "One said, 'There's an N-word over here.' Isaiah didn't say anything and they shot Isaiah," Craig recounted. Hearing the details of what happened to his son—the young man who had been so excited to be the first in his family to go to college that he kept a countdown calendar on the refrigerator—Michael tried to catch his breath as he wiped away a tear that had fallen from his left eye.

Craig told me he had played dead. When the shooters left, he and the remaining kids ran out of the library. Then they prayed for their brothers, sisters, and friends still inside. Craig's big sister never came out. The gunmen, Eric Harris and Dylan Klebold, killed 12 of their fellow students and a teacher before turning their weapons on themselves.

While Michael spoke, I instinctively put my hand on his forearm. Then as Craig told his story, Michael reached out and grabbed his hand. At a certain point, Jeff said in my earpiece, "Keep going"—meaning he wasn't cutting to a commercial.

Later, watching the show from the coffee shop in my hotel when it aired in Colorado, I noticed that the camera kept zooming in on my hand on Michael's arm, then on Craig's hand enveloped by Michael's. I pictured Jeff in the control room shouting at the director, "Go back to Katie's hand," "Get their hands," "Go back to the hands!" I understood all too well the power of a moment like that, but this felt exploitive. The connection we made didn't need to be manipulated.

The interview garnered accolades for its intensity and sensitivity. When I later learned that Isaiah had been buried in his cap and gown, holding his diploma, the horror of that day washed over me again.

I've kept up with Craig Scott through the years. We had lunch in

Aspen and a drink in New York; he's grown into a really fine person. As for Michael Schoels, I heard he'd moved to Texas, then Tennessee. Craig lost track of him after the tenth anniversary of Columbine. I will carry the sadness I witnessed that April morning with me the rest of my life and hope that wherever Michael is, he has found some peace.

43

The Nicest Pal a Guy Could Have

AT JAY'S FUNERAL, I had Emily ask those who knew him if they'd be willing to write letters to Ellie and Carrie. They are our most prized possessions—the linen-covered boxes we keep them in are the first things I would grab in a fire.

I sit cross-legged on the floor and oh so carefully lift the letters out of the boxes, one by one—some on flowery notepaper, others on thick ecru stationery, still others torn from yellow lined legal pads. I treat each as the precious object it is, sharing priceless details from all stages of Jay's life, creating a vivid portrait of the person he was.

His cousin Rich writes of his adventures with 10-year-old Jay, playing ice hockey on frozen ponds and putting bottle caps on the rails at the Plandome train station.

A friend from grammar school shares the unusually thoughtful get-well card Jay wrote him in third grade, signing off with "you're the nicest pal a guy could have." A letter from a classmate at Washington and Lee describes Jay charging down the lacrosse field, his ponytail—a rare sight at W&L—flying in the wind. A buddy from officer candidate school reminisces about the pitchers of beer they shared while writing songs for a revue. A law-firm colleague tells the girls that after our first date, Jay walked into her office and announced, "I just met the girl I'm going to marry."

One letter writer says how sweet Jay had been to his young son, Luke, when we came over for dinner—Jay picking Luke up by his belt and twirling him around "like a merry-go-round." He signs off with "Take care of one another, be good to your mom, and always be ever so proud that your name is Monahan. Your friend, Tim Russert."

Tim, to whom I owed everything, a journalistic giant, respected by all who knew and watched him—who himself would die (suddenly, of a heart attack) a decade later.

ON THE EIGHTH anniversary of Jay's death, I took Carrie to the cemetery, a place I never found comforting and didn't visit often. I'd let her skip school that day, picking her up from home after the show. We got in Jack's sedan and made the 45-minute pilgrimage to Holy Rood.

A year before, I'd placed two ceramic tiles bearing photos of the girls at the base of his tombstone. Miraculously, they were still there—the images now ghostly, faded from sun and snow. I felt the winter chill as I stood back and watched Carrie read the chiseled slab:

John Paul Monahan III
January 5, 1956–January 24, 1998

"Should we say a silent prayer?" I asked.
We bowed our heads.
Then we held hands and walked the frozen ground—patches of tired grass strewn with twigs. I pointed out some of Jay's afterlife neighbors. "This is where Gaga is," I told Carrie. "And here are Gaga's parents. Your dad is with his family."

After what felt like an appropriate amount of time in this strange and solemn setting, we scurried to the car.

When we reached Main Street, Jack pulled into Dunkin' Donuts. Carrie requested a toasted coconut; I got a coffee and brought one to Jack. Then he turned onto 495 and drove us back to our lives.

PART III

44

The Way It Was

MATT AND I WERE in a groove. We had a warm, friendly relationship—he often referred to me as "sweetie" off camera, in the nicest way. Matt was less of a chauvinist than Bryant and didn't make me feel on edge.

The crew loved him. He could get exasperated if something went wrong on the show, but he always kept his cool. On camera and off, he exuded decency and kindness. When Spence held its annual father-daughter dance for the fourth grade, Ellie didn't have a father to bring. So Matt offered to step in.

The whole idea of a father-daughter dance really stuck in my craw. I thought it was so insensitive to the families who didn't have fathers—two other dads in Ellie's class had died of cancer, and another had been out of the picture for years. When I complained to the school and suggested they change the name of the event to something like "Bring a Special Friend," the headmistress told me she had spoken to the mothers organizing the event and they felt strongly. "It's a tradition," she said.

"So was slavery," I responded.

Ellie ended up not going, but I was so touched by Matt's offer.

I often thought the key to our success was that we were opposites who respected each other's distinct skill sets. He was punctual, arriving at 4:50 sharp every morning, unfailingly well prepared. I often rolled in well past 6, and crammed for my interviews while the hair and makeup folks whirled around me. And we had that rare, special thing called chemistry. We anticipated each other's reactions and finished each other's sentences. Best of all, we made each other laugh—that good time the viewers saw us having was real. Yes, we were competitive, vying for the big interviews and building our respective teams of producers. Occasionally that created tension, which made us both better.

But chemistry can be a tricky thing. Add a cocktail or two or hurt feelings, and it can blow up in your face. I never wanted to take that chance, so I rarely socialized with Matt outside of work. We didn't tell each other our secrets, our fears, our business. It was more like the intense intimacy of being in a Broadway play together: after the curtain call, actors often go their separate ways, back to their lives, and so did we.

On top of that, Matt was just a very discreet guy, never putting his personal stuff out there. When he broke off his engagement to a local newscaster, I had to hear it from someone else. And I didn't really tell him the details of Jay's cancer treatment. We weren't close in that way.

Often, when the girls and I were on vacation, strangers would approach and ask, "Where in the world is Matt Lauer?"—a reference to his globe-trotting series. But I also got the sense they were actually wondering why he wasn't with us, as if he were a fourth member of our family. I'd laugh and explain, "We work together—we don't vacation together!"

You could hardly blame anyone for thinking otherwise. The *TODAY* show marketing machine, always in overdrive, heavily promoted the idea that we were super-tight; look no further than those goofy promos extolling America's First Family, with "Katie, Matt, Al, and Ann, first on your TV." We often rolled our eyes at those, joking, "Yeah, we're a family, all right—the Manson family." But Matt and I both knew our success was built on the perception that we were like brother and sister, and between the hours of 7:00 and 9:00 a.m., we were.

* * *

I'D HEARD THE whispers about Matt. And there were a couple of incidents that kept the office rumor mill churning. One involved an interview he did with Kitty Kelley, the queen of tell-all biographies, who'd just gone to town on the Bush family. A huge admirer of the Bushes, Matt was unusually combative. Afterward, a producer wrote him a "top line," a communication system within NBC, congratulating him on the interview. Rather than thanking her, Matt asked if she was trying to butter him up. The producer wrote back saying that wasn't her style; she wouldn't know how. Matt said he'd show her, suggesting she spread it on her thighs, invited her to his studio office, and asked her to wear that skirt that came off so easily (or something to that effect). The producer stared at her computer—then realized the message wasn't for her.

Minutes later, a flustered Matt appeared at her door. He handed her a book. "This might be good for the show," he said. They never spoke about the incident.

The producer called me and told me what happened. "Can you believe it?"

Then it hit us: The scuttlebutt was that Matt had a fling at the Olympics with a production assistant. She and the producer had the same last name.

My first reaction was *Wow, gross, he's cheating on his wife*. Not *That's not okay, he's taking advantage of a young woman on the show*.

The general rule at the time was *It's none of your business*. A don't-ask-don't-tell culture where anything goes, and apparently everything did. Assuming Matt was having a consensual fling, I didn't even consider talking to the young employee about it and embarrassing her. I just figured that's how she'd feel—embarrassed. I never got the chance to find out.

Another story that made the rounds: Matt's wife, Annette, calling the control room one Saturday morning, furiously looking for him, demanding the home number of an anchor he'd been linked with. When I heard about it, I felt humiliated for Annette. But I had no idea if the rumors were true and, if they were, what I would even do with that information.

Welcome to TV news pre-MeToo. Salacious tales about who was shagging whom were practically part of the news cycle. Most of the speculation centered around the men in charge: An ongoing affair between a high-ranking, married executive and a junior publicist. A tryst between a powerful producer and his assistant, who quickly jumped several rungs up the ladder. Open secrets about an anchor and his long-term mistress, giving his assistant the unenviable task of juggling his schedule and keeping his wife in the dark. The lurid tale of a director engaging in a night of wild sex with a young staffer in a hotel bathroom at the Sydney Olympics. Years later, I'd learn about a secret office they called "the Bunker"—where the only one with a key was a male anchor who used it for one-on-ones, and I don't mean interviews.

Then there was HR. Called Personnel back then, it was nothing like the zero-tolerance ethics bastions they'd strive to become, churning out sensitivity-training courses and surveys (with decidedly mixed results). If there was a three-ring binder stuffed in a dusty file cabinet containing some pro forma policy regarding the rules of engagement, no one bothered to share it with the employees. A former NBC colleague recently told me that at one point, even *the head of HR* was screwing a low-level producer.

I don't remember any policies about interoffice relationships, but I do remember an ever-replenishing supply of impressive young women. Increasingly well-educated and ambitious, they were the beneficiaries of everything the women's movement had fought for—graduating from college with every expectation of a serious and fulfilling career, not just a job to keep them busy before marriage and motherhood.

Now there was so much proximity between male and female colleagues—in meetings, at work dinners, on the road. Suddenly men were surrounded by exceptional young women seeking mentors, looking to impress and rise through the ranks and even compete with their male counterparts—women they were spending more time with than their wives. While there were plenty of guys who jumped on the 6:07 to Scarsdale and back to their families, many others felt perfectly within their rights to come on to their new colleagues.

Meanwhile, it fell to the women to navigate the situation. Some cheerfully deflected advances, defusing the moment with humor. Others willingly participated, having flings for the fun of it, a no-harm-no-foul mentality. Some leveraged the situation, accommodating a supervisor's desires for the sake of their careers. Still others objected and risked being marginalized, demoted, even fired for some cooked-up reason. In that culture, as dysfunctional as it was widespread, women had to adapt to survive.

As for Matt, his MO had a psychology and contours all its own that wouldn't be revealed for years to come.

45

Affable Eva Braun

WITH THE CULTURE wars raging, the '90s were an incredible time to be in the news business. Everything from abortion to religion to the National Endowment for the Arts sparked vicious debate, although nothing more so than gay rights.

Ellen DeGeneres had come out and *Will and Grace* was a huge hit—gay life was in the nation's living rooms like never before. But so was its equal and opposite reaction, homophobia. Pat Buchanan decried "homosexual rights" at the '92 Republican convention; the Defense of Marriage Act passed—defining marriage as the union of one man and one woman; and Focus on the Family launched a "conversion therapy" ministry, sending a message that one's gayness can and should be reversed. It was all so fraught. An ideological tinderbox.

In 1988, a month into his freshman year at the University of Wyoming, Matthew Shepard left a bar in Laramie with two high school dropouts who then beat him with the butt of a gun 19 times, fracturing his skull. Then they lashed him to a fence by a desolate stretch of prairie and left him to die.

Matthew was slight, just five foot two and 105 pounds, and he still had braces on his teeth. He was also gay, and his brutal murder made him a symbol of virulent homophobia. The story dominated the headlines as the nation grappled with the depraved violence that had unfolded that night.

I sat down with Matthew's devastated parents, Judy and Dennis, for *Dateline;* watching the interview now, I'm struck by how differently the subject of having a gay child was treated back then. Even by me.

> Dennis: I think it was hard for him initially to say, "Dad, I'm sorry but I'm gay."
> Judy: He was our son—we would have accepted him and loved him and supported him no matter what decisions he made.
> Me: Having said that, was it a bit hard to accept at all?
> Dennis: You want to see your son or your daughter have grand-children so that the family tree continues. It was hard to accept the fact that it stops here.

I interviewed Jim Geringer, then the governor of Wyoming, about the crime, specifically asking if conservative groups were contributing to an anti-gay atmosphere by promoting conversion therapy.

Geringer had a good answer. "I wouldn't trade one type of stereotype or hate for another," he said. "Don't categorize people unfairly. Deal with people individually, and let's approach this in a way that's more rational."

I'd barely said, "Thanks so much for joining us," when the NBC switchboard lit up. James Dobson, founder of Focus on the Family and one of the most prominent Christian conservatives at the time, had put out an APB, telling his acolytes to call NBC and raise hell. Which they did. And suddenly the rap on me was that I was an unabashed, agenda-driven liberal who hated Christians.

That came up again during my cage match—I mean interview—with right-wing femme fatale Ann Coulter in 2002. She'd been booked on the show to promote her latest screed, *Slander: Liberal Lies About the American Right*. Ann Curry had been slated to do the interview, and when I found that out, I offered my services. Not only was I pretty cer-tain that Coulter would eat Ann for lunch, but I thought it was only fair, since she had written some pretty nasty things about me in the book that we were promoting. One of her more pungent lines was that I was "the affable Eva Braun of morning TV"—as in Hitler's mistress, the cheerful promoter of a heinous agenda. Yeah, I didn't really get it either.

We were off to a rocky start—me introducing Coulter with "She's been called everything from a pundit extraordinaire to a right-wing telebimbo"—and it got rockier from there. We sat across from one another, each in a short black dress with bare, crossed legs and black heels, in mirror-image face-off mode. Coulter rolled out her thesis: that liberals grossly mischaracterize conservatives as a way of silencing them. "It's all the same lie," she said, her pin-straight blond hair hanging in sheets on either side of her face as she fixed me with that impassive stare, "which is that conservatives are either stupid or scarily weird, and therefore you don't have to deal with their ideas."

Apparently I was a culprit; Coulter claimed I'd tried to blame the savage dragging death of James Byrd Jr., a 49-year-old Black man in Jasper, Texas, on a culture of intolerance fostered by Christian conservatives.

In her defense, I'd misspoken; in the interview she was referring to, with Texas governor Ann Richards, I'd meant to say right-wing extremists. Although I doubt that would have changed things between Coulter and me.

She went on to accuse the Left of name-calling, despite describing Walter Cronkite as "a pious left-wing blowhard" because he'd criticized Moral Majority leader Jerry Falwell for blaming 9/11 on liberals, specifically "the pagans and the abortionists and the feminists and the gays and lesbians...all of them who try to secularize America."

I asked Coulter if perhaps she should have focused more on Falwell's incendiary claim than on Cronkite's reaction.

Her response: "What Jerry Falwell said there, whether you agree with it or not, is fairly standard Jerry Falwell Christian doctrine. Yes, he's against abortion, he's against homosexuality—"

"But," I cut in, "to blame them for the events of September 11th... you don't find that a bit disconcerting?"

She didn't and defended Falwell: "What he said was, the Almighty has stopped protecting America because America was no longer asking for God's help."

I found that kind of hate-based nonlogic hard to respond to.

Rarely had an interview put me in such a heightened state of alert. Depending on where viewers were coming from, some thought I cleaned Ann's clock, while others thought she cleaned mine. I'm just glad I was wearing deodorant.

THROUGHOUT MY CAREER, whenever I was in front of the camera, I tried to keep my personal feelings—and my politics—in check. Journalists see things through their own filters. The approach we take, the questions we ask, the sound bites we choose, are all colored by our points of view. As such, I faced a serious conundrum when I asked Ruth Bader Ginsburg what she thought about Colin Kaepernick taking a knee during the national anthem to protest the police killings of Black men.

"I think it's dumb and disrespectful," she told me, adding, among other things, that there was no law preventing people from being "stupid" and "arrogant."

I stiffened. It seemed unworthy of a crusader for equality.

Sure enough, the head of public affairs for the Supreme Court, who'd helped us secure the interview (and who was conveniently married to a friend of mine from high school), emailed the next day to say the justice had misspoken. Could we please not use that part of the interview?

I was conflicted. Personally, I was a big RBG fan and felt she was an essential counterweight to an increasingly conservative court. But as a journalist, my job was to share her views. I called my friend David Brooks at the *New York Times* for advice. He thought I should take the comment out, arguing that Ginsburg was elderly and probably didn't fully understand the question. But when I asked David Westin, the former president of ABC News who had clerked for Justice Lewis Powell, he thought I should keep it in. "She's on the Supreme Court," he said. "People should hear what she thinks."

I ended up splitting the difference, leaving in Ginsburg's harsh characterization of Kaepernick's actions but leaving out the following:

"It's contempt for a government that has made it possible for their parents and their grandparents to live a decent life. Which they probably could not have lived, in the places they came from.... As they become older they realize that this was a youthful folly. And that's why education is important."

I lost a lot of sleep over that one and still wrestle with the decision I made. Clearly, this was a blind spot for Ginsburg, and I wanted to protect her. If I'd been interviewing Clarence Thomas or Samuel Alito and they said something guaranteed to embarrass them, would I have granted them the same courtesy?

WALTER CRONKITE CALLING out Jerry Falwell wasn't the first time he tipped his ideological hand. When he shed a tear and took off his glasses while announcing that JFK had died, when he said from the anchor desk, "It seems now more certain than ever that the bloody experience of Vietnam is to end in a stalemate" (prompting LBJ to say, "If I've lost Cronkite, I've lost Middle America"), he was weighing in. Who knows how much more damage Senator Joseph McCarthy would have done during his Communist witch hunt if Edward R. Murrow hadn't sounded the alarm about his smear tactics?

Not that I'm comparing myself to Cronkite and Murrow. I just appreciate that even those pinnacles of the profession knew it was okay to let the objectivity mask slip from time to time. It can be damn hard to keep in place—like, say, when someone claims that same-sex marriage is a threat to our society. To me, that's not only woefully wrongheaded; it's dangerous, and I don't think it should go unchallenged. There comes a time when objectivity has to yield to standing up for what's right.

I reconnected with Matthew Shepard's parents several times over the long arc of his story, forever entwined with the culture's evolving feelings about what it is to be gay in America. Judy and Dennis have played an important role in that evolution. I so admire their continual willingness to share their son's unthinkable fate as a way of educating people.

I saw them again in 2018 at a memorial service at the National

Cathedral in Washington, where Matthew's remains—in a small square vessel draped in ivory damask, embossed with a red iron cross—were interred; the Shepards had always been reluctant to bury their son for fear that his gravesite would be desecrated. Now, in a safe and reverential place, Matthew, that heartbreaking symbol of the human cost of bigotry, was laid to rest. And if seeing him that way makes me biased, so be it.

46

The Booking Wars

JANUARY 1999. PRESIDENT Clinton's impeachment trial was underway, *The Sopranos* debuted, and ex-wrestler Jesse Ventura became governor of Minnesota. But the story that really got my attention: Diane Sawyer was moving to the morning.

Diane was everything I wasn't—tall, blond, with a creamy complexion; a former Junior Miss Kentucky. Like Daisy Buchanan's, her voice was "full of money," seductive and dramatic. And her resumé was top-drawer: a Wellesley graduate, a member of the Nixon White House (she'd later help the former president write his memoirs), the first female correspondent on *60 Minutes,* co-anchor of several news shows, including *Primetime Live.* I was a widow; Diane was in a high-wattage marriage with revered director/producer Mike Nichols. I was fun and feisty; Diane was sleek and sophisticated. But there were a few notable similarities: we were both at the top of our games, and we were both *very* competitive.

When Diane became a star, I was still a local reporter, covering fires and school-board meetings. I remember being both fascinated and envious watching her report from the State Department. I scrutinized her on *60 Minutes* as she conducted a rare TV interview with legendary four-star admiral Hyman G. Rickover, then a cantankerous 84. I couldn't get over how cool that was.

When I was working at WTVJ in Miami, she came and spoke at a luncheon at a downtown hotel. Afterward, she took questions from the audience. I can still feel my heart hammering in my chest as I approached the mic. I can't remember what I asked her, but I do remember thinking she glowed.

And now we'd be going head to head.

I liked Diane and I think she liked me, so it was sort of funny to be cast in the press as mortal enemies. But we definitely kept tabs on each other. It got back to me that on the set of *Good Morning America,* she always had an eye on the monitor tuned to our show. Apparently one day while watching me, she said to no one in particular, "That woman must be stopped."

A *TODAY* show producer gave me a pillow she'd had printed with the quote, signed *D.S.*

I loved that I was getting under Diane's skin. Not that she wasn't getting under mine. When she scored a huge interview with a woman who'd just given birth to twins at the age of 57, I said, "I wonder who she had to blow to get that."

A wisecrack, people! But when it turned up in the tabloids, it didn't exactly sound that way.

I'm pretty sure I speak for Diane when I say neither of us ever resorted to actual fellatio to land an interview, but we both engaged in the metaphoric kind—flattering gatekeepers, family members, and whoever else stood in the way of a big get.

Even before she was crowned the queen of *GMA,* Diane and I had been competing for years. And it wasn't just us. There was Jane Pauley, who co-hosted *Dateline;* Jane was so decent, she found the competition for bookings to be distasteful and played the game reluctantly. Doggedly competitive Connie Chung was in the mix, hosting *Eye to Eye with Connie Chung* when she wasn't co-anchoring the *CBS Evening News* with Dan Rather.

But we were all in the shadow of the OG, Barbara Walters. The first woman to co-host a morning show (*TODAY*), the first woman to co-anchor a newscast (the *ABC Evening News*), she'd been out there practically on her own since the 1960s, enduring a *Handmaid's Tale* level of institutional sexism while paving the way for the rest of us. When she was on *TODAY,* it was stipulated in her co-host Frank McGee's contract that Barbara had to wait until he'd asked three questions before she could jump in with one. When she was given the evening news, her co-anchor, Harry Reasoner, sat next to her wearing an expression that made it seem like he'd smelled something bad.

Of course, she'd go on to be the queen—we all owed her so much. Whenever I lost a highly competitive booking, I always thought, *Let it be Barbara.*

NEWS-MAKING INTERVIEWS WERE the name of the game. But the bar for what constituted news was getting lower by the second. After all, who wouldn't be fascinated by Lorena Bobbitt cutting off her husband's penis and throwing it out her car window? Who could resist the Tonya Harding / Nancy Kerrigan shitshow on ice? As a result, every organism in the media ecosystem—from network newscasts to tabloid shows like *A Current Affair*—went after the same stories, covering them like they were cultural watersheds as opposed to the straight-up ratings bait they were.

Getting the big get wasn't for the faint of heart. The lengths we all went to were often absurd, hilarious, and flat-out shameless; I heard that Diane's bookers would often cry on the phone to potential guests if an interview was starting to fall through. Here were these suddenly famous folks who'd often been through hell—the last thing they needed was a sobbing booker on the other end of the line.

Then there were the covert ops. We'd put up our guests in hotels in New York, and if *GMA* was able to figure out our undisclosed location, they'd call, posing as a *TODAY* show staffer, and tell the guest the interview had been canceled. Or they'd send a car to pick them up in the morning and whisk them to the *GMA* studios instead of ours. If a guest was booked on both shows and the *GMA* slot came first, the producer would corner the guest in the greenroom afterward, chatting, offering more coffee, basically holding the person hostage so he or she wouldn't make it to the *TODAY* show in time. Over at 30 Rock, we'd be left scrambling and cursing.

GMA was notorious for these tactics, but we got our hands dirty too. Jeff Zucker could be ruthless (and downright obnoxious): When Dionne Warwick performed for *GMA* at a live concert in Bryant Park, he redirected the local News 4 traffic chopper to buzz the crowd. His *GMA* counterpart, the formidable Shelley Ross, was apoplectic.

Bookers (most of them women) were typically responsible for developing friendly relationships with the lawyers (most of them men) representing the big gets, buttering them up with lunches, drinks, and schmoozy phone calls in between. The stakes were so high, anchors increasingly had to get involved in the booking process. Drop the well-known name and it was open sesame: The assistant's clipped voice would instantly turn sweet as syrup and you'd be put right through. If that didn't close the deal, we followed up with handwritten, hand-delivered notes on expensive stationery engraved with our names, sometimes accompanied by fruit baskets.

Often we'd book the lawyer himself for an interview, not only for his legal perspective but for ego-stroking purposes that might lead him to offer up his client. Ted Simon, a nerdy Philadelphia lawyer, was lapping up the unprecedented attention when everyone wanted a piece of his client Michael Fay, the so-called caning boy, sentenced to six lashes in Singapore for vandalizing cars. Suddenly, Simon had a passel of suitors. In a *Vanity Fair* piece called "Kiss of the Anchorwomen," he described Diane's telephone voice as "very languid and sexual, lingering, throaty..."

Of me he said, "Katie is very warm, very sympathetic."

Hmm—I wonder who was making more headway with the good counselor. Despite all the unctuous phone flattery, the interview went to—wait for it—Larry King.

Then there was the silver-tongued Southerner (turned rabid Trump supporter) Lin Wood, who defended Richard Jewell, a security guard on the scene at the 1996 Olympics in Atlanta when a bomb went off. At first hailed a hero, Jewell suddenly became the prime suspect. I'd interviewed him during the hero phase, and when Jewell was finally exonerated, he and his mom, Bobi, flew to New York for a *TODAY* show exclusive. Clearly, we'd found a friend in Lin—which proved monumentally useful when a 6-year-old beauty queen with candy-floss hair and the face of an angel was murdered in her Boulder, Colorado, home. The media was desperate for interviews with anyone connected to the JonBenét Ramsey case. Thanks to Lin, we got a long sit-down with her parents, John and Patsy.

Most male anchors seemed to think angling for interviews was beneath them—they had that luxury. For "the ladies of the night" (that's how Peter Jennings referred to the female co-anchors of evening newsmagazine shows), scoring a get not only gave you bragging rights but provided a degree of job security. The competition that resulted fed into the sexist notion that we were backbiting nutjobs, scratching and clawing and ripping out each other's shoulder pads like Krystle and Alexis on *Dynasty*. (I find it puzzling that turf wars involving ruthlessly competitive men barely register—David Muir sparring with George Stephanopoulos over who got to anchor special reports; Bryant Gumbel openly deriding fellow sports wiz Bob Costas. Maybe it's because they didn't have talons or wear heels and wouldn't make for juicy, gendered copy.)

When it came to snagging big interviews, Lori Beecher was my secret weapon. She had an unparalleled ability to earn people's trust. They wanted to either marry her, adopt her, or take her on their next vacation. And she stopped at nothing on the rocky road to yes.

One of our first coups was Lucille Bloch, whose diplomat husband, Felix, was now thought to have been a spy. Lori was trying to convince Lucille to do an interview with me for the short-lived newsmagazine *Now* I anchored with Tom Brokaw. Lori asked Lucille if she could come to North Carolina to meet with her in person. When Lucille said she'd be spending the day cleaning and playing tennis, Lori showed up with Pine-Sol and a tennis racket and promptly made herself Lucille's constant companion.

Shortly after she arrived at the Bloch residence, a call came in. Lucille was busy, so Lori answered the phone.

"Hello, is Lucille there?" came the sultry voice.

"May I ask who's calling?" Lori said sweetly.

"Diane Sawyer."

"Just a minute, please." Lori covered the receiver and paused for a few seconds, then got back on the line. "Hi, Ms. Sawyer, Lucille is unavailable right now, but I'll have her call you back. What's the best number?" Somehow, Lori forgot to give Lucille the message.

The next day, a letter-size FedEx arrived—return address ABC. Lori slid it under a big pile of unopened mail.

I'm guessing Lucille found the note from Diane a few days after my interview.

NOW THAT DIANE and I would be facing off in the morning, the *GMA/TODAY* competition started to careen out of control.

In August of 2002, Jacqueline Marris, 17, and Tamara Brooks, 16, were abducted, assaulted, and bound together with duct tape and rope in Palmdale, California. Somehow they managed to free themselves and smash their captor over the head with a whiskey bottle before the police showed up. The terrifying ordeal had all the elements of a morning-show blockbuster.

In an effort to secure an interview with Jacqueline and her mother, Nadine, Diane portrayed herself as a devoted family woman, just like her. And it worked; Nadine agreed to a sit-down. Meanwhile, our booker Gloria DeLeon, who was busily building her own relationship with the family, kindly pointed out to Nadine that Diane never even had kids—that she was a *step*mother, whereas Katie Couric was a widow raising two daughters on her own. *She* was the family person. Gloria wore Nadine down, and it was decided they would talk to me. (Excuse me while I go take a shower.)

The only problem, said Nadine, was that her daughter had nothing to wear for the interview, since the police had seized her favorite pair of Dickies as evidence. So Gloria took Jacqueline to the mall and bought her a new pair.

Diane must have had steam coming out of her ears (I know the feeling). Trying to salvage the interview, she called Nadine, who innocently told her Jacqueline was out shopping with someone from *TODAY. Good to know,* I'm sure Diane thought. (Paying for an interview was a major no-no, even though that rule was often skirted with flowers, fancy dinners, and free trips to New York with a Broadway show thrown in.)

Luckily, I happened to be in LA when all hell broke loose. My friend and West Coast producer Audrey Kolina and I headed to Lancaster to do the interview at a hotel in town. Cue the *Mission: Impossible* theme: *GMA* found out and showed up at Jacqueline's house, claiming they were there to take her to the interview. Jacqueline was confused and called Gloria.

"Don't get in a car with anyone," Gloria ordered. "I'm driving you." On the way to the hotel, Gloria noticed they were being tailed—by a *GMA* booker and cameraman, it turned out, who suddenly gunned it and tried to run Gloria's car off the road. She called 911.

Somehow we managed to tape the interview, which aired the next day. But if we got the story, *GMA* got the last laugh: An embarrassing piece in the *New York Times* said NBC was "forced to acknowledge" that one of our bookers "had violated NBC News standards by buying Ms. Marris a pair of pants on an excursion to a mall...and that the booker would face disciplinary action." (When what Gloria really deserved was combat pay.)

Bonkers. But the ridiculous machinations often obscured the human suffering—the battered wives, castrated husbands, grieving parents, molested teens, and disgraced figure skaters who had set it all in motion.

There was a very fine line between a revealing interview and the exploitation of traumatized people in service of tawdry tidbits and sensational sound bites. It wasn't a surprise to see a recent reckoning over the treatment of troubled pop stars—Britney Spears breaking down on camera, Whitney Houston claiming, "Crack is whack." Were we journalists or voyeurs, selling our souls for bragging rights and ratings? I was willing to be a soldier in the booking wars but often had to remind myself that, behind the headlines, these were real families, wounded and anguished, who would be left to pick up the pieces long after we had packed up our gear.

NOTHING SPARKED A booking frenzy like OJ Simpson, bringing out the worst in us all. At the time, it was almost impossible for me to get my head around the cultural significance of the tragedy and the racial division it exposed, since I was so busy chasing down lawyers and cops like an NFL running back sprinting through an airport.

When I heard Johnnie Cochran was representing Simpson, I knew we had hit the mother lode. Johnnie and I had maintained a friendship since my interview with Reginald Denny, and that would pay big dividends now. I'd interview Cochran multiple times, zeroing in on what he knew and when he knew it. He never tipped his hand. I could always tell he was stalling when he'd say, "Katie, you know, that's a very good question." You could see the gears turning as he crafted one of his famously smooth responses.

Reporters were crawling all over anyone even remotely attached to the case. We set our sights on (among others) Judge Lance Ito, who appeared to be enjoying his newfound fame. On his birthday, we had a cake topped with a chocolate gavel delivered to his chambers. It became known as Cakegate. "Ito Cake Collapses on NBC" bleated the *New York Daily News* headline. They reported that the confection had been purchased from a local bakery for $75, and that Ito had accepted it but didn't eat a slice because he had the flu. "Some of the cake went to Ito's law clerks," said the *News,* "who pronounced it 'moist' and the remainder ended up in the TV press room where it was devoured by reporters." I guess that's called feeding the hand that bites you.

After the stunning not-guilty verdict, the race was on to score interviews with members of Simpson's "dream team." NBC's Stone Phillips interviewed Robert Kardashian. Barbara nabbed Robert Shapiro, who fell out with Cochran after saying he'd dealt the race card from the bottom of the deck. And I got Johnnie for a *Dateline* special. A week later, I was told that OJ Simpson had agreed to a prime-time interview with Tom Brokaw and me. One hour. Live. No commercials. No ground rules. A Super Bowl–size audience. People were calling it "the interview of the century." Please pass the Mylanta.

The upside was big, but the downside was bigger. If we didn't open with "Why did you kill your wife, you monster?" OJ haters would say we were too soft and shouldn't have given him a platform. But if we bore down on his alibi, history of domestic abuse, and the DNA evidence— all of which made him look guilty as sin—his supporters would accuse us of retrying someone who'd been acquitted by a jury of his peers. Add to that the fact that we were two white anchors questioning a Black man at a time when racial tension was boiling over. (Bryant had made the case that he should do the interview, but Andy Lack said no, pointing out that he and OJ were golfing buddies. Bryant was irate.)

We took a chartered jet to LA, armed with reams of research, and started cramming for this fiasco in the making. Just hours before the interview, Johnnie called—the team got cold feet and the whole thing was off. To soften the blow, Johnnie sent me a flower arrangement as big as a Bronco. Little did he know I was practically popping champagne. I had never been happier about the get that got away.

It was all so unsavory. The idea of racking up professional wins and losses as a result of so much violence and misery—Nicole Brown Simpson was practically beheaded. I cannot defend the media mentality at the time, except to say we all got swept up, including the viewers. Looking back, the '90s were like this lurid last gasp—an orgy of tabloid excess to close out the millennium.

47

Tom-Tom

AS FAR BACK as I can remember, I liked being coupled up. I missed male companionship—someone to do fun things with, maybe even have sex with. For a year and a half, I'd been piling books and magazines on Jay's side of the bed to make it seem less empty. I thought, *Maybe the time has come to start thinking about filling that spot with an actual person.*

In the spring of 1999, I was finally dipping a toe in the dating pool. The water wasn't exactly warm. A friend had fixed me up with one of her Connecticut neighbors, and we made plans to meet for lunch. I waited. And waited. After an hour, I asked the waiter if I had waited long enough. He said yes. (I was a little out of practice.)

Wow, stood up. Why should I be any different from single women everywhere? Still, it was pretty jarring. That afternoon, my AWOL date called and apologized, explaining to my assistant that he'd been playing with his dog on his bed and fell asleep. I was more perplexed than pissed. "Is that what they're calling it these days?" I said.

Then a podiatrist friend set me up with an anesthesiologist named Arnie, telling me he was terrific. Okay, why not?

With some trepidation I walked into the Upper East Side hot spot Coco Pazzo and scanned the crowd, feeling a few diners staring at me, perhaps curious about whom I was meeting. After a few excruciating minutes, an attractive man approached. "Hi, Katie!"

"Hi!" I said. "You must be Arnie the anesthesiologist!"

"No, actually, I'm Dave the investment banker. Arnie couldn't make it."

Talk about a bait and switch. Dave the investment banker seemed nice enough. Then he told me that before he and his wife called it quits, she threw all of his belongings out a second-story window. Check, please.

There was also the plastic surgeon who reeked of private-school privilege. When word got around that I was seeing him, people started coming out of the woodwork with stories; items popped up in gossip columns about rough stuff in a previous relationship that involved the cops. Some woman even asked my sister Emily to forward a letter she'd written saying she was deeply concerned about the company I was keeping. I decided it just wasn't worth the free Botox.

Because of my job, dating was complicated. Whoever I got involved with would require not only my parents' approval but the public's as well and would become an object of media interest. Imagine navigating the tender early weeks of a relationship with heavy PR concerns and tipsters dropping a dime on your every interaction. I once had dinner with a man I found super-attractive. Then I learned his wife had taken her own life and decided it wasn't a good idea. He had two young kids, and I couldn't bear the thought of their tragedy becoming tabloid fodder.

I did the best I could and kept at it. There was a handsome man who caught my eye at a neighborhood diner. I sent over a cup of hot chocolate (cute, huh?). He was a big Wall Street type and I really liked him. We had fun dinners in the neighborhood; he even surprised me with a diamond pendant. But after a couple of months, he ghosted me. Poof. I'll never know what happened, although I do know New York City is full of crazy-eligible guys whose hearts, for one reason or another, aren't open for business.

* * *

ONE MORNING AFTER the show I picked up the phone. Rabbi to the stars Shmuley Boteach, Michael Jackson's spiritual adviser, was on the line. "Katie, are you seeing anyone?" he asked.

"Rabbi Shmuley, what's wrong with you?" I laughed. "You're married and have, what, like 10 kids?"

"Not for me, silly," he said. "For Michael. He'd love to take you to dinner."

What?

I'd met Jackson a few days earlier at his suite at the Four Seasons; he had taken the entire floor, plus the ones above and below for his entourage. There were stone-faced, wired-up security guys everywhere—stationed in the halls, at the elevators; a pair of them escorted me and my producer Yael Federbush to Michael's suite.

Everything about Jackson seemed soft and weak—his smile, his voice, but especially his hand, which felt like a dead fish when he offered it. He had medical tape running down and across what was left of his nose. There was a computer on the desk behind him with a screen-saver montage of beautiful children.

I'd gone in hopes of snagging an interview and possibly a performance for the show. But talking to Jackson was like talking to a wilting flower—I found it a little hard to get traction. I'd heard he was thinking about playing Edgar Allan Poe in a movie, so I told him Poe had attended my alma mater. Crickets.

After 15 minutes, Yael and I made our way to the door. As we said our goodbyes, I mentioned to Michael, "I'd love to interview you sometime." He smiled. More crickets.

That he was using Rabbi Shmuley as his matchmaker didn't add up. Maybe he thought being seen with wholesome me would be good for his increasingly sketchy image, although I had serious doubts it would be good for mine. My answer was easy as ABC: No thanks.

TWO YEARS AFTER Jay died, my agent, Alan Berger, set me up on a date with someone he thought I'd like: a big-time TV producer named Tom Werner.

I was vaguely familiar with Carsey-Werner, the powerhouse production company behind *The Cosby Show* (back before Bill Cosby was a convicted rapist), *Roseanne* (back before she fired off racist tweets), *Grace Under Fire* (back before Brett Butler had a meltdown on the set). But Hollywood wasn't my sandbox; Tom Werner the person was unknown to me.

Alan sent me a *Newsweek* story about Tom and his empire. Blah-blah-blah—I zeroed in on his photo. *Mmm, not really my type, but kind of cute?* Apparently he was funny, smart (Harvard), and unpretentious. He was born and raised in Manhattan, which I thought might be a plus; at least we'd have the city in common.

"Okay," I told Alan. "When he's in town, I'd be happy to have lunch." (My usual rule was coffee, lunch, or a drink. Dinner was a potential death trap.) Along with managing the details of my career, now Alan was handling my love life, which I thought was sweet (as long as he wasn't going to take another percentage).

Tom called and invited me to the Rainbow Room atop 30 Rock. He was dressed just how I liked a man to be dressed: navy blazer, powder-blue button-down shirt, khakis, Hermès tie. He was charming and entertaining, telling stories about antics on the sets of his shows, his lackluster tenure as owner of the San Diego Padres, and growing up on the Upper East Side.

As for the nitty-gritty, he verified that he and his wife had just split up after 28 years. They had three kids—two in their twenties and a daughter in middle school; Tom had found a place nearby in Brentwood so he could easily spend time with her. Which spoke well of him, I thought, although I was pretty sure the bicoastal thing would rule him out as a steady beau.

The next day, a floral extravaganza arrived at my apartment with a note along the lines of *I can't wait to see you again.* Nice.

That was just the beginning. I had never been pursued with such intensity. Producer that Tom was, he orchestrated everything. A few weeks later, he sent a printed invitation to the girls and me for a lobster lunch on the deck of his Del Mar beach house and a VIP tour of the San Diego Zoo. Included in the invite were Alan, Wendy (now living in Rancho Santa Fe and producing *Larry King Live* from her guesthouse turned control room), and their families. We were given a behind-the-scenes tour, where we got up close and personal with some penguins (one of which projectile-pooped all over Wendy's daughter's white polo shirt).

When I went to London to cover a story, there were silk Sulka pajamas in a fancy box on the bed in my hotel room and yet another gorgeous floral arrangement. When I arrived at our summer rental in the Hamptons, an envelope was waiting for me. Inside, a fancy notecard on which Tom had written the lyrics to "Night and Day"—*Like the beat, beat, beat of the tom-tom*—signing it with "This Tom-Tom beats for you."

Yikes. *How can that Tom-Tom beat for me when he hardly knows me?*

48

The Couric Effect

THE PROMISE OF a new relationship always brought me back to Jay. With every step I took toward building a new life, I became more committed to keeping his memory alive. I enlisted the help of Lilly Tartikoff. Her husband, the game-changing Brandon, the youngest-ever president of NBC Entertainment, had lost his battle with Hodgkin's lymphoma at just 48. As we talked about our dead husbands over lunch at Cipriani, Lilly, a transfixing former ballerina, suddenly said, "We have to save the colons! We have to save the colons!"

Maybe not our bumper sticker, but I knew if I joined forces with Lilly, who'd spearheaded the Revlon Run/Walk for women's cancers, we could make a massive push to raise money for colon cancer research.

All I could think was *Finally, this disease will get the attention it deserves.* For the longest time, it was the ugly stepchild of cancers, colons being the literal butt of jokes, lacking the erotic appeal of breasts, the mystique of the brain, the easy-to-comprehend essentialness of the lungs. Instead, colons dwell in the netherworld of the rectum and the anus and, we're told, have something to do with pooping. (They're even as ugly as you might imagine, resembling an earthworm on steroids.)

But if something goes seriously wrong with your colon, God help you. At the time, things were going seriously wrong with the colons of over 100,000 Americans a year. Colon cancer was (and still is) the number-two cancer killer of men and women combined.

Lilly and I partnered with Lisa Paulsen, who ran the Entertainment Industry Foundation, and the three of us created the National Colorectal Cancer Research Alliance. I took the lead in establishing the Jay Monahan Center for Gastrointestinal Health (another mouthful) at New York Hospital, where Jay had been treated. Having to go to so many different locations for things like radiology, chemotherapy, and ocular oncology during Jay's illness had only added to the sky-high stress. The Monahan Center, led by Jay's doctor Mark Pochapin, would treat not only the disease but the whole patient—with kindness and compassion, from the person who answered the phone to the surgeon who removed the tumor.

One of the biggest problems we faced: Colon cancer screening was critically important, and yet people were just so viscerally turned off by the idea of it. All they had to hear was that it involved sending a tiny video camera on a six-foot-long tube up their bums, and many were inclined to say, "I'll take my chances."

Then a light bulb went off: I'd get one myself and put it on television.

A YEAR AFTER JAY died, we'd done a series on *TODAY* called "Confronting Colon Cancer." Now, I told Jeff Zucker, I wanted to go even deeper (literally). I wanted to help demystify and destigmatize a potentially lifesaving procedure.

"Fantastic," said Jeff, who, in a bizarre coincidence, had also battled colon cancer at a young age. "Let's do it." We tapped Ken Forde, a well-respected doctor at Columbia-Presbyterian, to do the honors.

A few days later, a camera crew set up in my kitchen to capture the prep. My task was to consume a gallon of something vile, misleadingly named GoLytely—a cherry-flavored concoction that would get everything moving, so to speak. I'd been advised to suck on a wedge of lime before and after each glass, tequila-shot-style (which this decidedly was not). I held my nose throughout most of it.

Gulping an entire jug of the stuff was no small feat. The final glass taunted me; I approached it like I was about to attempt the seventh summit. In one swift motion I downed it—and threw up all over my kitchen floor. Then I begged Arron, the cameraman, to destroy the footage. "I'm trying to get people to do this," I said. "If they find out how tough the prep is, they never will." (Thankfully, the vomit tape never surfaced. And the prep has become so much easier.)

The next morning, we filmed in the endoscopy suite at Columbia-Presbyterian—me in a fetching hospital gown with a big opening in back. "Please, guys," I said to the crew, "if it rears its head, do not shoot my ass." I asked Dr. Forde to give me enough anesthesia to dull the pain but not enough to put me out—I wanted to be able to give the play-by-play for the cameras.

One of the nurses inserted an IV in my forearm through which Demerol would flow and make me woozy. "I'm a little nervous," I said. "Is that normal?" They assured me it was.

Soon, we saw a pulsating image on a screen of a glistening tunnel with many bumps and bends. "I have a pretty little colon," I said in my semi-dopey state, which got a chuckle from the team. "But you didn't put the scope in yet, did you?"

Dr. Forde laughed. "Yeah, we're doing it! We're almost done!" I thought that exchange, more than anything, might really convince people to get their colons checked out—when this much-feared procedure was underway, I didn't even know it. Dr. Forde pronounced my colon "clean as a whistle."

My up-close-and-personal colonoscopy was a hit, bringing reporter involvement to a whole new level. Not only did it receive a tremendous amount of press, but it brought colon cancer out of the closet. Stacks of cards and letters (and even a few X-rays of people's colons) were delivered to my office. I was overwhelmed by the intensely personal stories.

I wrote back to as many people as I could. Decades later, I still think about them. Did they have a recurrence? Are they still alive?

Meanwhile, Allison Davis, our head writer, who is Black, thanked me for choosing a Black doctor to perform the procedure. When we decided to go with Dr. Forde, it hadn't occurred to me that we'd be sending a powerful message. I understood the impact as soon as she mentioned it and was so glad we'd made that choice.

Of everything I've done in my career, here is the thing of which I'm most proud: Studying the impact a public figure can have on health issues, the University of Michigan reported a 20 percent jump in colonoscopy screenings as a result of my airing the procedure. They called it the Couric Effect. But even more gratifying was unsolicited feedback from Ellie when she was just nine. One night, while setting the table, she caught me by surprise. "Mom, I'm so proud of the work you're doing with colon cancer."

Our big-ticket fundraisers for the NCCRA, I say immodestly, set a new bar for benefits, including a *Titanic*-scale overnight aboard the brand-new *Queen Mary 2,* docked in New York Harbor. Passengers dined on truffled tenderloin as John Lithgow emceed and Jon Bon Jovi and Harry Connick Jr. performed. Beyoncé delivered a goose-bumps-inducing rendition of "You'll Never Walk Alone." Nathan Lane sang "My Favorite Things" with lyrics tailored for New Yorkers by the insanely clever Marc Shaiman:

Hot summer nights when the air's rank and smelly
Losing my lunch at the Carnegie Deli
Nightclubs where drag queens are treated like kings
These are a few of my favorite things…

Marc also wrote new lyrics for "I'll Take Manhattan":

I own Manhattan, the Bronx, and Staten Island, too
And yet I'm not a Jew
Who knew?

The crooner: Donald Trump. They rehearsed it on a gold-plated piano at his apartment in Trump Tower. "The Donald," as he was called before he became "the president," was a good sport. Believe it or not, back then, he was able to laugh at himself.

Years later, Lisa and I would again join forces, along with Hollywood heavyweights Sherry Lansing and Laura Ziskin, my college friend Kathleen Lobb, and several other type A women, to create Stand Up To Cancer. Our goal was to shift the cancer research paradigm—to get scientists to collaborate rather than compete. To date, we've raised over $600 million and our scientists have helped gain FDA approval for nine new cancer drugs. I don't like to think about my obituary too often, but when I do, I hope the first line will be "Katie Couric was a tireless advocate for cancer awareness and research."

49

Emily

POURING MY HEART and soul into cancer advocacy had a healing effect. It helped so much to realize I could turn my nightmarish familiarity with the disease into something positive—deploying the top-notch network of specialists I'd built, along with my media connections and my incredible friends and family. I'd never call it turning lemons into lemonade, but it definitely felt good. By now, Tom Werner had worn me down. He seemed gaga for me, and I gave in.

One time when I was visiting Tom, I decided to take advantage of the fact that I was on the West Coast and scheduled an appearance on *The Tonight Show*. I loved being a guest. Debbie Vickers, Jay Leno's longtime EP, was terrific; the writers were always great to work with; and the dressing rooms, complete with your name nicely lettered on the door, were stocked with fresh fruit and cheese plates and lots of snacks that I'd stuff in my purse for later.

After the segment, I was still high from the crazy energy of a live audience and the easy banter between Jay and me, which belied the acute stress of having to be on your toes every second, mind racing to find the wittiest possible comeback. Feeling like I hadn't embarrassed myself, I bounced back to the greenroom where I knew Tom, Alan Berger, and NBC publicist Allison Gollust were waiting to whisk me off to dinner at Mr. Chow.

Normally I'd be greeted by a chorus of "That was great!" But instead, Allison looked at me in a way that let me know something terrible had happened.

"Your sister Emily called," she said. "She needs to talk to you right away."

I fished my phone out of my bag. "Emily, it's me, what's going on?"

Her voice was strangely calm. "Don't worry, this isn't about Mom or Dad." She knew I was always anxious about my parents' health. "It's about me. I've been diagnosed with pancreatic cancer. It's all over my liver."

She said it again: "I have pancreatic cancer."

I started to shake. This couldn't be happening. Jay...now Emily... facing a ferocious kind of cancer. *All over my liver.* I knew from experience what that meant; it was almost certainly terminal. If I thought my crusading colon cancer work or the fact that I'd already been through cancer hell had immunized me, I was wrong.

Tom herded me to the car and we headed to Beverly Hills. I was practically catatonic at Mr. Chow, staring at the diamond pattern of the black-and-white floor tiles. Once again, I felt a jarring dissonance between the public, high-gloss side of my life and the feeling that my world was crumbling.

I KNEW EMILY'S NEWS would crush my parents. They'd felt Jay's death so deeply, and he wasn't even one of their own. For their first child to be diagnosed just a year and a half later, at 53...

By now I was well aware of the statistics, that one in two men and one in three women would be diagnosed with cancer in their lifetime. But for our family to be sucker-punched a second time so quickly—it felt profoundly unfair.

Emily and I looked alike. While she'd inherited our paternal grandmother's tall, thin frame, and her face was more angular, with an aquiline nose, we both had our dad's lively eyes that turned down at the corners and a wide, inverted-triangle smile that turned up at the corners. Both smiles were gummy—we were cursed with the same small teeth that must have afflicted some distant relative.

In college, she dated Clark Wadlow, who was at Dartmouth. In her senior year, she asked my dad if they could get married; he told her that if they did, she'd be paying her tuition. (In other words, no.)

After graduating, Emily taught biology at a girls' school to help with Clark's tuition at Harvard Law. As gifted and brilliant as Emily was, as encouraging as my parents were of her professional pursuits, they primarily wanted her to marry well. For most young women graduating college in 1969, a job was viewed as "something to fall back on," not a lifelong career. When I left UVA in 1979, putting a husband's aspirations before mine was the furthest thing from my mind. What a difference a decade made.

It turned out Emily would need "something to fall back on." My first summer out of college, our family was having dinner at my parents' house for Johnny's birthday when Emily blurted out, "I'm getting divorced." We were shocked. Dismayed. (And Johnny was pissed she ruined his birthday.) Divorce wasn't something you really did in our family. It felt like we'd been marked with the scarlet letter *D*.

A few years later she was on a plane, seated next to a divorced doctor, the head of cardiology at my alma mater. What are the odds? They fell in love and got married—Emily and her sons, Ray and Jeff, moved to Charlottesville and started their new life with George Beller. Finally! A doctor in the family.

Public service suited her. She went from the school board to state senator to running for lieutenant governor. What a thrill for our family to see Virginians everywhere feeling the same way about her that we did.

She was on her way—on track, many thought, to become the first female governor of Virginia (I often fantasized about interviewing her on the *TODAY* show after she won). Then cancer struck and she had to drop out of the race. Tim Kaine, who would become Hillary Clinton's running mate in 2016, stepped in.

And still, she focused on the future. The day Emily was diagnosed, she cleaned the house, took out the trash, and told her minister that she "was going to fight this thing." At first a cocktail of drugs worked wonders, shrinking the tumors down to practically nothing. Everyone was elated. Except me—I'd looked in the eyes of this devil before; I knew its ability to shape-shift and raise false hope.

Sure enough, the tumors roared back a few months later. At least Emily was able to stay politically active a bit longer, as chair of the state Democratic Party.

I wanted to do something special for my sister, so I asked Hillary Clinton's office if the First Lady might be willing to have us to tea at the White House. I knew how much Emily admired Hillary—early in their careers, both were especially dedicated to fixing public education—and I imagined the two would have plenty to talk about.

We were shown to the gold-trimmed neoclassical Red Room. I remember sipping my tea and watching these two smart, dynamic women dish about politics. Emily, in the throes of chemo, was wearing a brunette wig with bangs. Through it all she was so animated; Hillary was her kind of rock star, with her extraordinary mastery of public policy. I know that afternoon was a high point during a time of unthinkable lows.

We gathered at Emily's house for her 54th birthday. Earlier in the day, with Emily sitting on the toilet seat in her bathroom, I carefully applied rose-colored lipstick and gently powdered her gaunt face. My amazing, ultra-competent big sister needing this kind of help crushed me.

The family sat around the dinner table telling raunchy stories—I loved watching Emily laugh as Jeff, who'd flown in from LA, regaled us with stories of his dating misadventures. I was grateful for the return to normalcy, however fleeting it would be.

The next day as we pulled out of the driveway, Emily, emaciated but still beautiful, smiled and waved goodbye. Then she turned and threw up in the bushes.

50

Churro'd

ALMOST WORSE THAN A cancer diagnosis is the period that follows: the tests, the scans, the agonizing uncertainty. It was hard enough on me and my parents, Kiki, Johnny, George, and Ray (in medical school at UVA). But I was especially worried about Jeff, just 24 and on the West Coast, far away from all of us.

When the girls and I were in LA visiting Tom, we wanted to come up with something fun and distracting. So we grabbed Jeff and took him to—where else?—Disneyland. He had stepped up in such a huge way for us when we were facing the aftermath of something similar; now we all wanted to be there for him.

We all piled into Tom's BMW and headed to Anaheim. The girls loved every second of it—Carrie especially loved the churros. At 5 years old, she had never tasted anything quite like them before and demanded more. I indulged her. What could be the harm of mass-produced logs of deep-fried, sugar-coated dough piling up in the stomach of a 38-pound child before a rollicking ride down Splash Mountain?

On the way home from the happiest place on earth, the girls and I were in the back while Tom drove and Jeff rode shotgun. Jeff was playing with Carrie's Ariel doll, joking about whether the carpet matched the drapes, when Carrie started complaining that she really needed to go to the bathroom. We were in heavy traffic on I-5, so I asked if she could wait. She said she would try. Then she complained again.

"Tom, I think we may need to find a bathroom," I said. "Carrie, can you hold it a little bit longer?" Then the car filled with a stench the likes of which none of us had ever smelled before.

"I guess not," said Jeff.

When we reached a rest stop, I grabbed Carrie, holding her by the rib cage with stiff, straight arms, her legs dangling, as I hurried into the ladies' room, trying not to laugh. I stripped off her clothes and threw them right in the trash—she was coated with diarrhea. Then I cleaned her up as best I could and wrapped the sweatshirt I'd been wearing around her. The whole disgusting incident became instant family lore (*churro'd* is still our word for having dealt with...let's just say, a situation).

ON TOP OF everything else, I had to manage the fact that my relationship with Tom was lining the pockets of the paparazzi. The shots were popping up everywhere; photographers were lying in wait when we arrived at hotels and restaurants. One guy ambushed us in the hallway of the Four Seasons and snapped a picture on a disposable camera, which was unnerving. On November 27th, I was on the cover of *People,* looking smiley and satisfied, next to the blaring cover line "Katie's New Guy." Above, in the right-hand corner, a smaller photo of Tom in a tux. The reporter had a giddy time of it, tracking our budding romance and assessing the chances that it was the real deal. Much earnest analysis of how I was doing post-Jay as a single mom with a big job (I'll never get over the authority with which some reporters write about the inner lives of people they've never met).

A lot of space was given to the fact that I'd lightened my hair, started working out with a trainer by the name of High Voltage (a close friend who's a book in herself), and spiffed up my wardrobe—or, as the article described it, "the leather and Lycra outfits, flirty sandals, knee-high boots and funky '80s tie-tops...have displaced the sensible junior-exec suits a younger Couric used to favor."

I wasn't the only one. Workplace garb had been radically rethought.

Now stilettos and slinky blouses were a common sight in the C-suite; legs had replaced L'eggs. Everything was sexier. And I embraced the leap from frumpy to frisky.

Not everyone was buying the new me. Viewers who had gravitated to my unpretentious relatability saw me as a traitor. But as a widow in my forties, I knew I had to get back in the game, and wanted to look as good as possible. I'd had many years as "the girl next door"; now I needed to be the girlfriend next door.

51

"*TODAY*, Tuesday, September 11th, 2001"

A T THE LAST MINUTE, Tom had decided to fly down from Boston to New York City for a visit. He was spending more and more time back East because he was negotiating with a group to buy the Red Sox. Yeah, I know. That was what it was like dating Tom Werner. Later that morning, he'd be flying to LA. I jumped in the shower, picked out a black cotton summer-to-fall shirtdress, kissed him goodbye, and headed out the door.

Matt opened the show that morning with an airplane analogy: "Good morning, Air Jordan is taxiing for takeoff. Legendary basketball great Michael Jordan is getting ready to return to the game he loves *TODAY*, Tuesday, September 11th, 2001."

We rolled through the day's stories: A U.S. drone had been shot down over Iraq. President Bush was in Florida, promoting his education plan—on the agenda was reading a book called *The Pet Goat* to first-graders in Longboat Key. Tim Russert analyzed the administration's controversial proposal to slash social programs while cutting the capital gains tax, and Tracey Ullman hawked her new talk show, *Visible Panty Lines*. We discussed thongs for a good portion of the interview.

The 8:30 half hour unfolded in the usual way, with people jammed up against the barricades on the plaza waving signs (HUG A NURSE TODAY!, FIRST TIME IN NEW YORK!, MY NAME IS AL TOO!). Al called it "a perfect fall morning, even though technically it isn't fall yet." The kind that makes you happy to be alive.

While Matt interviewed the author of a new Howard Hughes biography, I was goofing around in the production area, where the mood was relaxed, as usual, unlike in the studio, where you had to tiptoe and whisper. Suddenly everyone was staring up at a monitor displaying a startling sight: a giant gash in the North Tower of the World Trade Center, belching black smoke.

"What the hell?" said one of the news writers. *"What the hell?"*

At 8:51 a producer was in Matt's earpiece telling him to wrap up the interview—that something was going on downtown. Matt said, "We want to go live right now and show you a picture of the World Trade Center where I understand...do we have it? No, we do not...we have a breaking story, though we're going to come back with that in just a moment. First, this is *TODAY* on NBC."

Matt, Al, and I hurried to our seats in the sofa area. Back from commercial, Matt shared what we thought we knew—that there'd been an accident involving a small commuter plane. Then he handed off to me. "It happened just a few moments ago," I said. "We have very little information available at this time, but right now on the phone we do have Jennifer Oberstein, who apparently witnessed this event."

"It's quite terrifying. I'm in shock right now...I heard a boom," she stammered. "The pieces of the building were flying down. It's horrible, I can't even describe it."

Then we went live with one of our producers, Elliott Walker, who lived in lower Manhattan and had been walking her young daughter to school. Her voice quavered as she described seeing "an enormous fireball 300 feet across."

In *The Year of Magical Thinking,* Joan Didion wrote, "It occurs to me that we allow ourselves to imagine only such messages as we need to survive." That morning, my magical thinking went like this: *That poor pilot must have had a heart attack and lost control of the plane.* One of the first wire stories I was handed cited an accident in 1945 when a military plane crashed into the Empire State Building in heavy fog, killing 14. *That explains it.* As I glanced at the red digits below the camera screen—8:53—I thought, *Thank God this happened before 9:00 a.m. People probably aren't even at work yet.*

"Elliott," I said, "have you seen any evidence of people being taken out of the building...of course, the major concern is human loss....Do you know if there were many people in the building—"

"Oh my goodness...ohhhhhhhh! Another one just hit, something else just hit, a very large plane just flew directly over my building and there's been another collision. Can you see it?"

We could.

With orange flames ballooning from the facade, we watched in horror as the second plane came into view from the right side of the screen and tore into the South Tower. It was one of the most sickening things I'd ever witnessed, this massive jet barreling headlong into an office building. Holding a pen, I noticed my hand shaking uncontrollably. Matt mouthed a single word to me: *Terrorism.*

We were lucky Al was with us. He had covered the bombing of the World Trade Center in 1993 when he worked in local news and knew a lot about the structure. He explained that the towers were built with a 2-degree sway to withstand the wind and stress, but this was likely more than they were designed for.

My mind raced to Ellie and Carrie. I was on the air, so I couldn't call the school or Lori Beth. Were they safe? Were they worried about me? If parents were fetching their kids, would they wonder where I was? But I also knew that Lori Beth was on it. (She'd manually part traffic for those girls. As it turned out, she ran-walked from NYU to Spence, 49 blocks.)

Then it hit me: *Oh my God—Tom.*

Had he gone directly from Boston to LA as planned, Tom would have been on American Airlines Flight 11, which crashed into the North Tower. Instead, he'd switched his flight and departed JFK at 8:00 a.m. But at the time, I had no idea how many other planes had been hijacked and converted into missiles. For all I knew, the skies were full of them, like something out of *War of the Worlds.* I was panicking—but I couldn't reveal that to the millions of equally panicked viewers.

At 9:39, Matt and I threw to Jim Miklaszewski—Mik, as we all called him. Reporting from inside the Pentagon, he said, "I don't want to alarm anybody right now but apparently there was—it felt just a few moments ago—like there was an explosion of some kind here at the Pentagon...It felt like a small blast of some kind. The building shook, the windows rattled..." A 757 had slammed into the first floor, collapsing a large section of the E-ring, my old stomping grounds. *How many people were killed? How many did I know?*

Tom Brokaw appeared like a vision in the studio. He was so adept at stories of historic import—no one was better at weaving together the analytical and emotional aspects. Tom's perspective and stature were exactly what the moment called for.

The latest: The White House was being evacuated; the State Department was being evacuated; the Capitol was being evacuated. Sirens screamed; loudspeakers blared, "Take cover immediately." My parents lived 15 minutes from the Pentagon.

I slipped out of my chair, ran to the production area, and picked up a landline. "Mom, Dad," I blurted into the receiver, "please get down to the basement." I still couldn't get through to Tom.

And then we saw it: The South Tower disintegrating—that sky-high pillar of glass and steel crashing to the ground, generating tidal waves of smoke and debris that thundered through the concrete canyons downtown as terrified pedestrians tried to outrun them. At the North Tower, something unthinkable was happening: People were breaking windows and jumping to their deaths to avoid being burned alive. Then that tower imploded too, its iconic antenna, 360 feet tall, sinking into the wreckage.

CNBC's Ron Insana rushed into the studio and debriefed us at the anchor desk, his bald head and dark suit covered in a ghostly layer of soot. Someone handed me some wire copy. Flight 93 had crashed in a field in Shanksville, Pennsylvania. We would later hear of the brave passengers who stormed the cockpit with "Let's roll!" as their battle cry.

TODAY went off the air at 1:00 p.m. Afterward, I retreated to my office, shut the door, and wept. All those people on those planes—

did they know what was happening? Did they feel the aircraft change course? And everyone in the towers…did the people on the floors above the gaping holes in the buildings realize they were going to die too? What was it like, falling a thousand feet through the air, moments from death?

Never before had I felt such an overwhelming sense of responsibility to stay calm and get it right, as an audience of millions watched, desperate for any new shred of information. When I look at the replay, my composure seems utterly incongruous with how I felt.

Outside, I was assaulted by the sharp smell of burning plastic and metal wafting up from what forevermore would be known as Ground Zero. I stared out the car window at the shell-shocked city—people looking dazed, wandering the sidewalks holding candles. In the coming weeks, Frank Campbell, the funeral home that took care of Jay, would become a hotbed of perpetual mourning—hearses, flowers, swelling crowds spilling onto Madison Avenue.

I finally heard from Tom: His plane had made an emergency landing in Kansas City; he and his seatmate were driving the 23 hours to LA.

But relief would never come for so many—all those whose loved ones perished that day: Tall, 20-something Annelise—so excited about her future—who lost both her fiancé and brother. Ten-year-old Kevin Hickey, who came on the show to talk about his father, Brian, a firefighter from Queens; I'll never forget his sweet face crumpling in grief and Matt comforting him. The widows whose husbands kept Flight 93 from crashing into the Capitol.

Some were spared by the capriciousness of fate: The father, heading to Logan Airport, who turned around at the last minute so he could take his daughter to preschool. The secretary who walked to work, just to change things up—her tardiness saved her life. Michael Lomonaco, who'd become the chef at Windows on the World (who'd laughed a decade earlier when I joked about Velveeta during his cooking segment), getting his glasses fixed in the lobby when his restaurant on the 107th floor was incinerated, along with his employees and every last diner.

When I got home, Lori Beth was at the kitchen table with the girls, who were happily digging into their mac and cheese—I envied how oblivious they were. I hugged them extra-tight, knowing how many children would never experience that kind of hug again, their parents' faces peering out of HAVE YOU SEEN...flyers hanging on chain-link fences across the city.

52

WWED?

A S AMERICA DEALT with the aftermath of the carnage, my family was dealing with its own private tragedy.

Driving down Route 29, I thought how strange it was to be back in Charlottesville. I had spent four glorious years at UVA, for the most part balancing my academic pursuits with the pursuit of fun, all under the watchful eye of our founder, Thomas Jefferson.

I made bookcases from cinder blocks and planks and stashed my record player under the bed, along with albums by those anguished truth-tellers we were all so obsessed with: Joni Mitchell, Linda Ronstadt, Janis Ian...*I learned the truth at 17 / That love was meant for beauty queens*...

My first-year roommate had lush golden hair in a feathered cut with a serene aura suggesting she might have been aware of how good she had it. It was a rude awakening when the freshman boys, having seen her beatific smile in our pre-Facebook face book, lined up outside our door asking, "Is Molly there?"

UVA introduced me to a different world, with its own language, customs, and dress code; the first time I ever saw a popped collar on the Grounds, it was being worn by Paul Hicks (future father of Hope). Many of the students radiated privilege and hailed from places like Richmond, Chattanooga, Atlanta, and well-heeled Connecticut suburbs.

My mother, Elinor Hene, as a preteen in her hometown of Omaha, Nebraska.

I was 10 when I found this photo of my dad, John Couric, in officer candidate school. I thought he was the handsomest man in the world.

The ever-stylish Nana. As a young woman in Alexander City, Alabama, my mom's mom was considered a great beauty.

My paternal grandmother, Wilde.
A devoted mother, teacher, and
product of her time.

Election night, 1952.
My dad, third from left,
covering the Eisenhower/
Stevenson race for
United Press.

Outside my future elementary
school in Arlington, Virginia, at
3 years old. Once a ham, always
a ham.

The Couric kids, left to right: Me, Emily, Kiki, Johnny, 1960. No wonder my sisters nicknamed me Smiley.

Johnny and me with our parents in Virginia Beach on a rare family vacation. I love my mom's serene expression—no laundry, no dishes, no vacuum in sight.

My first photo op, 1966: Janie McMullan, Diana Searlman, and I raised $11.65 for the United Way. The local paper came and took this picture.

The fact that I was a cheer-leader seems to shock no one. Yorktown High School, 1974.

Pre-gaming with my child-hood friend Sara Crosman on the Lawn at UVA. The school wasn't my first choice, but it turned out to be a great fit academically and socially.

With my lifelong friend Wendy Walker at the Radio and Television Correspondents' Association Dinner, 1980. Clearly we were jazzed to be there—partly because we had a close encounter with our idol, Jane Pauley.

If looks could kill....
Under deadline in Havana
with CNN, 1982.

The *Take Two* gang:
With my boyfriend Guy
Pepper and my mentors
Chris Curle and her
husband, Don Farmer.
Atlanta, 1983.

Out in the field with
my WTVJ cameraman
John Lang and sound
guy Jorge DeVega.
Local reporters often
form really strong
bonds with their crew.
Nice mullet.

In Tallahassee, covering my first political campaign, 1986. P.S. He lost.

After an exhausting night reporting on a hurricane in the Keys, my crew and I took down this fish from the wall of my hotel room. I had my way with him, and John Lang captured the afterglow.

My first headshot, for WRC in Washington, DC. Trying—hard—to look professional. *(Ray East)*

Interviewing Virginia governor Gerald Baliles at the DNC in Atlanta, 1988. My first time in a headset.

Sister, sister: Kiki and Emily at Jay's and my rehearsal dinner in Georgetown, 1989.

Our wedding reception, June 10th. Jay always made me feel like Ginger Rogers.

I loved marrying into the "Han Clan," as the seven Monahan kids were known. Jay is on the right.

The morning after. If I have the math right, I was about 12 hours pregnant.

In Saudi Arabia covering Operation Desert Storm. I got a lot of attention—I joked that I went there a 6 and came back a 10.

Katherine or Katie? My first day as co-anchor of the *TODAY* show, April 4th, 1991. Fun fact: my nose runs when I'm nervous—hence the tissue. *(NBC)*

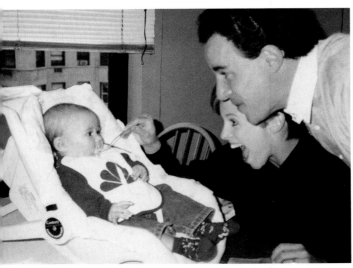

Proud as peacocks: In our first New York City apartment, Ellie seems skeptical as we introduce her to solid food.

On *The Tonight Show,* 1991. Bantering with Johnny Carson, the king of late night, was the thrill of a lifetime. A segment I'd recently done on how to properly use a condom provided some great material. *(Carson Entertainment)*

Getting camera-ready at the White House. My glam squad always had my back (and front).

With Jeff Zucker and Bryant Gumbel. Navigating the boys' club wasn't always easy.

Bush ambush, 1992: When the president showed up unexpectedly, talk of tea sets with the First Lady quickly turned to Iran-Contra. Clearly Mrs. Bush wanted to move things along. *(NBC)*

With First Lady Hillary Clinton in dueling shoulder-padded power suits on the White House lawn, 1993. *(William J. Clinton Presidential Library)*

August 1993: Once *The New Yorker* (and Eeyore) weighed in, my arrival in the zeitgeist was official. *(The New Yorker, cartoon by Danny Shanahan)*

"Katie Couric will do that to you."

The two Elinors and me: Three generations of Couric women, Maurertown, Virginia.

The West Wing, 1993:
During a commercial
break, I taught the
notoriously stiff Al
Gore the Pretzel. He
inscribed the photo,
"I think I've got it now.
Thanks! I'm ready for
the DANCE PARTY!"
(*Callie Shell, White
House photographer*)

With my friend Johnnie
Cochran, OJ Simpson's
defense attorney. He
liked me more than my
questions. (*Roger Sandler*)

Broadcasting from
Cannes, 1995. No
wonder I loved my
job.

From left: Kiki, Johnny, Emily, and me with our parents on their 50th anniversary.

Has there ever been a dad more excited to have a little girl? Jay and Ellie, 1995.

On our way to a state dinner, July 1995. I was seated at President Clinton's table. He told me he liked my hair, which I wore slicked back for some reason. *(Globe Photos / ZUMAPRESS.com)*

Jay during a Civil War reenactment—one of his many passions, and something our daughters have struggled to understand.

Pure bliss: Snuggling with Ellie and Carrie while Jay played Brahms on the Steinway we'd bought for each other, January 1996.

My dad and I both received honorary degrees from his alma mater, Mercer University, when I gave the 1996 commencement address. *(Mercer University)*

Meeting Princess Diana at a luncheon in Chicago, 1996. Marlo Thomas, me, and Anna Quindlen, practically genuflecting.

Fifteen months after I met the princess, I'd be in London to cover her funeral. I couldn't stop thinking about Jay. *(NBC)*

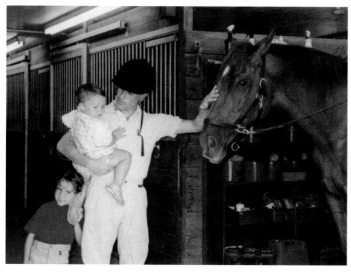

Jay wanted the girls to love horses as much as he did. A few months before he died, he said, "I'm going to buy Ellie a pony in the spring."

Pumpkin picking in Millbrook, 1997. Jay was so sick—whenever I look at this photo, I wonder what he was thinking.

Jay and Carrie. At his funeral, I saw Rosie O'Donnell crying as she passed this framed photo to the next pew.

Getting a tour of the Reagan Library. With her beloved Ronnie slipping away from Alzheimer's disease, Nancy and I quickly connected. She signed the photo, "I think my expression says it all." *(Reagan Library)*

They all seemed to have known each other before they got to UVA—from sailing camp, Miss Porter's, Foxcroft, or "the club." Secret societies were a big thing on campus, and no wonder: most of these kids had been in secret societies their whole lives.

I was curious about the sorority scene. Walking down the hallway to a meet-and-greet for interested first-years, I heard the high-pitched chattering of worlds colliding—the room teemed with pretty girls with perfect hair and names like Mitzi and Campbell and Kakie wearing wraparound skirts and Top-Siders. Even their Pappagallo purses had cool outfits—monogrammed covers that buttoned onto the bag just beneath the clacking wooden handles.

Suddenly I felt like everyone was staring at my flammable rayon blouse with the long, pointy collar that could send me airborne in a stiff breeze, my moss-green dirndl skirt and huarache wedges. Clearly, I did not know the secret handshake. I panicked and promptly left.

Then I got myself some headbands, khakis, and Fair Isle sweaters and rolled out Katie 2.0. Walking to class one day, I ran into my brother, who looked me up and down and said, "Katie. Who *are* you?"

I became a Tri Delt my fourth year. Which didn't stop me from moving easily between groups: the quirky, cerebral, cigarette-smoking staff of the *Cavalier Daily* and the preppy set I ran with at frat parties and semiformals. I loved debating journalistic ethics at the paper and refining my social skills at cocktail parties on the Lawn, where I was lucky enough to live my fourth year. I'll never forget sitting on blankets on the grass with my American Studies seminar, talking Twain, the '20s, and Horatio Alger, literally feeling my mind expand.

NOW I WAS in Charlottesville for another reason altogether. Emily and I sat on the porch of her white house on Rugby Road. She was so sick and yet still so engaged. I had brought my copy of *The New Yorker,* the one with the instantly iconic black cover that revealed a silhouette of the Twin Towers, and read a provocative essay by Susan Sontag about what America might have done to bring this on. Emily sat on the wicker chair across from me and listened intently. I thought about how much I would miss these conversations.

Three weeks later, Emily was in bed in the fetal position, her eyes closed, her breathing labored. I kissed her forehead and told her I loved her; she managed to mouth the words *I love you too.*

At the door, I turned and took in the scene: Our family on folding chairs encircling the bed, my mother clutching a tissue, my siblings with their heads bowed, Ray and Jeff quietly despondent, George pacing nervously. And I was struck by the universality of the moment: a family huddling, waiting, and watching as death looms, ushering a loved one safely out of this life and into whatever comes next. This brutal yet necessary rite of passage.

EMILY'S FUNERAL WAS held at St. Paul's Church in Charlottesville, across from the UVA rotunda. The grass was parched from a drought that summer, and the leaves were rustling.

It was standing room only. Mary Chapin Carpenter sang "Morning Has Broken." Tom was there, which my mom resented. A piece of my parents died that day, and they needed me. I shouldn't have brought him.

For years when I visited, my mom would look at me dolefully and ask, "Can you believe this happened to Emily?"

But her legacy would play out in myriad ways, including a scholarship fund for young women leaders and the amazing work being done at the Emily Couric Clinical Cancer Center at UVA Hospital.

For several years after she died, if I was in Charlottesville I'd still see the occasional Emily Couric bumper sticker from her senate campaign—it always grabbed me by the heart. Whenever I'm struggling on a personal level or with whatever's going on in the world, I wonder, *WWED?* What would Emily do? Quickly followed by *What would Emily be?* What would Emily have become if this hadn't happened?

53

Persona Non Grata

GEORGE W. BUSH and I got off on the wrong foot.

I loved his dad. He was gracious and charming and understood the role of the press—that it was our job to poke and prod. After that chance encounter at the White House, Bush 41 had sent me a nice note with a bumper sticker that said ANNOY THE MEDIA: RE-ELECT BUSH, which I put in a frame that still hangs in my office. Unfortunately, the Bushes weren't a case of like father, like son: W. was a bit thin-skinned and often held a grudge.

Just before his inauguration on January 20th, 2001, the morning-show anchors—well, the female ones—were invited to interview the incoming First Lady at stately Blair House on Pennsylvania Avenue, where the president-elect and his extended family were staying. (I love its origin story: One night at the White House at 3:00 a.m., Eleanor Roosevelt intercepted Winston Churchill, wearing a nightshirt and holding a cigar, wandering toward the private residence, looking for FDR so they could continue a conversation. Eleanor decided it might not be a bad idea to figure out a separate residence nearby for guests.)

We'd set up in the Jackson Place sitting room. Amid the American Empire furnishings, Laura Bush and I sat across from one another, two goblets of water on a small table between us. I asked her how she felt about the big day ahead. "I'm really thrilled," Mrs. Bush said. "I can't wait until we're actually on that inauguration platform and my husband is sworn in!"

If she sounded relieved, I'm sure she was, given the bruising Florida-recount drama. Of course, Tim Russert had predicted it would all boil down to the Sunshine State (the whiteboard on which he famously scribbled *Florida, Florida, Florida* on election night now lives in the Smithsonian).

With her lilting Midland accent and warm, steady gaze, Mrs. Bush was easy to like. I was eager to learn what she cared about and why. I was told there were no ground rules and I could ask anything. So I asked Mrs. Bush about abortion.

It wasn't out of the blue. Her husband had run on a pro-life platform, thought *Roe v. Wade* overstepped the Constitution, and had depended on evangelicals to propel him to victory. His pick for attorney general, John Ashcroft, whose confirmation hearings were underway, was fiercely opposed to abortion under any circumstances.

> Me: Do you personally believe that women in this country should have a legal right to an abortion?
>
> Laura Bush: I think we should do what we can to limit the number of abortions...and that is by talking about responsibility with girls and boys, by teaching abstinence, having abstinence classes everywhere in schools, in churches and in Sunday schools. I think there are a lot of ways we can reduce the number of abortions and I would agree with my husband on that issue.
>
> Me: But having said that, Mrs. Bush, they're not mutually exclusive. Even if you do advocate those things, do you believe women in this country should have a right to an abortion?
>
> Laura Bush: I agree with my husband that we should try to reduce the number of abortions in our country by doing all those things.
>
> Me: Should *Roe v. Wade* be overturned?
>
> Laura Bush: No, I don't think it should be overturned.

We quickly moved on to less contentious topics—how, as a former librarian, she cataloged her home library in the Dewey decimal system and the five best adjectives to describe her husband (*steady, funny, smart, quick, athletic*). Mrs. Bush seemed completely unfazed by our conversation, asking afterward if I could say hello to her mom, Jenna Hawkins, who apparently watched the *TODAY* show every morning. I said of course—the two sat on the carpeted stairs in Blair House as we chatted. When we parted, Mrs. Bush said we'd see each other again, when she officially became First Lady.

I called Tim in the car afterward and told him Laura Bush had differed on the record with her husband about *Roe v. Wade.*

"Katie, that's huge, huge," he said. "We've got to get it on *Nightly News.*"

I hustled back to the bureau and got the sound bite on in the nick of time.

Of course Tim was right; the First Lady's comments blew up, creating a giant headache for the Bush administration. Pro-life groups anxiously reasserted the president-elect's anti-abortion bona fides while Bush's designated press secretary, Ari Fleischer, repeatedly said he would not discuss the "personal views" of the president-elect's family. Someone on his team called Tim and claimed I had badgered the First Lady into making the *Roe v. Wade* statement.

Bush was steamed. When Andy Lack greeted him after the inauguration, he jabbed Andy in the chest with his index finger and said, "I can't believe *that Katie Couric* asked my wife about abortion!" Looking back, I can understand his anger; he hadn't even been sworn in and I was already raining on his parade.

Suddenly, I was persona non grata in the White House. After that, whenever there was a big interview, they swung the door wide open for Matt and closed it on me. It bothered me that NBC would let them call the shots that way, but I knew that if *TODAY* made a stink, we could be shut out of the rotation.

There was pressure *inside* the network too. Bob Wright once sent an email telling me I'd been "too tough" on Condi Rice and that they'd gotten a lot of complaints. I emailed him back and politely asked that he not interfere with my journalism.

Meanwhile, everyone knew where GE chairman Jack Welch stood. In 2000, he'd been accused of trying to sway election-night coverage by distracting editorial staff at the decision desk, doing his own analysis of voter data, and pressuring them to call it for Bush just as Fox had. He actually said at one point, "How much would I have to pay you to call the race for Bush?" When NBC finally did, a grinning Welch apparently brandished a thumbs-up.

54

Dear Katie

THE EARLY AUGHTS were a blur of busyness. *TODAY* was cranking away. The girls were at Spence, working much harder than I ever did at their age. Lori Beth kept the trains running on time—the homework humming, the playdates coming. I juggled it all as best I could—dashing out of the show early if there was a school performance or field trip. I'd always instruct Matt to share with the viewers where I had gone, hoping it would encourage employers everywhere to have family-friendly policies.

I made it my mission to instill in Ellie and Carrie the good values I'd learned growing up, which wasn't always easy amid the outrageous affluence of Manhattan's Upper East Side. Chauffeur-driven Escalades were lined up outside the private schools at drop-off and pickup; there were 12-year-olds with Prada backpacks, classmates with weekend homes...in Gstaad. And don't get me started on the bar and bat mitzvah arms race—parents feverishly trying to outdo each other with seven-figure shindigs: renting out Yankee Stadium or the Museum of Natural History, Flo Rida performing before a throng of screaming 13-year-olds, Beats headphones in the goody bags.

My daughters grew up so financially secure, around people with so much, I wanted them to understand the value of things. When Ellie begged me for a Baby-G watch, all the rage for a nanosecond, I said absolutely not, explaining that a $100 watch for an 8-year-old was just gross. In middle school, Carrie called from an outing with a friend and her mother and innocently asked if she could buy a bra from La Perla. I practically dropped the phone before delivering another hard no. (As if—I didn't even get *my* underthings from La Perla.)

Granted, sometimes the over-the-top perks of my job made it hard to keep everyone grounded. How could I not bring the girls to the Olympics in Salt Lake City, Sydney, Athens? They met gold medalists; Ellie interviewed sprinter Michael Johnson for a school paper, and he autographed one of his gold running shoes for her. When their idols Britney Spears, LeAnn Rimes, and, yes, Beyoncé performed on the plaza, they got photos with them afterward. Carrie rode on Hilary Duff's float during the Macy's Thanksgiving Day Parade. When the girls came to the show, they'd get the star treatment—their hair blown out, a little lipstick and eye shadow. The *TODAY* staff always made such a fuss.

Tom was incredibly sweet to them too. When he bought the Red Sox, we'd sit in the owners' box or front-row seats near the dugout; Ellie and Carrie would bring their American Girl dolls and stick their high-grade-polymer arms over the fence so Big Papi and Nomar Garciaparra could fist-bump Samantha and Felicity. And we took Robin Leach–worthy vacations—Costa Rica, Cabo, Hawaii, London, Paris, Venice.

It was a high-flying romance—until it wasn't. Tom went from hot to trot to cold and distant. It got to the point where I never knew quite what to expect from him, which kept me perpetually off balance. At one of my colon cancer benefits, rather than play the debonair co-host and help me welcome guests and gin up support for our cause, he spent the cocktail hour on his phone listening to the Red Sox game.

Tom had never actually finalized his divorce, which turned me into that slightly pathetic, needy girlfriend asking, "So, when..." I couldn't help myself; I had two girls, and I wanted them to have a father figure. I wanted to create a family. I'd even started asking West Coast friends about schools in and around LA.

One July, we traveled from Martha's Vineyard to Nantucket on a yacht that belonged to billionaire John Henry, principal owner of the Red Sox. Pulling into port, the opulent vessel all but screamed *Mine's bigger than yours.* That afternoon as we lounged on the deck, John's wife, Peggy, showed off a wide-brimmed raffia hat she'd just bought at Peter Beaton on the island. Some of the ladies tried it on; when it was my turn, everyone oohed and aahed (I have to admit, I've got a good hat head). "Maybe I'll get one!" I said.

A bit later when we disembarked, Tom turned to me and said, "Do you have your credit card?"

Yes, I had my credit card—I'd slipped it in my back pocket. I was more than willing and able to purchase my own hat. But that was beside the point. Did Tom think I was taking advantage of him? He was someone who loved spending money and giving gifts. I got the distinct sense this was about more than a hat. So what was he trying to tell me?

One night over dinner, I just came out with it: Did we have a future? I needed to know.

He seemed uncomfortable. After fumbling around, he finally said, "I have a chip missing."

I couldn't quite figure out what he meant. Was it the intimacy chip, the commitment chip, the piece missing from Chip, the teacup in *Beauty and the Beast*? I was tempted to suggest he find one at RadioShack but resisted—he seemed so morose and confused. I had assumed Tom was emotionally healthy, but if I had shaken a Magic 8 Ball, it would have come up *Don't count on it.*

The more distant he got, the needier I became. I started spending a lot of time in the self-help section of Barnes and Noble, reading books with titles like *Men Who Can't Love* and *Just Walk Away.*

As we did every year, the girls and I were going out to dinner the night before they headed off for seven weeks of summer camp. We were walking to a neighborhood restaurant when I checked in with my assistant, Lauren. "Hey, woman! Just saying hi. Any emails I should know about?"

"Let's see," she said. "Oh, here's one from Tom…uh…you may want to read it when you get home."

I assured Lauren, who was like a sister to me, she could tell me what it said.

"Maybe you should read this later, Couric," she said again, sounding weird.

"Laur, don't be silly. Go ahead."

She proceeded to read a "Dear Katie" email that basically said Tom was breaking up with me.

"Wow. Okay."

I felt a little sick. When we got to the restaurant, I forced a smile for the girls and pushed the food around on my plate.

The next day, a FedEx envelope arrived containing a handwritten card, expressing the exact same sentiments, word for word. In case the email had gone to spam, I guess.

Don't worry, Tom! Message received. I burned the note in my bathroom sink.

IT WOULD TAKE me a long time to fully realize what a textbook narcissist I'd been dealing with. Beware of men bearing gifts: What began as a lavish courtship (they now call it "love-bombing") ended with me in a puddle. It's a familiar cycle—idealizing, devaluing, and ultimately discarding. You're left wondering what you did to alienate someone who'd been so dizzyingly in love, when it was never really about you all along. If we had lived in the same city, had I been less vulnerable following Jay's death, I suspect I would have caught on much earlier.

At the time, the post-breakup miasma sent me reeling into a therapist's office. I drenched several tissues, fixating on the fact that Tom had rejected me—it felt so unjust. And I will never forget that nice woman sitting across from me in her leather chair, fixing me with her wise eyes, and saying, "Have you ever considered that maybe not everyone is going to like you?"

Honestly, I sort of hadn't. Since I was a toddler, I'd been such a pleaser, a master at recruiting people to Team Katie; I always knew the precise moment when I had them on the hook. On *TODAY,* getting people to like me was a job requirement, and pretty soon I was recruiting them by the millions. With that kind of positive reinforcement, it simply did not compute when somebody wasn't buying what I was selling. Especially somebody I'd invested in emotionally and had even considered marrying.

The therapist's words brought me back down to earth. I found it strangely liberating, this radical idea that not everyone was going to like me.

It was an epiphany that would come in handy.

55

Probing Colins

Jeff Zucker's feet may only have been size 9, but he left huge shoes to fill when he became president of NBC Entertainment. He'd hand-picked his friend Michael Bass, a fellow Harvard guy and longtime loyalist, to step in as acting EP at *TODAY*. Michael was incredibly nice and a solid producer but lacked Jeff's shrewdness and pizzazz (*yeoman-like* was a word that got used), which showed in the broadcast. Suddenly it felt slow, boring, blah.

Jonathan Wald—son of Dick, who'd run two networks—had been a producer at *NBC Nightly News* and seemed like a great guy. He was smart and quick-witted, albeit part of a TV boys' club that greeted each other with "Heyyy, buddddddyyyyy" and always landed on their feet professionally, often failing up. (One guy embezzled six figures and kept getting hired—even by people who knew about it.) Still, I was hopeful that Jonathan would be a little closer to the Jeff model than Michael Bass had been.

He wasn't. For starters, Jeff made everyone, from pages to VPs, feel like they were part of the most exciting enterprise ever (which, arguably, they were); Jonathan, on the other hand, could be hierarchical and inaccessible—people had to make an appointment to see him. He had guided us capably through 9/11 but didn't seem to have the fire in his belly to keep the show on top.

The ratings were tightening. Big bookings were more important than ever.

On July 24th, 2002, in Somerset County, Pennsylvania, nine miners were trapped underground after drilling through a wall that gave way, letting in millions of gallons of water. In a dramatic rescue four days later, all nine were lifted to safety. America was glued to the TV.

The next day, Diane had an exclusive with one of the rescued miners in the *GMA* studios. I flipped out. Then I called Jonathan from the production area and reamed him—with plenty of people in earshot on both ends. I couldn't believe we'd been completely scooped on a news story that was heaven-sent.

After the show, I dropped by Andy Lack's office. "Listen," I said. "I thought Jonathan was a good choice for the job but now I'm not so sure. I'm worried about the show staying competitive."

"I hear you" was pretty much all Andy had to say. After just 16 months, Wald was rerouted to CNBC.

As the senior person and a face of the show, I felt like the responsibility of keeping it strong, smart, and in the zeitgeist was on my shoulders. So I pushed the producers to stay on top of breaking news and interviews, but I also hatched ideas for the sort of fun, buzzy, unexpected segments the show had become known for. We did one called "Fantasy Jobs," where I sang cabaret at Caroline's Comedy Club with a surprise guest, Tony Bennett. Matt learned how to be a jockey, Al a cartoonist, and Ann went to astronaut school, which led to plenty of good-natured space-cadet jokes.

That turned out to be a dry run for a stunt we'd do a few years later for May sweeps called "Trading Places," which for me meant switching spots with Jay Leno. No one had ever taken his seat on *The Tonight Show* before—it was an audacious move. That morning on *TODAY,* Jay-as-me had awkwardly interviewed Colin Powell, providing material for my best joke of the night: "I have to tell you, I was really impressed with Jay—and then I got kind of upset, because, you know, probing Colins? I thought that was *my* area!" *Ba-dump-bump*. We got a ton of publicity out of it—we were back to being a hot topic at the watercooler.

But *GMA* was steadily closing in. So NBC tapped Tom Touchet, who'd been a producer at *GMA,* for EP.

There were a couple of warning signs early on, like hearing that people at ABC News were shocked Tom had been given such a big job. And he tried awfully hard to win everyone over, hosting ice cream and bowling parties. But he seemed indecisive and in over his head.

I regret not working more closely with him and offering guidance. I also should have lowered my expectations and wrapped my head around the fact that I'd never again know the kismet I felt when I worked with Jeff.

A NEW STORY LINE had taken hold: America's Sweetheart had become a bitch on wheels. (During commercial breaks, if we were playfully sparring, Matt would mock the moniker, saying, "America's Sweetheart—wouldn't you just like to backhand her?")

If caring about the show and expecting a lot from people made me a bitch, I could live with that. But the truth is, I was under a lot of pressure, and I'm sure I could have handled it better. For instance, with the miner story, maybe I should have met with Jonathan Wald in his office, *then* ripped him a new one—rather than humiliate him publicly.

The fact that I'd negotiated a contract for $65 million over four and a half years—leaked before the ink was dry—didn't help. Nor did the fact that I'd ramped up my look.

On their own, none of these things were a reason to make voodoo dolls in my image. Taken together, it made me look like I'd become a raging diva, a trope that the media found irresistible. It got to the point where they saw evidence of my supposed overweening vanity where it literally didn't exist.

Women's Wear Daily swore on a stack of Holy Bibles that I was scheduled to get an Endotine brow lift. I didn't even know what the hell that was and flat-out denied it, but they ran with the story anyway. Suddenly it was everywhere: *New York Magazine*, Page Six; talk-radio hosts were analyzing my decision to have the procedure. When I confronted *WWD*'s publisher Mary Berner, she actually said they stood by their story—as if they knew more about what was going on with my forehead than I did, presaging a kind of fast-and-loose approach to reporting that would practically become the norm. Only after I got Jay's colleague David Kendall to threaten legal action did they print a retraction, including my quote: "I can think of a couple of things that could use lifting, my forehead not being one of them."

The worst piece came courtesy of the *New York Times'* Alessandra Stanley. An NBC publicist called to apprise me of the bombshell that was about to drop on my head.

The next morning, I opened the newspaper just a crack...according to Stanley, I had grown "downright scary": "America's girl next door has morphed into the mercurial diva down the hall. At the first sound of her peremptory voice and clickety stiletto heels, people dart behind doors and douse the lights."

Media types ate up the clickety-stilettos line. Stanley went on to point out that our lead over *GMA* had shrunk from 2 million viewers down to 270,000—which, she seemed to say, was mostly my fault.

That night, I was emceeing a Conservation International gala at Tom Brokaw's request. It was a swishy affair packed with New York intelligentsia—probably all of whom had read the piece, mouths agape, in their town cars that morning. As I walked up to the microphone, I felt completely exposed. I just had to tell myself that most of the machers in that room had received their own share of bad press along the way. When you reach a certain level, the occasional takedown is to be expected. But reading mean things about myself never got easier.

What did help (a little) was understanding the huge role gender played in all of this. The short version: For so long, women were expected to be warm, friendly, nurturing. Meanwhile, to make it professionally, you have to be assertive, competitive, decisive—so-called male traits. When a woman dares to exhibit those traits by pushing her team to perform, demanding excellence and being ambitious for herself, it's seen as scarily norm-busting. Her punishment? She's called a *ballbuster,* an *ice queen,* or, in my case, a *diva* (I find it curious that there's no male equivalent for that word). Apparently, *friendly* and *warm* don't track with *strong* and *competent*. You're one or the other. You're either the cute girl who does features or the serious one who covers the Pentagon. You're either Katie or Katherine.

It bothered me that my fiercest critic was a woman. My dad used to say, "Women are their own worst enemies."

I often wonder about my part in this. While I took female writers, researchers, and producers under my wing, I was way less welcoming when a charismatic female correspondent entered my sphere. There were only a few coveted spots for women—I felt like I had to protect my turf. The system was run by men, and I knew the brain wasn't always the organ guiding their decisions. Case in point: One executive openly raved about the "bee-stung lips" of an anchor he wanted to hire, fantasizing about how sexy she'd look in a safari jacket while covering some war.

The fact that my mother kept such a close eye on my competition didn't help. "Who's that girl?" she'd say whenever someone sat in for me. "Why are they using her? She's trying to be like you." Getting territorial on my behalf, she made me even more paranoid.

All About Eve was never far from my thoughts, and I'd moved into Margo Channing territory: Someone younger and cuter was always around the corner. For a minute there, Ashleigh Banfield was the next big thing; I'd heard through the grapevine her father was telling anyone who'd listen that she was going to replace me. In that environment, mentorship sometimes felt like self-sabotage.

The idyllic phase where I could do no wrong was officially over. Although in terms of office politics, I hadn't seen nothin' yet.

56

One Big-Ass Rabbit

I ALWAYS LIKED LES Moonves, even though he was a close-talker with bad breath. I first met him in 1994 when he was head of Warner Bros. I'd been dispatched to LA to do a segment from the set of *ER,* the biggest show on TV at the time. That meant touring the County General set with sexy Dr. Doug Ross, aka an ascendant George Clooney. (It was a tough job, but somebody had to do it.) Then I visited the next soundstage over, where Les introduced me to the cast of a promising new show about six young, single Manhattanites. One of them, an actress with a fetching bob and a cute smile, said she was so excited to meet me—Jennifer Aniston before she became *Jennifer Aniston.*

Years later I ran into Les at a Knicks game. He came over, gave me a hug, and said, "If you walk down the aisle with that guy"—Tom Werner—"I'll be the first one to say, 'I object!'" Apparently, the bad blood stemmed from Les's abrupt cancellation of Tom's sitcom *Cybill* (years later, the show's star, Cybill Shepherd, would allege that Les pulled the plug shortly after she'd rebuffed his sexual advances, but I digress).

My taste in boyfriends hadn't prevented Les from pursuing me professionally over the years. Now, with my NBC contract set to expire in a matter of months, he was feeling out my agent, Alan Berger: Would Katie be interested in anchoring the *CBS Evening News?*

Wow. That was my first reaction. If this turned into something real, I'd be the first solo female anchor of an evening newscast. Ever. Barbara Walters with Harry Reasoner was a disaster. Connie Chung tried it with Dan Rather—another disaster. But me, out there alone...I suspended disbelief long enough to wonder, *Could this actually work?*

The courtship officially began at the Park Avenue apartment that Les and his wife, Julie Chen, were in the process of renovating. He greeted Alan and me at the door wearing his let's-make-a-deal smile—shrewd blue eyes, perfect veneers, skin burnished by the California sun (he was fully bicoastal, with a $28 million estate in Malibu). Then he guided us to the sofa, one of the few pieces of furniture in the place, and offered us red wine in delicate Italian juice glasses—not stemware, but the kind from which you'd sip fresh apricot nectar on the balcony of a palazzo overlooking the Amalfi Coast.

"I want to reinvent the *CBS Evening News*," Les said. "I want to energize it, give it new life." He talked about getting rid of the portentous, pretentious voice-of-God format and making it warmer, more accessible. Something smart and new.

I sipped my wine and listened, desperately scanning the place for cheese and crackers. "And I think you're just the person to do it," Les said.

I was flattered. And a little buzzed, although I didn't know if it was the pinot noir or the fact that he was massaging my e-spot (as in *ego*) so expertly.

Les went on: He thought I had the perfect personality and skill set to bring that kind of change, having mastered the tricky combo of being both approachable and able to hold people's feet to the fire in tough interviews.

Les said he wanted to make one thing clear: He wasn't interested in "blowing up" anything, as he'd been quoted as saying. He might as well have lobbed a grenade straight into the heart of the CBS newsroom, unleashing waves of fury and fear.

But he *was* looking to revamp a format that he believed had grown stale. Anachronistic. The evidence was hard to ignore: steadily declining ratings at each of the Big Three evening news broadcasts, with CBS stuck in last place for more than a decade.

It all felt a little surreal. While I could take a lot of credit for helping make the *TODAY* show a success, I was self-aware enough to know that I'd be a big departure from what people expected in an evening news anchor.

Of course, the gold standard was Walter Cronkite, whose authoritative, avuncular demeanor inspired worshipful reverence in millions of Americans. I couldn't imagine filling his wingtips.

Dan Rather's cowboy boots were another matter. He got the job in 1981 and held it for 24 years. Rather brought deep experience, authority, and a Texan folksiness, deploying election-night "Ratherisms" like "This race is as tight as the rusted lug nuts on a '55 Ford," "This race is hotter than a Times Square Rolex," and my personal favorite, "This race is tight like a too-small bathing suit on a too-long ride home from the beach." (Sometimes he just plumb ran out of gas, once saying, "This election swings like one of those pendulum things.") But when he reported a story on *60 Minutes II* about the supposed preferential treatment of George W. Bush in the National Guard, the whole thing blew up in his face when his sourcing came under scrutiny. Less than a year later, he was out.

The genial, much-loved Bob Schieffer, a fellow Texan who'd been with the network since 1969, filled in heroically and stabilized the broadcast while CBS figured out its next move. And that next move was apparently me.

I LEFT LES'S PLACE incredibly excited about the possibility of working with smart, strong producers on the evening news. He also said I'd have the opportunity to be a correspondent for *60 Minutes,* a lifelong dream.

This wasn't the first time I'd been approached about it. "Hey, kid," came the wiseacre voice through the phone a few years earlier—Don Hewitt, the show's legendary creator. He took me to lunch at plush Café des Artistes, with its murals of wood nymphs frolicking in the nude and leopard-spotted cushions. Our water glasses hadn't even been filled before he uttered the heart-stopping sentence, "I see you as the future of *60 Minutes*." A bit later, over Dover sole, he offered me a job.

It was such a big deal to me that a guy of Don Hewitt's stature thought I could bring something to the team. I wasn't ready to jump at the time, but we stayed in touch. Don sent a handwritten note:

> *If you ever want to stop "flirting" and talk about getting "married"...you and 60 Minutes...you know where to find us. As ever, Don Hewitt*

Little did I know CBS was paying a $5 million settlement at the time to a woman who'd accused him of sexual assault.

BY 2005 I WAS at a crossroads. I loved the *TODAY* show, but after 15 years, I was getting restless. I longed to be respected for my journalistic chops, and although I'd done many serious interviews in the morning, the fun stuff, which I had a blast doing—like flying across the plaza dressed as Peter Pan while flinging phosphorescent confetti, fulfilling my dream of being a backup singer for Darlene Love, hurling myself onto a Velcro wall—was what people remembered.

I felt like the show was getting softer, the hard news interviews getting shorter, the segments getting more sensational. The Laci Peterson story seemed to come on like clockwork at 7:35 every day, featuring her low-life husband, Scott, a prime suspect in her murder, not because there were new developments but because the story "rated." One morning, we had to wear goofy Jetsons-like outfits for something called "the *TODAY* show of the future." As Tom Werner drolly noted, "I don't think that's going to win you any Peabodys."

Under any circumstances, 15 years is a long time to be waking up every morning before sunrise. And I never forgot the cautionary tale that was Jane Pauley. I wanted to leave on my own terms, not because some TV executive decided I was no longer the flavor of the month. I wanted to jump before I got pushed.

* * *

RUMORS STARTED FLYING as early as November 2005, with a *New York Magazine* piece speculating about the next round of musical chairs at the Big Three: "New CBS News president Sean McManus, also the head of CBS Sports, has settled in quickly to his first-floor office suite and to the most thankless task on his to-do list: getting a star—preferably Katie Couric—to lift CBS News out of the bottom of the ratings race."

A steady drumbeat kicked in, with media columnists stoking a will she / won't she guessing game. One night, Ellie, Carrie, and I were passing out food to the homeless from the back of a mobile van. When I handed one guy his soup and an orange, he looked up at me and smiled. "Hey, everyone! That's Katie Couric!" he told the people in line. Then he turned back and leaned in. "So, are you going to CBS or not?"

NBC made it clear they did not want me to leave. Jeff seemed agitated at the prospect. Sitting across from him in his office, I remember how empowered I felt to be in demand and in charge of my own destiny. Given how instrumental Jeff had been in my success at *TODAY,* it was liberating to have a big opportunity outside the shop that had created us both.

I told Jeff I was really intrigued by the CBS job. That's when he started pulling a series of rabbits out of a hat. The first one: "I'd like to offer you a new contract, where you'd make 20 million a year."

I had to admit, that was one big-ass rabbit. Then the rabbits started multiplying—he offered me summers off, prime-time specials, and the opportunity to fill in for Jay Leno one week a year.

The other Jeff—Immelt, now the CEO of GE—got involved. He invited me to the 22nd floor of 30 Rock, where all the executives breathed rarefied air. He brought me into a conference room, stood at the head of the table, and planted an expensively shod foot on the gleaming surface, putting his crotch squarely in my sight line.

"You're so important to NBC," he said. "It's hard to imagine the place without you."

I directed my gaze northward and said I had loved my time at the network, but the CBS job was an extraordinary opportunity—"for me and for women."

Proving that we could do this, and do it well, meant so much to me. While I secretly wondered if I was really up to it (such a woman thing; has any man in the same position ever wondered that?), I thought maybe I could move the ball forward just a bit for my female compadres.

I KNEW IT WOULD be hard saying goodbye to NBC, my identity and my people for 20 years. I'd miss everything about that place: the Rockefeller Center Christmas tree (that tourist magnet we all secretly bitched about), the apple-cheeked ice-skaters, the red velvet stanchions at the deco elevators, the guards behind their podiums always greeting me exuberantly.

And the things I got to do, the mind-bending encounters. When Vladimir Putin came to town, NBC hosted a dinner at 21. I was seated to his left and took the opportunity to ask why he hadn't cut short his seaside vacation when a Russian submarine sank, killing all 118 sailors aboard. Through a translator, Putin said it wouldn't have made any difference. To which I said, "Perception is everything. At least you would have been seen as a compassionate leader." Putin just stared at me with those beady little eyes.

There was breakfast with my lifelong crush, JFK Jr. We met at a restaurant in Midtown so I could convince him to do an interview with me. He ordered cereal with fruit, and out came cornflakes topped with cubes of honeydew. We laughed—Kennedy had seen everything, but this was a first. (Tragically, the interview would be his last.) I also had the distinct displeasure of an irate Yasser Arafat snapping at me, "Who told you that?" when I asked him about the Palestinian charter that called for the destruction of Israel.

Then there was the time I interviewed King Abdullah and Queen Rania of Jordan at their summer palace in Aqaba. My producer/friend Nicolla—a master at nabbing world leaders for interviews—had spent months cultivating them. Afterward, the king and queen lent us their yacht. The camera crew, Nicolla, and I spent the day swimming and sunning on the Red Sea.

I GATHERED MY "KITCHEN cabinet" in my living room to take their temperature on the whole idea. Lori and Lauren, of course, but also Bob Peterson, an incredibly talented producer/editor I'd known since our days at WRC; producer Matt Lombardi, who infused any piece we did with something fun and special, like interviewing Tom Cruise while we were mountain-biking; Matthew Hiltzik, a personal publicist I had recently hired; and Alan. We plopped on the overstuffed sofas and took a collective breath.

"Welcome, and thank you for coming," I said in a mock-serious tone, as if this were a corporate board meeting. First, I told them about the NBC offer.

"Wow," Matt said. *"Wow."*

We all knew what that would mean: covering big stories, going to major events, scoring huge gets. I could see from my colleagues' expressions that visions of plum assignments were dancing in their heads.

Our conversation turned to the second option: CBS. "How long is the actual newscast, minus the commercials?" Matt asked.

"Twenty-two minutes," said Lori. Matt shot me a look like *You're going to hate that*—knowing I was always negotiating for more time for my stories.

Then Matthew piped up. "You'd be surprised how much damage you can do in 22 minutes."

I told Matt I knew what he was thinking. "But," I said, "I'll have *60 Minutes* to do longer pieces. Besides, Les wants me to do interviews as part of the newscast, so there's that."

Bob reminded me that I was loved at NBC. "Will CBS feel the same?" No one had an answer for that.

The H-word was brought up repeatedly (mostly by me), as in "Guys, this is a chance to make history." I told them I wanted Ellie and Carrie to see that they could do whatever they wanted, that it would be hugely symbolic to have a woman helming the anchor desk on her own.

Finally, Lori weighed in. "I'm not sure this is you. People love your personality. How much personality can you have while reading the news from a teleprompter? It sounds amazing and important going in, but then you have to do the freakin' job!"

I heard her. But ultimately, I knew I'd regret not taking the leap. Here was a chance to have the respect I craved: to be a real journalist, full stop, not a TV personality. I thought of the framed *New Yorker* cartoon that Tom had given me: two middle-aged women are ice-skating, and one says to the other, "Then one day I woke up and just couldn't *do* perky anymore." That's exactly how I felt.

And there was something else: my dad. When I first told him about the possibility, he said, simply, "Oh, my." I kept him apprised every step of the way and could tell how excited he was for me. In terms of our shared dream, this was the mountaintop. How could I not? For both of us.

My mind was made up. It was made up even before we sat down. I was ready for a change, and any cautions or caveats that had come my way hadn't really penetrated—not even one from Warren Beatty. After Jay died, I had become one of his phone pals, with whom he'd engage in long, rambling chats. He told me I was crazy. "Who cares about the evening news? Nobody even watches it," he said. "Mornings are much more important."

I told Warren Beatty to stick to acting.

A BIG ISSUE REMAINED. Moonves was offering $10 million—two-thirds of what I was making at *TODAY* and half of what Jeff was offering. But the morning show was the network's cash cow, raking in $500 million a year. The evening news wasn't printing money like the *TODAY* show. That didn't seem to matter to my mom.

"That's ridiculous," she said flatly. Then, channeling her inner Ari Gold, she said, "Tell him you won't take the job for less than what you're making now."

I've never been particularly motivated by money, but I saw her point and directed Alan to go back to Les. Alan laughed and said he would communicate Elinor Couric's terms. Les bumped up the offer to $15 million.

On April 5th, 2006, we made it official. A gushing press release went out: "With this move," Les said, "our News Division takes yet another giant leap forward."

Not everyone was excited. As I walked by the Brooks Brothers in Rockefeller Center one afternoon, a sweet, elderly security guard did a double take, then asked me plaintively, "Katie, why'd you have to quit us?"

57

Goodbye from Kansas!

WITH NEARLY TWO months left before officially joining CBS, I found myself in a weird bi-network limbo. I wanted to end my run at NBC with all the class the network had shown me. They had always been so generous—for instance, ordering town cars for Jay's funeral and hosting a reception at the Metropolitan Club afterward. But I had accepted a new job and I needed to support my future employer.

Lesley Stahl hosted a "ladies' lunch" in the back room of Michael's, the media hive, attended by the women who'd made it at CBS News—producers, reporters, and a few second-tier executives. In the pioneering class led by Barbara Walters, Lesley had been a TV-news fixture for as far back as I could remember, posing tough questions on *Face the Nation* in her sporty shirtdresses. We knew each other only casually, and I thought it was gracious of her to do this. Everyone seemed genuinely excited to have me on board, although I got a little nervous when Lesley pulled out a note Andy Rooney had asked her to read.

I'd always loved Andy Rooney's wry commentary at the end of *60 Minutes*. But he was as old and temperamental as his Smith Corona and didn't exactly greet the news of my arrival like the Wells Fargo wagon. In fact, a few weeks before the lunch, Andy was on Don Imus's radio show when Imus asked how he felt about the changes at CBS. Andy said he was "not enthusiastic": "I think everybody likes Katie Couric; I mean, how can you not like Katie Couric? But I don't know anybody at CBS News who is pleased that she's coming here."

Oh, boy.

Looking back, perhaps I should have heard the air-raid sirens going off and maybe even run for cover. At the Michael's lunch, though, Andy tried to make amends in the form of a note he'd pounded out on the aforementioned Smith Corona. It read in part:

> *In spite of reports to the contrary, I look forward to your coming to CBS. I did think Bob Schieffer went a little overboard when he said you were the best thing that ever happened to CBS News. Has he forgotten the day they cancelled the Dan Rather / Connie Chung co-anchor experiment?*

Then, in a kicker that would have gotten him in a heap of trouble today:

> *I kiss Lesley when I meet her in the hall now and I hope I get to know you well enough to kiss. I know we have a ways to go.*

These guys.

THE UPFRONTS—THE annual dog-and-pony show where networks parade their upcoming programs and talent for an audience of advertisers—was scheduled for May 15th, two weeks before my last hurrah at *TODAY*. CBS wanted me to be one of their headliners. Jeff Zucker seriously did not, since I was still collecting a paycheck from NBC. But Alan told him it was nonnegotiable. CBS was intent on showing off its new acquisition, making me feel like a car in a Christmas commercial. (At an affiliates' meeting, Les would smugly disclose how he finally got me to say yes: "We drank many bottles of expensive wine on the sofa in my apartment...Don't worry, my wife was in the next room." Hardee-har, Les.)

They asked me to say a few words about how excited I was to start this historic new venture. I wore a black pin-striped Ralph Lauren suit with a bit of a ruffle and just a dash of *Don't fuck with me, fellas*. I felt like I had officially gone to the other side.

Our apartment looked like my neighborhood florist, arrangements of hydrangeas and roses and ranunculus and towering white orchids crowding every surface. Cards and letters were pouring in. Well-wishers ranged from Bono to Claudette Howard from Schenectady. Helen Gurley Brown, *Cosmopolitan* editor and patron saint of sexy single gals everywhere, found a classically Helen Gurley Brown way to celebrate this triumph for women: "You have been such a classy little girl during all the hullabaloo (and there sure has been a lot)." Wrote Nancy Reagan, "God—just think—a whole new world! You get to sleep in—heaven!" Mike Wallace simply asked, "So when do the games begin?"

MAY 31ST, 2006. My last day on the *TODAY* show would be an unabashed victory lap. There were Olympics-scale banners on the plaza emblazoned with my picture, and people holding signs hand-lettered with messages like WE'LL MISS YOU! and GOODBYE FROM KANSAS, KATIE! There were endless clips of news-making interviews, of exotic locales, of my on-air escapades—serving a volleyball, snowboarding, balance-beaming, smoking a stogie with George Burns, shooting pool with Paul Newman, ice-skating with Michelle Kwan, dirty-dancing with Patrick Swayze. Hugh Jackman taught me how to swing a golf club; Liz Taylor showed me how to keep lipstick from getting on my teeth. Then there was Harrison Ford. After our interview, I whispered to his publicist, "Gee, that was like pulling teeth." That afternoon, I got a call from Ford. "I heard you thought I was a bad interview and I just wanted to apologize." I blubbered something about still waters running deep and got off the phone ASAP.

There were interview montages, hairstyle montages (note to self: If you don't look like Winona Ryder, do not cut your hair like Winona Ryder's). I paid my respects to Matt: "I know I'll never have a partner like you again," I said solemnly. "Because...I'll never work with a partner again." (Guffaws from the crew. And Matt.) "But truly, you have just been an extraordinary colleague and a wonderful friend...beneath this well-dressed exterior lies a huge and loving heart and I'm gonna miss you so much."

Then it was Matt's turn.

"They call us co-anchors and I hate it," he said. "I hate the term. We're *partners,* and we have been partners over these last 10 years—13 years in total—in every way possible..."

Wait, what?

Matt: Not that way!
Me: Wait a second...
Matt: That would be a little weird...
Al Roker: Page Six!

NBC THREW AN AFTER-PARTY at a rooftop space on 5th Avenue with champagne, canapés, and the neo-Gothic spires of St. Patrick's Cathedral jutting dramatically in the background. (Frankly, I was a little sick of Katie-mania by that point, although if anyone else was, they were nice enough not to show it.) The minute it wrapped up, Matthew Hiltzik and I had to fly to Las Vegas for a meeting with the CBS affiliates.

And just like that, after all those wonderful years at NBC, I was officially an employee of CBS News.

But due to a mechanical problem, we sat on the runway for four hours.

I passed the time with three bags of peanuts and two vodka sodas, joking a little nervously with Matthew about our failure to launch: "Do you think this is a bad omen?"

PART IV

58

The Dairy Depot

WITH MY FIRST evening news broadcast slated for September 5th, 2006, I had roughly three months to prepare. I dropped by the newsroom to introduce myself to the rest of CBS. It was cordial; the group seemed receptive, if a little reserved. I had no idea how on edge everyone was, how much raw paranoia was zinging around that place about the existential threat I apparently posed to their way of life.

Having worked at pretty much every network throughout my career, I learned that each has a unique personality. ABC is the slickest and shiniest, suffering from a slight inferiority complex because it's the newest kid on the block. NBC feels more urbane—proudly responsible for the winning team Chet Huntley and David Brinkley (my dad's and my onetime alter egos), followed by owlish, erudite John Chancellor. But NBC never took itself so seriously that it couldn't put a chimpanzee in the morning mix (J. Fred Muggs, the *TODAY* show, 1953–57).

Neither network would ever be described as venerable—that distinction went to CBS. It had been built from the ground up by the dynastic Paley family; Murrow, then Cronkite, brought dignity, decency, and heft.

The whole enterprise was so serious-minded, so immune to any kind of flashiness, that even creature comforts were an afterthought. Consider that the squat, industrial CBS Broadcast Center was once a dairy depot, where cows were processed and milked; the ramps used to transport them had never been dismantled. In the early '60s, they somehow converted the place into a news hub.

With their buzzing fluorescent lights and leftover rotary phones, the offices felt a bit like the FDA circa 1972. The halls were scattered with cardboard boxes, and random wires hung from the ceiling panels. There were rumors of mice in the control room and tobacco stains on the carpet from when Dan Rather missed the spittoon. The aesthetic was *Columbo*—trench coats and rumpled button-down shirts, versus the pricey suits guys wore at 30 Rock. It was a big change, but I admired the let's-get-down-to-the-business-of-journalism aura.

Although I did draw the line at the outdated, borderline-disgusting bathrooms near the entrance of the building (which were probably unchanged since Andy Rooney's first day). I went to Sean McManus and said, "Do you think it would be possible to upgrade the facilities?" It felt like a good use of my capital, sending a message about my desire to improve and modernize the place. A few months after my arrival, the stalls got an overhaul.

The team I'd brought with me from NBC—Lori, Bob, Matt, Nicolla, and Lauren—were ready to get to work. The network knew they were coming; they'd negotiated contracts, and their names and titles were stipulated in my contract too. But they were told there was no room at the inn by the broadcast manager, who'd been at the network in various roles for a quarter century. Her solution was to house some of them in a 9 x 12 space with no phone lines and a plastic folding table until she could find something permanent. Maybe she didn't like the fact that I had my own people...people like British-born Nicolla, whose statuesque, blinged-out fabulousness made her even more of a foreigner at that place.

My office was up a stairway on the second floor. Just outside was a balcony from which one could peer down on the newsroom—not a great look for someone staffers might have thought was on her high horse.

When Dan Rather had the office, it was dark and mannish—heavy furniture, a Royal typewriter on the desk (for show), a camo shirt from his days covering Vietnam. He kept a Bible on a pedestal; I heard he read a verse before every broadcast.

I enlisted a high-end designer friend to feminize the space. And soon, all traces of Dan were gone—during the renovation, they even hauled out his desk, chopped it up, and threw it in a dumpster. (We were all thinking, *Shouldn't that go to the Smithsonian or something?*)

The new look was something out of *The Devil Wears Prada:* glass desk with a stainless-steel base and a chic glass globe sitting on top; white leather chairs. The back area where Dan would huddle with his producers was transformed into a hair and makeup room, with a closet for several changes of clothes, like we had at *TODAY.* On the walls, black-and-white photos of trailblazing women—Amelia Earhart, Wilma Rudolph, Sally Ride. The office was chic and smart and would have looked right at home at NBC. But at West 57th, it stuck out like a Givenchy gown at a hoedown. A really dumb move on my part—one of many unforced errors.

Extreme Makeover: Office Edition bolstered the narrative that had been established before I'd even walked through the door. That $15 million salary had (of course) been leaked to the press, landing in a *Newsweek* cover story back in April.

The fact is, my salary *was* a story: the biggest paycheck in network news at the time. Now rumors were flying that some CBS staffers—and even stars—would have to take pay cuts as a result (notably Lesley Stahl, who I heard was furious and promptly resigned as president of my fan club). I never found out who the leaker was—possibly Alan Berger's agency, CAA, hoping to lure more clients, or maybe just some guy in Accounting. Whether or not the cost-cutting measures actually had to do with me, that's how people saw it.

WE WOULD NEED a new theme song. Bob Peterson, who was now the show's creative director, hired James Horner, the Academy Award–winning composer of soaring soundtracks for movies like *Field of Dreams, Titanic,* and *Apollo 13.* I suggested something Aaron Copland–esque, evoking amber waves of grain rather than the Manhattan skyline.

The result was both lilting and majestic, full of French horns, snare drums, and strings.

We also needed to reimagine the set. Bob had ordered a giant, curved flat-screen that would hang behind my left shoulder and be used for B-roll during opens as well as interviews with correspondents; it was radically new technology that didn't come cheap. And he commissioned a long, gleaming desk that perched on a platform; it had a monitor on the front that displayed graphic elements, like stock prices, and LED lights that changed colors. Embedded in the surface of the desk was flattering up-lighting (thank you, Bob).

We brainstormed how to change up the beginning of the show, including who might be the right person to announce me. Bob had an inspired suggestion: "How about Walter Cronkite?"

I loved the idea. Despite being from a very different era, he was the ultimate newsman, a towering figure who would bring a sense of continuity and the implication of endorsement, which we knew we'd need as we tried to win the viewers' trust.

He'd become a big supporter of mine both publicly and personally, inviting me to dinner shortly after I joined CBS. We'd met at the Pool Room at the Four Seasons; he brought along his lady friend, Joanna Simon, sister of Carly. I couldn't wait to pick Walter's brain about covering some of the biggest events in history. I really wanted to know how he was able to be such a symbol of fairness and objectivity. He told me, "I know I'm being fair when everybody's mad at me."

We talked about everything from my father's career at United Press to *American Idol*. We were having a wonderful time—that would have been more wonderful if Walter knew what I was saying; at 89, he struggled with his hearing, and the bubbling fountain abutting our table didn't help. I was practically screaming at him; Joanna cupped her hands around her mouth and repeated everything I said into Walter's ear. For so many reasons, it was a night I'll never forget.

He'd been retired for a while, and we thought he might get a kick out of recording the announcement. Bob and I called him from the back seat of my car.

"Hi, Walter, it's Katie Couric!" I said loudly. "I have a big favor to ask: Would you be willing to voice the new open? It would mean so much to me."

Cronkite replied, "Of course."

"Would you?" I said in disbelief.

"Of course, Katie, I'd be honored."

He would be honored?

Bob flew out to California to record the open. The problem was, Walter mispronounced my last name on every take, rhyming the first syllable with *door* rather than *her*. Finally, Bob said, "It's Katie *Kerr*-ick. Think of Steve Kerr" (a basketball player, apparently). Bob requested a few more takes. Slightly exasperated ("Now, listen, young man"), Walter acquiesced, and they nailed it (more or less).

SEAN MCMANUS HAD tapped Rome Hartman to be the executive producer. Rome emanated decency, and I was excited to work with him—despite the fact that he'd never helmed a nightly newscast before.

Determined to innovate the broadcast, we had endless meetings around a conference table, spitballing ideas. I pitched a weekly segment called "Free Speech," where we'd invite a variety of people, from politicians to pundits to everyday citizens, to weigh in on an issue they felt passionately about. The TV version of an op-ed.

Sean's number two, network news veteran Paul Friedman, piped up. "Why not do 'Free Speech' every night?"

Everybody thought that was a great idea. Privately, I had to wonder if we really could pull it off.

In August I spent a couple of weeks hanging out in the Hamptons with the girls to fortify myself. I'd sworn off sweets, determined to look as good as possible for my debut (I even turned down a piece of cake at my dad's 86th-birthday party—a literal first). Imagine my surprise when I learned I had miraculously dropped 20 pounds.

A heavily photoshopped picture of me from the upfronts had landed on the cover of *Watch!,* the CBS promotional magazine. Turns out some bonehead in the photo department had gone rogue. An eagle-eyed *New*

York Post staffer realized something was awry (respect). They published humiliating side-by-side photos; someone gleefully wrote that I'd gone on the "photoshop diet." (A year and a half later, a clueless speaker gave a lecture to Carrie's sixth-grade class on female objectification and used that very photo as an example of body-shaming in the media. How fun for Carrie that her mom was exhibit A.)

Given my practically lifelong struggle with weight, the whole thing hit me in a very vulnerable place. I hadn't even officially started at CBS and already I was at the center of a mini-scandal. The first in a series of unfortunate events.

59

Tick Tick Tick Tick

I WALKED INTO THE reception area at *60 Minutes,* located across the street from the Broadcast Center. What a thrill to see a huge stopwatch affixed to the wall. A senior producer named Michael Radutzky, who resembled Timon, the meerkat in *The Lion King,* gave me a tour. We stopped by offices and cubicles where he introduced me to producers, researchers, and assistants. As we walked down the hall, he casually shared the show's ethos. "The mantra here at *60 Minutes* is 'Someone else's success diminishes you. Someone else's failure elevates you.'"

I'm about as competitive as they come, but seriously?

A few days later, I was summoned back to the offices for a photo shoot. I was directed to a cavernous space where Bob Simon, Morley Safer, Steve Kroft, and Lesley Stahl were waiting. I wished I had brought a parka. I'd never gotten such a chilly reception anywhere for anything. No eye contact, no small talk, no nothing.

Jeff Fager, the executive producer of *60 Minutes,* ran the place like a fiefdom, with its own culture and self-serious identity. At first he seemed happy to have me. He gave me an office, which I really appreciated. But he didn't give me a team. Every other correspondent had one, researching stories and submitting "blue sheets," the system they used to determine who got there first and who would get to do the piece. But Fager decided I didn't need a team, despite the fact that I had another full-time job—anchoring the evening news. Instead, he said Radutzky would oversee my stories, and there would be a few other producers who would work with me on an ad hoc basis.

Okay, I thought. *Let's see how it goes.*

THE GEARS OF a massive PR campaign were cranking away. I did a ton of media, speed-dating a long line of reporters in 20-minute intervals, all asking the same questions. I was effusive with each one. When I voiced my concern to Matthew Hiltzik about all the press I was doing, he said, "Look, they're gonna write about you anyway; you might as well try to keep some control of the narrative."

In addition to print and TV stories and spots I'd taped with 48 different affiliates to run on local stations, my smiling (but warmly authoritative!) mug was plastered on the front of city buses—my stomach lurched every time I saw one lumbering and belching up the street. The launch was anything but soft. Expectations were sky-high.

Who knew that just a few months into the job, I would fantasize about being run over by one of those buses, the perfect O. Henry ending.

60

KC and the Sunshine Band

IF THE PAST few months had taught me anything, it was that everything I did my first night as news anchor would be under a white-hot spotlight. Starting with what I wore.

I asked Avril Graham, the fashion editor of *Harper's Bazaar,* to help me figure out "the look." We were going for serious yet accessible, classic but not boring, and nothing too feminine or sexy, which meant no pink, no shine, no ruffles, no bows, no froufrou, no unbuttoned buttons. And nothing too masculine; it was important that I wore clothes that didn't wear me. Avril brought in a rack of options.

We liked a white Armani jacket with a streamlined absence of lapels. "Is it really okay to wear white after Labor Day?" I asked, knowing there were rules about such things. But Avril waved off my concern. The jacket looked fresh, and it popped. Underneath, I wore a textured black shell and simple black skirt. Black pumps, pearl earrings. Who could find fault with that? For good luck, Avril suggested I wear a piece of jewelry from Jay, so I picked an antique gold bracelet he'd given me for my birthday.

Two hours before the broadcast, I settled into the makeup chair near the newsroom (my pimped-out dressing room was still under construction). The place crackled with nervous energy. Bob kept coming by, asking in his hyper-staccato way, "How's it going? How ya doin'?," referring to us all as KC and the Sunshine Band.

Since my hair had been such a focus in the past, we kept it simple here—a layered bob with a side part, bangs brushed across my forehead. My makeup artist, Josie Torres, was super-anxious, knowing that every eyelash would be scrutinized—as she put it to me recently, "We were on high alert. The press always criticizes women, and this was a really big night for women. None of us wanted to give them any ammunition."

At around 5:45, I was putting the finishing touches on my scripts when Rome and his wife, Amy, approached.

"Can we go upstairs for a minute?" Rome said.

I assumed they wanted to give me a pep talk. We climbed the carpeted steps to my office. Rome closed the door behind us.

Then he and Amy extended their hands.

"Let's pray," Rome said.

Wait, what?

They closed their eyes and bowed their heads. "Dear God, please help Katie, give her support and protection..." Then Rome asked God for a couple of other things.

I was surprised but also touched. While the network no longer wanted the *voice* of God, I wasn't opposed to a little divine intervention. Whatever worked. When Rome said, "Amen," I thanked them both— all three of them, I guess—and darted out, hoping some powerful force was with me.

EVERYTHING WE DID that night was intentional. For instance: Should I be sitting behind the desk at the open? Should I walk and talk? Should I stand? Ultimately, we split the difference, deciding I should start out standing in front of the desk, then take one small step (for womankind) before speaking.

But when I spoke, what would I say?

I settled on something radical: Instead of the traditional anchorman's "Good evening," I'd say, "Hi, everyone." Because who besides maître d's and Count Dracula says, "Good evening"? I wanted to talk the way people actually talk. The way I talk.

I started with the headlines, including a report from Afghanistan, "a gusher in the Gulf," and what it would mean for viewers at the pump. Then a "Free Speech" segment featuring Morgan Spurlock of *Super Size Me* fame on our increasingly polarized political discourse. And finally, for a new feature we called "Snap Shots," exclusive photos of newborn Suri Cruise, daughter of Tom Cruise and Katie Holmes.

Thump-thump, thump-thump—I thought my heart might leap out of my chest and land on my script. Somehow, muscle memory kicked in and I got through the 22 minutes without fumbling, stumbling, or throwing up. When we faded to black, I flung my script in the air as producers, assignment editors, and the crew came out from the shadows and clapped.

My friends had organized a viewing party on the roof of the Hudson Hotel a few blocks away. A hundred and fifty people were there, from old friends to boldface names: Tony Bennett, Connie Chung, Phil Donahue. David Kiernan and his wife, my dear friend Mandy, came from DC. At one point I saw David gazing up at Iman. He asked her what she did for a living. "I'm a model," she said. "Maybe you know my husband—David Bowie?"

Everybody cheered as I walked in and continued cheering as I headed straight to the bar and ordered my first cosmopolitan. Lauren grabbed my hand and pulled me toward the dance floor. Dancing was always our favorite way to blow off steam. We were having a great time doing some of our signature moves, like the Lotion, where we acted out dispensing some in our hands, rubbing them together, and slathering it all over our bodies. During yet another moment of post-show revelry, someone snapped a photo of me vogue-ing—hands on thighs, slightly hiking up my skirt—something I imagine neither Dan Rather nor Bob Schieffer ever did, at least not in public.

Ellie innocently posted several pictures from the night on Facebook. Someone grabbed one and sold it to *Gawker*. Lovely.

Meanwhile, most of the CBS folks were standing awkwardly on the periphery, watching us. It felt like the debate team looking down on the Breakfast Club.

Screw it, I thought. *I'm going to have fun.*

* * *

THE NEXT DAY at about 11:00 a.m., Sean McManus showed up in the fishbowl—the glassed-off work area where the people in charge sat. Typically reserved, bordering on diffident, he was now more animated than I'd ever seen him. Sean announced the ratings had just come out: We'd drawn 13.6 million viewers—up 86 percent from the previous year.

An elated Rome was standing next to Sean. "Doesn't it feel good to be number one?" he said to the newsroom. *Too soon,* I thought.

As the ratings came in, so did the criticism. Some focused on the new elements: We had shown a clip of Douglas Edwards debuting a photo of baby Prince Charles before revealing our Suri Cruise picture, "as if there were a grand tradition of baby pictures at the Tiffany network," my old friend Alessandra Stanley sniveled. Tom Shales, who'd been such a fan since I started at the *TODAY* show, declared that "Free Speech" was "the oldest idea in television: Have some well-known or obscure blowhard pop up and do a rant into the camera." Some critics claimed I lacked "gravitas," which I decided was Latin for *testicles.*

But the headline was what I wore. Shales opined that my blazer "buttoned in such a way as to make her look chubby, bursting at the button, which we know she isn't. It was a poor choice." Regarding my decision to wear white after Labor Day, that fashion arbiter, the *New York Sun,* admitted it "isn't a fashion crime anymore. But if Katie Couric really wanted us to focus on her reporting rather than her wardrobe, she shouldn't have flouted one of the oldest rules in the book." Keith Olbermann said my face looked Botoxed.

In terms of the format, I thought we were doing what Les had brought me there to do. Looking back, just having an anchor wearing lipstick would have been jarring enough; the changes we made were too much too soon. Standing at the top of the broadcast, axing "Good evening," leaning casually against the anchor desk and sharing a celebrity baby pic, doing video opinion pieces—it all amounted to sacrilege.

One bright spot was a downright chivalrous defense by the *Columbia Journalism Review* critiquing the critiques: "At least nine separate reporters noted the visibility of Couric's 'legendary' or 'famous' or 'celebrated' legs—startled, apparently, by the reality that when professional women forgo pantsuits for blazers and skirts, their legs *will* be visible. (For comparison, we had to look long and hard to find any media mentions of Brian Williams' physical appearance the morning after he inherited the *NBC Nightly News*)."

Unfortunately, the *CJR* isn't the megaphone the other media columns are. Still, I wanted to kiss the writer, Liz Cox Barrett, whoever she was, on the mouth.

61

... And I'm Katie Couric

I WENT BACK AGAIN and again to Radutzky's comment about what a backstabbing place *60 Minutes* was. But the more I thought about it, the more I realized that was just part of the show's fabled DNA. Don Hewitt was known to pit correspondents against one another, believing that fomenting intense competition yields the best work. I'd heard about the screaming fights and bare-knuckle politics. The standards were high; the margin for error wafer-thin. Membership in this exclusive club didn't come easy. It's hard to imagine now, but when veterans Lesley Stahl and Steve Kroft started out, executives held emergency meetings and complained bitterly that they weren't making enough of a splash. The place was notorious for hazing.

Yes, I knew *60 Minutes* was going to be a tough nut to crack. But I wasn't a kid—I figured my 15 years at *TODAY,* with my proven track record of scoring big gets and doing tough interviews, put me in a pretty solid position to win them over.

I was excited about my first piece, which I'd pitched. I wanted to explore why so many workers on "the pile"—the pulverized remnants from tons of steel and concrete crashing to the ground on 9/11—were getting deathly ill from the lead, asbestos, and PCBs that had been released into the air. I couldn't understand why the authorities weren't doing more to help the heroic first responders. A wonderful producer named Kyra Darnton would work with me on the piece.

Christine Todd Whitman had been the head of the EPA during 9/11 and faced a lot of scrutiny for not sounding the alarm early enough. Kyra and others didn't think she'd make herself available for an on-camera interview, but I thought I could get her to talk. I'd interviewed Whitman, the former governor of New Jersey, before and knew she liked me. So I reached out, then drove to her home in the Garden State to close the deal. I remember Kyra being excited by how involved I was willing to be in the booking process.

But I undercut my own legwork when I asked a freelance cameraman I knew from NBC to shoot the interview. I liked the way he lit me— an asset, given the *60 Minutes* style of shooting faces so tight you could practically count Steve Kroft's nose hairs. But still...another unforced error, advancing the idea that I required special treatment.

We called the piece "The Dust at Ground Zero." I remember how specific the notes were about how I should narrate the piece—to be conversational and subdued, not anchor-y. (Years later, when Oprah came on board as a correspondent, they so micromanaged the way she said her own name—repeatedly urging her to take the emotion out of it—that she decided to part ways with the program. As if Oprah needs coaching on how to communicate with an audience.)

Kyra convinced Jeff Fager to run the story in two parts. The first one aired the Sunday after my evening-news debut.

The girls and I tuned in. The piece was smooth, well reported, impactful. Although my favorite part came before my story, during the iconic intro: "I'm Ed Bradley"; "I'm Steve Kroft"; "I'm Lesley Stahl"; "I'm Scott Pelley"; "I'm Morley Safer"...

"And I'm Katie Couric. Those stories and Andy Rooney, tonight on *60 Minutes.*"

Jeff Fager sent a congratulatory email. My first piece was a success. If I was getting pummeled on the *Evening News,* perhaps Sunday nights would be the place where I could shine.

My next piece was a profile of Secretary of State Condoleezza Rice.

I'd interviewed her many times on *TODAY,* but this was an opportunity to go deeper, wider.

She defended the U.S. strategy of bringing democracy to Iraq by referencing racist tropes from the civil rights era. Rice saw a parallel between the misinformed idea that Iraqis simply weren't equipped to embrace democracy and the ignorant notion that Black people "really can't handle the vote."

"It makes me so angry," Rice said, "because I think there are those echoes."

I pressed her on WMDs and the faulty intelligence that propelled us into war. But I also wanted to access Rice's personal side. For this to be an in-depth profile, I'd have to get past her guarded facade. "Is it hard for you to have a social life? How does one go about asking the secretary of state out on a date?" And here I playfully held a finger-phone to my ear. " 'Hi, Madame Secretary, listen...' "

Which made Rice laugh.

We also got some great B-roll of a determined Condi in shorts and a T-shirt on an elliptical in her bedroom (she rose at 5:00 a.m. six days a week to work out to Led Zeppelin or Cream) and playing Schumann and Brahms on the piano with four friends on strings, something they did regularly.

Tough questions, personal insights, surprising moments. I thought we nailed it. Although this time the *Columbia Journalism Review* was less impressed, ignoring the serious conversation we'd had and portraying the interview as something befitting *Entertainment Tonight:* "The questions seemed more appropriate for someone like, say, Scarlett Johansson, rather than someone intimately involved in shaping our foreign policy in the wake of 9/11... To the head honchos at CBS News, we have one thing to say: Good night, and good luck." Clever!

That was nothing compared with the fire hose of derision aimed at me following my interview with John and Elizabeth Edwards. In March of 2007, Elizabeth went public with the dire news that her cancer had metastasized to her bones—and yet she had decided to continue the taxing work of campaigning for her husband in his quest for the

Democratic presidential nomination. This set off a coast-to-coast conversation about women, ambition, mortality, choices, and parenting. All issues I knew a lot about.

The morning of our interview, an article had come out in the *New York Times* analyzing Elizabeth's decision: "Some people—as demonstrated by responses to blogs and other forums—believe the Edwardses are stealing time from each other and their children, while others see a couple that has weathered the tribulations and assaults life brings to most families." For better or worse (worse), that sentence lodged in my head and became the template for my interview.

I intended to get to the heart of this deeply personal matter. But what was supposed to be a serious inquiry about their decision to stay the course came across as a heartless inquisition:

> Me: Some say, "Isn't it wonderful they care for something greater
> than themselves?" And others say, "It's a case of insatiable
> ambition." You say?...Some people watching this would say,
> "[I] would put my family first, always, and my job second."
> And you're doing the exact opposite. You're putting your work
> first, and your family second...Some have suggested that
> you're capitalizing on this.

You'd think I would have had particular empathy, given the losses I'd suffered from the same disease. But there I was, hammering away at their choices. I seem cold, callous. I can understand why people were irate. Here's a small sample of the comments from the *New York Times* blog:

> Some say Katie Couric should have quit her job to take care of her
> young daughters while her husband was fighting colon cancer.
> Some say Katie Couric is a no-talent hack who is an embarrass-
> ment to real journalists everywhere.

> Why o why have a lightweight like Katie Couric doing this type of
> interview. Wasn't the circus in town?

Edward R. Murrow must be spinning in the grave.

Once I picked myself up off the floor, I tried to analyze what was going on with me during this interview. I have a few theories: Perhaps I was reacting to the questioning of my seriousness, given that I had been a "morning-show host"—trying to compensate by being hard-nosed in a situation that warranted sensitivity. Maybe it was a subconscious reaction to criticism that I should have been tougher on Condi Rice. Or maybe when I read that paragraph in the typically beyond-reproach *New York Times* that started with "Some people," I thought it gave me permission to use the same squishy, non-journalistic device. Perhaps I was channeling my own guilt over Jay.

Elizabeth wrote me a lovely note assuring me she understood why I had to ask the questions I did. But the whole thing still stings. If I could have just one do-over, this would be it.

62

She's Toast

THE HEAT WAS on. Never in my working life had I been more in need of a diversion when the cameras weren't rolling.

After Tom's charming "Dear Katie" email, I had a steamy fling with jazz trumpeter Chris Botti. He was as sweet as he was cool, a good friend of Sting who worshipped Miles Davis. But two months in, when a paparazzo shot of us looking cozy at a Knicks game hit the tabloids, Tom came calling. He dumped me again after a couple of months. (A few years later, he popped up and presented me with a small velvet box over lunch. Inside, a giant chunk of cubic zirconia. Tom giggled, vowing there was a real diamond where that came from. Sad.)

In my final months at *TODAY,* I'd been seeing a guy named Jimmy Reyes—divorced with two kids, worked in his family's hugely successful liquor-distribution business. Jimmy had actually been engaged not long before we were set up—to Laura Ingraham. Yes, that Laura Ingraham. I couldn't imagine how one man could be attracted to two so radically different women. Granted, Jimmy was a Republican, but Ingraham, then a right-wing radio pundit, was next-level. (Once, after a breakup, she shoved a garden hose into an ex-boyfriend's mail slot in an attempt to flood his house. Adding insult to injury, he was apparently in the process of refinishing his hardwood floors.)

Jimmy was busy, I was busy, but when he came to New York or I went to Washington, it was nice to have a companion. The relationship was no-drama, which is exactly what I needed.

AS I PREDICTED, our big ratings the first day had been driven by curiosity. Now, as they sank to pre–Bob Schieffer levels, anxiety at CBS rose. The press was relentless, and a sense of *She's toast* started seeping into the newsroom. Sean had stopped coming by the fishbowl to inquire about last night's newscast with a hopeful "How'd we do?" The fantasy that I would come in and miraculously put CBS in first place had faded.

I started to dread going in. Each morning, I'd put on an invisible suit of armor over some inoffensive outfit and push through the glass doors on West 57th Street, braced for whatever heat-seeking missile was headed my way.

A month into my new role, a milk-truck driver entered a one-room Amish schoolhouse in Lancaster, Pennsylvania, with wire, plastic ties, sexual lubricant, and a small arsenal. He dismissed the 15 male students, bound the remaining 11 girls' ankles, and barricaded the door. Then he opened fire, killing four of the girls, ages 7 to 13 (another died at the hospital the next day).

It was depraved. And the third fatal shooting at an American school *that week*. I wanted to go to the scene—I knew that dispatching the anchor would help convey the horrific magnitude of the story. And it was precisely the kind of raw human tragedy that I'd become adept at covering.

"I should grab a crew and go down there right now," I said to Rome and the other producers sitting in the bowl, following the developments. "We can be in Lancaster in two and a half hours—we'll broadcast live from there."

Their vague nonresponse said it all. I could tell they were nervous about doing anything out of the ordinary, anything that might open us up to more criticism. "I think we should just cover it from here," Rome said in a better-safe-than-sorry kind of way.

Under normal circumstances, I would have pushed back; I was managing editor of the broadcast, after all. And yet I was starting to doubt my own judgment.

So I let it go. Later that night, when I glanced at the monitors, you can only imagine how it felt to see a somber Charlie Gibson anchoring ABC's *World News Tonight* from Lancaster.

The story reverberated across the country and was still very much in the headlines the next day. I decided it would be valuable to hear from someone who had experienced a similar tragedy.

Brian Rohrbough had lost his son Daniel in the Columbine massacre seven years earlier; I'd met him while covering the story for NBC. So I reached out and asked if he'd be willing to do a "Free Speech" segment about trauma and getting through tragedies like this.

We arranged with the Denver affiliate to tape Rohrbough; they'd feed us the video at 4:45. So there we were at 4:46—me, Rome, everyone, standing around watching the commentary as it came in—our jaws dropping as Rohrbough's attempt to grapple with yet another school shooting turned into a creationist, pro-life diatribe: "For over two generations, the public school system has taught in a moral vacuum... replacing Him with evolution... Abortion has diminished the value of children..."

Surprise turned to panic. The segment was guaranteed to bring more bad press, but what choice did we have? It was called "Free Speech," for God's sake. Were we seriously going to muzzle people in a segment called "Free Speech"? That sounded like a recipe for *really* bad press. So we went with it.

Incensed viewers took to the CBS website:

> Your free speech segment today was the biggest load of hogwash I have ever witnessed. How could you use an unspeakable tragedy to give a rightwing flat earth nut job a podium?

Then I got hammered from the other side for a blog post I wrote saying we knew that some might find Rohrbough's views "repugnant."

Gee, it had seemed like such a good idea. In retrospect, I wish

I had called Brian Rohrbough and said that while I appreciated his commentary, it wasn't really about school shootings.

After that fiasco, we decided to only let people speak their minds once a week, before deciding that we the people of CBS didn't have the constitution for "Free Speech."

"Free Speech" was dead.

63

So Hawt

WHEN I FIRST came to New York, I was a DIY / Loving Care kind of girl, until I realized I needed professional help. I started going to the lively Louis Licari salon on 5th Avenue. Louis is a doll, so in late October when he hosted a cancer fundraiser at the salon, I wanted to be there for him.

When I walked in, I immediately noticed someone standing at the makeshift bar: six foot one, dirty-blond hair, wearing one of those shirts with a band at the neck in place of a collar. "Who's that?" I whispered to Leigh, a freckle-faced brunette who did publicity for Louis.

"Right?" Leigh said in her Brooklyn accent. "He's so hawt!"

She gave me the lowdown: His name was Brooks Perlin. Super-WASPy, ran a hedge fund (which it turned out he didn't, although at the time, I admit it made him even more attractive). Loaded. (Even better, but again, not true.) Apparently, he and Louis did triathlons together.

I made my way to his general vicinity. When I got to the table, Brooks grabbed a cup of white wine, handed it to me, and smiled.

We made the smallest of small talk before I drifted away and started to circulate. When a good song came on, one of the male hairdressers and I started dancing a little. I was wearing a navy knit dress with a leather belt, and, as the kids would say, I was feeling myself. I sensed Brooks was checking me out.

A few days later, Leigh called and said Brooks was asking for my number. I told her to go ahead and give it to him, without thinking too much about it. I had other things on my mind—like continued public humiliation and the potential loss of employment.

In fact, when Brooks did call, I was so preoccupied with all the trouble at CBS that I didn't get back to him right away. So he called again. When I finally responded, he actually said, "I can't believe you didn't call me back!"

Clearly, he wasn't intimidated.

Brooks suggested we get together. "Do you want to do a sailboat race with me next weekend?"

Uh, no, thanks.

"How about rock climbing? Or we could go for a run in Central Park."

Maybe I looked like I was in better shape than I actually was. "Do you work for Outward Bound?" I joked. Dinner sounded a lot less strenuous, so we made a date for the following week.

At a Greek restaurant, in my usual third-wheel position with my friends Pat and Mark Shifke, I told them I had a date coming up that I was kind of excited about.

"Who is he?" Mark asked. Having lived through so many of my romantic escapades, they felt a certain investment in my love life. I also think they were eager for me to finally find someone so they wouldn't have to hear yet another chorus of "Breakin' Up Is Hard to Do" (and even harder to listen to).

"I actually don't know much about him," I said.

"Why don't you just google him?" Pat suggested. It was 2006—googling wasn't yet something you did 87 times a day.

"You do it, Mark!" I said.

Mark squinted at his BlackBerry. "Okay, got him. He's from Darien...he works at a hedge fund. Went to Williams...he was on the tennis team...he was actually *captain* of the tennis team..." Pause. "In 1996."

We did the math. I had a date with someone 32 years old. Seventeen years younger than me.

I was stunned, then slightly titillated. "Oh my God," I said. "Should I even go on this date?"

Then I answered my own question. "Why not? It could be fun."

Pat and Mark looked less enthusiastic.

"Hey," I added, "if I ever write a book, it'll make a great chapter!"

64

Lasagna Was Served

BROOKS AND I had our first date at Raoul's in SoHo. We ran through the standard get-to-know-you topics—work, college, childhood, family. He was easy to talk to. I liked the fact that he seemed close to his parents (they were his cheerleading squad at triathlons). And did I mention Brooks was handsome? I knew I wanted to see him again, but Jimmy was still in the picture.

The girls really liked Jimmy—he happily shuttled Ellie and her friends around the Hamptons before they had their licenses, and Carrie, at 10 years old, basked in the male attention. One night, while all of us were in the kitchen at the apartment, Jimmy was tossing walnuts for Carrie to catch in her mouth; she kept dissolving in giggles as they bounced off her cheek. In the middle of it all, Brooks called. I took the phone into the other room.

"You have to go outside," he said.

"What?"

"You have to go outside and look at the moon. It's a huge, orange harvest moon—it's incredible. You've got to go see it."

I told Jimmy and the girls I needed to walk Maisy and ran to the end of the block, where I could see the moon glowing above the rooftops. Brooks was right—it was incredible. The bright orange ball illuminating the city made me swoon.

That January, I was throwing myself the mother of all birthday parties. I worshipped Audrey Hepburn and couldn't think of anywhere I'd rather celebrate the big 5-0 than at Tiffany's on 5th Avenue. I wore a little black dress, with an out-of-character scoop neck that showed off my cleavage, and long, black satin gloves. Tiffany's had loaned me a diamond-studded tiara worthy of the royal family; it came with two burly security guards who were never far from view. The waiters served trays of "Tiffaninis" (a martini-type cocktail the color of Ty-D-Bol), mini–Maryland crab cakes, filet mignon on French bread, and that perpetual crowd-pleaser, pigs in a blanket.

Salespeople were stationed at the jewelry cases on the expansive first floor to help guests try on serious bling. Barbara Walters, Regis Philbin, Al Roker, and Jeff Zucker were there. Flipping through the pictures, I see Les Moonves and Matt Lauer were there too, wearing big, prelapsarian grins, oblivious to what their futures held. I'm looking pretty smiley too—you'd never know that at the time, my day-to-day existence was a dumpster fire.

Dinner and dancing happened on five. Bette Midler sang another Marc Shaiman ditty, this one to the tune of "Moon River": *Ms. Couuur-ic grew up on TV / but now AARP wants youuu…*

The Jersey Boys crooned "Big Girls Don't Cry" and Tony Bennett capped it all off with "The Way You Look Tonight." Dessert was a giant birthday cake in the shape of three stacked Tiffany boxes, along with single-serving blue-box cakes for each guest. And everyone took home an actual Tiffany pillbox. Ellie, Carrie, and I still keep ours on our dressers, and every time I look at mine I think of that spectacular night.

Jimmy had been there, hanging close by the bar while I flitted around. A week or so later, I went to DC to cover the State of the Union. He met me at the Hay-Adams afterward for a drink at the basement bar, Off the Record. Then we rode the elevator to my floor. At the door, I conveyed that I thought the state of *our* union was *not* strong…I said that I really liked him but that I didn't think we were a long-term thing.

Jimmy was so nice about it; I'm sure he already knew.

"Want me to come in?" he said, I assumed for one last roll in the Hay-Adams.

"I don't think that's such a good idea," I said, laughing, and gave him a hug.

Men.

WHEN CARRIE AND I baked cupcakes topped with gummy worms, I'd bring a few to Brooks's man-pad in the East Fifties. We played tennis and rode bikes in the park, even though he was one of those dudes who wore Lance Armstrong–y performance gear and kept yelling at me for not staying in his "draft." We even went rock climbing. I was horrified afterward to see the photos he had taken of me gamely ascending, my butt in a harness. (Not a good angle, ladies.)

After a lifetime of trashing older guys for squiring around much-younger arm candy, I had become the female version. I'd tell my girlfriends, "You know, watching Brooks walk around like Michelangelo's *David* in boxer shorts really takes the edge off." In Miami Beach, when the paparazzi showed up, I was more than happy for them to snap photos of him while I stayed Krazy-Glued to my chaise, clutching magazines and a beach bag to my midsection.

His nickname in college was "Woody," as in Woody from *Cheers*—he could be a little spacey. But he was sweet and fun, like a golden retriever, and completely unfazed by the fame part of my job, more than happy to be my plus-one at fundraisers, black-tie galas ... even dinner at Jeffrey Epstein's.

Let me explain. Peggy Siegal, Manhattan's PR doyenne, had billed it as an evening honoring Prince Andrew at the "largest single-family dwelling" in New York City. At the time, Jeffrey Epstein's nefarious behavior was mostly under wraps. I'd never even heard of him, but I had heard of Prince Andrew—I'd be covering the nuptials of Prince William and Kate Middleton the following spring, so getting some face time with the royal uncle didn't seem like a bad idea.

The place, 40 rooms over seven floors, was *Eyes Wide Shut* with a twist—creepy chandeliers and body-part art. I saw Charlie Rose, George

Stephanopoulos, Woody Allen, and Soon-Yi milling around. We also brought Chelsea Handler; she and I had dinner plans that night, and when this came up, she was game. Suffering from momentary amnesia, Chelsea actually asked Woody and Soon-Yi how they met. Meanwhile, in jeans ripped at the knee, velvet loafers, and an air of studied insouciance, Epstein nursed a drink and held court in front of a massive fireplace. Tables had been set up in the living room in a square where guests ate lasagna out of shallow bowls. Stilted mingling. An early night.

"That was pretty bizarre," Brooks said in the cab afterward. "Did you see how young the women were who took our coats?"

I couldn't imagine what Epstein and Andrew were up to, apart from trying to cultivate friends in the media. Which, in retrospect, they must have figured they'd need when the pedophilia charges started rolling in.

Thanks, Peggy.

LOOKING BACK ON the Brooks era, I realize it screamed midlife crisis (even more than the red Thunderbird I bought for myself in my forties). But I also think I was rebelling: During my half century on the planet, I'd never done anything particularly scandalous. Now here I was, being judged on a grand scale at every turn. I think Brooks was my way of challenging the increasingly oppressive idea of who I was supposed to be and how I was supposed to act.

On at least one occasion, I took the rebellion too far, like the time we went to a disco near Grand Central and started doing shots of ouzo— not really something I do. People were excited to see me, and I was lapping up the attention. I decided to show how young and down I was by performing this stupid party trick called a flaming Statue of Liberty, where you suck on your index finger, dip it into a shot of high-proof alcohol, light it on fire, raise it in the air, down the shot, and extinguish the flame in your mouth. (What could go wrong?)

The crowd was egging me on, doing flaming shots along with me. So rather than stop at two, I stopped counting.

My head was spinning like a mirror ball. Brooks and I made our way to the dance floor, where, after a few clumsy moves, I collapsed like a sack of potatoes. In a scene out of *Weekend at Bernie's,* Brooks helped me to the door, kept me from wiping out on the snowy sidewalk, and somehow got me to Lenox Hill Hospital, where he told the staff I needed help...and privacy.

I recall a stretcher, an IV, violent puking, Brooks snoozing in the chair next to me. When I wasn't retching, I was obsessing over the possibility that someone at the hospital might tip off the tabloids. I could just see the headlines: *Anchor Hits Rock Bottom! Lady Took Some Liberties! Blotto Katie Blacks Out!* By the grace of God, the whole thing stayed under the radar.

Turns out I hadn't heard the last of the party trick that damn near killed me. A few years later on *Jeopardy!,* Alex Trebek asked one of the contestants to share a fun story about herself.

Her response: "I once did a flaming Statue of Liberty at a bar with Katie Couric!"

I'll take "Embarrassing Moments" for $2,000, Alex.

IT WAS BAD enough that people were openly talking smack—Dan Rather told Joe Scarborough that I was "dumbing down and tarting up" the news. Almost worse was the internal sabotage.

One night after the broadcast, Rome grabbed a handful of people for a quick meeting in his office and shut the door behind him. He told them they had to cut back on taped pieces, like my in-depth interviews, because they cost too much, and they weren't resonating with viewers. Apparently they weren't resonating with CBS correspondents either, since those pieces ate into their airtime.

"Do it gradually," Rome told them, "and keep it to yourselves."

Everyone understood.

The next morning, there was a story about it in *USA Today.*

The situation was unwinnable—we were trying to bring change to a place that didn't want to change. We'd thought we'd be greeted as liberators; instead, we got an insurgency.

Bob had been trying to streamline the production of the broadcast, working closely with editors and tech folks. One afternoon, he entered his office and discovered a typewritten message that had been slipped under the door. It had the anonymous, herky-jerky look of a ransom note. It said:

```
Let me tell you that you're a fucking asshole . . .
There's a line of people who would love to kick
your ass.
```

Jesus.

65

The Wisdom of Samantha

PEOPLE SAY THE darnedest things. Once while I was on vacation, a woman approached me excitedly.

"When you started on the evening news," she said, "I picked up my daughter from school. She even skipped soccer practice so we could be home to watch your first evening newscast. I told her, 'This is such an important moment for women.'"

I was so moved—it was exactly the message I was trying to send.

Then: "After that night, we never watched you again."

One Saturday afternoon, on my way to Central Park with Maisy, a middle-aged woman in a sweat suit came toward me. "Are you Katie Couric?" she asked.

"Yes," I told her, happy to see a friendly face.

"Well," she said, "I don't care what anybody says, I like watching you on the evening news."

When I reached the reservoir, I called Alan Berger. I finally lost it, crying so hard I practically hyperventilated, and I didn't even care how many fit and happy runners on the bridle path saw me.

"Why is this happening?" I sobbed into the phone. "I just don't understand it. I'm doing the best I can."

Alan just listened.

At home I tried to keep things as normal as possible and not let the girls see me down. I wasn't always successful. Over dinner one night, as Carrie stuck pieces of roast chicken in her mashed potatoes, I started weeping.

"Mom, what's wrong?" Ellie said, alarmed.

"I'm sorry, guys," I said, blowing my nose in my napkin. "I'm having a tough time at work. I'm getting trashed left and right. It's just really, really hard to deal with, day after day."

Carrie piped up: "Mom, remember what Samantha said?" And then, in a spot-on Kim Cattrall, "If I worried what every bitch in New York said about me, I'd never leave the house."

I burst out laughing. It was just the right thing to snap me out of my funk. Then I began to seriously question my parenting if my fifth-grader could effortlessly quote a line from *Sex and the City*.

GOD, I WISHED Jay were here—to listen to me vent, read the tea leaves, and help me manage the politics of CBS. Not only had he been a loving partner, he was really astute and a great lawyer, so attentive to the finer points of my recurring negotiations with NBC. After he died, I found a legal pad on which he'd scribbled, in black felt-tip pen, things like *Insurance? Housing allowance? Five years?*—the terms of my first contract. I wondered what he would think of all this.

I'd been on the job less than six months when Alan and I were summoned to Les Moonves's office at Black Rock, the granite sky-scraper on West 52nd Street. I couldn't imagine what it was about, but I doubted it was something awesome.

Les had a gleaming corner office on the 35th floor with an "I'm king of the world" desk and the aroma of fine Corinthian leather. The place was so different from the news operation over at the dairy barn, and rightly so: CBS Entertainment was the profit center, thanks to money-minting hits like *CSI* and *Survivor*. Les himself was hauling in close to $40 million a year.

He was entertainment through and through; news, not so much. In retrospect, there was probably something kind of *off* about the way he wooed and anointed me for the anchor job without ever getting buy-in from some of the most important people in the news division. It's as if he were hiring me to star in yet another *CSI.*

Don Hewitt, my most ardent suitor, had retired. As the head of *60 Minutes,* the marquee show of the news division, Jeff Fager was probably the most powerful person in the organization. Obviously, I should have met with him before I accepted the job so he could feel like he was part of the process. But Les never brokered that meeting—and neither did Alan. I just assumed Fager was on board.

There was still a mountain of distrust between the hard-core newsies and the slick Moonves. So I'm sure it wasn't helpful when, early in my tenure, at a party at Tavern on the Green to celebrate the new season of *60 Minutes,* I hung close to Les. I saw newspeople eyeing us suspiciously. That chumminess probably reinforced the idea that I was Les's person. But he was the only one there I really knew and one of the few who seemed glad to see me.

Now at Black Rock, I wasn't sure Les was that glad to see me.

He and Sean greeted us with outsize bonhomie. He offered us a seat and got to the point.

"We've been thinking about you and what you're good at. The evening news really doesn't give you a place to showcase your talent." *Oh, boy, here it comes . . .*

"Would you be interested in going to the morning show?" he said. "You're so great at it, and they could really use your help."

I was taken aback. "Absolutely not," I said. "I didn't leave the morning show I helped make number one so I could go to the third-place morning show."

What I wanted to say was *I cannot believe you're giving up on me already.* That and *Why don't you have the balls to tell all the people undermining me to get with the program?*

Les was only thinking about Les. As I'd come to realize, he didn't want his legacy sullied by a glaring failure at the *CBS Evening News*—he'd do just about anything to make the problem go away.

I told them both that I had come here to accomplish something, and if it didn't work, it didn't work. I'd rather leave the network than retreat to the morning show, which at the time was a cheap imitation of the other two.

Les and Sean looked disappointed that I hadn't provided an easy solution to their problem, which was me.

"Okay," Les said simply. "Let's keep going."

66

The Fall of Rome

CARRIE WAS ALWAYS terrified of lice. Unlike so many of her class-mates, she'd managed to outrun the little buggers for years. But now they were having a field day in her chocolate-brown hair.

Who you gonna call? Licenders!—Orthodox Jewish women from Brooklyn who come to your home and cover your head in a tar-like substance that kills the lice and, more important, their eggs while instructing you to wash all your bedding and bag non-washable stuffed animals to suffocate the critters. When they found a few errant nits in my hair, it was decided I needed delousing as well.

Just as one of the women started slathering my scalp, the house phone rang. Rick Kaplan was downstairs.

"Oh God, seriously?" I said. Pause. "Okay, send him up." The whole scene (and, for that matter, my life) was so absurd, I thought, *Why not?*

Sean had suggested we meet. "I think he might be a good person to bring over," he told me—meaning a good person to replace Rome as executive producer.

"I like Rick," I said. "If you think it's a good idea, I'm all for it." At that point, I was willing to try anything.

The former EP of several successful newscasts, creator of *Prime-time Live,* and onetime president of CNN, Rick was an experienced, respected producer known for many things, including his ability to get the best out of strong-willed anchors and his steady (occasionally heavy) hand. We'd never worked together before, but we were friendly.

"Welcome to the lice capades!" I said at the door, my hair thick with goop.

Rick filled the door frame. At six foot six, in his trademark sweater-vest, gold chain, cordovan tassel loafers, and cologne you could smell in the next zip code, he was an imposing figure. He had seen it all and none of it fazed him.

Rick took a seat on the couch (covered in plastic) and cut to the chase.

"The show's a mess," he said. "It's just not smart. You're trying too many goofy things. Katie, you're an extraordinary journalist, and you need to be doing an aggressive, really substantive newscast. These are very serious times, and they need a very serious newscast."

"I hear you, Rick," I said, somewhat defensively. "But I was brought there to reimagine the evening news and make it less stilted. If you think we need to recalibrate, and clearly you wouldn't be the only one, I'm more than willing to give it a try."

I liked that Rick had a vision, and I was happy to make it my vision too. I was also relieved I'd be working with a seasoned pro. Rome was struggling. And Sean, son of *Wide World of Sports* host Jim McKay, was a sports guy who made it clear he didn't really like news, while his number two, news veteran Paul Friedman, was a huge obstructionist and an overall nasty guy (his nickname was Darth Vader). Rick knew what he was doing, and he was a fan at a time when I really needed one.

Les was on board as well, telling Rick, "Katie deserves better than third place—we need to change that."

Yeah!

"Or that's gonna be on my goddamn tombstone."

Oh.

ON A GLUM day in March, Rome gathered everyone in the newsroom. Fair-haired, with the look of a grown-up altar boy, he was the polar opposite of Rick.

Rome praised the staff and said how much he'd enjoyed working with them all. "But now," he said, "it's time for someone else to take the reins."

Gazes were lowered, shoulders sagged. Rome had fallen.

Then I said a few words. "I just want to thank Rome for being such an important part of our launch. He is one of the most decent people I've ever met, and I'm really going to miss him." Waterworks.

The staff seemed to view my tears skeptically. I could sense I was seen as the bad guy here, that if only I had been willing to do a more traditional newscast from the beginning, Rome would still be with us.

Everyone looked so beaten down. Our grand experiment had failed.

EVEN THOUGH RICK was moving us in a more traditional direction (he insisted I wear a jacket every night), he brought new energy and focus almost immediately, marshaling the troops, bellowing, "Do it!" whenever he heard an idea he liked. And we took some interesting risks; for instance, devoting the entire 22 minutes one night to the never-ending war in Afghanistan. It sent a signal about our commitment to hard news, even though it tanked in the ratings.

But if we thought Rick's arrival would instantly stanch the flow of bad press, we were wrong. A *New York Magazine* story titled "Alas, Poor Couric" detonated in July.

Let's start with the cover. A photographer named Platon (mono-monikered, like Madonna or Cher) came to CBS and spent several hours taking pictures of me in a space off the newsroom. He was lively and personable and convinced me to try some "serious" shots. I was fine with that; I didn't want a big smile to accompany a story about the challenges I faced at CBS. Platon had me sit on a variety of apple boxes, the go-to prop of photogs looking for a natural, no-frills vibe. The cover shot was someone I barely recognized: thin-lipped and dead-eyed, staring into the camera, filling the entire page. The explosive cover line: "I have days when I'm like, Oh my God, what did I do?"

And yes, I did say that—but they lopped off the second half of my quote: "I have days when I'm like, Oh my God, what did I do? But for some weird reason, they don't happen that often."

I felt like Carrie Bradshaw when she landed on the cover of *New York Magazine* holding a cigarette, looking seriously hungover, above the headline "Single & Fabulous?" I couldn't help but wonder, are magazine editors out to get us? One little editing decision—in Carrie's case, the addition of a snide question mark; in mine, a truncated quote—can change everything. We called Adam Moss, the magazine's top dog, and complained. He sheepishly conceded it was iffy. But the damage had been done.

The writer, Joe Hagan, threw me a few bones, giving our early broadcasts props for their "chatty, friendly vibe and a bright, casual atmosphere never before seen at 6:30 p.m." And yes, viewership was down, he wrote, but we'd doubled the number of female viewers between the ages of 18 and 49 in a single year.

Then he went to town on the negatives: that some thought I wasn't a true "newshound" like my predecessors, that my big salary required others to take pay cuts, that Bob Schieffer and Lesley Stahl had talked smack about me (anonymously) to the *Philadelphia Inquirer,* that I was so stressed out about the ratings, I beat up a news editor…

The assault-and-battery charge involving Jerry Cipriano was clearly a case of aggravated hyperbole, Your Honor. For the record: I was reading a story about tuberculosis that had been added during the broadcast when, much to my surprise, the creepy, hard-to-pronounce word *sputum* came up on the prompter. It's just not a term I use (falling into the category of words that gross me out, like *moist*), and Jerry hadn't warned me about it.

After the broadcast, I went up to him and basically said, "I can't believe you did that! You have to tell me when you're going to use a word like that!" and slapped him on the back in a half-annoyed, half-playful way. (I wondered if he was screwing with me, the way they say Tom Brokaw's writers sometimes screwed with him back in his local news days, writing *L-1011* instead of *DC jumbo jet* because they knew Tom had trouble pronouncing his *L*s.)

Jerry and I had a great working relationship. We traveled the world together; he saved my bacon on plenty of occasions and remains a good friend to this day. But at the time, everything I did or said could and was being used against me.

Ideally, the media sisterhood would have come to my defense. Instead, proud feminist Nora Ephron piled on, writing: "It's impossible for me to make any sort of evaluation at all about her. Because I cannot believe how bad her makeup is." Sigh.

After the *New York Magazine* hit job, I went on an epic crying jag. I remember looking at Lauren and blubbering, "I'm trying to cure cancer, I write children's books—I'm a good person. Why does everyone hate me?"

We laugh about it now, but at the time, I was drowning.

67

Business Trip

SOMETHING I'LL NEVER understand: affluent parents who scrimp on childcare, paying rock-bottom wages, not offering ample benefits and time off. You've entrusted this person with the thing you care about most in the world—why wouldn't you do everything in your power to make sure she (or he) feels respected and valued? With the women who took care of my kids, that was my highest priority.

During those incredibly stressful early months at CBS, I wondered what would have become of us if it weren't for Lori Beth. Work was so hard, my schedule so unpredictable, my romantic life so volatile, my stress level so high . . . Lori Beth was the glue, our rock, our savior.

She was also the secret police. One day when Ellie was in seventh grade, she told Lori Beth she was going to visit her friend Elizabeth on another floor in our building. Lori Beth smelled a rat and went down to the street, eventually spotting Ellie and Elizabeth tottering out in stilettos and makeup, on their way to meet some boys. The riot act was read, and Ellie was dragged home.

Another time, when Lori Beth detected cigarette smoke coming through the vent in the wall between her and Ellie's rooms, she told me about it, knowing I'd bring the hammer down: *"Your father died of cancer—why would you invite that into your body?"*

As you might imagine, tears. Lots. Of. Tears.

Lori Beth was getting a degree in English from Hunter College at the time and shared her learning with the girls. It wasn't always age-appropriate. When Carrie was 8, Lori Beth taught her every word of Emily Dickinson's "My Life Had Stood—a Loaded Gun," which cherub-faced Carrie would dutifully recite at the dinner table:

For I have but the power to kill
Without—the power to die—

My Little Pony it wasn't.

We were a family. In some ways funky and misshapen, but a family nonetheless, fiercely loving, happy more often than not. Of course we had our challenges—for example, when I had to inform the gang I was heading off to the most dangerous place on earth.

When I was still at *TODAY,* I'd told *Access Hollywood* that, as a single mom, I was reluctant to travel to Iraq to cover the war, saying that I didn't want to make the girls orphans. I got some blowback, but *TODAY* was such a mom-friendly show, I knew the audience would ultimately understand.

Now, though, in my glass-ceiling-smashing job, I really didn't feel like I could say no. Dan Rather had reported from many war zones, covering the Soviet-Afghan war in a mujahideen headdress. In my effort to make history, how would it look if I summarily said, *You can't ask a single mom to do that?*

So there I was, with a security expert tightening the straps on my 15-pound bulletproof vest and measuring my head for a helmet. Rick Kaplan had assured me that we'd be escorted by the military's top brass and would be safe. I knew how important it was to get out there and report on a war growing more unpopular by the day. But still— sometimes I wondered what the hell I was doing.

THE WAR HAD begun in March of 2003. Three weeks later, Baghdad fell, the statue of Saddam pulled to the ground. President Bush landed on an aircraft carrier—memorable both for the flight suit that made it look like he was wearing a sizable codpiece and his declaration to the troops, in front of a huge MISSION ACCOMPLISHED banner, that "because of you, the tyrant has fallen and Iraq is free."

We know what happened next: "free" Iraq in free fall; the preppy civilian Paul Bremer put in charge; ordinary Sunnis, including professors and teachers, ejected from their jobs, many locked up in that hell-hole Abu Ghraib. Insurgency, civil war, Bremer in way over his nicely coiffed head.

It would be impossible to cover the war well if I couldn't get a word with the president of the United States, and given the chilly state of things between me and the Bush administration, that was a distinct possibility. A year after my interview with the future First Lady, I pissed them off again when I interviewed Secretary of State Colin Powell on the first anniversary of 9/11.

I had gotten to know him when I worked at the Pentagon, and I did a warm profile of him on *TODAY*. But in the unedited interview, with the "war on terror" expanding rapidly and Cheney and Rumsfeld beating the drum about regime change in Iraq, I had to ask Powell about the specious attempt to connect Iraq with 9/11, the potential of a long-term commitment to the region, and our unbreakable loyalty to Saudi Arabia, where most of the hijackers were from. After the interview, Powell literally ripped off his mic and tried to slip out without shaking my hand.

Later, I interviewed Tim Russert about Bush's low-energy pre-invasion press conference; I quoted Tom Shales, who described it as "soporific." Tom Touchet received an irate call from the White House press office: "If she continues along these lines we will have to cut off access."

Finally, détente: Just before I left *TODAY,* David Gregory, who was well liked by the administration (Bush gave him the nickname "Stretch"), did me a solid, brokering a meeting with White House communications director Nicolle Wallace and adviser Dan Bartlett. I finally got to clear the air.

My second day at CBS, I was granted an interview with President Bush. By then, the war was three years old and going disastrously: 3,000 U.S. troops had been killed and over 20,000 wounded. Brent Scowcroft, national security adviser to Bush's father, said publicly, "Iraq is a failing venture."

We had a walk-and-talk (mostly in circles) through the halls of the White House. With the fifth anniversary of 9/11 coming up, I asked Bush what he recalled about that day.

"I remember the horror, and I remember the loss of life," he said. "I also remember the lessons...I resolved around that time I would do everything to protect the American people. And that, frankly, has defined much of how I think as the president. For me, it's not just a moment. You know, it's really been a changed life."

While it felt good to be back in the business of questioning the president of the United States, I was keenly aware that I was on thin ice. If I got too tough, I ran the risk of being blackballed again. If I soft-pedaled it, I didn't deserve to be the anchor of the evening news.

I noted that people admired him for sticking to his principles, but if circumstances changed, could that be seen as inflexibility?

"I am inflexible when it comes to making sure we don't get hit again," Bush said, "and you bet I'm gonna remain strong about making sure that the world we leave behind is a more peaceful world."

Despite the fact that the invasion has actually galvanized terrorists, I thought. But I kept that to myself.

THE REPUBLICANS WERE routed in the midterms—Bush called it "a thumpin'." Public support for the war cratered. Rumsfeld was out. Al-Qaeda had gained a foothold in Iraq, bombing a mosque, one of the Shiites' holiest places, hoping to exploit the havoc and escalate civil war.

Suddenly, a last-ditch effort was on the table—"the surge," which involved deploying an additional 30,000 troops to secure the population by having soldiers live among the Iraqi people and train their forces. General David Petraeus, who wrote the book on counterinsurgency (literally—his Princeton PhD dissertation), was in charge. I was deployed to interview him and find out how it was going.

Which brings me to the bulletproof vest. I wore it in Fallujah as

Petraeus and I walked the streets in triple-digit heat—my shirt was soaking wet beneath the Kevlar. It was September of 2007. We toured a place where, three years before, four contractors had been burned alive, dragged through the streets, and strung up, their tattered corpses dangling from a bridge. Now, looking at the footage, I fixate on my pearl earrings and half-pony. Like a lot of female journalists, I struggled with balancing the brutality of war with the pressure to be telegenic.

I remember fearing for my exposed body parts, especially my head. But Petraeus himself was so confident, intelligent, and smooth, it was hard to not be reassured. People hung out at open-air markets, excited children clustered around American soldiers who doled out candy, and Petraeus was greeted warmly by locals.

I still wasn't convinced. "Some people might be watching this and saying, 'Oh yeah, this is a nice dog-and-pony show; yeah, there are some areas of calm,'" I said. "But if you look at the country as a whole, it's still a nightmare."

Petraeus admitted there was still way too much violence but said that levels were dramatically down; I checked the army's records, which bore that out. Still, it was all relative. The crew and I had to be escorted by beefy, heavily armed security, and we went to sleep to the *rat-a-tat-tat* of not-so-distant gunfire, the sky lighting up as bombs went off, even though we were staying in the Green Zone, a supposed oasis of safety where officials and journalists were housed. At the end of a grueling day, my shirt soaked with sweat, I'd remove my bulletproof vest and lay it on the floor, picturing the girls getting home from school and slipping off their backpacks. I hoped they were keeping up with their homework, practicing piano, and not giving Lori Beth a hard time.

I was proud of our coverage, although some critics called it a desperate attempt to reverse sinking ratings and reassert my hard-news credentials. Then MoveOn.org went after me, calling my reports "puff pieces scripted by the institutions [CBS] purports to be investigating," and cherry-picked quotes, leaving out the tougher questions I'd asked. I suspect their real gripe was that I'd provided a platform for some positive news—the effectiveness of the surge—in a deeply unpopular war.

It felt strange being vilified by the Left; usually, I was accused of being in the tank for liberal causes. I thought back on Walter Cronkite's wise words to me at the Four Seasons: "I know I'm being fair when everybody's mad at me."

The success of the surge was short-lived, and the war continued to unravel. Years later, I met a commercial helicopter pilot who told me he used to fly Chinooks in Iraq. I asked him what, in retrospect, he thought about the war. "So many of my buddies were killed," he told me, shaking his head. "What a waste."

AFTER TWO WEEKS in the Middle East, I was exhausted, emotionally and physically—completely wrung out—and I'd never been so happy to be home. I couldn't wait to hug the girls and smell their hair. As I got out of the elevator, the first thing I saw was a big poster taped to the door. In bubbly letters filled in with stripes, polka dots, and hearts it read, WELCOME HOME MOM!

Underneath, in girlish print, *How was Iraq?*

68

The Twitter

B Y 2007, WITH the world pushing into the digital space and social media emerging in a big way, I wanted to help move the news division in the right direction so we didn't get left behind. I started ending live broadcasts of big events, like Super Tuesday, with "For our continuing coverage, please go to cbsnews.com." I began carrying around a flip camera that I busted out if I saw something or someone newsworthy, like Michael Dukakis at the Democratic National Convention in Denver, whom I grabbed for an impromptu interview as we were going through the metal detector. And I launched a series of online interviews called @KatieCouric, which would let me do what I did best: talk to people—something I rarely did in our 22-minute broadcast.

My first guest was right-wing radio host Glenn Beck, who tried, without much success, to explain why he'd called President Obama a racist. I also sat down with Malcolm Gladwell, Hugh Jackman, Ellen DeGeneres, Shakira, Bill Gates, Drake, Al Gore, Justin Bieber...big names who knew that being interviewed online was no longer a dis. (I'd come a long way since 1994 when Bryant, Elizabeth Vargas, and I were on the sofa trying to figure out the "World Wide Web"; the worst part was when I plaintively asked our head writer, "Allison, can you explain what Internet is?" We were widely mocked 17 years later when some nice person leaked the video.)

When Brian Williams joined Twitter in September of 2010, I decided to have some fun with it and reach out. I chirped:

> Hi @BWilliams! Welcome to @Twitter! Looking forward to following you. (Don't worry, I'm not a stalker) Your pal, Katie.

Pretty harmless, right? But CBS PR called a state of emergency. "What were you thinking?" they screeched at Erica Anderson, the young woman who helped with my social media. "Katie's ratings are lower than Brian's. It's never a good idea to engage with him!"

"They don't have a clue," Erica told me, rolling her eyes.

When the *Deepwater Horizon* rig exploded, belching oil into the Gulf of Mexico, I reported from the scene, then solicited questions on Twitter from viewers distressed about the environmental disaster unfolding in real time, including endless images of distraught birds coated in what looked like chocolate syrup. The team fanned out, finding answers, which I then shared on the broadcast.

Paul Friedman later sniffed to one of my producers, "I think it's beneath the anchor of the *CBS Evening News* to be on the Twitter."

Yes, *the* Twitter.

ACROSS THE STREET, things with Fager were starting to curdle. Perhaps he felt that the bad press I was getting would tarnish his show's sterling reputation. Perhaps it bothered him that I didn't need a Svengali. Perhaps I didn't suck up enough. Perhaps he was just an ass who didn't like strong women. (So many choices!)

Whatever it was, our relationship went from bad to worse. Two incidents stand out. In the fall of 2008, the catchy song "Poker Face" blanketed the airwaves, bringing a new level of attention to a fledgling pop singer. I called Vicki Gordon, a senior producer who'd shepherded countless big interviews during her tenure, and said, "Listen, I have an idea. Lady Gaga's going to be huge—the next Madonna. I think she'd make a great profile."

Pop stars in general weren't a slam dunk with the gray-faced newshounds of *60 Minutes,* but when someone rose to the level of phenomenon, whatever the field, I thought it was important to take notice.

Vicki said she thought it was an interesting idea and that she'd run it by Fager.

She called me back the next day: "Jeff said, 'Not for us.'"

I was disappointed but not surprised. I gave a mental shrug and turned back to my work.

A year later, Vicki called me at the *Evening News.* "Remember your idea about Lady Gaga? Well, now Jeff wants to do it."

"Great!" I said, feeling vindicated. But by that point she'd been virtually everywhere, including the cover of *Rolling Stone.* "We can try a different angle," I told Vicki. "She went to a Catholic girls' school near my apartment. We could go back and talk to her teachers."

A few days later, I walked across the street to check in at the production office, where they kept a big whiteboard listing upcoming stories and the correspondents who were doing them. I saw *Lady Gaga* on the board and scanned to the right. Under *correspondent,* it said *Anderson Cooper.*

What?

Back at my office I called Vicki. "I don't understand," I said. "I came up with that story a year ago."

"I'm sorry," she said. "They decided to give it to Anderson."

"Why? That was my story!"

"I'm sorry," she repeated.

The unfairness made me insane. I'm not sure why I didn't just storm into Fager's office and get it all out on the table. But I let it go.

The second bile-inducing incident came right after the 2008 election when Obama, in a true team-of-rivals move, chose Hillary for secretary of state. Fager told me, "I want you to do the definitive profile of Hillary Clinton as secretary of state." I had already interviewed her on the campaign trail for *60 Minutes,* so it made sense.

Lori Beecher began laying the groundwork. She reached out to Philippe Reines, Hillary's senior adviser at the State Department, to start figuring out the logistics.

Two weeks later, Lori walked into my office looking confused. "Philippe just called me," she said. "He told me that Scott Pelley's team had reached out about a profile of Hillary for *60*. He asked if we even talk to each other over here."

This time I confronted Fager. "Jeff, I don't understand," I said, standing in his office, with its crappy feng shui—for some reason, there was no seating close enough to his desk to enable a serious conversation. "You told me that you wanted me to do the profile of Hillary Clinton, but Scott Pelley's producers are calling, and it makes everyone look stupid."

"Oh," he said casually, barely making eye contact, "we decided to move things around."

What?

Fager looked down at the papers on his desk in a way that made it clear the conversation was over.

I was at a loss. Feeling screwed with, needing help, I called Les Moonves and asked if we could have lunch.

We met at a dimly lit Chinese restaurant near Black Rock—the kind of place executives bring their mistresses. Les greeted me warmly, as always, giving off the winning whiff of someone who'd just banked another 10 mil.

I cut the small-talk portion short. "Les," I said, "as you know, one of the reasons I came to CBS was to do pieces for *60 Minutes*. I need some advice on how to maneuver the politics over there." I told him what had happened with the Hillary piece. "Can you give me some guidance? Can you maybe talk to Jeff and find out why this is happening?"

As usual, Les was opaque—although for a split second I did catch him processing the fact that he had a problem. "I'll talk to Fager," he said, shoveling some more beef and broccoli onto his plate.

I'll never know if he did. In retrospect, I don't know why he would—his evening-news anchor, a bad-press magnet who had failed to move the ratings needle, was butting heads with the EP of the most revered program on television, a critical and commercial triumph.

* * *

AT LEAST THERE was one story Fager couldn't take away.

When a US Airways jet carrying 155 passengers and crew members made an emergency landing on the Hudson, suddenly everyone wanted to know everything about the pilot, Captain Chesley "Sully" Sullenberger.

The second the alert came in, Lori typed out a one-sentence blue sheet—"Katie Couric interviews the crew of US Airways flight 1549"—and submitted it to *60 Minutes*. Then she flooded the zone, making calls and sending emails to virtually anyone who had any influence with Sully: the head of the pilots' union, the copilot, the flight attendants, US Airways corporate communications...

But Fager's brush-cut lackey, Bill Owens, wanted his buddy Scott Pelley to do the story, natch. Pelley's entire team was working the phones. There was also Matt Lauer, equally desperate to bag the first interview for *TODAY,* and with CBS dicking around and competing against itself, he came close.

At a certain point, it was obvious Lori and I were the closest to the finish line—they had no choice but to let me get on with it.

"Don't fuck it up," Owens told Lori, helpfully.

I INTERVIEWED SULLY IN his hilltop home in Danville, California. A former air force fighter pilot who'd instructed flight crews on how to respond to crises in the air, he might well have been the perfect person on the planet to be confronted with this situation. I'll never forget him saying to me, "For 42 years, I've been making small, regular deposits in this bank of experience, education, and training. And on January 15th, the balance was sufficient so that I could make a very large withdrawal."

We also arranged to have many of the survivors and their families come to Charlotte, North Carolina, the aborted flight's original destination, to thank Sully and the rest of the crew. I thought it would be moving to see the passengers reunited with the man who'd quite literally saved their lives. Fager didn't want to do it, but I pushed back.

It was worth it—hugs, tears, grateful spouses, children, homemade signs, roses, a survivor who'd lost his brother on 9/11 and had prayed for his own life so his parents wouldn't lose another son.

I won an Emmy and got a pretty cool phone call a few years later.

"Hi, this is Clint," came the gravelly whisper. Clint Eastwood was making a feature film about the incident and wanted me to reenact the interview, replacing Sully with Tom Hanks.

Sure, I said. I also told Clint I could reenact the broadcast I anchored from the freezing banks of the Hudson that night.

"That's interesting," he said. "Maybe we should call it *The Katie Couric Story Featuring Sully Sullenberger.*"

I laughed. "I have no problem with that, Clint."

69

Damned If You Do

THE MOOD LIFT from a big win was always short-lived. In general, I felt embattled. Defensive. Misunderstood. I guess you could say I was feeling like Hillary Clinton.

I conducted her first White House interview in a prime-time special back in 1993. Rewatching it now, I'm struck by a number of things, starting with the title card: In a fancy, fussy *Donna Reed Show*–style script, the words *Hillary Clinton: America's First Lady* appear on-screen as if being written by an invisible hand. There are pink flowers, tinkly music, and a soothing voice-over befitting a feminine-hygiene ad.

I thought Hillary was smart and engaging; looking at it now, I find her strangely sphinxlike. I am amazed at how controlled she seems, determined to avoid doing anything that might inflame her detractors. In one conversation, she's wearing a light gray dress with white polka dots and a floppy bow tied tight at the neck. Her hair looks like Mamie Eisenhower's—primly styled, close to the head. It all seems market-tested for maximum inoffensiveness. I thought back to pictures of a groovy Hillary in her youth, in granny glasses and skintight bell-bottoms, or decades later, in one workhorse pantsuit after another…they make the dress-and-pearls-and-hose phase seem like a forced detour.

Her voice is different too—so precisely modulated, sometimes lilting in a way that doesn't sound quite genuine. It's impossible to picture the woman on-screen letting loose with the hearty, bawdy laugh she'd share so easily later in life.

At one point Hillary gives me a rare peek at their residence on the second floor of the East Wing, and her efforts to make like Jackie and own the role of lady of the house are a bit painful to watch. Entering a common space, she opens her arms stiffly and says, "Isn't this a beautiful central corridor up here?" Then she leads me to a painting she calls "one of my favorites": a Mary Cassatt of a mother cuddling two young children in soothing hues—an image of womanhood as maternal, nurturing, and reassuring as one could find anywhere.

Not that career women can't be maternal and nurturing and love a Mary Cassatt. But as the most prominent woman in America at the time and the face of a new breed, Hillary understood the threat she represented and seemed to be doing her level best to allay people's fears. Turned out that ladylike lawn strolls and house tours wouldn't really be enough.

AFTER MUCH "WILL she or won't she?" speculation, Hillary announced she was running for president in January 2007. A little-known junior senator from Illinois had formed an exploratory committee one week earlier.

A few years before that, while covering a story on Capitol Hill, I was standing on the corner with a camera crew when a car pulled up across the street and a lanky guy jumped out. He dropped his cigarette, crushed it under his shoe, and bounded toward us, hand outstretched.

"Hi, I'm Barack Obama—I'm a big fan!" he said, then headed back to his car.

"Who was that again?" I said as he pulled away from the curb.

"Don't ask me," said the cameraman.

Before the New Hampshire primary, we set up shop at the musty Wayfarer Hotel near Manchester, in a bungalow on the property that was normally used as a wedding chapel (Dan Rather broadcasted from there so many times over the years, it came to be known as the Dan Rather wedding chapel). Per custom, journalists and political operatives thronged the hotel bar, with everyone—including Hillary's own advisers—predicting she would lose big.

Everyone was wrong. The victory came down to a single, unscripted moment in a diner when a voter asked Hillary how she kept so "upbeat and so wonderful." Caught off guard, she actually got misty, replying, "It's not easy. I have so many opportunities from this country, I just don't want to see us fall backwards...you know?" Chin in hand, shaking her head. The crowd applauded.

On the debate stage just two days earlier, she had to field a question about the supposed "likability issue" she faced, prompting the faintest of faint praise from Obama: "You're likable enough, Hillary," he said, dismissively.

I found it all so frustrating. Ambitious women have always been required to project a certain toughness to head off the idea that they're simply "too emotional" to make difficult decisions, that their periods or their pregnancies or their hot flashes might cause them to behave erratically, rendering them unsuitable for leadership. Now, back at the diner, showing emotion—being vulnerable, even fragile—was the only way Hillary could break through. It was just another example of our whipsawing "damned if you do, damned if you don't" world.

I couldn't imagine where Hillary got her thick skin. Consider: Fox News anchor Neil Cavuto saying, "Men won't vote for Hillary Clinton because she reminds them of their nagging wives." Tucker Carlson admitting that "when she comes on television, I involuntarily cross my legs." Rush Limbaugh wondering whether the country was ready to watch a woman age in the White House—never mind how weary and gray male presidents become, time-lapse-photography-style. Then there was the Hillary rally in Salem, New Hampshire, where two protesters held up signs that said IRON MY SHIRT. Not to mention the Hillary Nutcracker sold in airport gift shops, complete with "stainless-steel thighs." It was shocking to me how socially acceptable sexism still was.

I was eager to use my position to fight that battle. As managing editor, I had a real say in what kinds of stories we were going to do, pushing the team to cover things like sexual assault in the military; dating violence, after UVA lacrosse player Yeardley Love was beaten to death by her boyfriend; the plight of Afghani girls who dared to attend school. I did a *60 Minutes* piece on college freshman Beckett Brennan, who'd been raped by three basketball players, and how terribly she was treated by the police and the university.

I also made sure that not-so-subtle sexism didn't seep into the newscast, always on high alert when our three male news writers described Hillary. More than once I asked Jerry, "Would you describe a male candidate that way?"

When Hillary lost, I used my daily commentary to talk about the misogyny I had witnessed, pointing a finger at "all the people who crossed the line and all the women and men who let them get away with it."

That caught the attention of high-strung Keith Olbermann, who, in a regular segment on his show *Countdown,* named me that week's "Worst Person in the World." I took it as a compliment.

70

If Jay Were Here

I WAS IN LONDON covering the G20 summit. After an exhausting day of speeches and breakout sessions on the breezy topic of the world economy, I called home to see how things were going there.

Ellie picked up. I heard cheering in the background. At that very moment, she was checking various admissions portals on her computer, getting her college acceptances: Yale, Harvard, Williams, UVA... there was laughter, the clinking of glasses—Lori Beth and our wonderful housekeeper, Rose, had opened champagne. Dancing broke out. I could hear it in Ellie's voice—complete happiness and relief.

I was so proud of her. If only I could have been there.

PARENTING ALWAYS POSED challenges but even more so once we got into the teen years. Yes, certain terrors like choking, drowning, and wandering off with strangers had subsided, but they were quickly replaced with new ones involving the mysterious inner lives of adolescents—the social turmoil, the pressure to achieve. I was blessed with extraordinarily grounded girls who didn't court danger. And yet, like anyone else, they had their struggles. And sometimes I wasn't there to help them as much as I should have been.

My mother was always there for us. She lived in a perpetual state of readiness to rush to our defense, find solutions, intervene.

It was different for me. Work obligations definitely got in the way, but I was also aware of how situations could be complicated by the fact that I was a public figure. When Ellie was bullied in high school, I proceeded cautiously. I asked the administration to handle it, then stayed out of the fray, knowing my involvement could lead to a juicy item in the tabloids. That would have made the problem even worse, especially for Ellie. At the time I remember thinking, *If Jay were here, he'd storm over to that school and raise hell.*

When Ellie went off to Yale, Lori Beth moved out. Carrie was too busy and too independent to need a live-in nanny, and Lori Beth was ready to do other things. I'd be indebted to her forever—by now, she was family. Meanwhile, Brooks had been spending so much time at the apartment, I suggested he just move in. Somehow, in a spasm of really bad parenting, I neglected to discuss it with Carrie. Which meant she had to handle the requisite teen angst with a 30-something man-boy strolling around the apartment shirtless. Even in front of her friends.

Please forgive me, Carrie.

71

Hockey Mom

IN THE WEE hours of August 29th, 2008, the phone in my hotel room rang and rang. Or so I'm told—I'd taken an Ambien and was dead to the world. My team nominated my producer Brian Goldsmith for the unenviable task of waking me up. He got the key from Lauren and was now looming over me with a big scoop.

"They're saying John McCain has picked a running mate," he told me. "It's Sarah Palin, the governor of Alaska."

"Who?"

"Yeah, good question."

We'd been in Denver covering the Democratic National Convention. Towering Greek columns had been erected at Mile High Stadium as the backdrop for Barack Obama's soaring oratory as he accepted the party's nomination. Republicans would go to town on what they viewed as the pomposity of it all.

It had been five exhausting days of going nonstop until 11:00 p.m., waking up early to do hits for *CBS This Morning,* grabbing interviews, and getting ready for the evening news while reporting from the convention. I was desperate to sleep in before heading to St. Paul for the Republican National Convention. Instead, we took off that morning and spent the day frantically scouring the Internet and working our sources for any and all shreds of information on Palin. We had detailed binders on everyone but her.

This much we knew: Palin was a straight-shooting mother of five with sky-high approval ratings; typically levelheaded pundit Bill Kristol called her "my heartthrob." And she was a dead ringer for Tina Fey.

I called Nicolle Wallace. I had recruited her to be a pundit at CBS but now she had a big job on the McCain campaign. "Talk to me," I said. "Why Sarah Palin? That came out of nowhere."

"We saw there was such excitement generated by Hillary Clinton's candidacy," she explained as I furiously scribbled notes in the margins of my evening news script, "we wanted someone who could tap into that."

That felt cynical to me—the assumption that Hillary supporters would vote McCain/Palin simply because there was a woman, any woman, on the ticket. Where Palin stood was definitely TBD.

Night three of the convention. The mood in St. Paul was giddy. The Republican faithful milled about, wearing GOP gear emblazoned with elephants and lots of red, white, and blue. It looked like the world's biggest Fourth of July picnic, when in fact it was Sarah Palin's coming-out party. Bob Schieffer and I watched from our booth as Rudy Giuliani delivered a red-meat speech, listing all the decisions Obama had apparently changed his stance on. "If I were Joe Biden," he said, "I'd want to get that VP thing in writing."

Nicolle stood just offstage with Palin, who was carrying a cup of tea and holding Nicolle's hand for support. She said, "Do I have to go out there now?"

"You have to go out there now," Nicolle answered. "You're going to be great."

An announcer worthy of the WWE introduced her. Palin let go of Nicolle's hand, surrendered her cup of tea, and emerged from the darkness into the glaring lights and deafening roar of the convention hall.

I'll never forget watching her walk across that stage. Not since

Geraldine Ferraro strode out in her suffragette-white suit in 1984 had we gotten such a powerful hit of female energy at a national convention. The fact that she was also drop-dead gorgeous made Palin look like a gift from God. No matter where you stood politically, it was a breathtaking moment for women everywhere.

The jubilant crowd shrieked its approval before she'd even said a word, waving signs with messages like PALIN POWER and HOCKEY MOMS 4 PALIN. TV cameras homed in on her kids, her husband, Todd, holding their infant son, Trig. The applause lasted three minutes and 15 seconds.

Palin was a former mayor, a PTA member, and, yes, a hockey mom: "You know they say the difference between a hockey mom and a pit bull?" And here Palin pointed to her own mouth. "Lipstick!" The crowd went berserk.

About 30 seconds in, McCain, who was watching backstage with campaign strategist Steve Schmidt, said, "She's good, she's good." A minute later: "Man, she's great." A couple of minutes after that, he looked at Schmidt, eyes wide, and said, "She's fucking great, right?"

Palin took plenty of digs at Obama's community organizing and positioned Michelle as unpatriotic for having said that, for the first time, she was proud of her country. Palin then praised the people who "grow our food and run our factories and fight our wars. They love their country in good times and bad, and they're *always* proud of America." The crowd sent up its rafter-rattling approval.

Nicolle came by the CBS workspace looking elated, and rightly so (although she might also have been a little high on Vicodin—the ultimate multitasker, she'd tried to squeeze in a root canal between conventions).

"What did you think?" she asked.

I had to hand it to her. "She was awesome," I said. "Wow. You must be feeling really good about it."

Nicolle told me that at a certain point, Palin's prompter had been completely blocked by one of the huge signs people were waving.

"Oh my God," I said. "What did she do?"

"She winged it," Nicolle said. "She just threw in the pit-bull joke."

Now, *that* was impressive.

Everyone in the media had underestimated Sarah Palin—myself included. The day of the announcement, while preparing an intro for a piece about her, I was reading some copy that mentioned her sons, Trig and Track.

"Where the hell do they get these names?" I said to a colleague, not realizing my mic was hot. Somehow the audio got out and circulated among right-wing news outlets, who'd later use it as proof that I was out to get Palin from the start.

WITH BOTH CAMPAIGNS in full swing, the fall of 2008 was go time. But the *CBS Evening News* was stuck in neutral. The ratings were struggling. *I* was struggling. I needed an attention-getting interview. I needed Sarah Palin.

Nicolle said they were going to do mostly network interviews, which sounded risky to me; why not start out in local and midsize markets, where the stage is smaller and the reporters are less likely to be aggressive? But that was their call. All I cared about was being first, and I was pretty sure my relationship with Nicolle would give me a leg up.

So there I was, sitting in the back seat of an SUV (my mobile office), when she called.

"Katie, I'm so sorry"—*Uh-oh*—"but the decision was made to give the first interview to Charlie Gibson."

Devastated doesn't describe it. After we hung up, I burst into tears.

Charlie delivered a solid interview, although he was criticized for his stern, professorial demeanor—the skeptical head tilt, the reading glasses perched on the end of his nose. I was determined to keep the focus on Palin when I got my chance.

But first, more bad news: the second interview was going to Sean Hannity at Palin-friendly Fox.

"What was your family's reaction," Hannity says, about learning McCain had picked her. "Was that time to huddle and have a hockey-team meeting?"

Toward the end, Hannity deploys the ultimate gotcha: "What motivates you?"

I felt confident there was more wood to chop.

I was riding in the back seat of Jack's car, on my way to the cemetery to check on Jay, when I got a call from Steve Schmidt. He said the words I'd been waiting to hear for weeks: "Okay, Katie, you're up."

72

You Betcha

THE DEN IN my apartment had a full wall of built-in bookcases painted cranberry red, so the girls and I named it the Red Room. But in the days leading up to my Sarah Palin interview, the Red Room became the War Room.

The floor was blanketed with research. I settled in for several marathon sessions with Brian Goldsmith—at just 25, a full-on policy wonk (in high school, he was grounded for sneaking out of his bedroom to…watch C-SPAN). We inhaled everything that had ever been written about Palin and her sometimes wacky views on things like evolution and global warming. Our goal wasn't to give her a pop quiz. Since she was totally unproven on the national stage, we wanted her to reveal her positions on the issues and her fitness for the presidency. If elected, John McCain, who'd been treated for melanoma four times, would be the oldest president in history.

We picked the brains of the smartest people we knew, including the head of the Council on Foreign Relations Richard Haass and former Georgia senator Sam Nunn, now focused on bioterrorism. The best advice came from former Secretary of State Madeleine Albright.

"She's really a blank canvas," Albright told me over the phone. "No

Our "manny," my nephew Jeff, brought much-needed joy to our home after Jay died.

Talk about making an entrance: On Halloween 1999, I flew across the plaza as Peter Pan (and accidentally kicked some poor man in the head).

This is *TODAY* on NBC, with Katie Couric, Matt Lauer, and Ellie Monahan.

In the aftermath of Columbine, I interviewed Craig Scott, who lost his sister in the massacre, and Michael Schoels, who lost his son. Some of the rawest grief I've ever witnessed. *(NBC)*

My on-air colonoscopy, courtesy of Dr. Ken Forde, prompted a 20 percent increase in colonoscopies. Researchers called it the Couric Effect. *(NBC)*

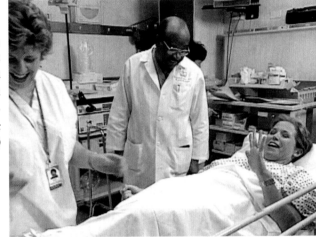

My mentor, the legendary Tim Russert, telling the nation what the 2000 presidential race would come down to. That whiteboard now lives in the Smithsonian. *(NBC)*

Visiting Emily for her 54th birthday in 2001, four months before she died of pancreatic cancer. She always thought she was going to get better.

At "the pile," two days after 9/11. I felt such a profound sense of responsibility covering that catastrophic event. *(NBC)*

Wendy introducing me at my induction into the Television Hall of Fame. We've been friends for — gulp — 40-plus years. *(Television Academy Hall of Fame)*

NBC relentlessly promoted the idea that the *TODAY* show was one big happy family, as if we spent every waking hour together. *(NBC)*

At the Olympics in Athens, 2004. Matt and I had a great relationship, but there was a lot about him I didn't know.

R&B royalty Mary J. Blige and Chaka Khan lit up one of our star-studded colon cancer fundraisers. *(KMazur / WireImage via Getty Images)*

My last day at *TODAY*, May 2006. They threw one heck of a going-away party. Tony Bennett sang "The Best Is Yet To Come." Oops. *(G. Gershoff / WireImage via Getty Images)*

When CBS put me on the Photoshop diet, the *New York Post* noticed and published the pictures side by side. *(New York Post)*

Making history—and apparently a bad fashion choice—as the first solo female anchor of an evening newscast. *(CBS)*

My assistant Lauren and me leading a conga line at the after-party following my debut. CBS veterans didn't join in.

Good times: Feeling (and looking) dwarfed by the giants of *60 Minutes*. *(John P. Filo, CBS)*

At a White House briefing during the Bush administration. One of these things is not like the others. *(Official White House Photo)*

Birthday at Tiffany's: Lori Beth, Carrie, me, and Ellie celebrating my 50th, 2007. *(Mia McDonald)*

Seven months after my CBS debut, Rick Kaplan swooped in and gave me back my confidence. *(John P. Filo, CBS)*

Trying to keep my cool in a bulletproof vest and triple-digit heat while touring Fallujah with General David Petraeus. *(CBS)*

Part of my CBS posse—Bob, Nicolla, Matt, Lauren (and Alexa Hirschfeld, who went on to found Paperless Post).

With Jeff Greenfield and Bob Schieffer, covering the DNC in Denver, 2008. Enthusiasm for Barack Obama was off the charts. *(John P. Filo, CBS)*

On the campaign plane with Sarah Palin, when she was flying high—before I asked her which newspapers and magazines she read. *(CBS)*

With my secret weapon, producer Lori Beecher. The blood, sweat, and tears we shed over landing Sully's first interview won us an Emmy.

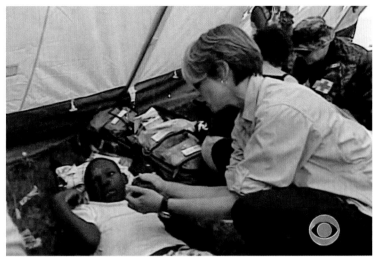

Trying to comfort Larousse Pierre, recently orphaned and badly injured in the Haiti earthquake. I will never forget the sound of him wailing in pain. *(CBS)*

Feeling less than heart-broken on my last day at CBS, May 2011. *(Heather Wines, CBS)*

With Brooks Perlin in Miami Beach. I stayed Krazy-Glued to my chaise when a paparazzo showed up. *(Splashnews)*

Meeting Queen Elizabeth, post-curtsy, on the occasion of her Diamond Jubilee. I think we really hit it off (for five seconds, anyway). *(Lewis Whyld / WPA Pool via Getty Images)*

Great expectations: On the set of my talk show, *Katie*, which premiered in September 2012. *(ABC, Ida Mae Astute)*

Feeling slightly adrift in a sea of bright colors. *(ABC, Ida Mae Astute)*

During the *Katie* era I felt most comfortable getting back to my news roots, reporting on stories like Hurricane Sandy.

An early date with Molner, at a Knicks game. *Us Weekly* said we were "piling on the PDA." *(James Devaney / FilmMagic via Getty Images)*

At Ellie's Yale graduation, 2013. I wish Jay could have been there.

Our wedding in East Hampton, June 21st, 2014. I loved it when John grabbed my mom's hand. *(Brian Dorsey)*

My bonus children, Allie and Henry. *(Brian Dorsey)*

After 16 years of being single, I'd finally met my match. *(Brian Dorsey)*

Philanthropy has its privileges: With Jon Hamm before a Stand Up To Cancer telecast. *(Image Group LA / American Broadcasting Companies, Inc., via WireImage)*

Introducing Yahoo CEO Marissa Mayer in Las Vegas. Suffice it to say, I didn't bleed purple. *(Ethan Miller via Getty Images)*

At the Supreme Court, interviewing Justice Ruth Bader Ginsburg. The crusader for equality surprised me with her comments on race. *(Mary F. Calvert)*

At Yahoo I got to interview everyone from Edward Snowden and Chance the Rapper to my feminist hero Gloria Steinem.

August 11th, 2017: I covered the "Unite the Right" rally for my National Geographic series, *America Inside Out*. My beloved Charlottesville, where I'd spent four glorious years during college, had been transformed into a hotbed of hatred. (*Tom Daly*)

For another episode in the series, Viola Davis and Julius Tennon told me about their efforts to open more doors for people of color in Hollywood. (*National Geographic, Hussein Katz*)

John's folks, Paula and Herby, have been like grandparents to my girls. Here they are at Carrie's Stanford graduation, 2018.

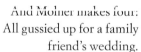

And Mother makes four: All gussied up for a family friend's wedding.

To help Carrie learn more about her father, I took her to Virginia, where she met two of Jay's reenactment buddies, Todd Kern and Mike Hickey.

Sealed with a kiss: Mark proposed to Ellie with the ring Jay had given me. *(Jenn Morse Photography)*

Molner's favorite photo of me.

After Alex Trebek died, I was honored to be the first female guest host of *Jeopardy!* and raise a quarter of a million dollars for Stand Up To Cancer. *(Jeopardy!)*

one really knows where she stands. My advice to you would be this: Just let her talk."

Those four words sank in. It's a natural impulse when you're interviewing someone to try to fill the dead air, and you end up letting them off the hook. So I made a mental note to avoid jumping in, no matter how awkward the silences.

We fine-tuned a list of questions, then role-played the interview, Brian doing a not-half-bad Palin. Meanwhile, in a hotel room across town, the real Sarah Palin paced the floor, holding a thick stack of cards full of facts she was trying to memorize. It wasn't going well.

I GOT UP AT 6 and jumped into the shower while my glam squad, Josie and Dana, filed in. Josie laid out brushes, eye shadow, and tubes of mascara and lipstick on my desk in the Red Room. Wrapped in a white terry-cloth robe, I took a seat and they went to work. Once I was camera-ready, I stepped into a navy pin-striped Hugo Boss suit that I always felt good in.

The day was glorious—crisp and crystal clear, reminding me how long it had been since I'd felt that jolt of early-morning energy. Brian, Rick, and another producer, Jen Yuille, were waiting downstairs. We piled into a black SUV and I started reviewing my questions for the first of two cracks at Palin.

I knew from watching Charlie's interview that Palin could respond with a baffling word salad—it was critical that I didn't let her wander off topic. I was also aware that my performance would be scrutinized almost as much as hers: what I asked, my tone, my demeanor would be pored over and picked apart. So I decided I would remain as expressionless as possible.

We settled into a makeshift studio at the Millennium Hotel. Palin walked in looking friendly but tense. As she was getting mic'd, she told me how much her parents liked me. Then she started futzing with her Elle Woods–worthy pink jacket, which was refusing to lie flat against her décolletage. So, in a surprise *Girlfriend, I got you* moment, I grabbed a piece of gaffer's tape from a crew member and offered it to her, which she appreciated (is there anything women bond over more quickly than a wardrobe malfunction?).

I felt like I was leading a lamb to slaughter.

THE CREW TWEAKED the lighting. Rick was sitting in my sight line, behind Palin and the cameras. I'd told him not to make any sudden movements; when we were out in the field, he was always signaling me like a base coach to do one thing or another, and I didn't want him distracting me.

The cameras started rolling.

We began with the financial crisis. Palin said that America was looking to John McCain to fix the system. I repeatedly asked her for evidence that he would lead the charge for more oversight and regulation. Palin offered a couple of non-answers.

> Me: But he's been in Congress 26 years; he's been chairman of the powerful Commerce Committee and has almost always sided with less regulation, not more.
>
> Palin: He's also known as the Maverick, though, taking shots from his own party and certainly taking shots from the other party...
>
> Me: I'm just going to ask you one more time, not to belabor the point: Specific examples in his 26 years of pushing for more regulation.
>
> Palin [*smiling*]: I'll try to find you some and I'll bring 'em to ya.

I sensed she was getting rattled. Clearly, Palin wasn't ready for prime time and a part of me felt sorry for her, watching her grasp for answers, trying to put sentences together that made sense. I kept going, asking why she thought Alaska's proximity to Russia enhanced her foreign policy credentials.

> Palin: Well, it certainly does because our next-door neighbors are foreign countries. There in the state that I am the executive of.

Me: Have you ever been involved with any negotiations, for ex-
    ample, with the Russians?
Palin: We have trade missions back and forth. It's very important
    when you consider even national security issues with Russia as
    Putin rears his head and comes into the airspace of the United
    States of America—where do they go? It's Alaska.

Brian was sitting close enough to a press aide from the Palin team to
see the message he was typing on his BlackBerry:

This is a fucking disaster.

BACK AT CBS, a puffed-up Rick walked through the newsroom
pronouncing the interview, "Huge. Huge." People barely looked up
from their keyboards. We'd turn around some of the interview for
that night's broadcast. Rick also asked Lori to reach out to *60 Minutes*.

"Tell them we'll just drop some bread crumbs throughout the week
and they can do a big piece on it Sunday."

"No, thanks," Bill Owens told her over the phone.

"Really?" Lori said. "It's a fantastic interview."

To which Owens replied, "Sarah Palin just isn't that in-ter-est-ing,"
o-ver-ly e-nun-ci-a-ting ev-er-y syl-la-ble, as he often did.

I didn't get it. Rick was dumbfounded. He felt it was the most
important political interview since 1979, when CBS anchor Roger Mudd
asked Ted Kennedy why he wanted to be president. Kennedy's rambling
response pretty much doomed his campaign.

I heard later that a high-ranking producer had walked into Fager's
office and urged him to run a chunk of Palin on Sunday. Fager said
he wasn't interested in my interview. When pressed, he responded,
"I don't need her on *60 Minutes*." I'm not sure if he meant Palin
or me.

The following Monday, I met Palin and her daughter Willow in the
hall outside their hotel room in Philly—Nicolle had thought the scene

would make good TV. I asked the 14-year-old if she was enjoying all of this.

"It's so fun," Willow said with a sweet smile. "I love it."

I imagined her mom, standing a few inches away, might be feeling differently.

We headed for Ohio on the McCain campaign plane. Palin was up front on the aisle; Brian and I were seated several rows back. Brian glanced in the governor's direction and noticed her manicured hand turning the pages of the *New York Times.* Funny—we hadn't pegged Palin as a *Times* reader. It made me wonder what else she read on a regular basis to stay on top of the issues.

After a rambunctious rally where the crowd ate up her every word, Palin and I wandered backstage to continue our conversation. We needed some B-roll of us walking and talking, so I asked a few more questions, including what newspapers and magazines she read.

> Palin: I've read most of them again with a great appreciation for the press, for the media—
> Me: But, like, what ones specifically? I'm curious that you—
> Palin: Um, all of 'em, any of 'em that have been in front of me over all these years. Um, I have a vast—
> Me: Can you name a few?
> Palin: I have a vast variety of sources where we get our news, too. Alaska isn't a foreign country where it's kind of suggested, it seems like, "Wow, how could you keep in touch with the rest of what Washington, DC, might be thinking and doing when you live up there in Alaska?"

I'll never know why Palin didn't just answer the question. No, she wasn't a big reader, but why couldn't she just wing it, like she did so brilliantly with the pit-bull joke? At the very least, she could have said the *New York Times,* although maybe Palin thought it would anger her conservative base. Or maybe she was just over it. And me.

It's funny—of all the serious things we discussed, this off-the-cuff exchange was the one that played on a national loop, marking a turning point in the campaign. Almost immediately, McCain's poll numbers started to sink.

The interview was a turning point for me too. Finally good press, and lots of it. And the people at CBS were visibly surprised by how well it went. Brian, such a great and loyal friend, was basically like, *Duh—have you* seen *Katie before? This is what she does.*

Then there was *Saturday Night Live.* A friend called at around 10:00 p.m. to say, "Make sure you watch tonight!"

Oh, boy, I thought. *This could go either way.*

I got in my flannel pj's and sat on the couch with Ellie in the Red Room. Sure enough, we were the cold open.

There's letter-perfect Tina Fey as Palin in the pink jacket and rectangle-lens eyewear—an American flag in the background, just like in our interview. And there's Amy Poehler playing me.

It's a hilarious bit, with Fey nailing Palin's impenetrable gosh-golly syntax and Poehler-as-me staring back and rapid-blinking incredulously. At one point she asks, "What lessons have you learned from Iraq and how specifically would you spread democracy abroad?"

After a long and comical pause, Fey/Palin cites the mayday option for contestants on the game show *Who Wants to Be a Millionaire:*

"Katie, I'd like to use one of my lifelines."

Which pretty much summed up the state of the McCain/Palin campaign.

Choosing Palin wasn't John McCain's finest moment. But when I watched him give his classy concession speech, I was reminded of what an incredibly decent guy he was. I'd always enjoyed being in his presence; he'd invited us to stay for a barbecue at his ranch in Sedona when I was there to interview him (unfortunately, we had to hit the road). He loved to goof around with reporters and really respected what we did. Those were the days.

Sarah Palin may have crashed and burned, but she launched a new era in American politics. Her plainspoken mean-spiritedness and her ability to tap into populist grievances planted the seeds of Trumpism that would grow and spread like kudzu across the land.

The interview won a coveted duPont-Columbia Award. And while it didn't provide much of an uptick in the ratings, rumors that I was about to get fired would never be whispered again.

73

Over Un-Easy

KATIE BOYLE WAS a senior producer at CBS and, for me, a rare bright spot—diligent and serious-minded, but I could make her laugh with a funny aside or an eye-roll when no one was looking. I called her Katie B.; she called me Katie C. In February of 2011, she asked if I would be willing to meet with a woman named Abra Potkin, who worked in the syndication department of CBS, the folks who brought you daytime staples like *Judge Judy* and *Dr. Phil*.

"You will *love* her," Katie told me like she was describing one of the cool kids.

We arranged to have lunch at the Greek Kitchen, my go-to in the restaurant dead zone surrounding the CBS Broadcast Center. Abra had straight raven hair and lively brown eyes that widened conspiratorially as she leaned in, gesturing broadly. She was one of the most enthusiastic people I'd ever met and won me over instantly. Abra wanted to feel me out about hosting a syndicated daytime talk show.

Syndication. The very word rang with lucrative possibilities. In a nutshell, a syndicated show is brought to market, and local stations have the option to pay a licensing fee to air it; if the show is considered hot, that can mean big money. The downside is syndicated shows aren't protected the way they might be if wholly owned and operated by a network. To a large extent, they're on their own.

I was raised on syndicated shows. I had my after-school snack of vanilla wafers in front of *The Dinah Shore Show* as she gently chatted with guests in her soft white blouse and even softer blond hair. Then there was the affable Mike Douglas (24-year-old Roger Ailes was a production assistant) and the equally affable Merv Griffin. Merv went on to create syndicated game shows like *Jeopardy!* and *Wheel of Fortune.* When he died in 2007, his net worth was a billion dollars.

But history was made in 1986 when Oprah arrived on the national stage. Her show quickly achieved mythic status, the pinnacle of what syndication could do—provide a platform for feel-good conversation while folding in hugely important topics like racism, domestic violence, and AIDS, minting money in the process.

For years, I had resisted the idea of doing a talk show of any kind. There had been many overtures, including a DreamWorks proposal for *The Katie Couric Hour,* an alternative to the fluff and "oversaturated, old-skewing" court shows that were proliferating at the time. In the middle of the pitch, they had a bunch of people show up outside the windowed conference room holding big signs that said WE LOVE YOU, KATIE! Jeffrey Katzenberg assured me it would be a hit.

It wasn't for me. I liked news. I was happy where I was.

But now it was time to reassess. For starters, Oprah had announced she was ending her 25-year run, leaving a huge daytime void to fill. And after five years of feeling muzzled at CBS, I was ready to live my best life and focus on big, relevant stories in a format that I would get to create.

"Is there a way to have a little personality and still tackle important, meaty topics?" I asked Abra.

"Yes!" she said emphatically, thrusting both arms in the air. "Ab-so*lute*ly!"

My good sense drifted up and away like the steam rising from my avgolemono soup. "Okay, maybe this could be interesting," I told her, leaving the door ajar.

It was nice to feel wanted.

In early February, Les's name popped up on my phone.

"Hey there," he said smoothly. "Listen, I wanted to tell you, I just promoted Jeff Fager to chairman of CBS News."

Of course I'd heard the rumors. Still, my stomach dropped. Here was Les, the guy who had wooed me with wine and promises, promoting my nemesis. "Les, you must know this is not good news for me," I responded.

He waved me off like a gnat circling his ear. "Oh, he'll be great!"

Right.

My contract was up in June. The idea of becoming a free agent terrified me. Playing the waiting game wasn't in my nature, and I wanted to perpetuate the narrative that I was still a hot commodity. If I didn't have someplace to jump to, I worried that I'd be seen as a failure, bumped off the glass cliff.

Les was on board with me doing a show—I'm sure he regarded it as a face-saving way to segue me out of the anchor chair. But I wasn't comfortable fully exiting the news business. I'd been in it for 32 years, and I wanted to figure out a way to continue doing big interviews and breaking stories. So I came up with an idea: If CBS was my syndicated home, why couldn't I still do pieces for *60 Minutes*? Yes, I realized it was a novel idea, temporarily forgetting CBS didn't like novel ideas.

Jeff Fager suggested breakfast at the Market Place Café and Deli at the corner of 57th and 11th. A diner, basically, that happened to be empty—not the sort of spot you'd choose if you're looking to convince someone you think they're all that.

He seemed even more uncomfortable around me than usual, if that's possible. Early in the conversation, Fager said he was making some changes at the *CBS Evening News*—something like "We're going in a different direction," that euphemistic favorite when someone's about to get canned. Not a surprise.

While he didn't name names, it quickly became clear he already had someone in mind to succeed me: square-jawed, stentorian-voiced Scott Pelley, rumored to have been Fager's first choice to replace Dan Rather all along. You'd have to look high and low to find an anchor less like me than Scott Pelley. I'd heard he entertained guests at his home on Connecticut's Gold Coast in an ascot and smoking jacket. One day, he showed up with two couples who'd paid big bucks at a cystic fibrosis benefit for a tour of the CBS newsroom. I greeted them graciously, always stunned that anyone would pay cash money to see us making the sausage, after which Pelley, in the poshest voice you could ever imagine, said, "Katie, by the way, I met your sister-in-law Clare at the Tokeneke Club in Darien last weekend. She is de*light*ful."

Clare's the best, but who talks like that?

Back at the diner, I stared at Fager's receding hairline and puffy eyelids, then tried to express my wishes calmly and sincerely. *Do not grovel, do not grovel, do not grovel...* "Some of the most gratifying work I've done at CBS are the pieces I've done for you," I began.

Nothing.

"I really love *60 Minutes*," I said.

"I know you do," he replied.

More dead air.

What a dick.

I thought back to another telltale moment: I'd been assigned to profile Andre Agassi. My favorite part of our conversation was when Andre talked about his hair...or lack thereof. At the height of his fame, his sex-symbol status was entwined with his flowing mullet. When his hair started thinning, he covered the bald spot with a toupee. As you might imagine, even the most secure hairpiece could be problematic if the wearer is diving for shots and reaching for overhead slams. Andre was hilarious, describing his fear of the toupee flying off while he was competing in the French Open, landing on the court, and lying there like roadkill. He was laughing, I was laughing—a genuinely funny, spontaneous moment.

But when Fager watched it during the screening, he said, "Enough of that. Take it out."

Fager seemed dead set against letting my personality emerge in any piece I did. Probably because he didn't like my personality.

Staring at my untouched, greasy, over-easy egg, I said, "Okay, well, thanks!"—and pretended I had an errand to run in the opposite direction. Anything to keep from having to spend another second with the guy.

I'VE OFTEN IMAGINED what I could have done differently at CBS. I think about the advice I've shared with fresh-faced (aka hungover) college graduates in the many commencement speeches I've given over the years: "Sometimes you have to leap before you look!" "Take a risk, try new things!" "Get out of your comfort zone...even if it's uncomfortable!" I dusted off the message on a notecard a producer had written me when I left *TODAY:* "A boat is always safe in the harbor, but that's not what boats are built for."

Maybe I should have kept my boat tied to the dock; maybe I should have looked before I leapt. When someone said the stains on the carpet at NBC were coffee while the stains at CBS were blood, instead of chuckling, maybe I should have listened. I know I should have spent more time getting advice from people who had my best interests at heart. I was so hell-bent on taking a stand for women, I didn't consider the woman who'd be at the center of the storm...me.

74

Take This Job and Shove It

A S I OPENED my mind to the syndication idea, one thing seemed clear: If I was really going to enter this alien fray, I'd need a partner—a really capable, trustworthy executive producer. My first thought was Jeff Zucker. The problem was, he'd become a controversial, embattled figure, having been pushed out at NBC as soon as Comcast bought the network.

He'd had a mixed track record, to put it mildly. NBC was known for its unparalleled tradition of hit scripted programming since the days of Brandon Tartikoff—responsible for '80s juggernauts like *Miami Vice, Cheers, L.A. Law,* and *The Golden Girls* (remember "Must-See TV"? It really started with Brandon). Instead of honoring that legacy, Jeff focused on the bottom line, leaning into cheap-to-produce reality TV like *Fear Factor.* (And let us not forget he spearheaded *The Apprentice,* making Donald Trump a small-screen star and positioning him for a successful presidential run. Thanks, Jeff!) And he got lambasted for bungling the *Tonight Show* transition from Jay Leno to Conan O'Brien and back again, publicly demoting and humiliating Conan. On Jeff's watch, NBC fell from number one to number four in a single season.

Jeff wasn't everyone's cup of tea. His know-it-all confidence could be really off-putting. When he moved to California to oversee the entertainment division, plenty of Hollywood heavyweights were incensed by the dismissive way he treated them during business meetings, never tearing his gaze from the minimum three monitors he had on at all times in his office. Tom Werner was one of those incensed heavyweights, once saying to me, "It's almost as if my dating you has hurt me." (I could practically hear the wheels in his head turning as he considered which relationship would be more advantageous.)

And yet, Jeff and I were sympatico. Our partnership at *TODAY* had been the envy of morning TV; who wouldn't want to replicate that? If we teamed up again, I thought the chances were good we could create something special and that, together, we could navigate the rapidly changing television landscape.

"Hey, I've got a great idea," I told him.

I went on to describe not only the talk show but the business we could create, where our show gives birth to other syndicated shows that we would basically own.

"That could be fun," Jeff said noncommittally. I told him we'd be 50/50 partners—both executive producers with equal influence and decision-making power. I'd give him half my salary, and our back-end stake would be 50/50 as well: whatever the profits, we'd split them evenly.

And yes, it might look like a step back—he'd been the BMOC at NBC, hobnobbing with big cheeses in the executive suites at 30 Rock, deciding the fates of EPs like the one I was now asking him to become—the one he'd been two decades earlier at *TODAY*. But the truth was, he needed a gig.

About two weeks later, he asked Alan and me to come see him at his apartment off Park Avenue.

We sat down at the white kitchen table. Caryn said a quick hello and headed out the door. The high-end stainless-steel appliances gleamed in the background—I wondered how the place could look so clean with a couple of little ones, a tween, and a teen running around.

I cut to the chase. "So, whaddya think?"

Jeff paused for dramatic effect. Then somewhat cavalierly, he said, "Okay, I'll do it."

I was a little stunned. "Really?" I asked. *"Really?"* I repeated, surprised but so relieved to have someone I trusted to ride shotgun.

Jeff looked around as if to say, *Am I missing something? Why isn't she getting this?* Alan chortled.

I probably should have been less grateful and more skeptical, interrogating Jeff's true level of interest. I don't think it even occurred to Alan to ask him a single question about this really consequential decision. Which I get; an agent's raison d'être is to close the deal. But still—he was there to represent my interests, and I think he owed it to me to at least kick the tires on this thing.

Then there was the question of Jeff's baggage. He and Les Moonves detested each other, so doing the show at CBS was a nonstarter (especially with Fager showing zero interest in using me on *60 Minutes*). NBC had pitched me hard with a video of my antics on the *TODAY* show that ended with an invitation to "come home to NBC." That tugged at my heartstrings—although with Jeff in the mix now, the invitation was basically rescinded. Suddenly, ABC was looking pretty good.

ABC honchos Anne Sweeney and Ben Sherwood arrived at my apartment bearing a PowerPoint presentation and a Wheaties box emblazoned with my high-school-cheerleader picture.

Ben talked about having an unparalleled stable of great talent that I would be part of. A former producer for Tom Brokaw, he said all the right things—about the high-profile specials I'd be doing, about me being part of the ABC family. I felt like he saw the possibilities.

Then Anne and Ben showed us the money: a whopping $50 million budget (more than twice what a show like this typically costs), including a back-end percentage and a salary of $20 million for me, $10 million of which would go to Jeff—an unprecedented payday for an executive producer. It was crazy in retrospect, but at the time, it was important to me to show Jeff we'd be equal partners in this venture.

I FELT LIKE THINGS were starting to gel, so imagine my surprise when I was puttering around at home one day and a call came in with the familiar 664 prefix—NBC on the line.

"Hey, Katie, it's Matt. I'm on the phone here with Jim." Matt as in Lauer; Jim as in Bell, the EP of *TODAY*. I really wasn't accustomed to getting personal calls from either one of these guys, much less on a party line.

"Hey, Katie," Jim chimed in.

"Hey, guys! What's up?"

"Well...we were wondering if you might be interested in coming back to the *TODAY* show."

Really?

Here I was, trying to reinvent myself, when a sure thing reared its handsome head—an opportunity to go back to doing what I'd proved I was really good at with none other than Matt Lauer by my side. Meredith Vieira had announced she'd be leaving, and Ann Curry would be replacing her. So how would this work? I'd been raised on the notion that there were two main anchors overseeing the action, long before there was a cast of thousands sitting around a table "laughing and scratching," as my mom would say.

"What about Ann?" I asked.

"We'll work it out," Jim said. If the plan was to sideline Ann, it wasn't clear; I just assumed they were envisioning a throuple, which sounded awkward.

I wondered how the interviews would be divvied up. Matt and I had already been competitive about who got what; with three of us, I envisioned the *TODAY* "family" turning completely dysfunctional, fighting over a drumstick on Thanksgiving. And I was pretty sure Ann wouldn't go for it either—honestly, it seemed a little unfair to her. But there was a looming chemistry issue: such a big part of that show is being able to hit the ball back and forth, and Matt and Ann just didn't have that kind of rapport.

It all seemed a bit half-baked, a little desperate, and tricky from a PR standpoint. Besides, I was already into it with Jeff—it would have been a huge slap in the face if I backed out of our deal to retreat to NBC, where he was persona non grata. Ultimately, I decided Thomas Wolfe was right: I couldn't go home again.

Back at CBS, I felt like a dead woman walking. For any doubters, there was this: On May 1st, when the most dramatic story of the Obama administration was breaking—SEAL Team 6 raiding the compound in Pakistan that was sheltering Osama bin Laden and taking him out—I wasn't called in to report it.

Here I was, the face of the *CBS Evening News,* and on this night of all nights for newshounds (and Americans and freedom lovers) everywhere, hanging out at home in my sweatpants. I even called in to CBS—"Hey, this is incredible, what's going on? Need me to come in?"

The EP was basically like, *Nah, we're good.*

MAY 19TH—MY final day at the anchor desk. While I'm not a huge fan of the sound of a door closing, it was a relief to be putting CBS behind me. In a demure black dress (a fitting bookend, perhaps, given all the crap I got for wearing white on my first broadcast), I teed up a highlights reel that was pretty darn chockablock, if I do say so myself. I had the team edit the end of the montage to "In My Life" by the Beatles—one last poke at CBS's stuffy style. We broke news, won awards, and held our heads high amid frequent indifference and flat-out resistance.

After the broadcast, the staff gathered in the newsroom. I thanked everyone, including my holy trinity of news writers, Jarod, Joe, and Jerry; cribbing from Dorothy, I told Jerry, "I think I'll miss you most of all." And as I reflected on the incredible experiences I'd had at CBS—interviewing Defense Secretary Bob Gates in a Humvee in Afghanistan; covering the barrier-breaking election of Barack Obama; gripping the hand of a wailing, badly wounded Haitian boy in a makeshift hospital tent in Port-au-Prince after the earthquake; shaking in a bathroom in a Tahrir Square hotel during the Arab Spring, terrified that the protesters below would storm the building; confronting the Holocaust-denying Iranian president Ahmadinejad with a photo of mangled bodies in a mass grave in Auschwitz; hitting the ground running at Virginia Tech on the heels of a massacre—I couldn't help but note the disconnect between the work we'd done and the fact that I never really belonged there. The body had rejected the organ early on, and no amount of immunosuppressants (or hand-wringing or course-correcting or belated ingratiating) was ever going to change that.

After the broadcast, a bunch of us pre-gamed at Nicolla's with champagne and martinis; someone had made up T-shirts bearing the *Survivor* logo. We toasted ourselves while listening to the playlist Nicolla had put together, which included "Take This Job and Shove It," "That's It, I Quit, I'm Movin' On," and "I Will Survive." I don't know how I would have gotten through those five years without my loyal, talented team.

Then we headed out to the nightclub Butter, where we colonized several couches and enjoyed the bottle service. It was an intense, bittersweet affair.

Apparently, I wasn't the only one feeling that way. When Susan Zirinsky, the EP of *48 Hours* and future president of CBS News, showed up, she confessed to my friend Charlie, "I let her down. I should have done more."

Yes, Z (as everyone called her) could have been a more vocal advocate. We had delivered some kick-ass hours together, including a tribute to the late Ted Kennedy and a glittery pre-Grammy special. But the truth is, it would have been risky. I was radioactive, and anyone who valued her position at CBS—like Z, the only woman who'd made it to the leadership ranks—knew better than to go to bat for me. And I'm not sure there was anything she or anyone else could have done.

A few weeks after I exited the dairy barn for the last time, I was at Reagan National following a visit with my dad. He was very sick, and I was bereft, knowing he didn't have much time left. A hospital bed had been set up in the living room. I showed him how he could play Scrabble on an iPad, and I read to him from Laura Hillenbrand's book *Unbroken* (word games and military valor—two of my dad's favorite things). He commented that the main character seemed slightly "braggadocious," which made me smile.

For a while now, my father had been too overwhelmed with illness to sustain a tactical conversation about my troubles at CBS. And the last thing I wanted to do was burden him. But I also think I was embarrassed. I felt like I'd let him down.

I pictured my parents taking their seats at the kitchen table at 6:30 to watch me on their portable TV with rabbit ears. I thought about how hard it was some nights to keep it together behind the anchor desk and wondered if they were falling for my everything's-going-great routine. I wondered how aware they were of the beating I'd taken in the press. They had kept meticulous scrapbooks from every chapter of my career—up until CBS. Maybe there just weren't enough positive pieces to fill one.

My heart was heavy as I headed to the airport. And just as I was about to get out of the taxi at the terminal, I spotted Jeff Fager 30 feet ahead of me, bounding out of a town car with the new president of CBS News, David Rhodes, both looking particularly pleased with themselves. The contrast between my father and these two self-satisfied schmucks couldn't have been sharper. I slumped in the back seat, taking my time fishing out my cab fare, giving thanks for my Fager-free future.

75

A Chap Named Parkinson

M Y DAD'S ILLNESS was progressing rapidly and taking its toll on my mom too. She had to do so much for him—button his shirts and tie his shoes—in addition to grocery shopping, cooking, laundry, ironing. Under the best of circumstances, she wasn't the most patient person, and my father's spiraling needs sometimes left her feeling anxious and angry. The scenes from their marriage would now feature bickering, exasperation, retribution, shame. Yet they loved and cared for each other without fail; after dinner, they'd make sure each had taken their assortment of pills, which they kept in a plastic Pepperidge Farm bag on the kitchen table. They were determined to stay independent and wouldn't accept any caregiving help, even though God knows we tried.

I hosted a big family bash in the Hamptons for my dad's ninetieth. Before the party, I took him for a spin in my Thunderbird; walking out to the driveway, he told everyone he was going for a ride with a "real star." As we drove along the glorious tree-lined streets of East Hampton, I was full of gratitude, so happy we could have that time together.

We made sure to have all the Southern foods he loved: honey-baked ham, fried chicken, cheese grits, biscuits, and a spinach salad (because I had to serve at least one healthy dish). Dessert was a seven-layer caramel cake from Caroline's in Annapolis, caramel being my dad's favorite. All of us—including his 10 grandchildren—gave speeches, and Carrie sang "I'll Be Seeing You," the World War II song my parents loved.

My dad gave a charming speech, explaining that he'd "outlined remarks mentally but did not commit them to paper because my constant companion—a chap named Parkinson—has inhibited my penmanship." Then he presented his great-granddaughter Emily, Ray's daughter, the grandchild my sister never met, with Emily's charm bracelet, tinkling with silver mementos, including some from his travels. It was such a tender, melancholy moment—a reminder that we'd lost Emily and that my father might not be here much longer either.

The next day, I heard a soft thud on the front steps. My dad had lost his balance and lay crumpled on the concrete near the front door. I helped him up, sick with worry, especially when I saw that his glasses had somehow cut his face. He assured me he was fine. My dad was so thin—his belt cinched on the last hole to keep his khakis from falling down, skin hanging in flaps from his bony arms. Once I got him inside, I ran to the bathroom and fetched some Neosporin and a Band-Aid. I helped him apply it, which didn't leave me a second to cry.

Johnny was the most reliable caregiver of us all, considering that he lived the closest to our parents and he's the nicest person in our family (I think we'd all agree on that). He'd clean the gutters, move furniture, reprogram TVs, trim shrubs...on Sundays he'd sit with them at the dining-room table and help pay their bills. Once when the basement flooded, he spent hours upon hours over the course of days moving furniture, taking up the old carpet, including the tackboard and the mat, cutting it all up and putting it in the garbage, repacking the stuff that had been in wet boxes, and renting giant fans to dry everything out. Throughout the ordeal, our mom sat on the basement steps, taking it all in.

"Wow!" she said. "We're working really hard."

To which Johnny replied, "What's this 'we' stuff?"

They laughed and laughed.

Kiki and I visited as much as we could. I remember one afternoon sitting with my dad on the front steps of their house, trimming his fingernails with the small, spring-loaded scissors in his red Swiss Army knife, taking each finger and holding it securely between mine as I carefully snipped, listening as my dad chatted about his college professors from 70 years earlier, recalling every name and what they taught as well as the other students in the class.

I looked out at the front yard, unchanged for 54 years save for the crab apple tree that had been cut down, the one that bore the arsenal of small projectiles with which we pelted the neighborhood boys. I thought about my dad carving neat patterns in the grass with his push mower. Calling down to the basement where I was practicing on our upright piano with the gummy keys, "Katie, play 'As Time Goes By'!" Surveying the cicada carcasses littering the soil around the boxwoods, a glass of scotch in his hand, telling me that since they came every 17 years, he probably would never see them again.

WE GATHERED AT the hospital, moistening my dad's mouth with a sponge on the end of a lollipop stick, kissing him, just being there. He'd been experiencing "sundowning," the late-afternoon confusion hospital confinement can bring, where he'd yammer on about crazy things— some even raunchy, which was so out of character. But now his body was surrendering too—he slept most of the day. Knowing that hearing is the last thing to go, I'd brought my iPod, set up a small speaker in his room, and played Frank Sinatra, Tony Bennett, and Benny Goodman on a loop. I told my dad I loved him so much, that he was the best father and that I never could have done the things I had without his love and guidance—as true a sentiment as I've ever felt.

Walking down the hospital hallway, drained and sad, I turned to my brother. "Johnny, I guess we need to write Dad's obituary."

He smiled. "Oh, Katie, no, we don't. He's already written it." He'd also written thorough instructions, back when he was in perfect health, for his funeral arrangements, including that the local Presbyterian minister should preside, that Kiki's son Sam should blow taps, and "under no conditions are you to purchase fancy urns"—for him, or when the time came, for our mother. Thrifty to the end.

On a steamy, sticky, southern day in August, we had a small graveside service in Eufaula. Each of us gave a eulogy. I noted that our father was neither handy nor sporty, but he was fair-minded, kind, and incredibly smart—"I now so regret teasing Daddy by starting to snore at the dinner table every time he tried to explain an issue or deliver some insight about history," I said. I went on for pages and could have gone on for several more but closed with gratitude for "his loving presence in our lives—even after his death."

I miss my dad.

76

Family Feud

AFTER BEING STUCK in second place for 852 consecutive weeks (more than 16 years!), *Good Morning America* finally beat *TODAY* in the ratings. Rumors about Ann's fate swirled. We'd later learn from media reporter Brian Stelter that the show's executives had hatched a secret plan, code name Operation Bambi: Marginalize Ann to the point of no return. Thirteen months after being anointed, she was out.

On the morning of June 11th, 2012, I curled up on the couch, still in my pj's, and tuned in:

"This is not easy to say," Ann begins, "but this is going to be my last morning as a regular co-host of *TODAY*." And suddenly she starts tearing up. Voice cracking, she tells the audience that they are "the *real TODAY* show family."

Meanwhile, Matt is sitting right next to her on the couch, legs casually crossed, right arm draped across the back of the sofa à la Don Draper in the *Mad Men* title sequence. Given the gossip, you couldn't help but conclude that he'd played a role in Ann's demise.

"You have the biggest heart in the business," he attempts, as Ann dabs her eyes with a delicate finger. "You put it on display *every single day* in this studio." The two are flanked by a somber-looking Al Roker and Natalie Morales. A choked-up Natalie reaches across Matt to grab

Ann's hand. Now there's an image for the ages: a tight shot of their grip inches from Matt's sternum.

Just as I was thinking/hoping/daring to dream we were done here, the most cringeworthy thing happens: Matt actually leans over and tries to give Ann a kiss, grazing her temple as she visibly ducks.

And so ended Operation Bambi. But NBC's troubles had just begun. Despite the declining ratings, Ann had some very loyal fans, and they rallied around her, threatening boycotts and ranting on Twitter:

> @todayshow stinks without Ann...Shame on u for how u treated @anncurry...WHAT A BIG MISTAKE THEY'VE MADE.

It reminded me of Jane Pauley's ouster 23 years earlier.

Handling on-air transitions is one of the toughest things in the business, partly because management often fails to understand the intimate relationship viewers have with the people who show up on their TV in the morning: smiling supportively, giving them a heads-up on the weather, reminding them what time it is, sharing news both good and bad, becoming part of the household hubbub. The audience learns about their lives and pet peeves—for instance, that Bryant Gumbel hated cheese ("I'd rather eat a pound of dirt") and that Matt was such a germophobe he made no bones about wanting to swim in a tank of Purell after greeting fans on the plaza. Viewers knew that I'd sing at the drop of a hat, that Al loved to draw cartoons, and that Ann's mother disapproved of her makeup. All that familiarity breeds deep loyalty in an audience, and if they feel one of their on-air friends has been wronged, they'll turn.

Ann's situation should have been handled differently. The *TODAY* show could have been straight with her rather than sabotaging her, but TV executives aren't known for honest conversations. By the time they offered her the soft landing of compassionate globe-trotting correspondent, parachuting into disasters natural and man-made—a role she perfected—there was too much bad blood, and all she wanted was out.

I wonder if Ann felt vindicated by the ferocious backlash Matt suffered. He could have avoided the whole thing if he'd taken us up on a pretty sexy offer: to co-host the syndicated show with me, an idea we'd hit him with *twice*. The second time, ABC got heavily involved, with Bob Iger offering a package of opportunities at the network and apparently ponying up even more than he was paying me. I knew they'd have to break the bank to pry Matt away, and they were willing.

Jeff and I were giddy at the possibility. But leaving the comfortable and well-compensated confines of the *TODAY* show for something completely unknown was a huge risk.

In early April, Matt re-signed with NBC. And no wonder: $25 million a year, a four-day workweek, and a helicopter to take him to and from his manse in the Hamptons. (He gave me a lift back to the city in that thing once, a scene straight out of *Succession*.) Yes, the compensation was obscene, but when you are the face of a profit-gusher like *TODAY,* the sky's the limit.

Jeff was livid. I got the clear sense he was much more excited about our show when there was a chance Matt would join us, partly because poaching Matt Lauer would have been a hell of an *FU* to NBC for showing Jeff the door—just as Les Moonves poaching me for the *CBS Evening News* was a great way to stick it to Jeff. The media runs on schadenfreude—it's not enough that you're able to attract big-name talent to enhance your operation; the real joy is in screwing the competition. What a business.

All Jeff and I could do was move on. We were in it now, and there was no turning back.

PART V

77

Nancy Knows

WE HAD A full year to prepare for the syndicated show. Our gap year, as I came to think of it, quickly got stuffed with glad-handing, lunching, and meet-and-greets designed to excite the local GMs and convince everyone Jeff was fully on board.

I also popped up in various places on ABC to keep myself in the public eye. The highlight was a special I did for *20/20* called "The Jubilee Queen," commemorating 60 years of Queen Elizabeth II's reign. I caught up with Prince Harry at a polo match in Brazil (still in his wild-oats-sowing phase—a strong aroma of alcohol and cigarettes seemed to ooze from every pore). On the subject of his social media–aware "granny," I asked Prince Harry if she'd friended him on Facebook. He said she hadn't, then asked if she'd friended *me* (um, no, unfortunately). At Clarence House, Prince William opened up about how difficult it was to not have his mother at his wedding, telling me he was "just very sad she's never gonna get the chance to meet Kate."

I donned a fascinator (which looked more like a Frisbee-shaped matzo) for a Buckingham Palace garden party: tea and scones on 40 acres for 8,000 guests ranging from landed gentry to "commoners," a sea of fanciful bonnets in all shapes and shades. Eventually, the queen approached in a peach coat with big buttons and a matching hat, one of her handbags dangling, in trademark fashion, from her forearm. I curtsied and told her what an honor it was to meet her. Then I said, "We're working on a special about you, Your Majesty."

To which she responded, "There's a lot there." That was clear (and we hadn't even seen *The Crown* yet).

I also guest-hosted *GMA,* a show that had been my mortal enemy for 15 years. Some thought that was downright treasonous, as if there were a codicil buried deep in my old NBC contracts demanding lifetime loyalty. *TODAY* retaliated by bringing in Sarah Palin, of all people, to guest-host at the same time (narrowly winning the week, so I guess she got me back).

By now, things with Brooks were wearing thin. The older I got, the younger he seemed. The relationship was way past its sell-by date, but for some reason I couldn't find it in me to end it. Turns out I didn't have to.

I was in Simi Valley, California, to do a Q & A at the Reagan Library. I had some time on my hands, so I got a pedicure, during which Matthew Hiltzik's name showed up on my phone. Page Six wanted my reaction to the fact that Brooks was moving out of my apartment. You really haven't lived until a tabloid informs you what's going on in your personal life.

Nancy Reagan had invited me. We'd become friends when she took me on a tour of the library for the *TODAY* show in 1998 soon after Jay died. She was especially kind to me that day. I think she felt we were kindred spirits: I had lost my husband, and she, in many ways, had lost hers—her beloved Ronnie was slipping away from Alzheimer's disease, something he called "the long goodbye." We'd also produced a beautiful piece about his love letters to Nancy. After President Reagan died, I brought her a Venetian glass vase I'd picked up in Italy.

Following my Page Six newsflash, I was sitting with Nancy when she inquired about my love life. She was in a wheelchair and very frail, although her appetite for dish was undiminished (I remember her digging into the topic of Warren Beatty during lunch one time at the Hotel Bel-Air).

"Oh, that handsome younger guy I've been with for a while," I said, "that's pretty much over."

Nancy paused, taking it in. Then she smiled sweetly and said, "Well, dear, at some point, I guess you have to talk."

78

That Molner Guy

ISHOULDN'T HAVE let it go on so long with Brooks. My mother openly disapproved—she thought he was using me and didn't like the age difference. And when I shared with *People* how great it was all going, calling Brooks "incredibly kind, caring and sensitive," my mom went berserk. My father called and begged me to reach out to her, which of course I did. But I will always regret the distance that relationship temporarily put between my parents and me. And Carrie and me.

Breakups triggered such awful feelings—of sadness and emptiness, of what might have been with Jay. It was a different kind of loss but it retraumatized me just the same—my friend Donna, a therapist, described it as reigniting my grief dendrites. So I always let things drag on longer than they should. I often told my girls as they were walking out the door, "Make good choices." Why was I making so many bad ones?

The upside: The breakup diet. By now, I had a much healthier relationship with food, but it would forever be entwined with my emotions. I couldn't eat or sleep, and the anxiety seemed to ramp up my metabolism. The skinny jeans I kept in the back of my closet fit again, and my clavicles felt like wings.

The downside: When the girls and I went to Puerto Rico a week or so later over the Christmas break, I was once again the third wheel (though with three other couples, I guess I was the seventh). Despite crushing an impromptu game of Name That Tune we'd played with our iPhones on the terrace of the hotel, I was pretty miserable. Alone again, naturally.

WOMEN HAVE OFTEN asked me for dating advice and I always tell them the same thing: "Be intentional." I remember seeing the 1984 movie *Falling in Love* with Robert De Niro and Meryl Streep as suburban strangers, married to other people, who meet at a bookstore. The serendipity of bumping into your soulmate while browsing bestsellers seemed a little ridiculous to me. In my experience, you had to make your own luck. So, after a few months of licking my wounds, I went back to singing the single-gal solo "Do you know anyone?" to every person who crossed my path.

One morning at Flywheel with my friend and dating adviser Pat, I spotted Molly Helfet hanging her jacket in a locker. Her elegant South African husband, Dave, was the chief trauma surgeon at the Hospital for Special Surgery.

"Hey, Pat," I said, "do you think Molly and Dave know any nice doctors I can go out with?"

"I don't know," Pat said. "Let's ask her."

We weaved our way through the tomato-faced, soaking-wet spinners from the previous class and got to Molly. "Hey!" Pat said. Then, in a low voice, as if we were sharing state secrets: "Katie has a question for you."

I mentioned what a great guy Emily's doctor husband, George, was and all the nice MDs I'd met through my cancer advocacy work. Other than my brief fling with the plastic surgeon, doctors were strangely underrepresented in my thick dating portfolio.

Molly flipped through her mental Rolodex. "A doctor? A single doctor? Not really," she said, then paused. "But we do know this banker named John Molner."

"Does he have a pulse?" I asked.

"Yes, he does." Molly laughed. "He might be seeing someone—other than that, John's great."

But John Molner didn't call. He didn't write. Every time I saw

Molly at spin class, I'd inquire without shame or subtlety, "Molly, what happened to that Molner guy?"

Trying to move this thing along, Molly said she could host a dinner party and invite us both, which sounded horribly awkward; one day on the golf course, Dave floated the same idea to John, who apparently disliked it as much as I did. Rather than be seated next to each other at a dinner with other guests looking on, trying to determine if a love connection was happening—like horse breeders standing around a paddock waiting to see if the stallion is going to mount the mare—he said, "Okay, okay, I'll call her."

On April 10th, an email came:

> Hey Katie,
>   Don't know what you did to upset Molly Helfet but she gave me your email.
>   I'm off for a long weekend on Thursday, but back next week.
>   Do you have time to meet for dinner or something?

He followed up with a phone call; I liked the warm, confident sound of his voice. I asked him if he'd like to meet me for lunch sometime. John laughed. "I don't really go out to lunch."

"Okay, then, how about a drink?"

"Come on," he said, "let's just have dinner."

He sounded funny and nice, and what did I have to lose? I also figured that nighttime restaurant lighting might be a little more forgiving than the sun streaming through the windows, blasting my face. (Did I mention John was six years younger than me?)

We made a dinner date for April 27th. He suggested the Danny Meyer restaurant Maialino in the Gramercy Park Hotel, which struck the perfect not-too-casual, not-too-fancy note.

A really strange part of going on blind dates when you're a fixture on TV is that the guy already knows exactly what you look like (and probably has some sort of opinion about you as a person too). The good news is that his face won't fall when he first lays eyes on you; there won't be any huge surprises. Once when I was really pumped for a date, I googled the guy and found his company's website along with a headshot of a model-handsome man and I thought, *Hello, Gorgeous!* But when I got to the restaurant, let's just say he looked nothing like his photo. Turns out the picture he'd used online *was* a model's.

Even if John Molner knew what I looked like, I wanted to appear as alluring as possible, so I resurrected the leather-skirt look that had worked pretty well for me back in the day and applied enough makeup to enhance my features, without it looking like I had used spackle.

The hostess was escorting me across the restaurant when, midway, someone appeared out of nowhere—he'd been waiting at the bar—and stuck out his hand. "Hey, I'm John."

He was wearing a chocolate suede jacket, a basic dress shirt, and nondescript slacks. I didn't love his loafers, but he had a nice way about him. We were led to a primo table for two in the back.

John ordered soft-shell crabs and their famous slow-roasted pork dish Maialino al forno. *This guy likes to eat,* I remember thinking approvingly. That, and *He may be Jewish, but he's definitely not kosher.*

I got the lemon pasta and decided to order a glass of wine. I'm not much of an oenophile, but I wanted to impress my date, so I asked the waiter if they had a Barolo, which I'd recently heard a friend order and knew was a step up from your average red. "Oh," he replied, clearly pleased. "Let me get the sommelier."

I made a quick accounting of the guy sitting across from me: Definitely cuter than when I googled him (which had done his perfectly nice nose no favors). He had a firm handshake, seemed comfortable in his skin. So far, so good. I joked about the fact that we were finally here, together, in the flesh, and said I hoped Molly and Dave hadn't twisted his arm too much. John laughed.

The sommelier suddenly appeared and bent at the waist. "I hear you're interested in a Barolo. Well, you're in luck! We have a very *fine* Barolo," he said. I couldn't tell the difference between a very fine Barolo and a medium-fine one, but he didn't know that.

"Great," John said. The sommelier decanted the wine tableside.

After we let it breathe for a bit, as we'd been instructed, the Barolo flowed, and so did the conversation. John told me about growing up in Chicago; I mentioned that my parents had met in Chicago and my mom had always wanted me to move there. He talked a little bit about his divorce and his two kids; I told him about the girls. What didn't come up during dinner: he was dating a 27-year-old.

The very agent-y William Morris agent Jon Rosen, who'd always been after me to be his client (eventually I relented), came over to our table to say hi and invite us to a party for Robin Williams that was going on upstairs. John got into a lengthy conversation with Williams, which impressed me. Even now, after all the famous people I've met and interviewed, I still sometimes get nervous around celebrities, but he seemed completely unfazed. I liked that.

Then we sat down on an ottoman to chat with someone else, and John put his hand on my back. It took me by surprise, but it also felt good. Later, when he hailed me a cab, I returned the favor by kissing him lightly on the lips before jumping in.

Little did I know John's girlfriend was waiting for him in the lobby of his building.

"How was your date with Katie Couric?" she asked.

Apparently, a friend of hers was at the restaurant and had sent her a text.

EMAIL FROM ME, April 27th, 11:01 p.m.:

> OK. First date evaluation: You are really fun and funny! Thanks so much for dinner and having blind faith in a blind date!

Email from John, April 28th, 9:31 a.m.:

> My evaluation: Excellent date. You have a great smile, bright eyes, and an edgy downtown black leather (Gucci no less) skirt! (for a woman who lives @ Park and 91st)

Upshot: Even though he thought my Chanel skirt was Gucci, date one had been a raging success. Well, except for one thing—apparently our very fine Barolo cost nearly $500. I hadn't seen the bill; John paid for dinner. I was mortified and to this day feel bad about it. I must have apologized 500 times. But as first-date stories go, we've gotten a lot of mileage out of that one.

A few years later, when John and I jointly formed an LLC, we named it—what else?—A Very Fine Barolo.

79

Are You Ready for This Day?

A LMOST IMMEDIATELY, JOHN broke up with his girlfriend. I couldn't believe he was bucking the trend, leaving a beautiful 27-year-old for a 54-year-old.

Our second date involved day-drinking. We went to Barbuto and shared a bottle of rosé on a Sunday afternoon (a day John and I now refer to as Rosé Sunday), then weaved our way to the West Village apartment where his older brother Tom and his longtime partner, Andy, lived. I tried to engage Tom in a conversation about Henry Kissinger's mistakes in Cambodia but had no real idea what the hell I was talking about; I marshaled whatever details I could from something I'd read in the *New York Times* that morning. Tom is uber-intellectual (and was roommates with Henry's son at Yale) and I am no match for him sober, much less with half a bottle of wine coursing through my bloodstream.

We said our goodbyes. In the lobby, John grabbed me and kissed me by the mailboxes lining the wall. I'm not sure if it was the wine or all that talk of Dr. K., but I was definitely in lust. Things between us progressed pretty quickly—so quickly that by date four, it was time for him to meet Ellie and Carrie (great idea for another *Meet the Parents* sequel—*Meet the Daughters*). One evening, John came to our place a little early to pick me up for a date. Ellie was there with two friends from college. She said, "My mom's running late; can I get you some tea?"

John said he was fine and took a seat on the maize-colored sofa. Ellie took a seat on the identical one facing it.

"So what are you guys doing tonight?" she said, taking on the parental role. Thank goodness she didn't ask him what his intentions were.

Next came dinner with John's kids—Henry and Allie, then 17 and 14—at Red Hat in Westchester, not far from where they lived. I remember them both being sweet but a little quiet, having kinda, sorta heard of me and yet not really sure what was going on. Shortly after we were seated, a platter of fried calamari appeared, followed by a caprese salad for six. My friends always laughed about the freebies that came my way when we were at restaurants, like a massive wedge of cake or extra sides. ("It's good to be an FOK"—friend of Katie—my pal Mandy would say.) But Henry and Allie seemed a bit overwhelmed. Luckily, they were hungry.

John had already passed a number of tests, but there was a big one up ahead: Could I peacefully coexist with him in my home-away-from-home, East Hampton? As much as I liked him, if you're with the wrong person, a weekend can be a very long time. So I invited my friends Kit and Laurie to chaperone.

We played Scrabble outside in our bathing suits; when John made a seven-letter word, scoring 50 bonus points, he raised his fists in victory and did a cannonball into the pool. It was funny. And obnoxious. And exactly like something I would have done.

More than anything, I was drawn to his sense of humor. When we were driving back to the city in separate cars, John followed me out of town in his sporty little Mercedes convertible. When we got on I-495, he pulled up next to me—with an open book propped up on the steering wheel, as if he were casually reading while driving. (Don't worry, he wasn't.) He just looked over, smiled, and waved before passing me, delivering an excellent sight gag.

A BLOSSOMING ROMANCE WAS a great diversion from the pressure of launching a hotly anticipated talk show. Apparently, Jeff and I were a huge get for ABC—the executives felt sure they had a winner on their hands.

But they didn't want to leave anything to chance. The network was conducting extensive research to figure out who our target viewer was. They came up with a detailed psychographic and even gave her a name: Lisa, from Elmhurst, Illinois, home of the former Keebler factory. Lisa is 45 years old. She has three kids and works part-time. Her household income is $44,000 a year, and her house is worth $179,000. According to the psychographic, Lisa struggles with "overs"—she's overworked, overweight, and overwhelmed. But she is "resilient" and "optimistic"; for Lisa, life is good, but life is hard.

Then they went to town on me, determining my appeal. The big takeaways were that I was sunny, funny, and smart, which became our mantra.

It was a little weird. With the *TODAY* show, I just kind of came on, and people responded. Here, there was product-testing. It didn't feel organic. At a certain point Jeff made a huge push to bring on Allison Gollust. When we worked together at NBC, she and Jeff cooked up ever bolder ways to draw attention to *TODAY* and later to Jeff himself when he moved to Entertainment. They were joined at the hip. The problem was, we'd already hired a PR person for the show. There really wasn't a role for Allison.

Jeff asked me to meet with her anyway.

One weekend when I was out in the Hamptons, I went over to her house and told her what I'd already told Jeff—that we had the communications piece of it covered and there just wasn't a job there. What we needed were talented producers. ABC was paying Jeff and me a ton of money; I was also an EP of the show, and my name was on it. I felt a certain responsibility to spend the money wisely and have some real agency in the decision-making.

I had to wonder why Jeff was angling so hard to bring Allison on board. She and her husband and kids had moved into the apartment right above Jeff and Caryn's—everyone who heard about the cozy arrangement thought it was super-strange. By that point, Caryn had become a close friend and it made me really uncomfortable.

"I don't want to force myself on you," Allison said reasonably that day in the Hamptons. She seemed disappointed, but that was the end of it. (Sort of. Not really.)

IN AUGUST, WITH our debut less than a month away, the marketing team rolled out a promo we'd shot around the city. It featured me passing out invitations to my new show—to ladies in a nail salon, to a crossing guard, to a class full of women doing yoga (I carefully inserted the invite between their toes as they executed their down-dog splits). Not real women in a nail salon or a yoga class, mind you, but actors they had cast. At one point I had to call in a favor from none other than Donald Trump to help us get a permit so we could shoot part of this thing in Central Park.

The idea was that we were introducing viewers to a lighter, more accessible side of me, which is what daytime TV called for. But the music, the mood, my face, my voice are all so relentlessly chirpy—watching it now makes me cringe. At the time, I put my trust in the promotional team. They understood that audience better than I did; I figured they knew how to position me. My mandate was to be warm, friendly, welcoming. It wasn't at all clear how that would square with the other side of me—the inquisitive, skeptical side. I felt a serious identity crisis coming on.

In the plus column, Sheryl Crow agreed to write and record the theme song. I went down to her home in Nashville and we played around in her recording studio. I told her I wanted the song to be upbeat and fun, and she delivered, with lyrics that hit the personal-growth note at the core of a lot of daytime programming. The only problem was a chorus lyric she'd written, *Are you ready for today?*—which called to mind another TV show entirely. So Sheryl changed it to *Are you ready for this day?*

Jeff sent me an idea for the open of the first show that involved a Matt Lauer cameo. I emailed him back:

Funny. would get a lot of buzz. He's kind of a pussy so probably won't do it though.

Jeff's response:

> right, i agree with u
> but i am willing to ask him
> just wanted to make sure ur comfy with it

Surprisingly, after spurning our advances twice, Matt agreed to do the spot.

Cold open. The sound of crickets. A shot of me in a twin bed wearing monogrammed pajamas, tossing and turning. Then, suddenly, my eyes pop open.

"Wow, I just had the weirdest dream! I had a dream I left the *TODAY* show to anchor an evening news broadcast and I did it for five years. And then I dreamed I was going to be hosting my own daytime talk show…"

At which point, in the twin bed next to mine, Matt, also in monogrammed pj's, rolls over, takes off his eye mask, and says, "That was no dream. And the talk show? It starts right now. So are you ready for this day?"

Cue the theme song:

I woke up to a new dawn breaking
You were on my mind
So many roads still worth taking
There's no more wasting time…
Are you ready for this day-ay-ay-ay-ay…

I'll never forget walking out onto that stage, greeting a live audience. They were standing, applauding wildly—they all looked so happy, like a casting call for Up with People (they'd been instructed by the audience coordinator to wear bright colors). Apart from greeting viewers on the plaza at *TODAY,* interacting with a live audience wasn't something I'd really done in my career as a journalist. I didn't know what to do with all that over-the-top energy. So I made these crunched little hand-puppet waves at the audience and smiled right back. It didn't come naturally.

"Stop!" I said, in my blue-gray cap-sleeve dress and steep heels. "I'm not wearing waterproof mascara!"

It was all a bit disorienting, especially the nearness of the audience. "I feel so close to you guys," I said, "literally! I'm going to have to remember to shave my legs more often."

I launched in. "In many ways this is a new beginning for me, which is both incredibly exciting and terrifying. But I think for all of us, life is often about new chapters and new adventures and learning how to handle and even embrace change."

A photo of Jay, the girls, and me appeared on the big screen behind me.

I mentioned losing Jay. On a happier note, I said that Carrie and Ellie—now 16 and 21—were here, on either side of my mom. The crowd cheered as the camera cut to the girls, seated in row three (Carrie, who apparently had missed the memo about bright colors, was literally the only person in the audience in black). "And I feel very lucky to have my mom here today as well. Mom, thank you." More cheers. It was an early, odd glimpse of how much the show would be based on me rather than the stories we were doing, which I wasn't entirely comfortable with. I'd always seen myself as a journalist with a personality—not a TV *personality.*

So, are you ready for this day?

Looking back, I guess the answer would be *Maybe not.*

OUR FIRST GUEST was Jessica Simpson. In retrospect, that might have signaled a fluffier show than I was intending; after all, she was the one who famously asked if Chicken of the Sea was tuna or chicken. But as a Weight Watchers spokesperson who'd been relentlessly ridiculed for not losing the baby weight fast enough, she might, I thought, appeal to Everywoman. She was also an entrepreneur, having built a shoe empire. At the end of the segment she gave me some black flats from her line, and I gave her a onesie for the baby.

But for anyone who thought pop starlets were going to be the norm

on *Katie*…my guest the second day was a complete 180: Aimee Cope-
land, the 24-year-old graduate student who'd lost both hands, a foot,
and her entire left leg to a flesh-eating bacterial infection. I guess you
could say I was figuring it out.

THE DIFFERENCES BETWEEN the newspeople we'd hired and the talk-
show people Abra had hired were growing more apparent by the day.
It wasn't the Sharks and the Jets, exactly; more like oil (Jeff) and
water (Abra).

Jeff had gone from barely tolerating Abra to pretty much loathing her.
She was our conduit to ABC, the bridge between us and the network
brass as well as the stations, and Jeff abhorred the idea of having to
listen to her. So he banished her to another floor of the building.

A big challenge was creating a show from scratch every day as
opposed to reacting to a constant influx of news. And we were getting
mixed messages: make the episodes topical so they're a good lead-in to
local newscasts, but make them evergreen enough to work as reruns. My
neck was getting stiff from the whiplash.

And then there was TiVo, DVR, cable, and Facebook, all fighting
for the same eyeballs. Getting them to look at us was tougher than we
thought.

A couple of months in, I met with Anne Sweeney. Perfectly groomed
in her tailored suit and pumps, she was the picture of the successful
female executive, the sort of person who looked like she smelled really
good. We exchanged niceties about our families before getting down to
it. A little sheepishly, I said, "I think the show's looking pretty good,
don't you? I think there's a lot of potential for it to grow."

Anne put it bluntly: "I didn't want you to have the number-one *new*
talk show; I wanted you to have the number-one talk show, *period*."

Oh, shit.

And it hit me that we'd broken an important rule of business:
underpromise and overdeliver. With all the hype surrounding the debut,
surrounding me, with all the money ABC was throwing at us, it was
clear: We'd overpromised and underdelivered.

The real issue for me: There was very little overlap between the kind of shows I wanted to do and the shows people typically watch in daytime. I was determined to hang on to my news chops—I'd worked too hard to establish myself as a journalist to suddenly play the Gidget Goes to Daytime role. So I broke another rule of business: I didn't give the people what they wanted.

Aggressively so, sometimes. One of my favorite producers, Molly McGinnis, reminded me of the time I called her into my office after hours to tell her I wasn't happy with the direction the shows were taking, saying they lacked substance. International Women's Day was coming up, and I said I wanted to scrap whatever we had planned to do an hour on empowering women instead.

"In the space of 45 seconds, you ticked off a new rundown that required five or six new bookings and a meaty video package on Malala," Molly said. She took her marching orders and was headed out the door when I apparently added, "Oh, and you know what would be good? Have someone like Christiane Amanpour come on and talk about Malala. She can narrate the package. You'll write it, but she'll narrate it. And she'll do the top of the show too." The producers had 48 hours to rebook, restack, and redo the entire thing.

Christiane had been at the Vatican; they reached her right as she was boarding a flight from Rome. Molly wrote the Malala package for Christiane to track an hour before air. Go, team! Go, me!

The episode tanked. Yet another serious topic the daytime audience didn't care about.

Molly, thank you. And I'm sorry.

THE PRESSURE WAS on to right the ship, but frankly, my executive producer seemed a little at sea. Jeff's gut, which had served him so well throughout his years at *TODAY,* was failing him. Furthermore, he found the prospect of reporting to anyone humiliating. On day one, when an excited Bob Iger dropped by to watch the first episode from the control room, Jeff promptly nixed that idea. He also hated getting feedback from the local GMs, who were fixated on the ratings in their respective markets. He'd put them on speakerphone and roll his eyes while they droned on about how newsy the show should or shouldn't be. ABC's confidence in him was flagging, and our relationship was fraying.

At the same time, speculation was growing about who would be the new president of CNN. Apparently there was a guy from ESPN they were seriously considering; Jeff told me he was a "total douche." Shortly after, it popped up in the press that Jeff was being considered for the job (everyone knew he and Allison had Page Six on speed-dial).

Jeff needed to be a big deal—his ego craved it. He clearly wanted out of a job that had become, for him, demeaning. I started to wonder if this had just been a way station all along, until he could land a bigger gig. While we should have been course-correcting, he was planning his exit strategy.

One day, I walked into his office and gave it to him straight: "Hey, this Page Six stuff isn't helpful. All these rumors you're planting isn't good for morale. It's distracting and creates uncertainty. Please cut it out."

"I have nothing to do with it," Jeff said unconvincingly. Reading his face, I was struck by how much he'd changed since we'd first met, 22 years earlier; that skinny guy with a tuft of mousy-brown hair in a gray sweatshirt and girls' sneakers had thoroughly morphed into a master of the universe–type, with the cold stare and regulation shaved head. As much as I wanted to, I couldn't say what I knew to be true: *You're lying.*

THE DIVIDE BETWEEN the newspeople and the daytime-talk people was growing deeper. The daytime folks were super-focused on stunts. Once a producer ordered—at considerable expense—a life-size plexiglass horse on wheels that I was supposed to straddle for our "salute to country music" episode (I also recall bales of hay that had been shipped in from God knows where). My response was "Get rid of it. Put the horse down! I am not coming onstage on a rolling horse." Although I did come out on a rolling piano once, wearing an evening gown, with Barry Manilow at the keys. I love Barry Manilow, but I wanted to crawl under the lid.

By this point, we were typically doing somewhere between a 1.6 and a 2—ratings anyone would kill for these days. But they weren't high enough to justify our paychecks and how expensive the show was to produce.

Anne Sweeney had lost all confidence in Jeff. One afternoon after we finished taping, he poked his head into the makeup room.

"They fired me," he said.

I was pissed—both at Anne for not giving me a heads-up, and at Jeff for having one foot out the door.

He called me a couple of weeks later. "Will you do me a favor?" he said, sounding uncharacteristically needy. "Will you call Jeff Bewkes"— then CEO of Time Warner—"and put in a good word for me at CNN? This is really my last chance to have a big job like this. And of course, if you want it, there will be a job for you too."

In those eight seconds while he waited for my answer, our time together flashed before my eyes: the excitement and fun, the teamwork, the unstoppable ascent. Yes, he'd been a huge disappointment. But in spite of everything, we'd been through so much together. I also knew news had always been his sweet spot, and CNN would be a much better fit.

Of course I would, I told him.

On November 29th, Jeff was named president of CNN. His first hire? Allison Gollust.

Oh, and I never did hear from him about that job.

80

Flop Sweat

FOUR MONTHS IN, with an ominous feeling rolling through the place, we pulled the staff together for a reset.

I recently stumbled on a notebook from that time in which I'd jotted down some takeaways alongside nervous-looking doodles. A few phrases jumped out:

> *Median age of viewer: 60!*
> *TARGET AGE = 45!*
> *RELATABILITY is a* <u>*MUST*</u>*! Women want to see themselves reflected in TV*

The meeting was also an opportunity to reconnect with Lisa from Elmhurst, Illinois. I'd scribbled in the notebook:

> *What does Lisa want from daytime TV? Why does she watch?*
> *1. time filler*
> *2. laugh, smile, relax*
> *3. entertainment*
> *4. information*

The idea that we were busting our asses every day to create "time fillers" was hard to swallow. And if there was still any doubt that the day-time landscape might not be the perfect place for me, there was this:

WHO IS KATIE?
  Read book The Hero Within
  All about archetypes
  We start out naive—Bambi in the woods
  We have to move forward to be hero
  From hero you become ruler, then wizard, all along you are wandering
  Lisa—what is her archetype?
  At home she's the ruler, at work the wanderer…

The thing had flop sweat all over it. I wondered, did Frustrated Talk Show Host count as an archetype?

WE WELCOMED A few new producers, who'd worked at places like *Ricki Lake, Dr. Drew's Lifechangers,* and *The Tyra Banks Show.* The lack of news experience at that level was a real problem with some of the topics we wanted to cover. Like my trans-disaster.

I always felt compelled to help people better understand what they may not. So when a producer pitched Carmen Carrera, the transgender model and reality star, I thought it was an opportunity to educate people, including myself, about something that had long been in the shadows.

When she came on, I was struck by her beauty: delicate features framed by cascading chestnut locks; ample cleavage in a black slip dress with spaghetti straps. The producer didn't provide much in the way of guidelines about what we could or couldn't talk about, so I began by asking Carmen when she realized she was in the wrong body; we flashed a photo of her as a sweet but confused-looking kindergarten boy. Then came the whammy—when I inquired about her anatomy: "Your private parts are different now, aren't they?"

"Shhh..." Carmen literally shushed me on national television, saying she didn't want to talk about it. "I still have my career goals, my family goals...I wanna focus on that rather than what's down there," she said, concluding, "there's more to trans people than just that."

Scrambling to recover, I explained that it's all still a mystery to a lot of people, and that's where my question came from, adding, "I hope you don't think it's prurient interest."

"No, no, no," said a really gracious Carmen. "At least I can say people are becoming more interested in learning these days, rather than judging without experience."

"And that's a good thing," I said.

"That's a great thing," said Carmen. "But just me, personally, I'd rather not talk about it."

"I understand that," I said, "and I totally respect that." Smiles all around.

After the break, I introduced Laverne Cox, the transgender star of *Orange Is the New Black.* I asked her if she felt as Carmen did, that people were preoccupied with "the genitalia question." Laverne enumerated the horrific statistics regarding the discrimination, unemployment, and violence that trans people face, pointing out that "if we focus on transition, we don't actually get to talk about those things."

After the taping, the producers asked me if I wanted to take out that awkward exchange with Carmen, but I said, "No, let's keep it in. I'm a fairly sophisticated, open-minded person, and if I could ask such a dumb question, I bet others might do the same." At the end of the episode I even said, "We want to hear what you have to say about the topics we discussed today. Head to our website, our Facebook page, or tweet me @katiecouric"—completely unaware of the fusillade of rage I was inviting into my feeds.

The next day, which happened to be my birthday, I flew to Las Vegas for CES—the Consumer Electronics Show—where I'd be introducing Yahoo CEO Marissa Mayer. En route, I noticed that my phone was blowing up. The trans community was in an uproar.

One of the many indignant tweets:

> I wonder how Ms. Couric would feel if someone cast aside her
> accomplishments & boiled her down to genitalia?

And the media scorn was equally ferocious. *BuzzFeed* called my interview with Carmen "invasive" and "cringeworthy," while *Slate* said it was "tone-deaf."

Holy hell—I knew I'd been a bit clumsy, but I had no idea how deeply offensive my comments were. I was so embarrassed.

Eventually I got over it, and I have Laverne Cox to thank. A year and a half later, she asked me to present her with her 2015 Fashion Media Award. In her speech, she said I'd allowed myself to be "teachable" and that I'd "demonstrated what ally-ship looks like" when I invited her back to the show and asked what conversations we needed to be having.

Two years later, I used the incident as a springboard for my documentary *Gender Revolution.* I explored what it is to be trans, chronicling the journey of, among others, a 5-year-old girl and a bullied teen, as well as a 70-year-old woman after she'd gotten gender-confirmation surgery. I learned so much and invited viewers to learn along with me. A grateful mother stopped me at the airport to tell me how helpful the documentary had been to her and her family as they sought to understand her trans son's experience.

MEANWHILE, BACK AT *Katie,* there were other speed bumps along the road to sunny, funny, and smart. Like my conversation with Joan Rivers. Can we talk?

Joan was a New York legend. I'd had dinner at her ornate apartment in the East Sixties—French Provincial, with heavy drapes and brocade everything, the spoils of a very successful life. I wanted to do an interview that got beyond the shticky one-liners she was known for and delve into her emotional, interior self. In the documentary *Piece of Work,* she'd shared her terror of facing an empty calendar, and to be honest, that reminded me of me.

The producer assured me that nothing was off-limits. So I decided to explore her decision to get plastic surgery. I heard the studio audience gasp.

"I want to look pretty. Don't you want to look pretty?" she said sharply, fixing me with those piercing eyes. (The exchange didn't make the final cut.)

In her dressing room afterward, she unloaded on our producers. "Who does she think she is? She's on her knees blowing 14-year-olds." (I guess she hadn't heard about the Brooks breakup.)

I wish it hadn't happened. Joan had been so kind to me after Jay died, sending me a note, widow to widow, that read in part:

> *You are the star of your movie or play and hard as it may be for you to believe this at this time, there is a glorious, golden life ahead for you and your kids. Xoxox, Joan Rivers*

Less than two years after our interview, she died unexpectedly. It was our last encounter. The whole thing remains a profound bummer to this day.

But I am happy to say there were many great episodes and memorable moments: Stoic Robert De Niro choking up during an interview with the cast of *Silver Linings Playbook*. Sam Berns, who would die at 17 of progeria, a rare genetic disease that causes children to age at warp speed, being presented with a game ball from his beloved New England Patriots (Sam blew me away). Ninety-year-old Irving Fradkin, an optometrist from Fall River, Massachusetts, who started a grass-roots scholarship fund, flanked by a dozen grateful kids among the hundreds of thousands he'd sent to college.

Other episodes brought me back to my news roots, like Hurricane Sandy, which sent me all over Staten Island to hear the stories of shell-shocked residents. One woman whose husband and daughter had been violently swept away by the floodwaters agreed to come on the show.

Then there was Sandy Hook. It happened on a Friday afternoon. Two producers and I jumped in a car and headed to Newtown, Connecticut, and attended a prayer vigil that night.

Jackie and Mark Barden lived there with their children, James, Natalie, and, until Friday, their darling, redheaded 7-year-old, Daniel. When I went back to Newtown on Sunday, I nervously knocked on their door. Someone opened it and I was surprised they invited me in.

There were at least 40 people inside, including Jackie's nine siblings, their spouses and kids. A fire crackled in the fireplace and the Christmas tree was up. As gently as I could, I asked Jackie and Mark, "Do you think you could talk to me about what happened?"

I was guided to the sofa in the family room. James, who must have been about 11, had tears streaming down his face throughout the interview—an extraordinary embodiment of pain and one of the saddest things I've ever seen. That uneasy dichotomy that every reporter knows, wanting to be respectful but also wanting to capture profound human drama in its purest, rawest form...I hadn't felt it this viscerally since Columbine.

My sit-down with the Bardens was one of the most powerful interviews I'd ever done. We became friends. They returned to the show on the one-year anniversary of the shooting; I emceed their Sandy Hook Promise gala, and John and I hosted them at the U.S. Open.

They were a big reason I made a documentary on gun violence three years later, *Under the Gun,* which featured Mark and Jackie. We saw them at Sundance, where the film premiered—I remember John giving Mark a hug when they met.

"Wow," I said, "you got a Molner hug? You're a member of a small club." Now Mark always makes sure to hug Molner whenever he sees him.

THAT TIME WAS full of firsts for John and me. We went to a B and B in Vermont where it rained all weekend; John made fun of me for wanting to leave early to visit the Ben and Jerry's factory. He introduced me to his parents in the summer of 2012 at the Aspen Ideas Festival— gregarious, flirtatious, handsome Herby, a former CEO turned ski instructor; gorgeous Paula, with her silver bob and sophistication, her boundless curiosity. They're really different, but such a great couple. At their 50th-wedding-anniversary party, someone toasted, "To Paula, who has all the questions, and Herby, who has all the answers." (Another thing I learned along the way: Look for a man who has a healthy relationship with his mother.)

It's so sad to me that my dad never got a chance to meet John, and vice versa, but at least my mom did. When we were visiting her in Virginia, John came to the Giant with us for a little grocery shopping. She needed Advil, so I sent him off to the in-store pharmacy to find some. He came back with a big bottle of the generic brand and pointed out to my mom how many more tablets she could get for nearly half the price. That, among other things, quickly won her over.

As fall gave way to winter, John and I were growing closer by the day. And I started feeling something I hadn't felt in quite a while: contentment. All those years of failed romances were behind me. Life was good.

I remember one especially tranquil afternoon, sitting on the floor of my dressing room at ABC. Cynthia, my live-wire stylist, had already gone home. Dana and Josie had packed up their hair straighteners and eyelash curlers. No frenetic chatter; the thrum of the fluorescent light had stopped. I inhaled the silence and scrolled through my messages. Then a text came from John.

Call me right away.

81

The Brady Bunch

JOHN WAS NEVER one to mince words, but his text was especially blunt. He hadn't been feeling well for several months. I never worried about it too much; I thought he'd just had a stretch of bad health—the flu or some other kind of virus. The flare-ups varied in intensity. But he would always get better.

Unlike Jay, John had an internist, so at my urging, he went to see him. The doctor told him it was probably acid reflux and prescribed Prilosec and Tums. He also said it might be "trapped gas."

We laughed about the imaginary illness and dubbed it "trapped-gas syndrome," joking that we should establish the Trapped Gas Foundation, or TGF, for people who were "suffering in silence." The doctor did recommend John see a nutritionist, who told him he was eating too many salads. (Why hasn't a doctor ever said that to me?)

Throughout the summer, he seemed fine.

Fine enough for us to drive three hours to the Hamptons on weekends, to visit friends in Nantucket, to travel to Iceland in July, where we strapped on crampons and walked across glaciers and rode out-of-control horses, but passed on *hákarl,* the Icelandic "delicacy" of fermented shark meat.

Early in our courtship, I had floated a trial balloon. "Do you think you'd ever like to get married again?" I casually asked.

"Not really," he said simply. He had married his high school sweet-heart and clearly didn't seem interested in the idea.

I felt the sting of disappointment, but I was so tired of coupling up and breaking up, I was just happy I was with someone who was normal—mature, kind, emotionally healthy. By this point I'd given up on the idea of some sort of magical Brady Bunch scenario. If John and I were simply "life partners" without the benefit of marriage, I could live with that.

Labor Day weekend, 2013. We were in the Hamptons with Tom and Andy, hanging out by the pool, when John asked me to go for a walk on the beach. I was perfectly happy staying at the house, so I took a pass. I told John he should grab one of the bikes and go by himself. But he looked so dejected, I finally said, "Okay, Molner, I'll go for a walk on the beach."

It was approaching the magic hour, late in the afternoon when the sky turns pink and the beach has cooled down. It's my favorite time of day, and John, not a big fan of "roasting in the sun," would often relent and walk with me through the shallows as sunbathers gave way to twilight wine-drinkers and barbecuers. John carried an L.L. Bean canvas tote that looked a bit precious; there was a bottle of rosé and two glasses inside. We walked for a bit, then nestled into a pocket of sand protected by seagrass with a perfect view of the ocean. John poured us each a glass of wine. We toasted each other and the end of summer.

"I really love you," he said.

"Aw, thanks," I said with a slight undercurrent of *Duh*. "I love you too."

John soldiered on. "No, I *really* love you."

"Molner, I really love you too." *Why is he being so weird?*

"I really love you and I want to spend the rest of my life with you," he said.

"Of course! I want to spend the rest of my life with you too!" I said sweetly.

Then something crazy happened: He stood up, got down on bended knee, and opened up a small green leather box.

"Couric," he said exasperatedly, "I'm trying to ask you to marry me."

In the box was a sparkly cushion-cut diamond encircled by smaller diamonds staring me in the face. The exact ring I wanted if this day ever came.

My confusion showed in a series of "What?"s. Finally, Molner said, "Well, you haven't answered my question."

I knew I wanted to marry John, but I had totally given up on the possibility of it ever happening. So I was in a state of semi-shock.

Finally, I said, "Yes, of course. Yes!"

We stopped by my friend Charlie's house. After years of listening to sob stories about boyfriends gone bad, she deserved to be one of the first to hear the news. Chatting with her and her husband, Ralph, about nothing in particular, I waved my hands around a little more than usual.

"Wait!" she said finally. "Wait! Is that an engagement ring on your finger?"

"Yes!" I shrieked. We all laughed and hugged. It started to feel more real and right.

John hadn't told a soul what he was up to. On the drive back to the house on Amy's Lane, we saw Andy and Tom taking a walk. John slowed down. When we shared the news, we high-fived and cheered. Then I saw catering trucks rolling up and waitstaff with linens and chafing dishes moving in. John had arranged a feast and had invited some of our closest friends. Ellie, Carrie, and their boyfriends were running late, thanks to bumper-to-bumper traffic. Suddenly, panic. *Ellie and Carrie don't know yet. Oh my God.*

I wished he'd talked to them first. My fantasy was the guy in the Kay Jewelers commercial asking permission to marry Julie, when the camera suddenly cuts not to Julie's dad, but to her young son.

When the girls arrived, I asked them to meet me in the sunroom. They looked so confused when I walked in, sitting close together on the sofa. I decided to rip off the Band-Aid and flashed my ring. "What do you think, guys? John and I are getting married."

They both burst into tears. Not the happy kind.

Ever since he met them, John was careful not to impose himself on the girls—if anything, he held back, because he didn't want them to think he was trying to be their father. And I wondered if those good intentions were backfiring now—if that self-imposed distance made Ellie and Carrie think he didn't care (which couldn't have been farther from the truth).

"Don't worry," I said, looking into their tearstained faces. "Nothing's going to change!"

Losing their father so young, they'd been through so much, and I couldn't bear thinking I might be putting them through more.

I knew there would be bumps in the road as we integrated our families, but I was determined to make it work. For everybody.

JOHN WAS STILL in a frustrating cycle of feeling fine and feeling lousy. In the fall, he called me from his apartment and said he was lying on the bathroom floor, unable to stop vomiting. Ugh—more food poisoning, I figured, or maybe the flu again. I wanted to help him out, but the truth is, I was too distracted by something else: Carrie, now 17, in her senior year of high school, suddenly went from being a healthy teenager to dangerously sick.

Complaints of back pain turned to fever—which led to a Cipro prescription that didn't work and a fever spike of 104...me carrying a pajama-clad Carrie downstairs, putting her in a cab, and racing 20 blocks to the emergency room. An IV drip...temperature of 105...the words *concerns of impending septic shock* scribbled on her chart...blood pressure plummeting; a powerful antibiotic that we desperately hoped would fight the bacteria in her bloodstream. Doctors fearing organ shutdown... *This can't be happening...God, please help Carrie...*

The sheer terror, the acute sense of aloneness being a single parent... When John called in the middle of it all to tell me he wasn't feeling well, I just didn't have the bandwidth to help. The best I could do was have a friend drop off some saltines and Gatorade at his apartment.

I kept vigil for five days in Carrie's hospital room, sleeping in the vinyl recliner. And finally—she sat up and ate some Jell-O. The antibiotics were working, the whole thing the result of a raging asymptomatic UTI.

Now it was John's turn.

82

Déjà Vu

CHRISTMAS 2013. I decided I would try to make a fancy meal—a rare occurrence. I bought a standing rib roast from the hot neighborhood butcher, Evan. I also whipped up some creamed spinach (my mom's recipe, which meant squeezing the water out of frozen cooked spinach and adding a can of Campbell's cream of mushroom soup). A salad of Bibb lettuce, sliced pears, and Gorgonzola, even Yorkshire pudding! By the time we sat, I was exhausted.

After dinner, John said, "I need to lie down."

Wait a second—I made the entire meal and you aren't even going to help with the dishes? I was so annoyed.

At the Sundance Film Festival, he spent most of the time sleeping. In early February, at a baby shower back in New York, he couldn't manage appetizers or a Bloody Mary.

"You look really thin," one of John's golf buddies remarked. When I seemed surprised, he added, "It's not something you notice when you're with someone every day."

Where had I heard that before? Managing a busy life and a demanding career, too distracted to see changes in the person you live with . . .

"Molner," I said, "this is insane. Please go see Felice."

Felice Schnoll-Sussman, MD, the director of the Monahan Center.

Imagine what that was like, sending my sick fiancé to the facility named for my dead husband.

The minute John walked in, Felice knew he was seriously unwell. When she pushed on his abdomen, she couldn't feel his internal organs. *Had his regular doctor not even put a hand on his belly?*

Felice went into her office. She thought she was going to throw up. Then she collected herself, returned to the exam room, and told John, "You need to go across the street and get a CT scan."

Felice ordered a "wet read," a fast peek at the results the minute they have them. She called John and asked him to come to her office. He assured her she could say whatever she had to say over the phone.

"We found a mass," she said. What she didn't tell him was that it was a tumor.

Call me right away.

Déjà vu. As I sat on the floor of my dressing room, trying to absorb this terrible news, I thought, *Wasn't I in a dressing room at work when I received terrible news about Jay? Are you kidding me, God?*

John's fear came pulsating through the phone and directly into my heart—I was having trouble breathing. I realized I'd have to start consulting with doctors, devising a plan, white-knuckling it as we waited for lab results and surgical outcomes. After Jay, after Emily, all I could think was *I can't do this again.*

I'll do this again.

THEY SCHEDULED JOHN for an upper endoscopy. Tom met me in the waiting area, along with our friend Dave Helfet. When John went in for the procedure, Dave whispered to me, "God, I hope it's not liver cancer."

I felt like he'd punched me in the gut and seriously considered returning the favor.

When John came to, we met him in the recovery area. His eyes were damp. I touched his cheek.

"It's going to be okay," I whispered, having no idea if that was true.

All I knew was that John had a tumor on his liver the size of a coconut. Jay's mass was the size of an orange; Jeff Zucker's, a plum. In my early thirties I had a fibroid tumor they compared to a lemon. I was so sick of the fruit salad of tumors.

John's small intestine was also inflamed and appeared ulcerated. And he had horrible esophagitis. ("His esophagus looked like raw meat from vomiting so much," Felice told me later.)

In other words, John was a mess. And he was in trouble.

The tumor had to be removed, pronto. Since Dave was a trauma surgeon, he knew just the person for the job.

We went for a consultation with Peter Allen at Sloan Kettering. Not *When my baby smiles at me I go to Rio* Peter Allen but a brilliant surgeon who'd done a yearlong tour of duty sewing up wounded soldiers in Iraq.

Once inside the nondescript building on York Avenue, we waited to go up to Dr. Allen's office on the third floor. As people piled into the very slow-moving elevator, John whispered, "Please keep your head down and don't do your Katie Couric thing."

And of course, that's the second someone did a double take and said, "Hey, aren't you Katie Couric?"

I smiled and mouthed the words *Yes, I am.* I thought John was going to kill me.

The truth is, I wanted to keep a low profile for my sake too. If this got out, I could just picture the tabloid headline: "The Black Widow Strikes Again!" with my head photoshopped onto the body of a spider.

SURGERY WAS SCHEDULED for after Presidents' Day weekend. Somehow John had the presence of mind to go to his lawyer beforehand and rewrite his will to include Ellie, Carrie, and me. Such a loving gesture—and yet what it implied was so upsetting. He also made a generous gift to Stand Up To Cancer and the Michael J. Fox Foundation for Parkinson's research, among other causes. But even in this profoundly mortal moment, there was a little levity: John bequeathed an all-expenses-paid golf trip anywhere in the world to the seven guys he regularly played with.

February 24th, 2014. John's family, Wendy, and I gathered at the hospital and tried to make small talk. I glanced at a smiling Steve Harvey on the TV mounted to the wall. The minute hand on the clock seemed frozen.

Meanwhile, John was laid out on an operating table being flayed with a scalpel, his skin and muscle peeled back so Dr. Allen could slice his liver in half and remove the tumor (and resect an ulcerated piece of his duodenum). If a giant tumor had to take up residence anywhere, the liver was a good place, because it regenerates, like some kind of super-organ. If all went well and it was an isolated mass, John's liver would miraculously grow back in a matter of months.

"Why is this taking so long?" I must have asked at least 20 times.

Four hours later, a hospital coordinator came up and said the operation had gone well—"They got it all." But we really wouldn't know what "it" was until the pathology report came in. Had it spread? Would John need chemo?

As Paula, Wendy, and I were leaving, exhausted from the day, a nurse chased us down with some scary news: John was bleeding internally, a potentially fatal situation. Dr. Allen was on his way home to Chappaqua; by some miracle they reached him just before he got on the Willis Avenue Bridge, where a U-turn would have been impossible.

A major blood vessel had sprung a leak. I panicked, knowing that when patients die, it's usually in recovery, not on the operating table. Two interminable hours later, Dr. Allen came and told us they had stopped the bleeding.

John recovered on the 16th floor—basically the liver-cancer floor, where so many patients were living out their last days. There was a man in his thirties with bile-duct cancer; he and his wife had two young kids. They reminded me of Jay and me. There were rooms crowded with ultra-Orthodox Jews in their fur-trimmed hats. There were emaciated, ghostlike figures hooked up to IVs walking the halls, going through the motions. The 16th floor of Memorial Sloan Kettering must be one of the saddest places on earth.

A few days in, John was on the move, holding on to his IV pole. He'd do laps around the floor, gingerly at first, increasing the distance every time. The more he walked, the sooner he'd be able to give a positive answer to the standard post-op question posed by nurses multiple times a day: "Have you passed gas?"

"No," John would reply. "Have you?"

Finally, one night at around 2:00 a.m., he was walking the halls when he emitted a sound he was convinced could be heard all the way to lower Manhattan. "A patient in a nearby room muttered, 'Show off,'" John joked.

Soon it was like he was training for a 10K—increasing the number of laps, warning other patients that he was passing on the left, greeting his new friend with bile-duct cancer (who looked healthier than he was; he would live only a few more months) with a thumbs-up. One afternoon when John was feeling particularly peppy, Tom and I trailed behind him and his stainless-steel little buddy, the IV pole, belting out a medley of our favorite tunes from *West Side Story, The King and I,* and *Gypsy* to cheer him on, hoping that everything was in fact coming up roses.

If there was any question about whether or not John wanted out of the hospital…he started showering and putting on his street clothes each morning and sitting in the chair in his room to greet his medical team. "Hey," he'd say, "you gotta dress for success." Once, he actually went to a nearby diner for pancakes. When he came back, the team was waiting for him, Dr. Allen's arms crossed in mock anger.

"Ladies and gentlemen," Allen told the team, "we've got a runner." John was discharged the next day.

When the pathology report finally came, we had reason to feel optimistic. John had a carcinoid tumor, this one "indolent," which meant it hadn't spread. ("Leave it to me to have a lazy tumor," John said.) But I still needed reassurance. Given my experience, I did not trust cancer in any form. What I did trust, more than just about anything, was the opinion of Mark Pochapin.

We met at a café on Lexington Avenue and I passed the pathology report across the table.

This time, Mark smiled.

83

"And YOU Get a Vacuum!"

*K*ATIE RECEIVED A less favorable prognosis.

After a taping one day in November, Abra came to my dressing room. "Katie, they're not renewing the show," she said. It was just too expensive to produce at a time when audiences were getting smaller by the day.

I was okay with it. I had been pretty ambivalent about the whole thing from the beginning, which probably isn't a great way for the host and namesake of a show to feel. It just wasn't my calling. John told me I should have just embraced the genre and had fun with it, but with George Watson's words—*Don't be typecast as the cute girl who does features*—ringing in my ears, that was easier said than done.

No, the mortician-like prompter reading that was expected of me at the *CBS Evening News* wasn't right either, but the softness of daytime was a wild overcorrection (an episode devoted to "*Redbook*'s Hottest Husbands" may have been the nadir). We never really figured out the balance.

Finding somewhere you can put your multidimensional self on display is tough. I don't think I fully realized at the time just how unique the *TODAY* show was—the only place I could comfortably converse with the Senate majority leader and the Teletubbies on the same morning.

The day we taped our Christmas show, I summoned the staff to the set to deliver some unjolly news—that there wouldn't be a third season. No one seemed especially surprised. Deflated, maybe, but not shocked. It had only been two years, not 10. And yet we had developed the kind of camaraderie that comes with working deep into the night and on weekends together, changing things at the last minute and somehow putting on a show every day.

Once again, I'd already found a safety net: The previous April, I was a featured guest at Yahoo's lavish retreat in the Turks and Caicos, an orgy of fruity cocktails, twinkly lights, over-the-top dinners, and high-end swag. The idea was to position the company as a thought leader in the world of new media for an audience of CMOs. John Legend performed (Yahoo flew in a special piano).

At some point I got the chance to meet with Marissa Mayer one on one and pitch her an idea. I told her Yahoo had huge pipes, but the stuff going through them was sludge—decidedly lowbrow and unsubstantial. With people increasingly turning to their laptops and mobile devices for news and information, it seemed like such a missed opportunity.

"Do you want to keep serving up stories like 'Meet the Boy Who Lived on Ramen Noodles for 13 Years' or do you want to create meaningful content?" I said, oiling my escape hatch. "Yahoo has the potential to be a really important destination. I'd like to help you do that."

Marissa's eyes widened. I could tell I had her on the line.

JUNE 12TH, 2014—our last taping. At the top of the show, Morgan Freeman's reassuring visage appeared on-screen. "Today on *Katie,* we look back together," he intoned. "It's been quite a journey, hasn't it?"

Yes, Morgan, it has.

For our final show, the staff had arranged a number of surprise guests; the theme, apparently, was alcohol—I did a tequila shot on-air with Susan Sarandon and had a glass of red wine with Martina McBride. Josh Groban came by, and so did Valerie Harper. It felt a little like attending my own wake.

I guess it's fitting that we ended the show with a giveaway; we called it Katie's Ultimate Swag Bag. Mucho free stuff for the studio audience:

a camera ("You're going home with one!"), a handbag, scarves, a travel hair dryer and flat iron, Bliss products ("Bliss wants everyone to have luxuriously smooth skin, so they're giving you their hot salts scrub!"), a Vitamix blender, headphones, a gym membership, a cordless vacuum that I hoisted over my head and shoulder-pressed, demonstrating how light it was.

Before signing off, I had the staff and crew come onstage. Each held a flute of champagne; I teared up as I thanked them for their hard work. "It's been a bear, but you made it bearable," I said. I wasn't doing the happy dance I did when I was finally sprung from CBS, but there was none of the momentousness of when I left *TODAY*. A long line of people had tried and failed at this—Bonnie Hunt, Megan Mullally, Queen Latifah, Anderson Cooper, Bethenny Frankel, Kris Jenner, Carnie Wilson, Magic Johnson, Martin Short, Caroline Rhea, Tempestt Bledsoe, Harry Connick Jr., Chrissy Teigen, Tony Danza, Jane Pauley…and now they could add my name to the list.

In my mind, I'd already moved on. Besides, I had a big party to throw in just nine days.

JOHN HAD LOST 25 pounds; he had a huge S-shaped scar snaking down his abdomen. The acute similarity to what I'd gone through with Jay—the terror, the waiting, the praying—almost did me in. But there was one big difference: With Jay, it ended in a funeral. With John, a wedding.

While he was sick, the thought of canceling the whole thing was never far from our minds. John had even asked Dr. Allen if he thought it was okay for us to get married—the last thing he wanted was to make me a widow a second time. Dr. Allen gave him the green light.

In other words, the show would go on—even if *Katie* would not.

84

I Will

I ASKED A FANCY-PANTS designer to create a fun wedding dress, shorter in front and longer in back (knowing the legs are the last thing to go). But when I checked myself out during a fitting, I looked like a leftover piece of meringue, which wasn't what I was going for. An expensive mistake.

Less than a week before the wedding, my friend the designer Carmen Marc Valvo dropped off a white, sequined, floor-length number with a bit of a train; it had a halter-type bodice that showed off my shoulders, toned from doing gymnastics in my youth—thank God for muscle memory. Chic, simple, pretty. Perfect.

June 21st—the summer solstice, the longest day of the year (John figured there had to be some significance to that). I woke up, jumped in the Thunderbird, turned the radio on full blast, and sang along with the American Authors, *This is gonna be the best day of my life*...I felt like I was driving on air.

Later, we had a casual lunch in the backyard where John's mother, Paula, met my mom for the first time. I had grown to love my soon-to-be mother-in-law so much, but my mom was my mom, and I was eager to share her. When I saw them sitting close, chatting over tea sandwiches and chilled pea soup, it filled my heart with joy.

The ceremony was at 6:00 p.m. Rows of white chairs had been

set up in front of the pool and a white runner laid out on the lawn so I wouldn't aerate the grass with my heels. A trio of guitar, violin, and cello played some of our favorites: lots of Beatles—"In My Life," "Blackbird," "Here, There and Everywhere"—interspersed with Bach, Handel, and Vivaldi. Our guests milled about, drinking champagne and admiring the garden, which was exploding with color and beauty and life (special shout-out to the dahlias).

When I came downstairs, John was there to greet me. He looked so dashing in his navy Zegna suit—no longer gaunt, just trim and handsome. He whispered in my ear, "I'm the luckiest guy on Amy's Lane."

I melted. Then he added, "Well, this side of Amy's Lane." And I burst out laughing.

"Okay," I told him. "Let's do this thing."

We walked out together, holding hands. As a 57-year-old bride, I was a little self-conscious, but when I saw all our friends beaming at us, I just went with it. We strolled toward John Ellis, a friend of John's and a cousin of George W. Bush, who'd gotten credentialed online as a Universal Life Church minister for the occasion. Imposing and patrician, he would make a great Reverend Hale in a summer-stock production of *The Crucible.* As we reached the brickwork surrounding the pool, I heard the crunch of sequins under the heels of my strappy silver sandals.

John and I had written our own vows and wanted them to be funny and sincere. Here's one of mine:

"I promise not to stay mad at you for more than 72 hours in the event you do something colossally stupid—such as take my car key with you 140 miles from our home on the Monday of Memorial Day weekend, while I have teenage girls and a flight in four hours to the West Coast for a *BIG* interview the next morning."

Yes, that happened.

For his part, John said, "I promise to remember to hold the camera at 'eye level' (not lower) when taking photos of you and your fans."

He was learning!

Carrie sang the Beatles song "I Will." *What a blessing,* I thought, remembering that upsetting afternoon nine months before when the girls had burst into tears. Time heals—they were totally on board now.

After John Ellis pronounced us husband and wife, we walked back down the aisle to the musicians' rendition of Pharrell's "Happy" (hey, it was 2014! And we *were* happy!). As we passed my mom, John reached down and squeezed her hand. She smiled approvingly. For me, it was one of the most beautiful moments of the whole ceremony.

Afterward, I learned that Matt Lauer and Howard Stern had cooked up a plan to crash the wedding—apparently, they were going to submerge themselves in the pool in scuba gear and pop up at some point. Luckily, they'd shared their plan with *TODAY* EP Don Nash, who told them, "That's a terrible idea."

I had imagined this day for years, wondering how conflicted I'd feel—if I'd have one foot in the past, remembering that other June day 25 years earlier at the Navy Chapel in Washington.

I wondered how Jay's family would feel about me getting remarried. I wondered what it would be like for my girls . . . our girls.

I'd invited Clare and her husband, Jeff. After the ceremony, she grabbed my arm and looked at me with her beautiful ice-blue eyes and said, "I want you to know, we are all so happy that you've met someone. I've prayed for you to meet a wonderful man. And I couldn't be more thrilled for you." It was an extraordinary gift, giving me permission to love John while still loving Jay.

Clare being there was so important to me. The person who'd helped me grieve my husband—her brother—was now here to help me celebrate my new life.

After Jay died, I tried to maintain a bond with his family, and yet the Monahan diaspora extended to Delaware, Kansas, New Mexico, and beyond. Distance and busy schedules made getting together a big challenge, especially without the linchpin—Jay. Even though we have drifted apart, I'll always love the Monahans.

I understood how they might feel. When Emily's husband, George, remarried, I was so happy for him. But at the ceremony at the St. Regis Hotel, it was impossible not to think about Emily and what might have been. At the same time, I had great empathy for George, knowing what it felt like to be trapped in that purgatory between loss and finding love again. My parents, though…they couldn't come. They simply couldn't.

They say when you marry someone, you marry their family. I hit the jackpot in that department. Ellie and Carrie had already lost three grandparents, and now they had a new set in the divine Paula and Herby, who immediately started referring to the girls as their granddaughters. It meant so much to me when, four years later, they came to Carrie's Stanford graduation. Meanwhile, I had always wanted more children, and here they were: Henry, who inherited John's sense of humor, wowed us with his hilarious wedding toast, and Allie, sweet and self-possessed, welcomed me into her life without hesitation. Add Tom, Andy, and John's bon vivant little brother, David, and we had the makings of a thoroughly modern family.

It took me 16 long years and so many false starts. After all this time and all my searching, it felt like I had made my way home. Of course, I thought about Jay that day. But I was excited about this new chapter of my life. With another John Paul—another JPM. This one John Paul Molner.

After a reception at the Topping Rose House in Bridgehampton, we plugged in an iPhone and had a spontaneous dance party (I love John, but he doesn't move his feet when he dances, which makes him look like one of those gas-station windsocks). My friend Kathleen brought my mom back to Amy's Lane. Standing at the kitchen island, they ate wedding cake and relived the highlights before Kathleen helped my mom into bed. The next day, she told me how happy my mother was that finally, after all these years, I seemed settled and content.

85

Labor Day

FIVE WEEKS AFTER tying the knot, we were in Martha's Vineyard at Laurie David's bucolic spread, Wise Owl Farm, formerly known as Camp David. She and her husband, Bart, grew sweet potatoes by the thousands there, plus tomatoes, kale, garlic, parsnips, edamame, shishito peppers, and these twisty-looking shiitake mushrooms that sprout from holes drilled into logs.

On Saturday, we took their Boston Whaler on Menemsha Pond to Bart's secret spot, where we dug clams out of the muck with our toes. Laurie's ex, Larry David of *Curb Your Enthusiasm* fame, had a house nearby that Bart built and Laurie decorated—how's that for an amicable divorce? Larry wasn't there at the time, so Laurie decided to show us around (pret-ty, pret-ty, pret-ty invasive—sorry, Larry!). That night we steamed the clams and washed them down with rosé.

The next morning I went out to the chicken coop and gathered fresh eggs, with which Laurie made a killer kale-and-mushroom frittata. Then the four of us headed to the tennis court. As I was picking up the fluorescent green balls that littered my side of the net, I saw my phone, which I'd set down on the brick wall encircling the court, light up.

My childhood phone number. Feeling a familiar pang of anxiety, I answered immediately.

"Katie, please come take care of me."

My mother's quavering voice alarmed me. It was the first time I ever heard her sound helpless. We hightailed it to the ferry.

After our dad died, my mom didn't want to relocate to Boston to live with Kiki or to New York to live with me. She may have bitched about how small and basic our house was, growing up— referring to it derisively as "the box"—but there was no place she'd rather be, surrounded by her needlepoint pillows and my dad's books, even the bathroom wallpaper that had been installed upside down so it looked like the butterflies were doing an airborne back-stroke.

But I worried about her spending so much time alone. Navigating airports got to be too much, so when my mom wanted to visit, I'd ask Amro, who drove me and was like a member of the family, to pick her up in Arlington and provide door-to-door service. (She'd make ham sandwiches for the trip and could never understand why Amro always saved his for later. He didn't have the heart to tell her that as a Muslim, he didn't eat pork.)

When I arrived at 40th Street, the door was open, which seemed strange.

"Mom?" I said loudly and walked in. I found her sitting in her usual place at the kitchen table in her chenille bathrobe, eating a bowl of Corn Chex.

"Katie!" She seemed surprised to see me. "I just don't feel well," she said and put her forehead on the table.

"Don't worry, Mom, I'm here," I said, rubbing her back.

I wished so much that I lived nearby or that I could move in. But Carrie was heading off to college, and I had a demanding professional life and a brand-new husband...so instead I had meals delivered, that well-meaning default of the sandwich generation.

My mom got up to take her bowl to the sink. Believe me, I tried, but she responded with an exasperated "No, I'll do it!"—something I'd heard many times before.

Then she said this: "I don't want you to be sad when I die."

My heart stopped. It was my worst fear since I was a little girl—one that only increased with time.

I'd do almost anything to have that moment back so I could tell her the truth—that I was going to be more than sad. Untethered, like a helium balloon that had escaped a child's grip, drifting, aimless. I wanted to tell her that when she died, a piece of my heart would be forever buried with her and my father in a cemetery in Eufaula.

I spent the next few days just being there and helping out, picking up her watch from the repair guy at the jewelry store, buying her a salad, running to the drugstore.

That Tuesday, I was doing my first interview with Ruth Bader Ginsburg at the Supreme Court for Yahoo News, this one about the so-called Hobby Lobby ruling. I got back to Arlington at about 5:00 p.m. and opened the door, which, as always, got caught on the carpet protector. My mom was sitting in a chair by the staircase, clearly furious.

"What took you so long?" she said. "I've been waiting for you for hours!"

She got upset over the littlest things. When the neighbors repaved their driveway, she insisted they'd gone an inch over our property line; a Hatfield-and-McCoy-level feud ensued. Perhaps spending all those hours alone gave her too much time to stew.

Still, I got so mad at myself for lingering over a cup of coffee with my producer and not rushing home. That's time with my mom I will never get back.

IN AUGUST, JOHN and I took a red-eye to Italy for a belated honeymoon. We made a side trip to Banfi winery in Montalcino, Tuscany, where we stayed in a medieval castle. We rode bikes around the country-side beneath a glowing sky the color of an Aperol spritz. We took a cooking class and learned how to make pillowy gnocchi with brown butter and sage, and a meat sauce that tasted like the kind your chubby Italian grandmother would make if you had one. We dressed for dinner and drank the region's delicious, fruity wines on the patio beneath a dramatically up-lit castle wall.

But when we arrived in Florence, I got word that my mom was running a fever, and the home health aide she'd finally allowed in the house had called 911. Johnny rushed over and found her gripping the banister, screaming, "No, no, no," refusing to go. The paramedics had to carry her downstairs. I have thought about that disturbing scene so many times, it's almost as if I were there.

We tried to go to dinner, but I could barely carry on a conversation. Our next stop was supposed to be Portofino for a two-day stay at the apparently very splendid Splendido hotel, which John had been excited about. Instead, I said, "I can't stay here. I want to go home." My mom was in the hospital telling the doctors the same thing.

We called in hospice. Those incredible people—Kiki told me that one night, our mother said to the nurse on duty, "Hold me, I'm afraid." That angel on earth did exactly as she was asked, cradling Mom for hours as she slept.

Back on 40th Street, I'd lie with her in bed, rub her feet, and stroke her silky white hair. I'd hold her hand and feel the loose skin over the raised blue veins that formed tributaries from knuckle to wrist. I fed her droplets of Coca-Cola from a syringe I'd bought at CVS, as though she were a bird with a broken wing.

"Mom, I love you so much," I said. "You're the best mom in the world."

I kissed her forehead a dozen times and raised her hand to my cheek. Her eyelids fluttered; I like to think she felt both my touch and my love.

My heart hurt as the girls and I walked out the front door—the door I'd flown through to run and catch the bus, that I opened to greet Emily's date as he stood nervously on the front steps or to flirt with the paperboy Ralph Janafska, whom I had a crush on at the age of 7. The door I opened so quietly when I'd stayed out past my curfew; the same door my dad swung open when I was kissing Ernie Sanders in the driveway a little too long. The door I carried Ellie and then Carrie through on their first visits to their grandparents, that I'd stumbled through as a toddler. The gateway to my future that always welcomed me back and made me feel safe like nothing else. The door where my parents stood and waved goodbye, watching me drive away time and time again.

This time would be the last. I'd never see my mom standing in that doorway, or anywhere else, again.

My mother died on Labor Day, which somehow seemed fitting, given the four labors she'd endured and what a tireless worker she'd been throughout her life. It weighs on me that I wasn't there—that I wasn't there with my dad or Emily either. Death frightened me too much. Maybe it had something to do with being the baby and knowing everyone I loved most in the world might well die before me.

I thought back to a time my mom was driving me to my piano lesson, and I told her I wished people didn't have to die.

"Well," she replied, "if they didn't, it would get pretty crowded down here."

True, although by now I was feeling numb from all the loss, thinking that maybe the Courics had experienced more than their share. Yes, our parents reached ripe old ages. But Jay and Emily hadn't—and neither had Johnny's first wife, Marilyn, who went into septic shock, her organs shutting down in a matter of hours. She was just 54, the same age as Emily. As Kiki sadly noted soon after, among us four kids, she and her wonderful husband, Jim, were the only couple still intact. For the other three, our marriages ended when death did us part.

My mom once told me, "There are worse things than dying." I think she meant suffering. In her case, at 91, perhaps death meant deliverance. For me it meant devastation. My minister reached out when he heard the news and offered this thought: "Those who love deeply, grieve deeply." At least for a minute, I was filled with gratitude to have known that kind of love.

I called the reporter at the *Washington Post* who'd edited my father's obituary. "I wanted to let you know my mom died, and I'd love to have an obituary for her," I said.

"Well, what did she do?" he asked. "Tell me about her."

The question caught me by surprise.

"She did everything," I replied. "Raised four kids, who all went on to be very successful people. She was the heart and soul of our family. She was ahead of her time, volunteering at Planned Parenthood. She worked at Lord and Taylor in the gift department; she arranged flowers for weddings."

I'll never forget the sound of silence on the other end.

That's when it really hit me, how undervalued mothers are in our society, especially the full-time kind. I was incensed that somehow my mom's accomplishments, her amazing life, were deemed not worth writing about.

86

#Ladydouchebag

A NURSE HANDED ME two blue latex gloves filled with ice and tied at the wrist—frozen, hand-shaped water balloons with which to cradle my new, smaller breasts.

I'd always wanted to have them reduced. They were heavy and fibrocystic (the surgeon told me it was like cutting through concrete), not to mention saggy, causing deep bra-strap grooves in the flesh on my shoulders. So despite my fear of needles, scalpels, and anesthesia, I decided to take the plunge.

I came home groggy and bandaged and settled into bed.

John approached solicitously. So sweet. Then he brought his lips close to my ear and said softly, "There's a problem with the documentary."

"Why are you telling me this now?" I snapped.

"There's a problem with the way it was edited. The gun group in Virginia is saying there's a pause in the movie that never happened."

UNDER THE GUN was my second documentary with director Stephanie Soechtig. Our first, *Fed Up,* focused on childhood obesity—I was proud of the way it reframed the root causes of the epidemic (in a word: *sugar.* In everything). After Sandy Hook, I told Stephanie I thought we should zero in on guns and explore why, despite overwhelming public support, stricter laws were never enacted. We profiled a number of families whom I'd gotten to know, all shattered by gun violence, among them the Bardens; Lonnie and Sandy Phillips, whose daughter Jessie was killed in the movie-theater massacre in Aurora, Colorado; astronaut (and, later, senator) Mark Kelly and his wife, Gabby Giffords, after her near-fatal shooting. I was grateful they trusted me to share their experiences. But I also wanted to hear from gun owners to understand why they were so hell-bent on preventing any safety measures.

I flew to Virginia to interview members of the Virginia Citizens Defense League (VCDL), all of whom were packing heat. One woman described her gun as "pretty." Another told me she carried a firearm for personal defense, adding, "I really enjoy target shooting and I really enjoy working with people to show them that this piece of metal is not as scary as the movies make it look." Another said, "I have a machine gun that's *really* fun to shoot." They all opposed background checks, which someone described as a registry that would allow the authorities to knock on their doors and confiscate their weapons.

"If there are no background checks for gun purchasers," I said, "how do you prevent felons or terrorists from purchasing a gun?"

During the editing, Stephanie showed me a segment in which that question was followed by eight seconds of silence, and two of the subjects looking down pensively.

"Did it actually happen that way?" I asked.

Stephanie admitted she might have added a beat for dramatic effect, but I trusted it hadn't altered the essence of the exchange. She'd spent the early part of her career in news, and I assumed she wouldn't play fast and loose with the facts.

Little did we know, VCDL had recorded the whole thing.

"Audio Shows Katie Couric Documentary Deceptively Edited Interview with Pro-Gun Activists" read a headline in the conservative *Washington Free Beacon*.

I'd later learn that the pensive reaction shots were taken from an entirely different part of the interview. Which was ridiculous; the documentary was compelling enough without the sleight of hand. I was furious. Unfortunately, when Matthew Hiltzik put out a statement claiming I stood by the filmmakers, I was in post-op Lalaland and in no condition to approve it.

I told Stephanie to temporarily pull the film off the streaming service, Epix, and redact the pause. But Epix insisted on showing it the way it was. Of course, I'd be the one getting trashed.

We spent Memorial Day weekend at John's brother's place on Fire Island, where I was glued to my phone the whole time, crafting and recrafting a statement on Twitter—a labored explanation with just a dash of mea culpa for not expressing my concerns "more vigorously" during the editing phase.

Instagram took note:

Good job on editing your shitty documentary. You just proved that the media is a bunch of fucks with an agenda

Liar presstitute whore

Your terrible at journalism

#Ladydouchebag

You still have those amazing legs

Fuck off with this anti gun bullshit...you are not taking our guns PERIOD

Then came a tweet:

Katie Couric, the third rate reporter, who has been largely forgotten, should be ashamed of herself for the fraudulent editing of her doc.

This from Donald Trump. The NRA had endorsed him for president and donated more than $30 million to his campaign; this was his way of nakedly sucking up. So much for our decades of friendliness. I'd even attended his and Melania's wedding at Mar-a-Lago (I had jury-rigged my clutch with a small video camera to nab some footage for the *TODAY* show—I called it "Purse-Cam"—but it was confiscated by security).

Two weeks later, John and I were having dinner with friends at the Polo Bar, Ralph Lauren's clubby restaurant a block and a half from Trump Tower. Right before we ordered, a team of poker-faced guys wearing earpieces started moving through the dining room, casing the joint. Then Trump lumbered in, jaw jutting over his extra-long red tie, trailed by a subdued Melania and Barron. A waiter whispered to us that he was there to celebrate his 70th birthday.

They were seated at a banquette maybe 12 feet from us. I was directly in Trump's sight line, but he refused to look at me. To be fair, I refused to look at him too. John thought I was being as much of a baby as he was, that all was fair in love and politics, and why not be the bigger person? But I was fuming.

Andy Lack and Jack Welch were on the other side of the restaurant, and at a certain point they made their way over to genuflect before Trump (Andy, who was back as president of the news division, needed to be on decent terms with him for access reasons, and Jack was an unapologetic Trumper). Soon after, Trump walked past our table—and turned his head sharply to the right to avoid any possibility of eye contact.

I had fantasized about strolling over and pouring a glass of water on his head to see what would happen when it interacted with his hair; I imagined the elaborate comb-over disintegrating like wet cotton candy. But I decided that was probably not a great idea for so many reasons (getting tackled by Secret Service agents, the *New York Post* headlines, possible prison time…).

That foolish eight-second pause in the doc led to a $12 million lawsuit filed against me personally, probably because it would garner more press. It was ultimately dismissed. Philip Van Cleave, president of the Virginia gun group, would later get duped by Sacha Baron Cohen posing as an Israeli security expert. Somehow Baron Cohen's character,

Colonel Erran Morad, convinced Van Cleave to film a bogus infomercial called "Kinder Guardians." There's Van Cleave promoting firearms for toddlers concealed in stuffed toys, like the "puppy pistol." Yes, it's as insane as it sounds. I felt vindicated.

Back at the Polo Bar, I watched Donald Trump head for the exit, on his way to becoming the leader of the free world.

87

Palooza on the Plaza

THE WEEK OF January 2nd, 2017, I filled in for Savannah Guthrie while she was on maternity leave. It was weird sitting in my former *TODAY* show dressing room, now full of photos of Savannah and her friends and family, her trinkets, her books (including an inscribed copy of Megyn Kelly's *Settle for More;* yes, I peeked), her clothes, her stuff. But I loved seeing the crew, so many of whom had been a part of my daily life for 15 years. It was crazy to hear that Rope, one of my favorite cameramen, was now a grandfather; that Mark Traub, the stage manager I adored, whom viewers could often hear laughing heartily in the background (even when we hadn't said anything all that funny) was thinking about retiring. That Jennie, the teleprompter operator, whose banged bob had turned silver, was planning her daughter's wedding and wanted me to do a video message for the reception. "Where'd the time go?" we asked, shaking our heads.

At the top of the show, we told viewers not to adjust their sets. I shook Matt's hand, greeting him with a salutation worthy of the Kiwanis Club: *Hi! Katie Couric! Damn glad to meet you!* I said getting back in the anchor chair was like riding a bike.

But things were different. The set had been given a facelift— the brass-trimmed wooden desk that I'd sat behind was now modern and white with an orange *TODAY* show logo in front. In addition to the greenroom, they now had an "orange room," where viewer feedback and Twitter posts were shared, a nod to new media. And rather than divvying up interviews, the co-anchors conducted them together, which I found odd. It was hard to get into a rhythm and ask follow-ups. But it was no longer my show, so I got with the program.

The main event came Friday—Matt's 20th anniversary at *TODAY,* for which the team had planned a Lauer-palooza on the plaza.

When we headed out at 8:30, he trotted through a gauntlet of cheering staffers wearing navy T-shirts bearing a big white number 20, with their hands out for him to slap and grab—a manscaped Odysseus returning triumphant from the Trojan War (I half expected them to start chanting *All hail Matt!*). Just like my final *TODAY* show 11 years earlier, it seemed a bit much. But to be a constant presence in the world of morning TV for two decades is a major accomplishment, and I was happy for him.

A no-holds-barred lovefest ensued. I teed up a greatest-hits montage: Matt with some of the biggest names in news and pop culture, from Michelle Obama to Miss Piggy, against a backdrop of the biggest stories of the past 20 years. Matt's unparalleled ease and range were on full display.

The next day happened to be my 60th birthday, and my friend Jerry, who managed the props, wheeled out a cake. I turned the thick wax candle shaped like a 6 upside down and said, "Better than 90!"

Everyone laughed. To think I'd wandered onto this set for the first time in my early thirties...

When Savannah showed up to surprise Matt and they hugged and mugged, I moved to the side, well aware that America's First Family wasn't polyamorous.

At some point that week, I remember sitting next to Matt on the sofa during a commercial when he took a call. He was brief, saying only, "That's great news," before returning to the business at hand. My intuition told me it was Andy Lack with news about Megyn Kelly. At the time, there was frenzied speculation that Kelly would be leaving Fox News, which sparked a bidding war, a mano a mano fight among the network heads.

Turned out I was right—Megyn was coming to NBC, fresh on the heels of working for one of the biggest sexist pigs in the business.

88

Fire! Fire!

FOX NEWS OVERLORD Roger Ailes was the very first high-profile casualty of the MeToo movement. A lawsuit filed by Gretchen Carlson sounded the death knell—she'd secretly taped Ailes making bizarrely smutty remarks like "I think you and I should have had a sexual relationship a long time ago, and then you'd be good and better, and I'd be good and better." Soon, Ailes, who'd created the network 20 years earlier, was the target of dozens of allegations of sexual harassment (in one instance, he offered a woman a higher salary in exchange for sex on demand). With that, even Ailes superfan Rupert Murdoch admitted he had to go.

The significance of his sudden demise couldn't be overstated. Such a powerful media figure being taken down by female underlings—and for something that had been greeted with a yawn in so many workplaces for so long—marked a radical shift.

I knew Roger from my earliest days at TODAY. Back before he became the great and powerful Oz of right-wing media, he and his ideological opposite Bob Squier had a regular segment where they would opine about the political news of the day. Roger was always a gentleman to me, although he had no choice; I was an anchor and he was a guest.

A member of the crew once overheard Ailes chatting with Bryant before his segment, telling him about being at home in bed with a woman who wasn't his wife. When his actual wife (at the time) pulled up unexpectedly, a panicky Ailes tried an interesting diversionary tactic—setting a small fire and running out yelling, "Fire! Fire!" so the lady *in* the house could avoid the lady *of* the house by slipping out the back door. Apparently, a big laugh was had by all in the studio.

In 2014, when John and I were at the Breakers over Presidents' Day weekend trying our best to get some R and R before John's surgery, we saw Roger sitting in an enclosed courtyard with his doting, enabling third wife, Beth. He looked awful—wheelchair-bound, drawn and pasty, like the late-stage Charles Foster Kane. We went over and said hi, and, as always, he was friendly and kind. Who knew he was such a monster?

THE DIZZYING MONTHS following Ailes's departure had a two-steps-forward-one-step-back quality. There was Trump's "Grab 'em by the pussy" tape—which somehow wasn't deemed offensive enough to keep him from being elected president of the United States. But it *was* enough to inspire five million fed-up pink-pussy-hat-wearing women to take to the streets in cities around the world for the first ever Women's March, the largest single-day protest (MESSAGE TO TRUMP: KEEP YOUR TINY HANDS OFF MY UTERUS; A WOMAN'S PLACE IS IN THE RESISTANCE; GRAB 'EM BY THE MIDTERMS) in American history.

On January 10th, the *New York Times* broke the story that Fox had quietly settled a sexual-harassment lawsuit against pugilistic populist Bill O'Reilly. In a letter to Fox News, attorneys for anchor Juliet Huddy alleged she'd been subjected to relentless come-ons (including constant calls and masturbatory sounds on the other end of the line) and that O'Reilly punished Huddy's noncompliance by picking apart her work and sidelining her. Fox settled with Huddy just weeks *after* Ailes went down, *after* the network had vowed that such behavior would no longer be tolerated. But Bill O'Reilly kept his job. Then four more women and a collective $13 million payoff surfaced. Advertisers fled and protesters descended on News Corp headquarters. The jig was up. Fox had no choice but to part ways with their biggest star.

Five months later, with a book to promote, Bill O'Reilly was ready to do his first post-Fox interview. He decided to do it with...Matt Lauer.

The set was sober and spare, just Matt and O'Reilly sitting on a pair of gray chairs.

"You were accused of sexual harassment," Matt says, pronouncing it "*hair*-ess-ment," for some reason. "You said at the time you did absolutely nothing wrong. You stand by that?"

"I do," O'Reilly replies almost breezily. Then things get strange.

Glasses on, Matt bears down. "You were probably the last guy in the world that they wanted to fire. Because you were the guy that the ratings and the revenues were built on. You carried that network on your shoulders for a lot of years. So doesn't it seem safe to assume that the people at Fox News were given a piece of information or given some evidence that simply made it impossible for you to stay on at Fox News?"

If Matt sees any potential parallels between himself and O'Reilly, he doesn't show it.

O'Reilly, meanwhile, is glowering and harrumphing, counting the seconds until he gets to plug his book, offering cynical responses like "Those lawsuits involved many other people, not just me."

After nearly five minutes of this, Matt says, "Over the last six months since your firing, have you done some soul-searching? Have you done some self-reflection? And have you looked at the way you treated women that you think about differently now than you did at the time?"

Matt's final question, delivered in a low, somewhat pitying tone: "Were there any self-inflicted wounds here, Bill?"

THE DRIP-DRIP-DRIP OF speculation about other prominent, powerful men became a full-on deluge. In October, Jodi Kantor and Megan Twohey's investigation of movie mogul Harvey Weinstein exploded on the front page of the *New York Times,* tracing his nearly three-decade pattern of (among other things) luring actresses and female employees to his suite in the luxury hotels where he did business, stripping naked, and pressuring them for massages; allegations of sexual assault and rape would come next.

Harvey and I crossed paths a fair amount. Of course, he pushed relentlessly for coverage of his movies on *TODAY*. I saw him at Super Bowl XLVIII in Woody Johnson's box at MetLife Stadium, where the mix of people had a bar–scene–in–*Star Wars* feel—Quentin Tarantino, Dick Cheney, Lorne Michaels...My main memory, beyond the shrimp cocktail tower and sushi platters, was how inattentive Weinstein was to his gorgeous wife, Georgina Chapman. Harvey was such an operator, nothing diverted him from working a roomful of players.

After Weinstein came the parade of pervs, everyone from Mario Batali to Louis C.K., nailed for jerking off in front of up-and-coming female comics looking to be mentored. Maybe I shouldn't have been surprised; two years earlier, he'd reached out to see if I'd appear on his FX show *Louie.* In the scene he pitched, I'm on TV, reading the news, while Louie watches. And suddenly I break from the broadcast to speak to him directly: "Louie, just do it. You know you're gonna do it. So just take off your pants and get started...I'm gonna go back to my story. Just watch my mouth and do your disgusting thing." Louie unbuttons his pants.

And...scene. I guess life *does* imitate art. Even though John was a big *Louie* fan, I passed.

With women coming forward like never before to tell their painful, often ruinous truths, you couldn't help but think about Anita Hill. I'll never forget how alone she seemed, back in 1991, as she testified before the Senate Judiciary Committee—this poised, serious-minded, Black law professor being stared down by a tribunal of white male legislators, some as old as 88. Howell Heflin drawling, "Are you a scorned woman?" Joe Biden and Arlen Specter prodding Hill for the most embarrassing thing Clarence Thomas had ever said to her. Orrin Hatch waving around a copy of *The Exorcist* as supposed proof that Hill's reality was actually a fever dream, cribbed from the pages of a lurid bestseller.

I'd interviewed Hill shortly before the hearings and asked a number of questions that in retrospect are pretty tone-deaf, such as: If Thomas had repeatedly disrespected her at the Department of Education, why did she take a job with him at the EEOC? Her answer: She liked the work. It was an opportunity to put her skills toward civil rights initiatives, she said, which is what she'd always wanted to do. And in those days, it's not as though women—even talented, well-educated ones—were juggling tons of options. Particularly women of color.

As for leaving the position, Hill noted it would have been hard to find another one, especially since she wouldn't be able to count on a reference from her current boss, Thomas.

"So," Hill said, "it would mean I had no job."

What women have had to put up with because they needed the job.

The morning of Thomas's testimony, we were wrapping up the first hour of *TODAY* with some cross talk. I was in the Rotunda at the Capitol, and Bryant and Faith Daniels were in New York, maxing on the sofa on a Friday morning; "a getaway morning," as Bryant always called them. Wearing a charcoal-gray blazer with the peaks of a starched white hankie poking out of the breast pocket, he wondered how long people were going to remain interested in the judicial drama. He and Faith ticked off a few high-profile confirmation scandals, noting how, in each case, the media circus eventually moved on. Tossing back to me, Bryant said, "When do you think the public hits burnout on this one?"

I smiled into the camera. "I think it's going to be a good, long while before they will."

Part VI

89

The Last Supper

IN THE FALL of 2017, a couple of reporters reached out: *Can I talk to you about Matt Lauer?*

I took their calls and told them the truth—that it had been widely assumed Matt had a lot of problems in his marriage. Infidelity and talk of divorce had been tabloid fodder for years.

I knew Matt loved beautiful women; I knew he was an unabashed flirt. He could charm the pants (as it were) off any celebrity—I'd heard that Julia Roberts always requested that he be the one to interview her. And any time he was chatting up Sandra Bullock about her latest movie, I wanted to shout across the studio, *Get a room!* He told me a hilarious story about the time he'd just taken his first big glass of colonoscopy prep and was gearing up for a long night near the john when Elle Macpherson called and invited him out for a drink. Matt tried to make himself throw up but couldn't, cursing his lousy timing.

I knew he was a "player," but I didn't know his extracurriculars were happening inside 30 Rock. I had put the "spread some butter on your thighs" incident out of my mind, convinced it was a creepy one-off.

I'd later hear from friends who still worked at *TODAY* that things turned frattier after I left. While Meredith had a wealth of experience and didn't take any guff, it was now Matt's show. He'd become cocky and reckless, which changed the tone of the place, the control-room guys opining loudly about the anatomy of female guests and staffers and openly playing the crude game Fuck, Marry, Kill. At a certain point, all the PAs seemed to be pretty young women; when passing out the rundown, one of them would plop in each guy's manspreading lap.

By the time Ann Curry was at the big desk, Matt was the highest-paid anchor in TV history and the top dog in every sense.

November 3, 2017

ME—8:33 P.M.
Hey! John is going out of town (bone fishing) next week. Want to grab dinner on Wednesday? I'm trying to fill my dance card while he's gone. Lmk! Ps nice dolly outfit. I'm starting to get very worried...
MATT—8:36 P.M.
Wednesday is good!

November 5, 2017

ME—2:36 P.M.
Excellent
Let's go someplace kind of healthy not your weird burger place!
MATT—2:42 P.M.
You pick it

I was glad we had a date on the calendar. I'd been feeling a bit lonely and nostalgic—I missed the camaraderie of a network news organization. I missed the rhythm of a daily show and working with Matt. And I had an idea I wanted to run by him.

We met at Elio's, a scene-y Italian restaurant on the Upper East Side. Well-heeled Manhattanites bustled in, unbuttoning their coats and unwrapping their scarves. One of them was Matt. I thought he looked tired, older. I probably did too, but he also seemed a little on edge, without his usual easy smile. As diners whispered and stole glances, I have to admit it was fun to be seen with him again out in the real world.

We exchanged the latest on our kids, our travels. I gingerly asked about Annette.

"She's great," Matt said, "she's doing really well."

I hoped that was true. Whenever I saw Matt at parties, Annette was MIA. I never knew why—maybe she was antisocial or even agoraphobic. Or maybe the two of them had some sort of "understanding," whatever that might be.

A few years earlier, when John and I had become serious, I invited friends for dinner in East Hampton: Howard and Beth Stern, Matt and Annette, and a few others. I always liked Annette, even though I didn't know her well; I was looking forward to getting better acquainted after all these years. So I was surprised when Matt walked in alone.

"Where's Annette?" I asked.

"She isn't feeling well," he said. Disappointing, but not surprising.

At Elio's, our conversation quickly turned to the topic that was dominating dinner parties all over town—Harvey Weinstein and the cascade of allegations roiling the media.

"This MeToo stuff feels like it's getting kind of out of control," Matt said. "It feels like a witch hunt."

I took it that Matt was worried about a lack of due process, people's livelihoods and reputations being destroyed by anecdotes and innuendo—something I wondered about too.

I was watching his slender fingers as he carefully cut his chicken paillard when he said to me, quietly, "You know, women come into my office, and sometimes they're crying and want to talk to me. Now, if they sit next to me on the sofa, I can't even put my arm around them."

I tried to imagine such a scene taking place. "No, Matt, you cannot do that. You cannot put your arm around them."

He looked concerned.

I asked about Andy Lack, an ally to both of us in the blood sport that is TV news. For some reason Matt said, "Andy is my best friend."

Coming from a 59-year-old man, that sounded a little odd. "Matt. Let me give you some advice," I said. "Work friends are not best friends. Work friendships are mostly transactional. You can't necessarily count on them."

Something like worry flitted across his face.

Blame the pinot noir, but during dinner, I got a little teary-eyed telling Matt how much I missed live TV and working with a partner like him. He nodded and smiled; I could tell he knew what I meant and was feeling nostalgic too. I don't think we'd ever had such a vulnerable, honest conversation.

Then I described my idea for a show in which we'd revisit some of the biggest news stories of the past several decades. Matt seemed intrigued. "Do you want me to talk to Andy about it?" he asked. I said sure. Out on the sidewalk we hugged and went our separate ways. I felt closer to Matt that night than I had in all my years sitting next to him at the anchor desk.

November 8, 2017

ME—9:02 P.M.

Omg what the hell did you put in my drink?? Phenobarbital?????
Thank you for being such a good friend. I treasure you. Oy. Xo.

MATT—9:10 P.M.

The length of our friendship and the comfort that comes with that is more powerful than any drug in a drink! We have and always will have that ease and connection. I adore you back!

November 9, 2017

ME—7:30 P.M.

Yikes they're saying Charlie Rose is in the crosshairs. Yikes

MATT—9:00 P.M.

I know. It's out of control and it will only get worse!

MATT—10:09 P.M.

Where did you hear about the Charlie stuff?
Been brewing for a bit

November 10, 2017

ME—2:32 P.M.
Former CBS people

Less than two weeks later, amid stories of a long history of fondling, groping, breast-squeezing, thigh-caressing, and emerging from bathrooms stark naked with young female colleagues present, Charlie Rose was expunged—first from CBS, then PBS.

A smooth operator who oozed Southern charm, Charlie was an inveterate bachelor and fixture on the social circuit. And incredibly thin-skinned, as I had discovered. Back in 2007, I moderated a Q & A following a screening of *The Kite Runner* for members of the media. In my introductory remarks I remember saying something like, "Please ask your questions in the form of a question—that means you, Charlie," a humorous (I thought) reference to his penchant for long-winded wind-ups during interviews on his PBS show.

Charlie's long face got longer. He wasn't amused.

As clouds rolled over the sunny *CBS This Morning* logo, reporters were hard at work on a story that would jolt another network to its core.

90

No Bueno

ME—2:32 P.M.

All good w you? I was thinking about pitching that flashback series. Would you be interested in participating? I think it could be really fun and people would love it. Let me know what you think! Xoxo

MATT—2:33 P.M.

Hi sweetie.

Sure, who are you thinking of pitching it to? Andy? Burke?

ME—2:40 P.M.

I dunno! Maybe you can help me figure it out. No rush maybe we can talk about it after thanksgiving!

MATT—2:46 P.M.

Let's have a second chat after the holiday. Off to London for the weekend. Back Monday. My best to you guys!

ME—4:32 P.M.

Have fun and happy thanksgiving! Xo

MATT—7:32 P.M.

You too!

Just before the holiday, I received an email from my former assistant Meredith asking if I'd be willing to talk to Amy Brittain, a friend of hers from Columbia Journalism School. The same Amy Brittain who, with Irin Carmon, had just broken the Charlie Rose story in the *Washington Post*. She wanted to talk to me about Matt.

I told Meredith I'd be glad to. I was a young reporter once too.

It was a chilly Saturday in East Hampton. I nestled in the white Pottery Barn sofa with a cup of tea and stared at the skeletal trees outside. I had just built my first fire of the season.

When Amy called, I gave her my standard response: "I really didn't know that much about Matt's personal life. I think there was a fair amount of fooling around going on at NBC in general, but I don't really have anything for you about Matt. I'm sorry I can't be more helpful."

I could hear the disappointment in Amy's silence on the other end.

"But, off the record," I said, "I've worked at many networks, and I found CBS to be the most misogynistic—especially *60 Minutes*."

I heard her typing.

"If I were you, I'd look into that. And," I added, "Jeff Fager."

ON MONDAY, NOVEMBER 27th, I flew to the West Coast. I was knee-deep in a six-part documentary series for National Geographic about some of the most pressing issues of the day—tech addiction, Islamophobia, and white anxiety, as well as gender inequality. I'd started working on it in the summer of 2017. Before Harvey, before Charlie, before Matt. Before MeToo had become a movement.

I was particularly interested in understanding a culture that was preventing women from making greater strides in the workplace. Tech journalist Kara Swisher and I walked around Fisherman's Wharf discussing the bro-y vibe of Silicon Valley start-ups. To learn more about Hollywood's uneven playing field, I interviewed Julius Tennon. He's married to Oscar-winning actress Viola Davis; together, they formed JuVee Productions in 2011 with a mission to open doors for people of color in all facets of the entertainment industry. I sat in on a production meeting with the staff of JuVee to hear how they were working toward their goal.

The team explained that when casting, the roles shouldn't be limited to a particular ethnicity or race, even if the writer specified it. The producer used the example of casting a doctor: "Why not just say the character is a doctor; he's tall, handsome—"

"Wait," I broke in, "you just used the word *he* to describe the doctor. You made the doctor a man!"

The producer looked surprised, then embarrassed. Everyone laughed. Even at an enlightened company like JuVee, implicit bias is a hard habit to break.

November 28, 2017

KARA SWISHER—10:46 P.M.

Hey have you heard a not so nice story coming out about Matt Lauer? Curious if it has gotten out.

ME—4:56 A.M.

I know a lot of folks have been digging. I don't know much more than that and only know about rumors of playing around. I was happily oblivious or just too focused on my job! What have u heard?!

KARA—7:42 A.M.

Focused on interns. Not Charlie Rose level but no bueno.

ME—7:45 A.M.

Ay ay ay ay ay

91

Morning Has Broken

N OVEMBER 29TH, 2017, 4:00 a.m.
I was sleeping soundly in a high-thread-count cocoon at the Four Seasons Beverly Hills; Ellie, now living in LA, had spent the night. We often had slumber parties when I was on the West Coast so we could hang out but also so she could enjoy the luxurious bedding and spa-like shower that only a four-star hotel can provide. My phone went off and I squinted to see who could be calling me this early. My old friend Dana Keller.

"Hello," I croaked.

"Matt Lauer has been fired."

"What?"

In a matter of seconds I went from unconscious to feeling like I'd chugged eight cups of coffee. Alerts were coming in fast and furious. *Politico:* "Today Show Host Matt Lauer Fired for 'Inappropriate Sexual Behavior.'" The *New York Times:* "NBC Fires Matt Lauer, the Face of 'Today.'" *Vanity Fair:* "An Emotional 'Today' Grapples with Matt Lauer's Sexual Misconduct Allegation."

I turned to Twitter and watched a clip of the most bizarre open in *TODAY* show history. Live from studio 1A, there was Savannah, with Hoda Kotb sitting next to her, on the verge of tears as she shared the news they'd just learned—that Matt was out. I could only imagine how impossible it must have been to process what had happened and share it with the world.

The sun hadn't even come up in Los Angeles and my phone was exploding.

Kara Swisher—4:09 A.M.

And there we go on Lauer

Norah O'Donnell—4:26 A.M.

Hey. It's Norah. What do you make of this???

Joanne Lipman—5:00 A.M.

Shocking news . . . If you're up for it, USA TODAY's audience would love an op-ed by you, or a video op-ed (new thing we're doing). Let me know. Thanks!

Matthew Hiltzik—6:33 A.M.

Call me pls

Megyn Kelly—2:26 P.M.

Hey there—hope you're well. Getting the show together for tomorrow—do you have any interest in coming on to react to the ML news? Would be a thoughtful discussion. What a day, KC. Wow.

Xoxo

In the blink of an eye, "Where in the world is Matt Lauer?" had become "What in the world is up with Matt Lauer?"

My first impulse was to call Debbie Kosofsky, perhaps Matt's closest friend at *TODAY*. They had worked together in Boston and he adored her, as did I. We shared a birthday and were the same age; she was a grown-up. Surely Debbie would know what was happening.

"Debbie, my God," I said when she answered.

"It's a mess," she said, sounding distraught. "It's a real mess."

"Where are you?" I asked. "Are you with him?"

"I'm picking him up and driving him to see Jack. He wants to speak to him in person."

Jack, the oldest of Matt's three kids, was in boarding school. My heart sank as I contemplated the conversation they were about to have.

I couldn't imagine what it was like to be Matt at that moment, with practically the whole world reacting to your plummet from grace. Your family—your *children*—having to process something so painful and public. Had Matt seen this up ahead—had he been fearful that the MeToo movement was coming for him next? Was his on-air indignation with Bill O'Reilly all an act, a preemptive bid for plausible deniability? Was our conversation at Elio's just three weeks earlier his way of preparing me—grooming me—to be sympathetic?

I called Terry Schaefer, a producer I'd known since my early days in Washington; she'd overseen a finding-my-roots piece in Eufaula featuring my dad and me.

"Oh my God, Katherine. Oh my God." Terry always called me Katherine.

"What the hell, Frances?" I always called her Frances.

We sat on the phone and compared notes on the Matt we knew.

"He was always so sweet to me," she said. "When I needed money to finish a documentary I was working on, he sent me a check. No questions asked; he didn't want any credit. He just did it."

I reached out to Jennie Thompson, who'd produced a slew of great stories for me, especially during the Olympics.

"Jennie," I said, "did you know this side of Matt? This super-sleazy side?"

"No, never," she said. "I remember whenever we flew back to New York after a long trip, he got a cab for me and made sure I was taken care of. He didn't have to bother with that. He was always such a gentleman."

There was still a part of me that wondered if it was just a rumor running wild. Preposterous stories were regular tabloid fodder, like the photoshopped tabloid cover years ago that featured me, Jay, and Matt under the giant headline "Caught in a Love Triangle!"

Incriminating footage would start to surface. TMZ unearthed a piece of video from Andy Cohen's show *Watch What Happens Live* where he asks me what Matt's most annoying habit was during our time as co-anchors.

"He pinched me on the ass a lot," I say.

I thought it was pretty obvious that I was joking, given our sibling dynamic on-air. But the clip went viral, and so did one of Matt sitting on the sofa during a commercial break, eyeing Meredith as she leans in to grab a script from the coffee table in front of him. Says Matt casually, "Keep bending over like that, it's a nice view."

But nothing cast Matt in a promiscuous light quite like his 2008 Friars Club roast. Martha Stewart starts things off with "I hear NBC executives call Matt 'the Cock of the Rock.'" I do a Letterman-like top-ten list. *Number ten: According to his wife, he's not really an early riser, if you know what I mean. Number two: He loves to eat Curry.* The ballroom at the New York Hilton erupts; Ann blanches. "What? Indian food! What's wrong with you people?"

It was pretty raunchy—uncomfortably so in places, but standard fare for a roast. And it only got raunchier when Matt stepped up to the podium. Now, as people pored over every Matt-related clip and utterance with forensic intensity, two of his lines suggested to some that he had sex-with-co-workers on the brain.

Referring to my on-air colonoscopy he cracked, "Let me just say I saw that colon a lot before the rest of you saw it." And later: "What's with all the small-dick jokes?...It's fun to look over and see Ann Curry laughing—like she doesn't know how big my dick is." Oh God.

Meanwhile, some of Matt's interviews, which might have seemed merely flirty at the time, suddenly felt skeevy. During a sit-down with Anne Hathaway following a really unfortunate up-skirt paparazzo shot, he said with a touch of lasciviousness, "Seen a lot of you lately." Talking to Sandra Bullock about *The Proposal,* Matt seemed less flirty than horny when he couldn't stop mentioning her semi-nude scenes: "You're naked for most of this movie!" he said. And "Did I mention you have a nude scene in this movie?," adding that he'd made it his screen saver.

Taken together, the salacious snippets painted a damning portrait of

Matt—but it just wasn't how I saw him. All I could hope was that more information would come to help me understand exactly what he had done.

November 29, 2017

ME—12:16 P.M.

Matt,

I am crushed. I love you and care about you deeply. I am here. Please let me know if you want to talk. There will be better days ahead.

Love,

Katie

MATT—4:15 P.M.

92

Hero to Zero

THE IRONY WASN'T LOST on me that I was in LA investigating the mistreatment of women in the workplace. But it was hard to focus. An hour or so after I'd reached out to Matt, a friend forwarded an article in *Variety:*

> As the co-host of NBC's *Today,* Matt Lauer once gave a colleague a sex toy as a present. It included an explicit note about how he wanted to use it on her, which left her mortified. On another day, he summoned a different female employee to his office and dropped his pants, showing her his penis. After the employee declined to do anything, visibly shaken, he reprimanded her for not engaging in a sexual act.

Jesus, Matt . . .

The allegations were part of *Variety*'s two-month investigation. The piece included the reason Matt was fired: an NBC employee had gone to management with a complaint about "inappropriate sexual conduct" that started at the Sochi Olympics in 2014 and went on for months.

THURSDAY, NOVEMBER 30TH. I sat down to breakfast on the terrace of the Montage Beverly Hills. It was a typically cloudless, blue-sky day in

LA, completely at odds with the storm raging back east. A copy of the *New York Times* lay alongside my poached egg and coffee. And there it was, staring back at me: "Longtime Face of NBC's 'Today' Is Fired as Complaints Multiply."

One particularly appalling paragraph jumped out: Matt had called a producer into his office on the pretense of discussing a story, pushed a button under his desk that closed the door, pulled down the producer's pants, bent her over a chair, and had sex with her. Then she passed out. Matt instructed his assistant to take her to the NBC nurse.

This took place in 2001. My office was next to his. Our assistants shared a reception area. *How had this happened right under my nose?*

Matt put out a statement expressing "sorrow and regret" for the pain he'd caused. He added that, while some of what was said "wasn't true or has been mischaracterized, there's enough truth in these stories to make me feel embarrassed and ashamed."

As I walked down Wilshire Boulevard to a meeting with my agents at WME, I tried to process what I'd read. And suddenly a paparazzo appeared out of nowhere, clicking away. I was feeling out of sorts but mustered a weak smile, having been played so many times by the tabloids when they captured anything less than a happy face ("Woe Is Katie"; "Katie's Heartbreak"). So of course the headline accompanying the Page Six item this time was "Katie Couric Can't Stop Smiling After Matt Lauer Gets Fired."

Andy Lack reached out to me, which I appreciated. We arranged to meet at my place a few days later, when I'd be back in New York. The whole thing felt urgent for both of us.

He walked in looking more rumpled than usual. We took a seat in the den.

"I was shocked," Andy said. "I had no idea it was going on. I never saw this coming." Yes, they were friends, but apparently Matt didn't share the details of his life with Andy, despite the amount of time they spent together on the day-to-day. Despite Matt calling him his "best friend."

"Andy," I said, "can you explain what Matt did? Was this sexual assault? Because that's really important for me to know."

He answered immediately: "No."

"Then what is it? Were there pictures?"

Andy clearly felt uncomfortable giving me details. "It's really an age thing," he said. "The age difference is really troubling." Although I wonder if what Andy meant was *power*. As in, the power imbalance was really troubling.

He told me he had gone to Matt's apartment the night before to fire him. Matt did not protest. "He knew I had no choice," Andy said. "It was one of the hardest things I've ever had to do."

And I'll never forget what he said next: "Matt's gone from hero to zero, literally overnight."

We sat there in stunned silence, marinating in the shock and sadness of it all. Then Andy grabbed his coat, hugged me at the elevator, and hit the button. I later heard that the day before Matt was fired, the men in charge of the show walked out of a conference room, grim-faced and stoop-shouldered. As the director passed a producer's desk, he said under his breath, "The *TODAY* show will never be the same."

Even though I had read about all the awful things Matt had done, I was worried about him. I imagined him sleepless, haggard, depressed...maybe worse. And how were Annette and their children holding up? So I reached out again and asked how he was doing, which I realized was a very dumb question.

Matt got back to me two and a half hours later. He gave me his new number "for my files." He said he was struggling and would like to hear my voice.

Before I could respond, I heard from him again—at 4:04 a.m. He said he had tried to leave me a voice mail but (true to form) my mailbox was full. He repeated that he was struggling and that he'd like to hear my voice. I told him I would call him later that morning.

John thought I should just jump in the car and drive out to East Hampton to talk to him. I wanted to, but I didn't know what I would say. If I'm being perfectly honest, I was worried about my reputation. Matt's situation had created a feeding frenzy the likes of which I'd never seen before—there were paparazzi camped out at his house. If I was spotted there, it might have looked like I condoned the behavior. (I guess I could have visited in the dead of night, like Jennifer Aniston's character on *The Morning Show* after her colleague, played by Steve Carell, had an eerily similar crash and burn.)

I was confused, and simply not ready to take on the role of sympathetic friend and colleague just yet.

93

Addie

December 14, 2017

MATT—3:36 A.M.

Tried you yesterday but went to voicemail. Give a ring when you can.

ME—8:45 A.M.

Hey was in Erie PA all day and have two shoots today. This afternoon? Around 5? Will that work for you?

MATT—8:46 A.M.

Yep

ME—8:49 A.M.

Ok great will call then.

MATT—9:10 A.M.

Have a good day

I was glad we'd finally nailed down a time.

That afternoon, a friend sent a link to another article in *Variety*. It was about a woman named Addie Zinone.

Addie.

Zinone was her married name. I knew her as Addie Collins.

Nearly two decades earlier, Addie, then a broadcast journalism major on scholarship at Temple University, had sent me a fax (remember those?). She said she loved the show, loved the profession, loved me, and wondered if she could shadow me for a day or however long to see what it was really like behind the camera.

"This is the kind of person we should be helping—she has no connections and she wrote to me out of the blue," I said to my assistant, and asked her to call Addie.

She took a Greyhound bus from Philadelphia and found a cheap room through the Salvation Army. Addie's day with us led to an internship, which led to production assistant jobs on a number of shows. I remember seeing her diligently handing out scripts and working late in the edit room—I was so proud of her.

Now I was reading that Addie had been one of Matt's conquests. After four years at NBC, she'd been hired as a local anchor/reporter in her West Virginia hometown. Once he learned she had only a few weeks left at 30 Rock, he summoned her repeatedly to his dressing room, his office, a bathroom at the Staples Center in LA during the Democratic National Convention for wholly transactional sex. It nauseated me.

ME—5:59 P.M.
Let me call you in a few days

December 22, 2017

ME—6:42 P.M.
Hi you.
I'm sorry I haven't been in touch. It's been a bit confusing for me.
How are you?
ME—7:08 P.M.
Can I call you tomorrow? I'm heading to Aspen in the am but will arrive tomorrow afternoon.

December 25, 2017

ME—2:26 P.M.
Merry Christmas Matt.
Hang in there. Xoxo.

January 2, 2018

ME—6:35 A.M.
Hey.
MATT—7:57 A.M.
Hi
ME—7:59 A.M.
Thinking of you
MATT—7:59 A.M.
Thank you

94

The Leon Trotsky of 30 Rock

I KNOW. I WAS a mess.

By this point, it seemed clear that Matt had done some terrible things. It was awful. And yet... it felt so heartless to abandon him, someone who'd been by my side, literally, for so many years. Reading these texts and seeing my halting efforts to connect, I feel as if I was trying to salvage my relationship with the Matt I thought I knew.

It had been more than a month since he was fired, and I had yet to say anything publicly. To some, my silence was deafening. Maybe even incriminating.

Finally, I gave a statement to *People* about how upsetting and disorienting this all was to me and that it didn't reflect my experience with Matt. That way, every time I was asked about it, I could tell reporters I'd said what I had to say.

I truly had no interest in piling on. Already, Matt was the Leon Trotsky of 30 Rock: Photos of him had been taken down, his image had been scrubbed from social media and *TODAY* show retrospectives, his nameplate had been removed, his office demolished. It was as if Matt never existed.

In the karma-is-a-bitch department, Ann Curry resurfaced, revealing that she'd been approached by a tearful staffer about Matt's sexual advances, which Ann then reported to NBC management. It made me wonder why no one had ever come to me.

FOR MONTHS, MATT'S fate was topic A. At dinners, the grocery store, Starbucks...everywhere I went, there were incredulous looks, opinions, fresh anecdotes. People shared stories about him testing the waters—even with the wives of friends—via text. One woman told me that after she and her boyfriend, a well-known TV journalist, had dinner with Matt and Annette, Matt started reaching out to her, asking if she'd like to bring her son to see his horses. No mention of the boyfriend. She found it bizarre and so not cool.

Jill Rappaport, who had dated Matt for several years in his single days, reminded me that during the course of their relationship, he cheated on her all the time, then wrote her apologetic letters saying he was "like two people." As though his sexual appetite were beyond his control.

I wondered what his life was like now, how he spent his days. I hoped he was getting help.

That spring, Matt and John met up for a round of golf; they'd forged a cordial relationship before all this, so John reached out. As they walked down the fairway, John tried to extend an olive branch.

"Katie really cares about you," he said.

Matt's reply: "Don't go there."

ON A SATURDAY night in January, 14 months after Matt was fired, David Zaslav, the president of Discovery, was celebrating his birthday at the Palm in East Hampton. John and I had become friendly with David and his wife, Pam; they had invited us to join them at the French Open, and we would have dinner together a few times a year. We decided to spend that weekend in the Hamptons so we could go toast David.

There were about 60 of us in the cozy, wood-paneled space, all the cozier for the fact that it was bitterly cold and a fire was going in the fireplace.

For me, anyway, things got a lot less cozy when Matt walked in. I had no idea he'd be there, although I did know that David and a handful of others were rallying around him as best they could.

It had been over a year since I'd seen Matt in the flesh. My heart was thumping as he came toward me. His smile was tight, his gaze level—there was so much to say, but the time to say it had passed. So we defaulted to bone-dry, fake-nice conversation. He told me his son was starting to look at colleges. I updated him on Ellie and Carrie. It was so strained. The whole conversation lasted less than three minutes before we each pretended there were other people in the room we needed to talk to.

I'd see him again seven months later at an engagement party for CNN's Don Lemon and his partner, Tim Malone, at Ron Perelman's spread in East Hampton. Matt walked in with Lorraine Bracco. When he got close enough that he couldn't pretend he didn't see me, he leaned in with a kiss so perfunctory and stiff, it almost bruised my cheek. The conversation that followed was even more stilted than the one at the Palm.

Later, John strolled up to a kibitzing threesome in the middle of the room: Matt, Jeff Zucker, and Allison Gollust. They gave him three ice-cold shoulders. John laughed about how awkward it was.

I'm Gonna Miss This

ON YOM KIPPUR, the day of atonement, nearly two years after Matt's implosion, my inbox was once again flooded with emails. Ronan Farrow's book *Catch and Kill* was about to drop; among other things, it discussed the allegations by Brooke Nevils, then Meredith Vieira's assistant, whose anonymous complaint had prompted Matt's firing. The details of what happened at the Sochi Olympics were harrowing, including the image of Nevils lying facedown during sex, tears soaking the pillow.

That morning on the *TODAY* show—Savannah and Hoda, once again looking shaken.

As if the day couldn't get any more surreal, Matt's "open letter" flew into my inbox next. As he attempted to set the record straight, you could feel the rage radiating from every word...words I never imagined Matt (or pretty much anyone else I'd ever known) having to say publicly:

> We performed oral sex on each other, we had vaginal sex, and we had anal sex. Each act was mutual and completely consensual...

Whoa.

Matt went on to characterize the women who'd gone public about him as liars and opportunists (Nevils was said to be shopping a book). He added, "I will no longer provide them the shelter of my silence."

What was this—the fury of a man who felt his accusers had gone too far? Slut-shaming? I couldn't believe how sordid it had all become.

DECENT. KIND. GENEROUS. Conscientious. The epitome of a good guy. That's how I always described Matt.

My partner in crime. We had so much fun: Matt getting the GM at the Breakers to festoon my room—the minibar, my pillow, the underside of the toilet seat—with his headshot; me almost running him over while we were snowmobiling at the Olympics in Salt Lake City; the two of us plus Al singing horrendous backup for Stevie Wonder...Seamlessly supporting each other during breaking news, my constant companion in the morning.

Did I imagine all that? Was Matt a bad guy all along and somehow I'd failed to see it? I don't think so.

The MeToo reckoning taught me a lot, including the fact that people aren't all bad or all good. In many ways, Matt *was* decent. His dedication to the job, his love for his co-workers, friends, and, of course, his kids were real, I'm certain of it. Every bit as real as what he did to those women.

So many of us were blindsided, never imagining that a dashing, witty, beloved TV star had such a dark side. I've come to realize that Matt could be an excellent professional partner, a good friend, *and* a predator.

A few months after his demise, I reached out to Addie when I was in LA. She was living in Southern California, where she had moved in 2003. I'd watched her share her story with Megyn Kelly, but I wanted to see Addie in person and make sure she was okay amid the media firestorm. Over a glass of wine by a heat lamp at an outdoor café, we filled in the blanks of the past several years. How she had joined the army and served two tours in Iraq, gotten married, and had two children, a boy and a girl.

Then the conversation turned to Matt. Looking at me with those large, aquamarine eyes that matched her paisley peasant blouse, Addie told me how devastating that chapter had been, how much it had impacted her life and thrown her off course. Yes, the relationship was consensual, technically, but what does that really mean when it's between a 24-year-old production assistant and a wildly powerful 42-year-old?

Then she told me about sex in the bathroom at the Staples Center: Afterward, Matt tapped her butt and said, "I'm gonna miss this."

To put it mildly, there were aspects of Matt's character I didn't know at all and would never fully wrap my head around.

I asked Addie why she never came to me. The look on her face told me she hadn't even considered it. "I was so ashamed and humiliated," she said, adding Matt knew he was the only person she could talk to. Their shared secret kept her isolated and silenced. Addie feared coming forward, telling me she thought she'd be "swallowed whole" by NBC, reminding me what a different era the early 2000s were.

IN THE WEEKS that followed, I kept trying to resolve the cognitive dissonance. Why was I so conflicted? Was I concerned about the fact that Matt's exploits had been happening on my watch? Was I worried about my legacy, which had become so entwined with his? Having come of age in the business at a time when men behaving badly was commonplace, had I somehow become inured to it?

There were so many things swirling in my head: Our relationship. My own moral outrage. The weight of a long-overdue movement bearing down, expecting me to excoriate Matt. Anything I said would be scrutinized, weaponized, taken out of context, and used to further a whole host of agendas.

I also wrestled with the tricky notion of agency. I kept asking myself, *Why didn't these women just tell Matt to take a hike?* But the more I thought about it, the more I realized not everyone is built for that kind of confrontation. And maybe they aren't in a position to deal with the consequences of speaking up, which, for too many women, includes losing their jobs.

And why should the onus be on women to navigate men's advances and not on men to stop making them? In the case of Matt, people still tell me, "Oh, women were always throwing themselves at him." And maybe some of them were. But Matt shouldn't have interpreted that as a green light. As Peter Parker in *Spider-Man* reminds us, "With great power comes great responsibility," and Matt seriously abused his.

Time passed. Our chance to connect evaporated, along with our friendship.

I know Matt thinks I betrayed him, and that makes me sad. But he betrayed me, too, by how he behaved behind closed doors at the show we both cared about so much. He'd done incredible damage—to himself, to his family, to *TODAY,* to NBC. As for the women...I connected with some in addition to Addie, and all these years later, I could hear the pain in their voices.

I've thought a lot about the talented women who left TV news because of situations like this. There was the former associate producer who told me she had volunteered to go to Haiti to be part of the team covering the earthquake. The problem: She'd be working with an anchor who was a serious lech, always hitting on female colleagues when the show was on the road. So her EP sent a male producer instead, depriving her of a potentially career-making assignment.

And that was cable. Imagine the accommodations they'd make for a huge network star. After I left *TODAY,* a producer friend told me that when Matt was on location for a week, a pretty PA was sent home early. "We had to bring her back—for Matt's sake," a male producer explained, alluding to the trouble Matt could get into if she stayed. The trickle-down effect of sexual harassment: young women paying for the sins of their bosses.

Matt was seen as indispensable. Did that make him feel invincible?

That level of fame and power, where you're surrounded by smiling yes-men and -women whose job it is to keep you happy and make you believe you can do no wrong, can lead to your downfall.

One summer day in East Hampton, John and I were taking a walk when a white Jeep drove by: Matt. I'm sure he saw us; needless to say, he didn't stop. I knew in that moment we'd never speak again.

96

The System

ANOTHER RONAN FARROW special dropped in July of 2018. The eye-popping *New Yorker* piece detailed Les Moonves's alleged pattern of vile behavior toward actresses, writers, and producers; if they rebuffed him, he actively set about derailing their careers. People like Illeana Douglas, who'd been cast in a CBS sitcom called *Queens* and was summoned to Moonves's office, where, Farrow wrote, he lunged at her, pinned her down, and thrust himself against her. When she broke free, he warned Douglas to keep it to herself. (A moment from the story I'll never forget: When a visibly shaken Douglas leaves the office, her skirt askew, Moonves's assistant asks if she needs her parking validated.) Ultimately, he fired the noncompliant Douglas from the sitcom, which she saw as retaliation. Moonves later admitted he had tried to kiss her, but denied everything else.

Then there was the medical appointment at UCLA where, according to the article, Moonves grabbed the doctor and tried to force himself on her; when she pulled away, he stood by the exam table and proceeded to jerk off. Can anyone explain to me the impulse among so many otherwise smart, functional men to whip it out and do their business in front of women? I mean, what the hell?

As for Jeff Fager, Amy Brittain and Irin Carmon interviewed dozens of women for a *Washington Post* investigation into the culture he had fostered at *60 Minutes*. Now it was time to give Fager the chance to respond to a particularly repellent allegation: that he once said to a woman at a company party, "Grab my dick. I'm hung like a horse."

As Carmon tells it, CBS pushed back hard. The editor of the *Post,* Marty Baron of *Spotlight* fame, received several impassioned calls from people like Lesley Stahl and producer Ira Rosen (who'd had his own brushes with MeToo), claiming Fager had been wrongly accused. CBS threatened to sue, and Baron insisted the reporters' sources go on the record. When none were willing, the story was scrubbed of any references to Fager. (The *Post* would later refute Carmon's claim that the paper had succumbed to external pressure, calling it "baseless and reprehensible.")

It was a big blow to the two reporters, although Carmon got the last word, in dramatic fashion. Accepting an award for their reporting on Charlie Rose, she said from the podium:

> The stories that we have been doing are about a system. The system has lawyers and a good reputation. It has publicists. It has a perfectly reasonable explanation about what happened. It has powerful friends that will ask if it's really worth ruining the career of a good man based on what one woman says, what four women say, what 35 women say. Indeed, the system is sitting in this room…The system is still powerful men getting stories killed that I believe will one day see the light of day.

Jeff Fager—aka the system—was, in fact, sitting in the room.

Farrow's *New Yorker* piece made good on Carmon's belief—calling Fager out, describing how he enabled the bad behavior of male executives (including Michael Radutzky, who once threatened to throw a chair at a producer. Lori Beecher told me he'd backed her up against a wall until his face was an inch from hers and unloaded on her at the top of his lungs). Fager enabled the serial sleaze of Charlie Rose and others and got "handsy" with female staffers at parties after one drink too many (a high-ranking producer once told me about being in a cab with Fager when he asked her to "touch it," apparently not talking about his elbow). I'd later learn they handed out NDAs at that place like candy on Halloween—part of the settlement for complaints about sexual harassment. Not a great look for a supposed bastion of truth-telling.

Ultimately, what took Fager down wasn't the crime but the cover-up (also ironic—you'd think the head of a legendary investigative unit would know better than to make that mistake). With the internal probe underway, Fager sent the following text to Jericka Duncan, who was covering the story for the *CBS Evening News*:

> If you repeat these false accusations without any of your own reporting to back them up you will be responsible for harming me...Be careful. There are people who lost their jobs trying to harm me.

Duncan read the veiled threat on the broadcast.

By year's end, Fager was out, and so was Moonves. No wonder Les couldn't recognize Fager's misogyny—they were cut from the same cloth.

I think a lot about the onion that was *60 Minutes*. The whole experience is a huge source of disappointment to this day. Whenever I hear that ticking stopwatch on TV, I wince, remembering Don Hewitt saying I was the future of the show...until I wasn't.

Being a valued member of that team, practicing journalism at the highest level, would have been the pinnacle of my career. But Jeff Fager wasn't having it—a well-known, fully baked female journalist threatening the power structure, the male cabal in charge. I was one in a long line of very capable women who were drummed out of that place or left, too demoralized and fatigued to keep putting up with the BS, no matter how fulfilling the work could be.

Some who stayed went along to get along. As Lesley Stahl told the *Hollywood Reporter,* "I just wanted to be a survivor." Mission accomplished.

Aren't you glad that kind of retro, sexist office culture is finally on the way out?

Me too.

97

Bleeding Purple

S INCE LATE 2013, I'd been global news anchor of Yahoo News. John couldn't believe the grandiosity. "Why not call you intergalactic news anchor?" he said.

Yes, it sounded a little silly, but they were offering me a network news anchor's salary, and I was jazzed to be a part of the tech giant's expanding empire, telling *Politico,* "It almost feels like a start-up, but with a very established distribution platform. So it's the best of both worlds."

Even before I arrived, Yahoo's fearless leader, Marissa Mayer, was hauling in big names to helm various verticals they were launching: makeup magnate Bobbi Brown and fashion guru Joe Zee for beauty and style; David Pogue of the *New York Times* for technology. Marissa also shelled out for impressive print talent: *Times* political reporter Matt Bai, indefatigable Michael Isikoff, *Newsweek* veteran Dan Klaidman.

My first week there, I had an idea. Along with creating content, I could help forge powerful partnerships with people I knew socially, had worked with, or had interviewed. People like Starbucks CEO Howard Schultz.

"Howard," I said, during a visit to his jumbo spread in East Hampton, "wouldn't it be cool if the Yahoo home page was the default setting when you logged onto the Starbucks Wi-Fi?"

I added that we could join forces on content that tackled big social issues, something I knew Howard cared about. And we could set up screens in every Starbucks across the land so that people could lap up the latest news while waiting in line for their skinny caramel macchiatos.

Howard told me he had been kicking around that very idea with Tim Armstrong over at AOL.

"Don't do anything until you talk to Marissa," I said.

I connected them on an email; Howard replied all, saying he was excited to meet. Not a peep from Marissa.

So I reached out to Sandy Gould, head of Global Talent Acquisition (I mean, *Intergalactic* Talent Acquisition), who looked like a grown-up Jimmy Neutron, in cool specs and designer kicks from his vast collection. My email was a nudge with a smidge of WTF.

Sandy assured me "MM is definitely excited" and "going to follow up shortly," signing off with "Be well."

Three weeks later, another email arrived:

> I never heard from Marissa. But, no worries.
> All my best,
> Howard

Are you kidding me?

I'd later learn this was Marissa's MO. Not returning emails (and certainly not anything as old-school as a phone call), showing up for dinners with clients when they were already on dessert, leaving powerful people waiting for hours outside her office. Apparently there was a long line of major players who'd left the sprawling Yahoo campus in Sunnyvale, California, feeling less sunny than irate.

Our video group was small but mighty. I tapped Tony Maciulis, a quick-witted and talented writer/producer who was by my side at the *Evening News* and *Katie,* to lead the charge. Together, we assembled a fantastic, mostly female team. We did strong work right out of the gate, including short-form video explainers called *Now I Get It* on complicated topics like immigration, fracking, 3D printing, the Armenian genocide, artificial intelligence, and March Madness. I sat down with disrupters and game-changers like the founder of Airbnb and the hilarious women of *Broad City*. I went to LA to interview Betty White on her 95th birthday and to Nashville to talk happy marriages and corny jokes with Dolly Parton. I was particularly proud of a beautifully crafted piece we did about *Go Set a Watchman,* Harper Lee's newly discovered prequel to *To Kill a Mockingbird,* and the controversial fact that she was in failing health in a nursing home when it was decided the manuscript would be published.

That piece was part of Yahoo's *Viewfinder* series. Which would have been fine, if viewers could find it. In fact, there was just one problem with the great content we were producing: no one could find any of it.

That's because algorithms were making the decisions, giving placement to whatever brought clicks and revenue, prioritizing news partners like the *Huffington Post* over content from their own people (us). We started joking—darkly—that we were in the witness protection program—that's how hard it was to find us or our work.

I quickly learned that the journalism I lived for just wasn't in Yahoo's DNA because Yahoo was more about the delivery system and ever-mutating tech functionality than the news itself. Building an operation with a true editorial mission that would become a go-to for original content would prove to be an exercise in...well, *frustration* doesn't do it justice. After I hosted the Yahoo Superstar Awards, where the company handed out honors for things like "targeting user profiles for full funnel analysis across search data," John said, "If you're still wondering if Yahoo is a media company or a tech company, I think you have your answer."

A year and change into my tenure, Marissa invited me to have soup with her at her favorite spot in Midtown.

Soup? Sure, I like soup.

We met at La Bonne Soupe on West 55th, the eatery time forgot, specializing in lady-lunch food like crepes, quiche, and, yes, all kinds of soup. Kind of a weird choice, I thought.

I walked up the narrow stairs to the atelier-like second floor and saw Marissa sitting at a small table staring at her phone, looking surprisingly svelte for someone pregnant with twins. She suggested I have the tomato basil soup, her favorite.

As we slurped at a cramped two-top, I told Marissa our team needed a stronger, more coordinated effort getting our stories out there.

"I know you're expecting me to land big interviews," I said, "but it's really challenging if people need Magellan to find them." I didn't say that exactly, but that's what I meant. "It's a bit of a cycle: You do an interview, you make news, people see the interview, you get metrics that convince other people to do interviews." Conversely, if you conduct an interview in the forest and no one hears it, did the interview really happen?

Marissa nodded.

Yahoo was a strange place for me, culturally. I'd come up in energetic newsrooms with police scanners and excitable news directors providing the soundtrack, the place popping with a shared sense of purpose we all got off on. Here, the "newsroom" was pretty much silent—people wearing hoodies and earbuds, staring at screens in their own virtual pod-worlds. I know it makes me sound like I'm 110, but it was a huge adjustment (that I never really made).

There was institutionalized bonding, like yodeling for Yahoo's 20th anniversary and staff-wide purple-shirt-wearing. I never really liked the color purple (even though I loved *The Color Purple*). It would have made a great TV show. Wait, it did—*Silicon Valley*.

I tried my darnedest to give Yahoo journalistic cred, and what better time to do that than an election year? Especially a doozy like 2016. One of my first assignments was heading to New Hampshire to interview John Kasich. The Ohio governor was considered a new breed of Republican, very much his own man. As the crew and I made our way to the back of the campaign bus where the interview would take place, Kasich said he wanted to speak with me privately. I had no idea what this was about.

"Katie, can I ask you a question? You used to be the anchor of the *CBS Evening News*," he said with reverence and gravity. "Now you're with Yahoo News," he said with a bit less reverence and zero gravity. "What is that like for you?" Well, Governor...

I proceeded to explain how the media landscape was changing, how digital news was growing, blah, blah, blah. He listened, expressionless.

Post-election, Kasich came to the Yahoo "studios" in Times Square to hawk his new book. And again, he asked to speak with me privately. We ducked into the hallway.

"Katie, can I ask you a question? You used to be the anchor of the *CBS Evening News*—now you're with Yahoo News. What is that like for you?"

I'd just about had it with this tool. "I don't know, Governor Kasich," I said. "You used to be running for president of the United States, and pretty soon you're going to be out of a job. What is that like for *you*?"

I got time with almost every candidate. Ted Cruz talked my ear off for an hour; Carly Fiorina accused me of being sexist when I asked her if she was positioning herself to be vice president (I responded that if a male candidate was polling at 1 percent, I'd ask him the same thing). Bernie Sanders strolled in solo carrying a Saran-Wrapped sub he'd bought at a deli, while Marco Rubio and I chatted over arroz con pollo at the Cuban restaurant Versailles in Miami.

Getting an interview with Trump was much tougher. After an embarrassing number of unctuous calls and emoji- and *XOXO*-laden emails to his longtime secretary Rhona, I was finally granted the opportunity to grovel at his 5th Avenue office and pitch him the idea myself.

Trump came out and greeted me warmly (this was before our fun encounter at the Polo Bar). "Great to see you!" he said. "Come on in."

Radiant city views filled the windows. Trump's desk was the size of a dining-room table, and it was covered in magazines, all bearing his mug (or a facsimile thereof). Stacks of magazines, six copies deep: *Time, New York, Rolling Stone,* the *Economist, Esquire, People, GQ*...

"Can you believe this?" he said, waving a hand. "Can you believe this?"

"No. I really can't," I said honestly. Then he told me how much "the evangelicals" liked him as I glanced at a framed, blown-up copy of him on the cover of *Playboy.* Knowing I didn't have much time, I quickly explained Yahoo, telling him about our metrics and how many people were consuming news online.

Trump stared at me blankly. "What channel are you on?" he asked. "I'm not big on the computer stuff." The future Twitter president told me he didn't use email.

The interview never happened.

Surely Hillary will talk to me, I thought; we'd known each other for 25 years. And yet here, too, it was endless calls and emails and dropping by her campaign headquarters in Brooklyn. We got a date on the calendar for February 3rd in New Hampshire—which was promptly canceled, no reason given.

I emailed her campaign chairman, John Podesta, reiterating my desire to talk with Mrs. Clinton. I wrote that I thought she'd benefit from a more relaxed conversation where her warmth and sense of humor could come through—I told him I was interested in "showcasing her personality." And I shared a social media idea with viral potential called "10 Things You Don't Know About Hillary Clinton." Then Podesta's email was hacked.

The Hillary haters wasted no time dropping bombs in my inbox:

Nice to read your email from Wikileaks. You are a piece of shit. Better sleep with your eyes open. Lucifer

Katie,

You are the most phony, smug, fraudulently deceitful personality I've ever suffered through the experience of observing—in any profession. Everything you do to veil the person beneath the perk fails...You are an embarrassment to real Americans. This is how those beyond your circle at Yahoo feel about you. Christian P.

Katie, I just wanted to drop you a note to tell you what vile communist scum I think you are. So happy your television career is over. You always sucked anyway. You are shit just like your pal Hillary.

I googled the scribe behind that last one. He's a cardiologist in New Jersey. All heart, that guy.

The hassle of changing my email was bad enough. What really frustrated me was how impossible it had been to land the two interviews everyone in media wanted. The Yahoo folks were counting on me to bring in the big names that drove traffic. Particularly Trump, who was the clickiest of clickbait. And I wasn't delivering.

Marissa, meanwhile, seemed completely unaware. Disengaged. Although in April while covering a stem-cell conference at the Vatican, I do recall thinking that maybe she'd seen the light. Her office had gone to extraordinary lengths to arrange a phone call, factoring in the nine-hour time difference, then letting me know her meeting was running a few minutes long and that she'd reach out the second it wrapped up. I was excited, figuring this had to be big news—maybe a game-changing new partnership with an established streaming service?

Turns out Marissa had two extra seats at her table at the Met Ball a few nights later and wanted to know if John and I could join. Yeesh.

Despite the challenges, I got to do so much at Yahoo. I went to Davos for the World Economic Forum summit and to Moscow to interview Edward Snowden (where I used a burner phone and showered in darkness, terrified the Russians were spying on me). I ate hot wings at Harold's Chicken Shack on Chicago's South Side with Chance the Rapper; I covered the norm-busting early days of Trump's reality-show presidency with a top-notch group of Yahoo journalists.

Then, four years in, Tim Armstrong became the new CEO, absorbing Yahoo into Oath (which to me sounded dangerously close to *Oaf*). When the middle-aged mogul started wearing hoodies and hipster stubble and giving virtual pep talks, I knew it was time to go.

And thus ended the Yahoo era. I did a lot and learned a lot (and made a lot), but I never really felt like our stars were aligned. What I did feel was a bit of an existential crisis coming on.

98

Gone with the Wind

IN THE FALL of 2018, two decades after Jay died, I decided to take Carrie to Virginia to learn more about her dad.

Jay had become an almost mythical figure to her, his image sketched posthumously in photos and anecdotes. Ellie and I, who are so similar in temperament, were bonded by loss and our memories of Jay. But Carrie, just 2 when he died, knew her father only from the stories we would tell. Any memories she might have had vanished with the passage of time.

For a while that protected her. Ultimately, it made her feel like an outsider among us—unable to share our grief.

When Carrie was 12, we gathered to watch an incredible video tribute Jay's brother Chris had made. Through stories and recollections, it painted a portrait of Jay—his insatiable curiosity, his fastidiousness (on visits home from college, he organized his siblings' sock drawers), his compassion, his pet peeves, his loyalty, his love of history, his complexity. Carrie saw herself in him. Watching the video, she heard his voice for the first time and burst into tears.

Now, sitting next to her in our rental car as we headed south, I took in Carrie's amber eyes, ridged brow, and sweet Stan Laurel smile, all gifts from Jay. I hoped our sojourn in Virginia would help her better understand her phantom father.

We drove through Middleburg, a horsey town where my uncle used to run the Tally Ho pharmacy—I don't know what made me think it would still be there. He was married to my father's sister, Charlotte, a competitive ballroom dancer; they'd raised two sons and named one of them Couric.

We stopped in Maurertown, the bucolic idyll that kindled our marriage and fed Jay's obsession with the Civil War.

By the time Carrie came along, in 1996, we'd sold the house. But the new owner was happy to show us around. We peeked into the bedroom where Jay and I (mostly) slept and the adjoining room where we kept a fire going and watched TV with our toddler, Ellie.

A wet morning mist deepened the colors of the leaves. Carrie and I walked down to the river, where I took some pictures of her—I pointed out where her dad and I would go look for tadpoles. I imagined how delighted Jay would be to see his beautiful grown daughter standing by that river.

When it started to rain, we hurried to the rental car and left Valhalla behind.

Our next stop was the home of Todd Kern, who'd read the Sullivan Ballou letter at Jay's funeral. He had some things belonging to Jay that he wanted to give me. And I knew he'd have some good stories for Carrie.

She'd graduated from Stanford in the spring, an American studies major. Her senior thesis was a reckoning with her ancestry and the role played by race, particularly on my side of the family. In the introduction, Carrie writes of Jay's fascination with the Confederacy, something she wanted to learn more about.

We navigated the muddy driveway to Todd's, passing burnt sienna horses munching in the fields. Mike Hickey, another reenactment buddy, was there too. Both looked like men from another era in their cowboy hats, vests, and bandannas tied around their necks, their facial hair unfussy. I hadn't seen either man since Jay's funeral.

"She looks just like her father," Todd said, gazing upon Carrie, who smiled shyly.

Todd opened a wooden trunk, releasing a musty aroma. We picked carefully through the items, taking them out one by one: a tin plate, a drinking cup, a two-pronged fork and a weathered knife tucked in a canvas pouch. A wooden comb. A toothbrush with yellowed bristles. A leather holster. Gauntlet-like riding gloves in butter-colored leather. Two flasks—one with the faint, oaky smell of bourbon; we pictured Jay taking a swig while camped out on a chilly night. The other was brass, designed to hold gunpowder. The items had been kept in a grain sack stenciled CSA—CONFEDERATE STATES OF AMERICA.

At the bottom of the trunk was a long, waxed-canvas riding coat that Jay would have used in inclement weather. Fishing around in the pockets, Todd found half a roll of Tums, the white tablets crumbling, now 20 years old.

Tums—with which Jay self-medicated before his cancer diagnosis.

"An artifact within an artifact," Carrie said.

Todd told Carrie about how he'd met her father in the early '90s. One day at Hupp's Hill Civil War Park, where Todd was the curator, Jay wandered in. They started talking and quickly realized they shared many interests. Todd invited Jay to the next reenactment.

Almost immediately, Todd recalled, her father got swept up in the scene—scores of men in historically correct uniforms, aiming their muskets at the enemy across the field, unflinchingly in character. But Jay noticed that one thing was missing—a bugler. He volunteered to fill the role.

Jay began collecting antique brass bugles in every size. He also found some sheet music and practiced at all hours. Once, on vacation in Anguilla, we got a call from the front desk. Apparently, Jay's attempt at reveille was disturbing the peace.

Jay played the trusty bugler Corporal Monahan, Company H, Fourth Virginia Cavalry. Todd and Mike told us about his last reenactment, four months before he died—the ferociously bloody Battle of Antietam, claiming more than 20,000 casualties in a single day. They spared no details describing Jay's painstaking preparation, his stoicism, and his bravery in the face of a dire prognosis, so thin and so weak from yet another surgery. Carrie and I cried.

Mike reminisced about coming to Millbrook to help us put up the Christmas tree that year. He remembered Jay having trouble driving, having trouble seeing, having trouble eating a piece of pie at the Millbrook Diner. Which made both Mike and Todd choke up too.

The four of us drove to the Wayside Inn, where Jay and I sometimes went on date nights, famous for the Virginia peanut soup we never ordered. Soon I got an alert on my phone: There'd been a shooting at the Tree of Life synagogue in Pittsburgh; 11 killed, six wounded. I shared the horrific news with the group.

Todd and Mike were skeptical about the whole thing, seeming to suggest this might be fake news. That maybe it was part of a larger plot to undercut the Second Amendment and take away people's guns. And just like that, the mood turned.

Against my better judgment, I asked Todd and Mike what they thought about the debate currently raging over the fate of Confederate statues. To which Todd responded, "It's cultural Marxism." He also referred to the *Washington Post* as "*Pravda* on the Potomac." And when I asked about the lionizing of Robert E. Lee, who fought to preserve slavery and owned slaves himself, one of them responded, "He *inherited* them." I saw Carrie stiffen.

"Well, that was interesting," I said as we drove away.

I was conflicted; Todd and Mike had been so good to Jay, but their positions were hard for us to swallow. And yet I felt protective of Jay's memory, and I wanted Carrie to be proud of him. We rode in silence, with an unanswered question looming like a hitchhiker in the back seat: *If Jay were here, what would he think?*

In the summer of 2017, while Carrie was digging up so much about our family's past for her thesis, I was conducting some research of my own for a National Geographic documentary about the Confederate-statues controversy. The mammoth, oxidized likeness of Robert E. Lee astride his trusty steed Traveller in the middle of Charlottesville was ground zero for a debate that would radiate throughout the South. In fact, the entire country.

I interviewed Black Lives Matter activist Don Gathers, who contrasted the majestic scale of the bronze effigy with a small sidewalk plaque that read SLAVE AUCTION BLOCK…ON THIS SITE SLAVES WERE BOUGHT AND SOLD.

"You can't convince me that's by accident or happenstance," Gathers said. "It's a mindset."

Gary Gallagher, an American history professor at UVA, stated in no uncertain terms the reason Confederate states left the Union and entered into war: slavery. After their defeat, they tried to recast the effort in a positive light. "So what's the best thing we can talk about?" Gallagher said. "Robert E. Lee!" Setting forth the Lost Cause narrative, revolving around states' rights and the preservation of the Southern way of life, with Lee the heroic figurehead.

I started hearing rumblings of a "Unite the Right" rally scheduled for Saturday, August 12th. The night before, I attended a packed service at St. Paul's, across from the Rotunda. Charlottesville residents and clergy from around the country had gathered to peacefully oppose the hateful ideology of the alt-right marchers amassing on the edge of the Grounds.

As attendees sang and listened to speakers like Cornel West and Missouri pastor Traci Blackmon, a prominent voice after Michael Brown was gunned down in Ferguson, someone said to me, "There's something going on outside." People were quickly ushered out the back door while I went to the front steps overlooking the Rotunda across the street.

Throngs of young men, many dressed in white polo shirts and khakis, the "uniform" of the neo-fascist Proud Boys, were carrying torches and marching down the Lawn, where I lived senior year—a fiery gash running through the heart of the university. At the church a woman had approached me and said, "I wish Emily were here. She'd know exactly what to do."

The next morning, angry young white men gathered at the base of the Lee statue, then began chanting, "F— you, faggots," "Blood and Soil" (a Nazi slogan), and "Jews will not replace us." A phalanx of clergy locked arms and tried to drown them out by singing "This Little Light of Mine."

A thin blond man screamed out menacingly, "The country is ours. Your time is coming," drawing a symbolic finger across his throat.

And suddenly a jostling mass of mostly men poured into the streets. I grabbed interviews where I could amid the chaos, finding an 18-year-old self-described white nationalist who told me, "We need someplace that can be a white homeland or we will be bred out."

I wondered, *What happened in this young man's life to make him so afraid and full of hate?*

Many of the protesters were waving the Stars and Bars; some carried Nazi flags, some had AK-47s strapped to their backs. Confrontations turned violent—I remember the sound of screaming, the smell of smoke. And then, out of nowhere, a car came roaring into a crowd of counter-protesters, mowing some down, badly injuring several, and killing one—a 32-year-old paralegal named Heather Heyer. Sickening. Tragic.

So many people of my generation in the part of the country where I grew up were raised on the good-ol'-boy archetype and the romantic atmospherics of *Gone with the Wind*—the gentility, punch bowls, and picnics, Scarlett O'Hara flirting with the Tarleton twins, and the "happy slave" roles of Mammy and Prissy.

In our own home, I treated Jay's passion for the Confederacy with amused tolerance, seeing it as a benign hobby. For his 40th birthday, I threw him a party with an Old South theme. The invitation read:

> *Please come to a Very Civil Gathering to mark the birthday of Bugler Jay Monahan. WARNING: Anyone divulging this infor-mation will be considered a traitor and will be hanged! (In other words, it's a SURPRISE!!!)*

Virginia ham and biscuits, gas lamps, a Christmas tree decorated with blue and gray glass ornaments and toy soldiers, topped with a Scarlett O'Hara Barbie doll. Jay loved it.

I always told Ellie and Carrie that their dad was a history buff, which explained the Civil War memorabilia. As for the reenactments, he was an equestrian who relished the outdoors and enjoyed being with a cross-section of people of the type you found at these events—slipping off his jacket and tie and getting down and dirty with plumbers, dentists, and contractors who loved history as much as he did. I told them the wallpaper in his boyhood bedroom, covered with the faces of U.S. presidents, had sparked that passion, while his time at Washington and Lee had stoked an interest in 19th-century politics.

But now that script was wearing thin. With the culture fixated on historic wrongs in need of righting, with my brilliant daughters bearing down, I wondered if a reassessment was in order.

In her Stanford thesis, Carrie wrote: "Aside from his petulance and rigid jawline, he seemed to have left me nothing but artifacts—remnants of a life that wasn't even his."

Carrie's family research was unsparing. She excavated forgotten documents, letters, photographs, and a speech her dad had written that crushed her.

It was a reaction to the United Daughters of the Confederacy being denied the renewal of a patent for their logo, which featured the Confederate flag. Freshman senator Carol Moseley Braun, the first Black woman to serve in the Senate, had called the insignia "an outrage. It is an insult. It is absolutely unacceptable to me and to millions of Americans, Black or white, that we would put the imprimatur of the United States Senate on a symbol of this kind of idea."

Jay was incensed. He later delivered a nine-page single-spaced speech to the Daughters, vilifying Moseley Braun's comments as "venomous" and the press as being "obsessed with appearing politically correct." He also shared how he'd come to love the South:

> To make a long story longer, I married a native Virginian—indeed a University of Virginia graduate—who is the direct descendant of two Confederate veterans: one, a member of the Eufaula, Alabama Rifles, and the other, a member of Nathan Bedford Forrest's Cavalry. That means, by the way, that both of my daughters will be eligible to join the Mary Mildred Sullivan Chapter some day.

He was laying it on pretty thick. And he left out the fact that Nathan Bedford Forrest was the first Grand Wizard of the KKK, an ancestral association that disgusts me.

It's all a bit mysterious to me. Jay's parents, good Catholics, were liberal Democrats who cared deeply about civil rights and school integration, which started to happen when Jay was in third or fourth grade. They invited Black families to dinner and encouraged playdates (back before they were called that) with Black children. For their trouble, the Monahans had "n— lover" hurled at them more than once. Not that it kept them from doing what they felt was right, which included inviting their Black housekeeper's great-niece to live with them for several years until she went off to the University of Michigan. Jay's dad was so proud of her.

Then Jay himself went to college in the Blue Ridge Mountains and fell in love—with the land, the history, the people. Carrie wrote:

I am not sure if twenty years of collective reckoning and revision would have changed him, but I am hoping, urgently, that it would have. I cannot ask him questions about why he wrote what he wrote or played bugles on horseback in reproduced battle scenes. I'd like to give him a chance to explain things to me.

Here is what I know about Jay: He was openhearted and generous, always rooting for the underdog. He was drawn to people with integrity and character, and his friends, who came from all backgrounds, reflected that. But the romanticism that surrounded the Civil War for so long—the regalia, the accoutrements, the pastoral settings—kept him from acknowledging the brutal realities that undergird the Lost Cause narrative.

I wonder how Jay would feel about nearly 80 percent of the faculty at his alma mater voting to strip Lee's name from the school. And how would the conversations with his grown-up daughters go? Would he listen and learn from what this keenly sensitized, incredibly well-informed generation had to say? I hope he'd be moved by racial justice pioneers like Bryan Stevenson, author and founder of the Equal Justice Initiative, who told me, "My interest in talking about our history is not to punish America for this history…I want to liberate us. And there is a way to be a white Southerner"—even by marriage—"and proud of who you are and acknowledge the pain of this past."

I know it sounds like an excuse to say, "It was a different time." But—it was a different time. And Jay never got the chance to live in this one.

99

It's C-o-u-r-i-c

I'D DONE TIME at just about every major network. I'd joined forces with a digital behemoth. I'd worked for pretty much every middle-aged white guy at the top of the TV food chain. Now I wondered—with some urgency—what I would do next.

For the first time in my career, I didn't have a game plan.

I started to question everything. Shortly after the 2016 election, Andy Lack reached out about a nighttime show on MSNBC. The idea of going back to the network—which still was in my blood, which still saw me as family—was appealing. But it would have meant getting home after 10:00 p.m., hopped up on Diet Coke and adrenaline, and never having dinner with my new husband. It would have left my Yahoo colleagues in the lurch, and besides, I wasn't completely comfortable entering the cable fray, which seemed to rely more on opinion than reporting. Maybe I should have just done it anyway.

Maybe I shouldn't have done the syndicated show, with red flags flapping from day one. Did my fear of being perceived as washed up after CBS blind me to how wrong the genre was for me?

While we're at it, maybe I shouldn't have gone to CBS. At the very least, I should have been more mindful of the culture and the politics of the place and done my due diligence. At the time, I was riding about as high as a human can (by TV standards). Maybe I thought I was failure-proof and didn't consider how much it would hurt if I fell on my face.

But... where would saying no to CBS have left me—staying at the TODAY show the rest of my life? That didn't sound like such a great idea either. If there is one thing I've always been dead set against, it's staying too long at the party.

I started thinking about what I love to do: Talk to people. Tell their stories. Use those stories to help others better understand the world.

I started thinking about what I *hadn't* done. The obvious answer— I'd never been entrepreneurial. Never done my own thing, never not worked at some monster company with a big bronze logo affixed to the wall.

I started thinking about how to create the content I loved but in a new, more nimble, modern way, taking what I'd learned at Yahoo and combining it with my decades of news-gathering and storytelling experience.

I could picture it. But that would require a workspace, staff, production, marketing, promotion, a budget, a regular influx of cash... how could I make it a viable business and not just a vanity project? Who could help me do this?

Luckily, I had an excellent finance guy—a wiz at raising capital, managing people, bringing good ideas to fruition. And he was right there in the kitchen in his boxers, serving up the scrambled eggs.

John and I launched Katie Couric Media in 2018. I am so grateful for his business acumen—something he's apparently had his whole life. In fourth grade, he made a killing selling Burpee seeds door to door. When he was 14, he drained his savings to buy a snowblower at Sears, then signed up neighbors for his fledgling snow-removal service during a historic Chicago winter; late adopters were subject to surge pricing.

John knew what it took to build businesses, and now he'd thrown himself into the business of me. He says, "I want to help Katie keep doing what she loves to do."

It's a unique business model: We partner with companies that care about the same issues I do—gender equality, the environment, racial justice, entrepreneurship, health and wellness—and they underwrite our content. The idea is to reach people where they are (on their phones), with a daily newsletter, a podcast, digital series, documentaries, even scripted projects. One morning at my neighborhood coffee haunt, a woman came up to me, earbuds in, and said, "This is so weird—I'm listening to you right now. And here you are!" I love the sense of community we've built.

While social media can be blamed for many of society's ills, I appreciate that it lets me communicate in a quick and agile way, direct to consumer. Every day, I'm grabbing interviews with consequential people: elected officials, scientists, and heroes, like the hospital chaplain bringing peace to the dying during a pandemic. I've virtually made cocktails with Ina Garten, baked cookies with *Queer Eye*'s Tan France, and talked Hollywood, religion, and parenting with Jen Garner. Sometimes I'm Katherine, sometimes I'm Katie—now my work allows me to be both.

I've got a new lease on my professional life. It always galled me how anchormen could look like shar-peis and still be stars while newswomen were kicked to the curb the minute their AARP cards arrived. Thankfully, I don't have to let some network bozo decide if I still have value or tell me what kind of stories I can do. There's truly no limit to the content I can create. These days, I'm much less concerned about media's holy grail—relevance—than I am about being able to continue flexing my journalistic muscles.

As you might imagine, working with your spouse isn't always easy; when John and I told friends what we were doing, one said, "Good luck with that." We try to maintain some sort of boundary between work and real life and joke about not letting our newsletter subscriber base become pillow talk. We're both strong-willed and have been known to butt heads. So far, no concussions.

PRACTICING JOURNALISM IN the post-Trump era is challenging. Trust in the media has crumbled, and no wonder; people consume news in echo chambers, with algorithms serving up content that aligns with their POV (a bit like Netflix saying "If you liked [X], you'll love [Y]"). As a result, we're getting affirmation instead of information, with bogus news packaged up to look like it's coming from a reputable source. "Truth decay" has officially set in—a clear and present danger to our democracy.

Cable news exacerbates the problem with its eye-rolling, soliloquizing anchors who abandoned any pretense of objectivity long ago. Unfortunately, feeding the outrage machine has proven really good for ratings. I wish I could talk to Tim Russert about all of it.

On this frightening new frontier, I'm glad I am viewed as an honest broker, bringing old-school rigor and ethics to the job, using my skills to sift through the warring agendas and help decipher what's real.

Yes, it's hard, sometimes, not being part of a network news organization. Watching coverage of the 2020 presidential election from the comfort of my couch, I felt regular pangs; during the debates, I had to resist the urge to crash through the screen and shove aside the very capable moderators (moderating a presidential debate being one of the few things I never got to do). But it's a thrill to see a new and diverse generation of women handling it all so skillfully, neither as tokens nor window-dressing, but as formidable journalists in their own right.

Increasingly, women are getting the top jobs, making real decisions and setting the tone, not just playing second banana, propping up their male bosses. As president of CBS News, Susan Zirinsky was one of the first, followed by Rashida Jones at MSNBC, and Kim Godwin, a colleague of mine at CBS, who became head of ABC News. It's about damn time women are rewarded for their leadership and smarts, and not how they look in a safari jacket.

But old habits die hard: After I covered the white supremacist rally in Charlottesville, I heard that one of the top executives at National Geographic chastised my producers on a conference call, telling them, "I never want to see her on camera without makeup again." I'm sorry my face wasn't riot-ready. As far as I know, they haven't invented tear-gas-proof mascara yet.

My success may have come with a side of BS, but I like to think it did some good. When Norah O'Donnell became the big kahuna at CBS, I hope I'd smoothed over some of the bumps in the road by having been first.

THE REAL FEATHER in my cap is having raised two extraordinary daughters, although I'm not sure how much credit I can take. Ellie is a thriving TV writer—a tough industry to crack—in LA. Having dated for a decade since meeting at Yale, she and her perfect match, Mark, finally tied the knot. Among other things, he's a calming presence (yes, my girls can be intense; wonder where they got that from). Carrie is my social justice warrior. She got her master's in journalism from Columbia, and writes about important issues with wisdom and depth beyond her years. What I'm proudest of is the fine people they have become: kind, caring, unpretentious.

I always felt like one of the best things I could give my daughters was the example of someone living a full and fulfilling life—both as a mom and as a working woman. That meant being away from home a lot and missing some key moments. But it also meant sharing experiences I never had as a kid: picnicking on the Great Wall and seeing the cherry blossoms in Kyoto; bodysurfing at Bondi Beach; navigating the Pyramids at midnight by flashlight. I always wanted to give my girls the world, and in many ways, my work let me do that.

When all is said and done, though, I am my mother's daughter, becoming more like her by the minute: when I neatly peel a pear and present the girls with the tidy slices on a china plate, or when I fix them lunch and declare, "A sandwich always tastes better when someone else makes it for you." Or when one of my children feels slighted or wounded, and I rear up like a Kodiak bear on its hind legs, ready to maul whoever's crossed her. My mom may be gone, but her essence is very much alive in me.

IT'S AN ADJUSTMENT when the white-hot spotlight moves on. The ego gratification of being the It girl is intoxicating (*toxic* being the root of the word). When that starts to fade, it takes some getting used to—at least it did for me. I remember watching the '91 movie *Soapdish* starring Sally Field as a has-been soap star who heads to a mall in Paramus whenever she needs the endorphin hit of being recognized. Thankfully, I haven't resorted to hanging out at the food court…yet.

John helps me keep everything in perspective. Whenever a hostess at a restaurant looks at me blankly or I have to repeat, "No, it's C-o-u-r-i-c," he laughs and says under his breath, "It's over." The upside? I don't have to worry about those "Stars! They're Just Like Us!" photos of me in ratty sweatpants looking like I've been on a five-day bender.

But a lower profile doesn't mean I can't still create some serious dust-ups. When I was hosting the opening ceremony at the 2018 Olympics in Pyeongchang, I caused an international incident when I noted what good speed skaters the Dutch were, adding that when the canals freeze, the residents have been known to skate on them "to get from place to place." Twitter blew up, accusing me of suggesting that skating was a primary mode of transportation in Holland, sharing memes like a pack of speed skaters with a windmill backdrop under the caption *Rush hour in the Netherlands.* The Dutch embassy jumped in, inviting me to visit so they could "show me all the innovative ways the Dutch get around."

More thin ice: In January of 2021 when I appeared on *Real Time with Bill Maher,* he asked how I felt about the members of Congress who refused to concede that Joe Biden had won the presidential election. I lamented the fact that so many were consuming online misinformation. "How are we going to really almost deprogram these people who have signed up for the cult of Trump?" I said. Sean Hannity ran with it. Suddenly, I was being accused of wanting to send Republicans to concentration camps. I was also called the C-word more times in two weeks than I had in my entire life—and those were the nice comments. While being the occasional lightning rod is something I'll probably never get used to, at least people still care what I think.

Something else that's difficult to get used to: the creaks and cracks of aging. When I see the crepey skin on my thighs during downward dog, *Om* becomes *Omygod, how the hell did that happen?* (Although I'm happy to report my trademark calves are still hanging in there.) By now, squeezing my softening midsection into a formfitting sheath feels, well…exhausting. As my friend Carol put it, "I think we've officially entered our caftan years."

Wendy called the other day.

"Can you believe I'm 68?" she said.

"Can you believe I'm 64?" I responded, so grateful for this friendship that began all those years ago when we were babies together at ABC News.

The TV career that followed exceeded every dream I ever had. And yet I'm happy where I am now, still learning, still growing, still asking questions. I'll never forget Rod Stewart's response when I marveled that he'd fathered his eighth kid in his sixties: "There's still lead in the ol' pencil, Kate."

I may not have a pencil, but I've still got plenty of lead.

I also have more time for the things I love: Going to museums and country inns with John. Picking cherry tomatoes, arugula, and basil with the girls and whipping up a summer feast. Clipping dahlias the size of my head and arranging them in antique glass bottles.

Sometimes I'll post a video on Instagram of me showing off my garden's bounty—makeup-free, bedhead, still in my pajamas.

Once someone commented, "Wow, she got old."

And all I could think was *Aren't I lucky?*

Epilogue

Dear Katie,

Tomorrow will be the third anniversary of Jay's death—a time of sadness for all of us, especially you. Time heals and diminishes grief but the period is much longer and more intense when death comes to a young person, and, even more so, to a spouse. Your mother and I send our loving sympathy.

You have done a marvelous job of not letting your sadness hinder you in any of the duties which you now must carry out alone. You have two beautiful, intelligent and loving daughters and every day they continue to grow in mind and spirit—a reflection of your own personality and rectitude.

And your tough mindedness in navigating your career through the quagmire and land mines of the network environment also is admirable.

But enough of this pompous talk. Your mother and I love and admire you most of all because you remain wise, sensitive, righteous, beautiful, and because you adhere to a policy of Illegitimi non carborundum (Don't let the bastards grind you down).

Smaht and purty, too.

Your appreciative father,
JMC

Acknowledgments

Writing this book—excavating my life, reliving it, and mining it for meaning—has been one of the most challenging and gratifying things I've ever done. The pandemic felt a lot less lonely with my trusty iPad always waiting for me (if I could remember where I put it), welcoming my latest thoughts, memories, and dreams.

But what truly made this possible were/are two amazing women:

First, my collaborator, Lucy Kaylin. To say we've grown close through this multiyear process is an understatement. The late-night anxiety calls and early-morning check-ins; the constant Zooms; Lucy's Socratic lines of questioning that always pushed me to think deeper about my life and find the courage to, yes, go there. Then there were the etymological debates over things like the pronunciation of *dour* (she says *do-er* and I say *dow-er*), *jury-rigged* versus *jerry-rigged*....I relished having found someone who gets as excited about words as I do (even though she did once accuse me of being an "infinitive splitter"). Lucy is one of the hardest-working, most hyper-focused, and most talented people I've ever met, and she never wavered in her commitment to helping me tell my story. And it was so rewarding to share and analyze our experiences as two women who came up through the ranks of media at roughly the same time. Lucy, you have found in me a friend for life. I'm confident I've found the same in you.

I met Adriana Fazio in the fall of 2018, her last year at Notre Dame, when she came to interview me about her thesis: "Katie Couric's Career and Shifting Perceptions of Femininity in Broadcast Journalism." Once

I got past feeling flattered, I quickly realized that Adriana knew more about me than I did, and I hired her to help me with this book. Immediately, she proved to be irreplaceable—the third leg of our very sturdy stool. Not only is she a crack researcher, but she is organized, whip-smart, and indefatigable, somehow tracking down every interview, letter, photo, and speech. Then, when I was hit with the dual pressures of a deadline *and* a lockdown, she became another member of the family to help me round the clock. Adriana is wise beyond her years, and her editorial input was invaluable. She is a joy to work with—and live with—and I can't wait to see what she does (hopefully with me) next.

Lucy, Adriana, and I spent countless—and I mean *countless*—hours around dining-room tables in East Hampton and New York City, typically in our pajamas, barely lifting our noses from our laptops long enough to have a bite of a bagel. We've seen the seasons change together more times than we ever imagined. Thanking you both from the bottom of my heart is woefully insufficient. You ladies are the best.

Now, for the man in my life, John Molner. When I'd get nervous about how candid I was being, he'd set me straight by saying, "If you're not going to be honest, don't write a book." He is my steadfast, trusted partner in all things. I'm so grateful for his love, his wicked sense of humor, and his tolerance of my whirling dervish ways. John (mostly) cheerfully put up with our aforementioned dining-room tables piled high with the detritus of my life and multiple pairs of reading glasses. No wonder so many of my followers on Instagram (hopefully the single ones) want to clone him. John is a big reason I feel so lucky.

To my exquisite daughters: Thank you, Ellie, for your guidance, feedback, and encouragement (while you were working insane hours and planning a wedding), which kept me strong; thank you, Carrie, for your sharp wit and intellect, and for helping me understand our family heritage in a much more enlightened way, through your (award-winning!) Stanford thesis. Every day I am dazzled by the women you have both become.

Heartfelt thanks to my loving sister Kiki for her astute edits and for being the family historian, so adept at keeping all our ancestors straight. To Johnny, for his support and steadiness, and for helping me remember our parents' quips and quirks. To my nephew Jeff, a constant source of fun, who also revisited painful memories in service of honoring his mother, my sister Emily. To the always compassionate Clare Meyers, my primary source of Monahan lore, who was willing to relive a heart-breaking time in our lives. I am so blessed with family, both nuclear and extended.

A special shout-out to my BFF, Wendy Walker, for being there since day one of our careers and every time I have ever needed her, including while writing this book. David Kiernan, Jay's partner in crime at Williams & Connolly, time traveled with me back to our days with Jay—from the night we all met to the day we said good-bye. And speaking of the night we met, thank you to Mark Levinstein, who recalled every detail of that epic party (some of which I couldn't include).

Needless to say, I am indebted to the incredible doctors in my life: Mark Pochapin and Felice Schnoll-Sussman were my therapists, my shoulders to cry on, my saviors. I owe you both so much. Along with Joe Ruggiero and Peter Allen, they were my walking medical textbooks and trusted guides through this complex, often terrifying journey.

Writing about huge societal issues that I've witnessed throughout my life requires a deep understanding and educated perspective. For this I am grateful for the extraordinary insight of Marianne Cooper, professor of sociology at Stanford. And I so appreciated the guidance of forensic psychiatrist Dr. Barbara Ziv, and also Robert Draper, who helped me sort through the morass that was the Iraq War.

Endless gratitude to my posse of pals who fielded countless calls and texts, and took so many walks down memory lane with me, with plenty of liquor nearby: Bob Peterson, Matt Lombardi, Lori Beecher, Lauren Osborn, Nicolla Hewitt, Brian Goldsmith, and Tony Maciulis. (If these walls could talk—oh wait, they just did....) I couldn't have done any of this without you. A big thank-you to Matthew Hiltzik, Mark Traub, Molly McGinnis, Kaye Foley, Jerry Cipriano, Lisa Licht, and Anne Sweeney for the memory-jogging and clarity.

To the network archivists, especially at NBC, who pulled hours and hours of footage without complaint: Joe Depierro and Art Hogan, you are my heroes. Susan Zirinsky got the ball rolling with Michele Crowe at the CBS News archives, while Michele Mustacchio at ABC News was so responsive and helpful. Matt Glassman, assistant news director at WRC, went way back into the vault of news stories past, as did the WTVJ crew. Many thanks to my mentors from CNN, Chris Curle and her late husband, Don Farmer, who gave me the confidence to pursue my dreams (Chris, I'm sorry I lost the thumb drive…twice). Thanks also to Gail Evans, Elissa Free, Lisa Napoli, and, of course, Guy Pepper, who supplied plenty of laughs during this whole process.

As for the other men in my life, I am indebted to my loyal and much-loved friends Kevin Goldman and Dave Price, whose steadfast support has seen me through so much, including this book. I greatly appreciate the time and attention taken by Carol Naggiar and Cheryl Gould, who read the manuscript so carefully. Thanks also to Brittany Jones-Cooper, Lisa Henricksson, and Jodi Kantor for their inspired feedback. To those who prefer to keep their contributions off the record, I will simply express my profound gratitude for the effort you put in.

Thank you to the women who launched this book: My literary agent, Suzanne Gluck of WME, who set me up for success and introduced me to Lucy; and my editor at Little, Brown, Judy Clain, who believed my story was worth telling and made sure we stayed on top of every deadline. Thanks also for the dedication of Karen Landry and Sabrina Callahan of Little, Brown. Much gratitude for the hard work of our intrepid fact-checker, Heather Samuelson, and for Carolyn Levin's legal expertise. Thanks to Mario Pulice for his careful work on the jacket, and to Andrew Eccles, who always makes me look better than I deserve.

Finally, to the many, many extraordinary people I've had the privilege of working with and sharing my life with through the years—you have brought me immeasurable joy and comfort when I needed it most. In the immortal words of Debby Boone, "You light up my life."

Everyone has a story. I encourage all of you to preserve yours so that it can be cherished by those you love for years—even generations—to come.

Index

About the Author

Katie Couric (@katiecouric) is an award-winning journalist, a *New York Times* bestselling author, and a co-founder of Stand Up To Cancer (SU2C). Since its launch in 2008, Stand Up To Cancer has raised more than $600 million to support cutting-edge collaborative science, and its research has contributed to nine new FDA-approved therapies.

In 2017, she founded Katie Couric Media, which has developed a number of media projects, including a daily newsletter, a podcast, digital video series, and several documentaries. KCM works with purpose-driven brands to create premium content that addresses important social issues like gender equality, environmental sustainability, and mental health.

Previous documentaries produced by KCM include *America Inside Out with Katie Couric,* a six-part series for National Geographic; *Gender Revolution: A Journey with Katie Couric,* for National Geographic; *Under the Gun,* which aired on Epix; and *Fed Up,* available on iTunes, Amazon, and YouTube. Couric was also the executive producer of *Unbelievable* on Netflix and is developing other scripted projects.

Couric was the first woman to solo anchor a network evening newscast, serving as anchor and managing editor of the *CBS Evening News* from 2006 to 2011, following 15 years as co-anchor of NBC's *TODAY* show. She also hosted a syndicated show, *Katie,* and served as the Yahoo Global News anchor until 2017.

She has won a duPont-Columbia Award, a Peabody, two Edward R. Murrow Awards, a Walter Cronkite Award, and multiple Emmys. She was twice named one of *Time* magazine's one hundred most influential people and was a *Glamour* magazine Woman of the Year three times. She has also received numerous awards for her cancer advocacy work and has been honored by both the Harvard and Columbia schools of public health, the American Cancer Society, and the American Association of Cancer Researchers.

In addition to writing *The Best Advice I Ever Got: Lessons from Extraordinary Lives,* Couric is the author of two books for children.